The Quicksand War:
Prelude to Vietnam

Patti — p.221

The Quicksand War:
Prelude to Vietnam

///

by LUCIEN BODARD

Translated and with an introduction by
PATRICK O'BRIAN

(not an exact word for word translation — see the Introduction)

An Atlantic Monthly Press Book
LITTLE, BROWN AND COMPANY · BOSTON · TORONTO

Published in France in two volumes, *L'Enlisement,* and *L'Humiliation.*

ATLANTIC—LITTLE, BROWN BOOKS
ARE PUBLISHED BY
LITTLE, BROWN AND COMPANY
IN ASSOCIATION WITH
THE ATLANTIC MONTHLY PRESS

*Published simultaneously in Canada
by Little, Brown & Company (Canada) Limited*

PRINTED IN THE UNITED STATES OF AMERICA

Introduction

LUCIEN BODARD is one of the best-known French foreign correspondents and he is an expert on Indochina; he knows the Far East as few Europeans can know it, for not only has he spent a great deal of his working life there, but he was born in Chungking. Indeed, one of his earliest recollections is intimately connected with Asian politics — lopped-off heads in a basket, exposed to discourage the opposition. And as it happens his wife, who is a journalist too, also has an Eastern background, for she was brought up in Saigon. Lucien Bodard, therefore, possesses a vast store of knowledge, the immensely detailed ramifying knowledge that comes from having been there for years and years with open ears and eyes and a sharply intelligent, trained inquiring mind — knowledge of a very different kind from that which is amassed in a few weeks by newspapermen who fly into Saigon with a load of hurried reading and preconceived ideas.

But he was not only very well placed for receiving information; he was also exceedingly active in going out in search of it. He is a big, wonderfully energetic man (in some ways he reminds one of his friend and former colleague Graham Greene), and he has been everywhere and has met everyone — he knows the people, he knows the country, he has the right contacts — innumerable contacts — and he has a digestion that has withstood uncounted Asian feasts. And, perhaps the most important qualification for a man who wishes to see every side of a question, he is very good company — a man to whom people speak freely. He has poured this great wealth of information into two books passionately concerned with Vietnam, *L'Enlisement* — The Bogging Down — and *L'Humiliation;* they are close-packed books, factual and crammed with vitality; they provide an intensely living, detailed picture of that complex, many-sided country, an unrivaled background to the present situation; and they form the basis for this present book.

They are the opening books of a series designed to carry the history of Indochina up to the moment when the French were finally replaced by the

Americans, and these first two volumes deal with the return of the French to Indochina after the Japanese defeat, the deliquescence of that unhappy country's institutions, administration, morale and cohesion; with the efforts of the French, and particularly of the French army, to grapple with a situation that had escaped their moral grasp and their intellectual comprehension; and with the extraordinary rise of a new Asia unsuspected by the old colonial authorities. They deal with the difficult, confused early days when in spite of American opposition the French were trying to recover what they regarded as their own property; with the repressive action that grew and grew, progressively corrupting the repressors, until it was a war — a war that might perhaps at a given moment have been won had there been better leadership, more intelligence and above all more vision; with the French army, its heroism and stupidity, and the squalid, fatal quarreling among its leaders. They deal with the extraordinary lack of understanding of the meaning of Mao Tse-tung's victory and the significance of a Red China on the country's northern frontier, and with the steady rise of the opposing forces — poor, ill-equipped and living from hand to mouth, yet possessed of an inner strength that no mercenary army, however conventionally brave, no self-seeking body of colonialists and no mildly benevolent administrators could hope to rival.

They show the state of mind of an army that does not have the nation solidly behind it, whose heart is not wholly engaged and whose approach is merely professional — an army that is to some extent both geographically and morally cut off from its own people and that is fighting what at least some of its own nation calls "the dirty war."

They follow the vagaries of French and native Indochinese policy, the military successes and defeats, the rise of the centrifugal forces that are still tearing the country to pieces, and they reach the point at which the realities of the situation were forced upon the French command in 1950, when the well-trained, well-armed regulars came flooding into North Vietnam from their bases in Communist China, utterly destroying the fragile screen that had been set up along the border; and the full-scale, modern-style war was on, with Dienbienphu looming on the dark horizon and all the elements of tragedy close at hand.

It would be difficult to think of anyone better qualified to write about those years than Lucien Bodard, not only because of his local knowledge, training and long experience, but also because from the very outset his attitude was entirely objective. He was committed to no party; he was afraid of no sacred cows, nor even of generals, though in France, where everyone either is or has been or is about to be a soldier, a general is a more awe-inspiring figure than he is elsewhere. But these books, *L'Enlisement* and *L'Humiliation,* were written for an informed, deeply-involved French audience, perfectly acquainted with even the minor figures and fascinated by the play-by-play accounts of scandals that never reached the outside world at all; they therefore contained a great deal of material that had virtually no relevance for the English-speaking reader — it might even be said that for the outsider it fogged the general picture so that it was difficult to grasp it at all. The problem, therefore, was to find a way of telescoping the two volumes and of shortening them in such a way that the resulting book should still be truly Bodard, with his direct Breughelish detail and sweep, and yet not confront the reader with any parish gossip that would need footnotes of equal length to explain it.

It seemed to me that the first thing to do was to separate the purely ephemeral events from those of more lasting interest. It was a sound principle, but it was one that was difficult to put into practice, for the more carefully I looked into it the less it seemed to me that anything was purely ephemeral — the scandal of the piasters, the squabbling of forgotten generals, and the foolish greed of Bao Dai may seem unimportant now, but without any one of them the situation would have developed along different lines. However, some degree of selection there had to be; so, having discussed it at length with the author, I traced out the essential themes of the book and then chose typical passages and examples from the wealth of material at my disposal — some four hundred thousand words — to illustrate the attitudes of mind, the good will and idealism, the incompetence, muddle and plain graft that were characteristic of Indochina in the years between the end of the Second World War and 1950, and to illustrate them in their true proportions. This called for a great deal of cutting, condensing, and linking together, particularly in the earlier parts of the book. I have made these cuts silently, with no dots or square brackets; the same applies to the connecting pieces that I have written to bridge the gaps and to the occasional explanatory passages that I have inserted. I think it will be agreed that this was the right way of proceeding, for I was not working on the text of a dead author but, on the contrary, collaborating directly with one of the liveliest writers that can be imagined.

Then, in setting about the fine work, the actual turning of the book from one language to another, I allowed myself something of the same freedom, and, particularly in dialogue I have made no attempt at literal conversion; for "a translator who would write with any force or spirit of an original must never dwell on the words of his author," as Dryden says, ". . . he who copies word for word loses all the spirit in the tedious transfusion"; and to have translated Lucien Bodard so that he seemed tedious would have been a very gross betrayal.

PATRICK O'BRIAN
COLLIOURE, 1966

Contents

List of Maps

(Prepared by Henri Jacquinet)

PART I

Bogging Down

I T was all over in the summer of 1954. Dienbienphu had fallen in May. In July, at Geneva, the two independent nations of North and South Vietnam had come into being, and from now on throughout the Far East, the French were to count for nothing.

At Hanoi, in the Normandy bar, I sat next to three officers who were drinking champagne with some Eurasian ladies, and I recognized one as a famous captain of paras who had survived Dienbienphu.

"It was all for nothing," he was saying. "I let my men die for nothing." His glare was as blind as a sleepwalker's.

"In prison camp the Viets told us they had won because they were fighting for an ideal, and we were not. I told them about my paras at Dienbienphu. I told them how they fought. And they said, 'Heroism is no answer.'

"In prison camp we faced the reality of the Vietminh. And we saw that for eight years our generals had been struggling against a revolution without knowing what a revolution was. Dienbienphu was not an accident of fate, it was a judgment."

In Hong Kong, an American journalist said to me, "You have the rottenest army in the world, but we could have made you win at Dienbienphu, and I think we should have." One of his friends said hastily, "But I admire your army. They know how to make a *beau geste* . . ." It was kind of him, no doubt, but he really meant that the French army, like a Louis Quinze armchair, was the masterpiece of an extinct civilization. What could I answer? The Americans would never have fought as we did. They would have fought a different war. And by crushing the country and the people under a hail of bombs and dollars, they might very well have had more success than we.

Yet in the beginning, at least, the French had all the odds. The Vietminh were no more than scantily armed guerrillas, who lived off the Expeditionary Force, procuring their weapons by ambush and by theft. In those days,

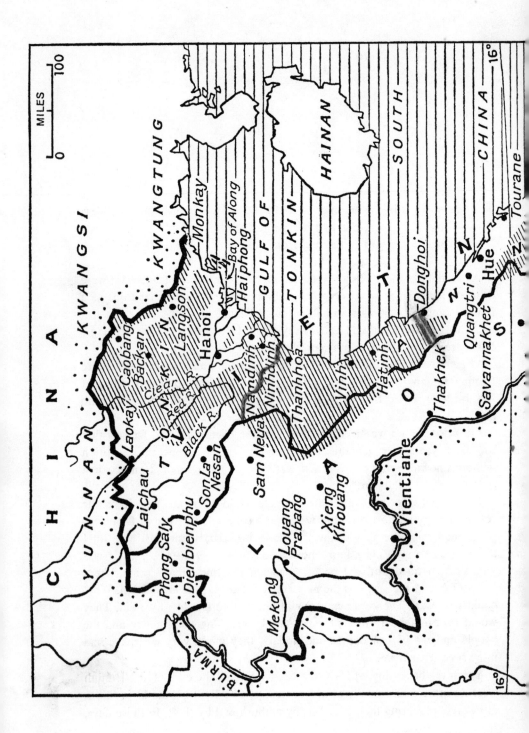

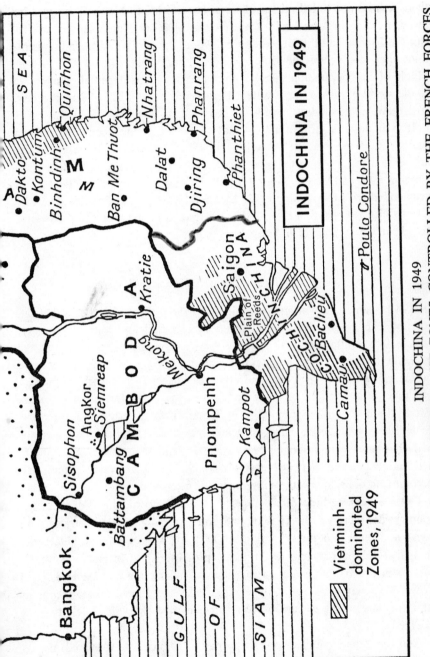

INDOCHINA IN 1949

VIET GUERRILLAS WERE PRESENT IN THE ZONES CONTROLLED BY THE FRENCH FORCES.

there was no one to help the soldiers of Ho Chi Minh. Mao's China was far
away, fighting in Manchuria against Chiang Kai-shek's enormous armies.
But the French had the Expeditionary Force, the police and the administration; they controlled the flow of money; they manipulated the piaster.
Much of the population sided with them; they could get all the native
soldiers and partisans they wanted. Paris fed the war a billion francs a day.
And then American dollars and supplies began to flow in.

It is impossible now not to wonder how the French could have been
beaten. And my reason for writing this book has been to discover the
answers. I am going to tell the story of the crucial years 1946–1949, the
years of folly and illusion, and of 1950, the year of humiliation. That harsh
year ended with the coming of de Lattre de Tassigny. Before his death he
was to give the army back its pride, so that, for four more years, France
could carry on her brave and hopeless enterprise.

The failure of the men of good will

IN 1948 I came as a war correspondent to Saigon. Everyday life in that fat,
corrupt, enchanting city was made up of blood, death, sensual pleasure,
weariness, splendor, idleness and overflowing profusion. There was savage
guerrilla fighting in the countryside and murder in the streets; but the
businessmen waded in riches, and even the *nha-qués,* the working masses,
had reached a standard of living that was unbelievable for Asian peasants.
Far to the north, in the mountains of Tonkin near the Chinese border, the
Expeditionary Force was struggling with Ho Chi Minh's regulars; but nobody bothered to talk about it. The war was endless; the war was routine;
and Indochina was a chessboard on which the innumerable pieces had
become immobile. It was the *enlisement,* the bogging down.

Outside Saigon, Indochina belonged to the Expeditionary Force; in the
countryside, there was no civilian state to be seen — no administration, no
laws, no courts, no public services. On those who were not killed, the
campaign rained rewards, decorations, promotion. After each operation,
successful or not, the army, as they put it, "shook the banana tree," and
everybody decorated everybody else. And in the Rue Catinat, the main
street of Saigon, the elegant officers came in from their rural fiefs to strut
like lords.

And the money counted too. Army pay in France was wretched; not so
in Indochina. A rifleman from French North Africa could save up enough
to buy a farm and a wife in his native land. Many officers established

dowries for their daughters. And since all military personnel enjoyed the automatic right to transfer piasters for francs at the unduly favorable official rate, real fortunes could be made in money changing. Apparently in 1947 the total transferred by the army was higher than its entire pay.

Business was very good indeed. Yet here in Cochinchina, the richest and most bourgeois of the five states which had formed French Indochina, and the longest under French domination, nationalism was rife. Vietminh partisans prowled the Plain of Reeds just outside Saigon. And even the carefully chosen ministers of Cochinchina's "separatist" government had suddenly begun to call for unification with Annam and Tonkin, and to term themselves "the government of South Vietnam," with the idea that it would one day be the government of all Vietnam and an independent Vietnam at that.

The old Indochina hands were indignant. "Monsieur, if we had had the sense to cut off a few dozen heads at the right moment there would still be a French Indochina. After all, before 1940 absolutely any Frenchman could travel wherever he liked, even in the wildest districts, without carrying a weapon. The village notables were only too happy to welcome him with deep bows."

The speakers were men of standing, respectable, worthy, jovial citizens with fat little bellies — the "colonial egg" — on spindly legs. They described the old Indochina, the Indochina of the sixty years' Protectorate, as an earthly Paradise. "What didn't we do for the *nha-qués?*" they said to me. "We rescued them from abject poverty, we gave them schools, roads and hospitals; and what is even more important, we brought them justice and security."

"But how can a country so overwhelmed with kindness possibly have blown up in our faces like this? Did not these happy people really want independence more than anything else?"

They were not in the slightest degree ashamed of their colonialism. "It was those newcomers," they cried, "those people de Gaulle sent us in 1945. We should have saved Indochina if it had not been for their notions." They were referring to soldiers like Sainteny, who had openly sympathized with Ho Chi Minh's nationalism, and General Leclerc, who had come to pacify the rebellious country but had ended by concluding it was pointless to try to return to colonialism. Even Admiral d'Argenlieu, the first high commissioner, had, as they saw it, made dangerous and unnecessary concessions. His successors Bollaert and Pignon, who were trying to persuade the Emperor Bao Dai to return to his throne and to become a rallying point for all the Annamese, had dangerous leanings toward independence. "If they had only listened to us! We who understood the Annamese so well — we who loved them and were loved in return. But these people accused us of exploiting the Annamese: indeed, they very nearly took their side against us."

"Don't you think that your Indochina really died long ago? You thought it was solid enough, but it only needed a push to bring it tumbling down."

It was sad to think how these men had striven to hold "their" Indochina, and how appallingly they had suffered. In 1941, at a time when the dogma of the white man's superiority was practically sacrosanct, it called for a great deal of courage in these colonists to collaborate with Asians. Yet when the mother country, seven thousand five hundred miles away, collapsed, and when Indochina lay helpless before the Mikado's land and sea forces, the French admirals, generals, civil servants and colonists voluntarily accepted the Japanese occupation: they hoped that by this desperate wager they might save the essential — the presence of the French flag.

For a long time they thought that they were going to bring it off, seeing that although the Japanese furiously annihilated all forms of white rule in Asia they did make this solitary exception: they respected the French sovereignty under Admiral Jean Decoux, the governor appointed by Vichy. The French administration continued to function; French citizens were free: the tricolor flew from every mast. By the spring of 1944 they only had to hold out for a few months or a few weeks for the game to be won.

Everything collapsed in a single night. On March 8, 1945, Saigon was seized with panic: the people of the town, jerked from their sleep by a great din, shrieks, rifle fire and shouting, asked one another "What can this disaster be?" They soon learned. The faithful night watchmen, big dark-skinned men, quietly warned their French employers. "Monsieur, put out the lights as fast as you can. The Japanese are killing all the whites." Terrified families rushed out, carrying their children into the garden, hiding until dawn in trenches. Meanwhile Japanese soldiers emerged from the darkness, crushing all resistance and smashing everything they found. From Saigon there arose the hideous noise of the lamentation of women, the shrieks of the dying and the clatter of breaking crockery.

The Japanese announced the deposition of the French in proclamations posted up on the walls. As the people heard the sound of the glue being slapped up for the posters they imagined that some inflammable liquid was being spread, so that the whole city should go up in flames.

This was the Japanese coup d'etat, the liquidation of Indochina, the bringing down of the whites and their systematic humiliation. The Kempetai, the Japanese Gestapo, carried out searches everywhere. They arrested the French and flung them into prison. They shut them up in the grim buildings of the Sûreté, the criminal investigation department, in the same place where the "imperialist" police had "questioned" generations of Annamese revolutionaries. What a revenge! The white prisoners had to squat, poised on their toes for hours on end; and they were beaten as soon as they lost their balance. And there were more sophisticated tortures, executions, massacres. The whole garrison of Langson was put to the sword. Only a few units in Tonkin escaped. Alessandri's column reached Chiang Kai-shek's China by a long and dreadful march through the jungle.

It was impossible to hide in Saigon. Every house had to have a wooden panel on its door with the name, identity, calling, nationality, sex and age of each person living in it. One of the last things that made people smile was the fact that feminine vanity had not entirely vanished — few women confessed to being forty, and those few cursed their simple-mindedness.

Labeled in this way, shut up in their houses, not allowed to go beyond certain limits and forced to observe a curfew whose time varied according to the whim of the Japanese, the French had the feeling of being caught in a trap. They were walking targets, and dread was the atmosphere in which they lived their daily round. How could they even understand what was happening to them, cut off as they had been all these years from their own country and from the rest of the world? How could they imagine that Hiroshima and Nagasaki were close at hand?

The Japanese, with foreknowledge of their coming defeat, intended, as a final stroke of revenge, to destroy Indochina entirely. And in order to make sure that it should never rise again they loosed the fury of nationalism among the mass of the Annamese population, who in their turn set themselves to hunting down the defenseless whites.

The French were at bay and this was the kill. To the savagery of the Japanese police and military there was added the hatred of the people of Saigon. The French were not merely terrified; they were beginning to feel a total loss of any hope — complete desperation.

The atomic bomb was the miracle that saved their lives. Indeed, the whites had their moment of exaltation, in which they believed that the Annamese would grow meek and harmless once more. They had not understood that they were going to come up against new and unrelenting forces; for at this time they still had no notion of what nationalism and Communism meant.

The appalling disappointment, the cruel and bitter disillusionment, was that the Annamese turned out to be infinitely more hostile without the

Japanese than with them. In a few days the flames of the revolution covered the whole of Indochina.

A certain Ho Chi Minh, a political agitator whose name was noted in the files of the police, suddenly appeared from the jungle with a handful of companions, and seized Hanoi. He founded the People's Republic of Vietnam and in doing so he became the Father of the Nation. Responding to his call great crowds assembled everywhere, in the towns, the villages and the rice fields, wildly celebrating their freedom. Everywhere there sprang up committees and militia bands. The Vietminh rising swept the whole of Annam, spreading as far as Saigon, seven hundred and fifty miles to the south.

That city too was in the hands of the Vietminh. For a month on end life there was a nightmare. During the day everything seemed quiet. The only question was that of getting food. Making the most of the outward appearance of sluggish calm, the French women would slip out as far as the market, where the sharper kind of merchant allowed them to buy fag ends of meat and vegetables at outrageous prices.

Fear came back with the twilight. At dusk there began a strange migration: neighboring families gathered stealthily in one of the houses — never the same — and there they united their joint lack of power. Every time it was the same interminable night. The darkness outside was full of prowling Vietminh. Their harsh, shrill voices could be heard coming from everywhere, their cruel laughter, their shouts and the sound of their whistles. Sometimes an assault group would go by, padding along to the *moc ai* rhythm, one-two, one-two: and then, when they stopped, that was the sign that a villa was going to be attacked.

It was an endless vigil. In every house the waiting had the same aspect. The rooms were lit for the sake of face. The men played cards, with their only weapons, the kitchen knives, within hand's reach. From time to time they broke off to calm their wives, overtaken by hysteria. The children, all put into the same bed in a next-door room, trembled with fear and were sick on the mosquito netting.

The terror mounted. From mouth to mouth there ran the names of men who had been hacked to pieces, of women who had been raped and cut open, of children who had been maimed. The shrieks of those who were being tortured to death could be heard. The Vietminh had set up "resistance camps" in the suburbs, and there they took their hostages, burying them alive, with only their heads showing above the ground. The horror reached its culminating point in the massacre at the block called the Cité

Hérault, where some hundred Frenchmen were dismembered, slashed to pieces, in unimaginably horrible circumstances.

Even the dogs ran mad, and they bit children, who had to be taken to the dispensary — a dispensary that had no medicines left.

At last one day the French of Saigon, wild with delight, heard that "they" were about to arrive. "They" were the people of the outside world, the whites from whom the Saigonese had been cut off for so many years — the whites who had won the war. The townspeople awaited their saviors. And indeed the British landed with their Gurkhas, and they were followed by the French parachute troops.

The British soldiers were effective. But what utter astonishment at the attitude of the "paras"! They looked upon these Frenchmen of Indochina, who thought themselves so deserving, as so many traitors. The liberated were cut off from their liberators by a vast moral chasm. The gulf was so great that the troops from France could only just bring themselves to the point of going to the help of the Saigonese, who were still being attacked by the Vietminh. The soldiers interfered unwillingly, as a last resort, when they could not possibly do otherwise.

Once a Frenchwoman, when the house was being set upon by the Vietminh, ran to the paras, whose quarters were close at hand: she succeeded in rousing the men, but their commanding officer, a colonel, refused to send any help. For he too, like the old colonialists, was a man of good will.

These paras, the first to come, equated the position in Indochina with that which they had known in France. For them there were just two categories, the collaborators and the members of the Resistance. Here the traitors could be none other than the French of Indochina: had they not worked with the Japanese for years? The Vietminh seemed the more deserving. They continually repeated that their rising had been directed against the Japanese: on the other hand, they loved the French, they told the paras, and the only people they had attacked were the imperialists, who had come to terms with the enemy forces.

The paras acted in good faith. Their intentions were of the best — they did not wish to force the Annamese to come to heel but rather to make a peaceful reconquest of their hearts. And yet a few weeks later there they were plunged into the bloodiest of wars.

Leclerc had arrived with his armored division, the famous 2ᵉ DB (*division blindée*), and as his orders required he sent columns out from Saigon for the peaceful reoccupation of the country. But they were attacked. Presently captured French soldiers were found hacked to pieces, and presently Annamese villages went up in flames. For violence answered violence. How short a time was needed for the dreams of sweetness and light to yield place to the intoxicating savagery of cruelty! In a series of destructive thrusts the French retook Cochinchina, Cambodia, Laos, central and southern Annam. But the Red *tieudoi** and all the guerrilla formations continually reappeared, as though they sprang from their own ashes. There was fighting throughout the whole of the rice-growing country.

Nothing made sense. After a few months Leclerc's own diagnosis was that it was impossible to reconquer Indochina by force. The uprising of the Asian masses, who were carrying on a "people's war" according to the principles of Mao Tse-tung, was something that could no longer be overcome. And to try to do so would mean utter exhaustion in endless warfare.

The French tried negotiation, and by the spring of 1946 they succeeded in coming to an agreement with Ho Chi Minh for the reoccupation of Hanoi: but this was only because the Chinese Nationalist troops who had entered Tonkin to disarm the Japanese had no intention of leaving the country. Roosevelt had had no wish to see a French Indochina, and the idea had been that as soon as it was convenient the Communist Ho Chi Minh should be knocked on the head and Tonkin taken over, either directly by the Chinese or indirectly by their friends. Faced with two evils Ho Chi Minh chose the lesser and called in the French to expel the Chinese, who had already squeezed him dry and who were preparing their take-over. Their departure was speeded by French bribes and by the trickery of Chiang Kai-shek. (The Chinese in Tonkin were the irregular army of Lu Han, the warlord of Yunnan. While they were busy pillaging Tonkin, Chiang Kai-shek sent two loyal divisions to take over Yunnan. Then he dispatched Lu Han's army to Manchuria, against the Red troops of Lin Piao, by whom they were promptly annihilated.)

But of course in the end negotiations came to nothing, especially with the Chinese gone. Ho Chi Minh wanted nothing less than a sovereign state, a Red Vietnam based on the "dictatorship of the people," whereas the French did not wish to concede independence at all, but at the most the setting up of a humanist, somewhat socialistic state very closely connected with France — an integral part of the French Union.

After a furious battle the Vietminh were beaten off and an apparent calm was restored: but from now on there was no hope of a peaceful solution. Indochina sank down into its war; and it sank down into oblivion too — nowhere on earth did anyone take the least notice of it.

* A *tieudoi* was a platoon in the Vietminh army.

But for me this was the exploration of a self-contained world — the world of murderous stagnation that was called "the happy war." Gradually I discovered the factors that made up the equipoise which the French and the Annamese had reached. Month after month, day after day, they were living in the common round of the piaster and of killing.

This bogging down did not occur immediately. On December 19, 1946, in Hanoi, the Vietminh failed in an attempted massacre: now in their turn the French tried to bring off a single great decisive blow. They tried a military operation to crush Ho Chi Minh and his guerrillas within a matter of days. It was an operation on the greatest possible scale. And it too was a failure.

It was supposed to be a triumphantly successful hunt. Ho Chi Minh was to be taken in his hideout on the Chinese frontier, where he had no more than a few thousand fever-stricken and ill-armed supporters.

It very nearly succeeded. In order to put an end to the Vietminh once and for all the French high command had made a prodigious effort: they had gathered all the available shock troops and all the war materiel that could possibly be assembled — materiel that had already served in the Italian campaign. It was a combined operation, planned according to all the rules of the respective staffs. Parachute troops were to be dropped over Backan, a wretched little town that served as Ho Chi Minh's headquarters and that stood almost in the middle of his jungle fastness, a hilly quadrilateral about one hundred and fifty miles square. And at the same moment two columns were to race forward and make contact with the paras, one column being the armor, which was to thrust along the R.C. 4 (route coloniale No. 4), and the other a column of boats, which was to go up the Clear River.

The expedition began amid general enthusiasm, and everyone was convinced that this was to be the end of the Viets. Technically it was almost perfect. But the boats could not get up the river: and above all the paras who were dropped over Backan with orders to take Ho Chi Minh dead or alive at any cost whatever, missed him by an hour. It was because of that one hour that the war in Indochina went on and gradually turned into a relentless tragedy.

From that time on there was no longer to be any question of catching Ho Chi Minh. For the future he was to be a being wrapped in mystery, and never did the French manage to track him down. So completely did he vanish into his jungle that there were times when the army intelligence believed that he was dead. He became a wanderer, changing his resting place every night, guarded by a whole battalion. A wall of secrecy surrounded him. Even his generals and ministers were not to know where he was, for might there not be a traitor among them who would tell the French?

With the escape of Ho Chi Minh the war began to go downhill. The Expeditionary Force most bitterly experienced the truth of the first great rule of the war in Indochina, the rule which states that every undertaking which is not a total success is fated to become a total disaster.

Pacification

THE war on the Chinese frontier might have been won if the French of 1947 had imitated their forefathers of the days of the colonial conquest and had plunged into the jungle to fight the enemy hand to hand. But they clung to the roads; they were the prisoners of their own cars and trucks; and they therefore condemned themselves to failure. The R.C. 4, without even a land link to the Tonkinese delta, had to be supplied from Haiphong by sea. Against all the elementary rules of strategy, this precarious 200-mile jungle road, crushed between the rugged Vietminh quadrilateral and the Chinese frontier, was garrisoned by thousands of French soldiers, whose duty was to keep it open for truck convoys. The reason given for maintaining the R.C. 4 was that it would bar the frontier and separate the Vietminh from the Chinese. In fact, Chinese technicians and Chinese arms and ammunition passed freely across it, to supply Ho Chi Minh's growing forces, which eventually amounted to ten solid regiments, based on a complex of military schools, workshops, supply dumps, printing presses, and arms factories — all made of bamboo, all easily movable. From the air, this jungle seemed deserted; in fact, it seethed with activity.

Yet what did the R.C. 4 and the Vietminh quadrilateral amount to in comparison with the rest of Indochina, that vast area, larger than France, which was being brought under control? The new watchword, the new idea, was Pacification.

It was in 1948 that the French thought this up, because they were unable to bring the Vietminh to a pitched battle and destroy them. Henceforward the great idea was to leave Ho Chi Minh in his patch of jungle and to win all the rest away from him. When the Vietminh no longer had the fertile areas and the close-packed mass of the people on their side they would be more entirely crushed than by any military defeat. They could no longer

ontinue to subsist, and Ho Chi Minh's regulars would then perish, starved
nd cut-off, on the Chinese frontier.

In Indochina itself, apart from their fastness in Upper Tonkin, the Viets
ad complete possession of only two Red areas, two enclaves on the coast
f Annam — Quangngai and Quinhon. And even there Ho Chi Minh only
ad some three million men and a very little in the way of rice and salt.

So what was at stake was French-occupied Indochina. It was a vast
xpanse of country that stretched out under the tricolor, and it was here
hat the bitter struggle between the forces of Pacification and those of the
Resistance was to take place.

This meant that the two sides were to be brought face to face in every
ossible sense, a confrontation in which weapons were only of secondary
mportance. To work upon the people and to win them over the French
rought everything they possessed into play; and the Vietminh did the
same. The two juxtaposed, intertwined civilizations were at grips with one
another in total warfare. At their disposal the French had everything that
showed on the surface, the whole of the established society founded upon
law. The Vietminh, on the other hand, were just underneath everywhere,
present in everything that was hidden. Two sides appealed to two
opposing instincts in mankind, the French holding out a normal life, with
prosperity and the benefits of the West, and the Vietminh offering pride
and revolt. The one side favored the wealthy and those who owned
property; the other side the poor. In this bid for twenty million *nha-qués*
both the one and the other also made use of terrorism. Between the two
huge machines the private individual was crushed.

On the R.C. 4 the French were fighting the Communists, an antlike foe:
they were fighting the Red concept of the world. Elsewhere, in the Indochina of the Pacification, they were primarily fighting against a form of
resistance, a kind of romanticism. The god of these members of the
Resistance was Ho Chi Minh, and they worshipped him with an extrava-
gant devotion. But they invented an Uncle Ho of their own: they did not
know him, for in Indochina the distances precluded knowledge. For them
Uncle Ho was above all the Patriot, the Hero who was expelling the
French. As for themselves they were not quite sure whether they were
Communists or not. They avoided asking themselves, preferring to say that
they were "Socialists," just as Ho Chi Minh must be.

Nguyen Binh, whom Ho Chi Minh had sent south in 1945 to build the
Resistance in Cochinchina, was not a Communist. He had learned his
revolutionary's craft from the Nationalists he met at the prison island of
Poulo Condore in the early 1920's, and gained experience thereafter in

Moscow and as an agitator in China. In the Plain of Reeds, near Saigon, ▌ eventually created a formidable headquarters, complete with camps, d▐ pots, workshops, schools, presses, and even a radio station; and his trad▐ routes reached through the jungle as far as Siam. Cruel, indefatigabl▐ pitiless, authoritarian, he was nevertheless a generous and romantic idea▐ ist; and, to the people of the south, he became a hero, almost a saint.

It was not really an army that this Resistance possessed, but rather ▐ number of commandos, of groups, and of intelligence networks tha▐ branched out in never-ending complexity. In order to kill the French the▐ lived parasitically upon them, right next to them. Yet although the resis▐ tants hunted their prey, at the same time they themselves were bein▐ hunted. For the French, thanks to their money, were able to recrui▐ informers, partisans and Vietnamese soldiers: there were a very grea▐ many of them, and they were exceedingly dangerous to the Vietminh —▐ they too had to be wiped out.

In order to deal with so many enemies, therefore, the Vietminh made ▐ systematic use of trickery and cruelty. In this war, as in all wars in which ▐ Resistance is concerned, there was a kind of fascination with death. Th▐ Resistance was not the stronger side as far as sheer strength was con-▐ cerned — they could not even storm the French posts fortified with▐ bamboo, nor the police stations. Assassination was the answer that re-▐ mained. Indeed the Vietminh's official name for their political committee▐ was "assassination committee."

This side of the Resistance delighted in blood. The real Communists,▐ those of the R.C. 4, killed without taking pleasure in it, out of necessity.▐ They would analyze a given situation and decide that the good of the Party▐ called for liquidation. But it was always a question of clearly designated▐ individuals. There were no mistakes: it was not a matter of chance; and▐ usually the Party preferred to set about the reeducation of the guilty men.

The rest of the movement, however, scattered death at haphazard: they▐ believed in pure terrorism. They exploded bombs in the midst of Asian▐ crowds, in the markets and in the cinemas. They paid boys to throw▐ grenades that they made themselves in their workshops: these "home-▐ produced bombs," as they were called, did little damage. But sometimes,▐ when they wanted a particularly striking effect, they would use really▐ dangerous grenades bought in Bangkok or Singapore, and then a whole▐ dense mass of the crowd would be mown down. One of these bombs▐ slaughtered sixty children in a single school.

The night belonged to the Vietminh. But at dawn the French patrols▐ came out. What quantities of corpses they found. How often a detachment, on reaching a village that had put itself under the unit's protection, would find ranks of heads neatly lined up in the central square. Some bodies bore warning notices, but there were others, quite unknown, who floated along the irrigation ditches, swollen like bladders, the skin a tightly stretched parchment. Sometimes a river would suddenly begin to bring corpses down on its current. No one would be able to tell where they had come from or who they were: no one would ever know. Among the bodies, women, old people, children: usually tortured and burned.

The only corpses that the French never found were those of the Vietminh. The enemy always carried away his dead and wounded: there were coolies for that very purpose. All physical traces of Red losses were done away with and for their propaganda the French were forced to rely upon guesses and to talk about "the grass covered with bloodstains."

It was a profitable war. To establish a French post, even in Red-dominated country, was to strike oil. Like mushrooms, little straw huts would spring up around it, belonging to concubines, snack sellers, bistro keepers, informers, interpreters, "boys" and "beps" (cooks). Even the neighboring Vietminh would take time from ambushes and murders to go marketing next to the enclosure. The first duty of the chief of a post was to set up a market.

The life was exciting. I remember visiting a splendid villa at Cantho, inhabited by a group of charming young officers fresh from Saint-Cyr and their amiable pet python. "Don't worry if the bangs wake you up," they said, conducting me to my room. "The Viets over the way usually machine gun us about two in the morning, and we answer them. It's sort of a ceremony. If you can sleep through, do. But if you're disturbed by a sound of footsteps, take a grenade — we left you a little pile of them, right by your bed. Just pull the pin, and put your hand out between the window bars, and let it drop. Then go back to sleep, and look at your bag in the morning."

Next day we went to a coconut grove, a high green vault on smooth columns, a warm silence broken by the young men's laughter. Bare to the waist, some cut trees; a few stood by with tommy guns for protection. Little Annamese boys shinnied up like monkeys to bring down the fruit, and we split it with machetes for its miraculously cool milk.

Building their simple fort, patrolling the villages, fighting their way out of ambushes, these young men were healthily happy. They were models of keenness, they had a splendid soldierly dash, their manners were aristo-cratically simple, and they looked like young seraphs. They had already taken casualties, but the war's horror had not yet deformed their minds. And enthusiastically they were getting to know this exotic world of village notables, *nha-qués,* naked children, partisans, and the graceful little *congai.*

But that evening in the villa, dinner was somber when a recent tragedy was recalled: a wounded man had had to be abandoned when a patrol was ambushed by a hundred Viets, and the post's medical officer had insisted on staying with him. Next day both were found with their heads cut off. The young officers began telling other stories of heroic sacrifice, and it developed into a kind of litany of *la belle mort,* an army ritual celebrating its martyrs to Duty.

But I was reminded of all the martyrs to pride, of Colonel de S——, who, for a point of honor, let himself be killed and hundreds of his men as well. It was just after I arrived in Indochina, in a convoy on the Dalat road. Hearing of a tremendous ambush, the convoy commander, a lieutenant, wanted to stop. But the colonel declared, "I will not tolerate showing fear of the Viets," and charged on, followed by the rest, into a hell of fire for mile after mile. They were all killed.

I complained of the panache that cost France a whole class of Saint-Cyriens every year in Indochina. Viet officers were indistinguishable from their men, even by the "command presence" these young men talked about. Wasn't it more sensible not to be deliberately a target?

There was a chorus of protest, and one boy said, "We command men of every race. Of the one hundred and twenty thousand men of the Expeditionary Force, only fifty thousand are Frenchmen. We have Negroes, Arabs, Asians, the Legion. All these mercenaries — and that's what they are — are held in line only by the respect and admiration they feel for "their" officer because he's a man, a chief. In the midst of the fighting, he's as relaxed as if he weren't fighting at all, quietly doing his job, with his map, his binoculars, his stick and his stripes. And his apparent contempt of death.

"In this Indochinese war, everything is based on the officer; he has to master himself, to be a hero all the time, even in everyday life. He is not entitled to make the smallest slip. I tell you this: here in Asia the French officer has never been closer to attaining his military ideal."

To me, this damned the Expeditionary Force. I wanted to say, and did not, "Just be decent technicians of war, not paladins. And try to understand the world you live in."

Later — but how could I have foreseen it? — these young aristocrats, or those who survived, were to become political commissioners, convinced of the worth of the people, of the people's war, and of the army's place in the

idst of the people. They would be converted by deaths, defeats, humilia-
ons, to something they had never conceived of. It would take years, but
ven then they would never really understand; they would go on to new
agedies, even greater humiliations, and they would end up being "lost
oldiers."

Army life was still good, but even in 1948 people spoke regretfully of
ne really good days, Leclerc's time, when the war was amusing. I was the
uest of a noncom's field mess, a *popote* of real old sweats, strapping and
ed-faced, who told me that the war had been slipping badly.
"The Expeditionary Force is all red tape and stuffy administration.
'hink of the time of P——'s commando . . . They were all Frenchmen
n it, and they were lions! Nothing they couldn't do. Their specialty was to
ttack naked, but well greased all over, with their ammo slung round their
ellies. One night P—— was reviewing a detail in combat order; he was in
he raw, everybody was. He saw the chaplain in line, in the same turnout,
nd he was *shocked*. 'Father, not you! At least put your shirt on!'"

Everyone in the country carried arms; villages created their own militias;
ig and little warlords sprang up; "protection societies" roamed the towns;
nd the Expeditionary Force created and paid for a fantastic mob, three
imes its own number, of partisans, condottieri, assassins, and adventurers.
Most of the partisans were left alone, with nothing much in the way of
defensive weapons, in the little guard towers scattered along the roads.
Costing only about a hundred thousand francs ($300), these were built of
brick, with a hole for an entrance, ten or twelve feet above ground level. At
night the partisans would pull up the ladder and join their women and
children in the one small room. Armed with a few grenades and their ancient
guns (since French regulations denied them tommy guns or automatics,
which might attract the Viets to buy or kill) they would lie all night by their
loopholes, waiting for dawn. Almost daily the high command would announce the loss of a few guard towers; but they were easy to build, and
there were plenty of *nha-qués* available.
It was a pitiless war. The Viets were carrying out a policy of atrocities:
but this atmosphere of torture bore its own corruption and contagion with
it. In the end cruelty was practiced on all sides. The Expeditionary Force's
Asian partisans, continually threatened with a hideous death, killed the
Vietminh with the most sophisticated torments — unless of course they
came to an understanding with them. Often it happened that even the
French were caught up in this intoxication of torture and death. It was in

the air one breathed, it arose from the country itself, forming part of its ways and customs: it emanated from the landscape, from weariness, over-excitement and example. Great strength of character was needed to keep it down. The Viets knowingly urged the French on to commit excesses, for they were well aware that as far as torture was concerned they were far beyond the French, both in efficiency and skill. For them torture as a form of warfare finally became a technique that allowed them to gain an ascendancy over the people and to win.

It was a cruel war, and although at this stage it had not yet reached the huge scale of the later years, when regular armies slaughtered one another in pitched battles, it was nevertheless fought with the utmost tenacity and bitterness: it was a many-faced war, and perhaps the best way of describing it, of conveying something of its unique atmosphere and quality, is to speak of some of the different fields in which it was fought, the jungle, the countryside with its perpetual guerrilla warfare, the deltas, the far-off mountains and the R.C. 4, that disastrous road that was supposed to cut the Vietminh off from China.

The war in the jungle

APART from the two human ant hills of the Tonkin and Cochinchina deltas and the densely populated coastal strip of Annam, Indochina is an almost uninhabited jungle. In an area nearly the size of France each side fought in the twilight, without seeing the other; handfuls of men, lost in the enormous landscape, tried to creep up on one another through the darkness and the leaves, to kill at point-blank range. But it was not only the French and the Vietminh who hunted one another down. They had also drawn the little western kingdoms of Indochina, with their scores of different races, into the butchery. The jungle turned into a chaos of hatred in which men varying in civilization from the Stone Age to the utmost refinement of Buddhism wiped one another out. All the primitive enmities between clans and tribes were exploited, and between the imperialists and the Communists they exploded spontaneously.

It was an inextricable tangle. Wars dating from every century were all going on at the same moment: the weapons ranged from blowpipes, spears and spells to machine guns and mortars. There were also economic wars for the possession of salt, that essential commodity for forest dwellers, and above all for opium. Both the Viets and the French bought up the drug, outbidding one another in order to win over the Meos, those formidable mountaineers, who produced it.

And there was not a single nation that was not divided against itself. The King of Cambodia's government was pro-French: so was the government of the King of Laos. But in Cambodia Dap Chuong's mystical Issarak Khmers, allied to the Vietminh, were camping in the holy places of Angkor. In Laos the gouty old king at Luang Prabang, the city of a hundred pagodas, was pious and faithful. His son, Prince Savang, wanted to transform the kingdom of a million elephants into the super-Monaco of the Asian forests, and he wanted to do so remaining close friends with the French. But out of jealousy the feudal lords of the younger branch of the family fomented the Red rebellion of the Pathet Lao. Even the savages were drawn into the battle, from the tribes of elephant-hunting magicians on the Burmese frontiers to the naked Mois of the Annamese highlands. The French gave some of these primitive warriors tommy guns, but there were others who served as guides to the Red detachments. From mountain peak to mountain peak it was a Fenimore Cooper kind of war.

But even among the most backward little tribes the conflict was primarily ideological. The clash of ideas stretched out to reach even the earth-eating pygmies in the unexplored regions, mere white patches on the map.

Throughout all this vast stretch of country the French were in contact with the petty rulers: everywhere they explained to the natives that the Vietnamese were the enemy, the Vietnamese and the Vietminh. They practiced the policy of encouraging minorities and they set up principalities, confederations and autonomous states. Each of the squares on this jungle chessboard had its own flag, its own decorations, its own army, and above all its own financial needs. In Tonkin, on the coast of the bay of Along, the pirate Vong A Sang raised his Nung battalions, whose emblem was an umbrella handle. Along the Red River, Deo Van Long, the son of the man who led the Black Flags when they killed Sergeant Bobillot at the siege of Tuyenquang half a century before, became the great opium lord thanks to French protection. And in the remote valleys and clearings of the everlasting forest there were many other little rulers set up in this way.

To begin with everything went well. The Expeditionary Force established posts on the peaks, above the peaceful, close-packed jungles, above the forest and the wild tumbles of rock that looked like a petrified storm at sea. The airplane made everything possible, for it overcame distance, mountain chains, impenetrable vegetation. The old Junkers perpetually flew to and fro, dropping food and supplies to garrisons at the far end of the world, places that were at some weeks' or even months' march from the nearest civilized village.

In these remote posts there was always to be found an NCO of the

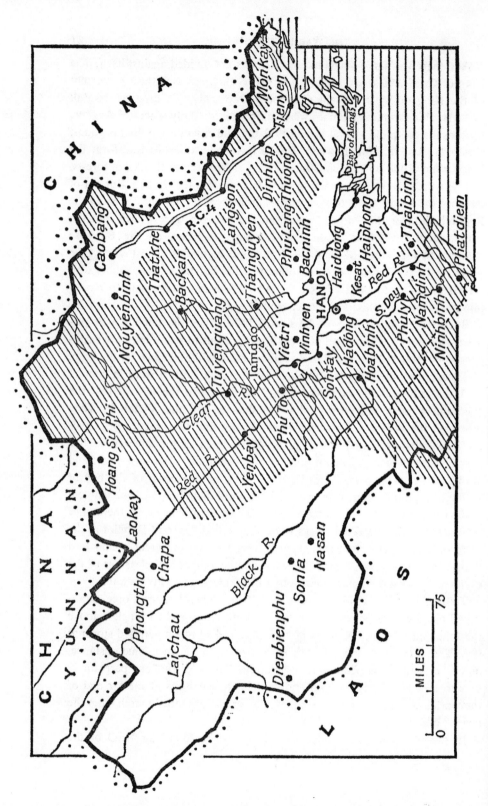

TONKIN IN 1949

Colonial Army, somewhat given to drink and infected with malaria. But he would know how to pay the petty kings in salt or ingots, and turn naked men with silver collars around their necks into passable soldiers with bush hats, belts and submachine guns: but being an experienced man he would refuse to put the Meo and Man highlanders into the regulation boots, for barefoot they are the finest marchers in the world. This Admirable Crichton of the jungle could turn his hand to everything. He might compose national anthems or design a royal standard. But above all he would continually reiterate, "I will never abandon you to the Vietminh."

The French chief of the post would imagine that these Vietminh of whom he spoke were far away. But they were there, on the spot. And they only let him know it when it was too late, by an ambush, by dead bodies lying on the ground. The good life was over.

For in fact the jungle was not impenetrable at all. It was crisscrossed by secret tracks. Ho Chi Minh's columns and his agents traveled along them through the limitless mountains and forests, marching as though time did not exist. Sometimes a political commissar would stop in a clearing and make his headquarters in some wretched hut. Soon afterwards a region of stronger Communist influence would come into existence all around it.

Everything that belonged to the French — the plane, the dropping zone, the fortified post — was formidable; but it could all be seen. Everyone knew where and what it was. But these secret Red movements, this hidden creeping influence that was so undetectable — that was something else again, and like everything that cannot be clearly grasped it was terrifying.

The Vietminh's chief weapon was their success in carrying the war of ideas to even the most primitive and brutish little tribes. The French promised the savages that they would free them from the Vietnamese. But everywhere the Vietminh forestalled them, promising another kind of freedom — freedom from the French. They set up the Resistance deep in this same jungle where the Expeditionary Force was conferring with the rulers. Ho Chi Minh's agents worked at the level of the common people, saying to the wretched jungle dwellers whom they found undermined with fever, superstition and undernourishment, "You do not even know it, but you are the People. All rights belong to you. You think life is harsh and difficult. It will be easy and delightful if you kill the people who are exploiting you, the imperialists and the traitors."

And then, when the forest tribes were sufficiently infected and won over, the Viets began the war of the jungle trails against the French. It had its own rules, laws far more rigid and merciless than those of the war in the rice fields.

The only way of moving was along the tracks. They were so narrow that two columns running into one another head-on could not manage to deploy and fight — only the men in front on either side could fire. So one had to set about it another way, fighting in the American Indian fashion, not clashing directly with the enemy but getting ahead of him and suddenly appearing on his flanks. The right tactical approach was to vanish, to be as it were nonexistent, and only to show oneself at the last second, the moment of striking down the quarry.

The two opposing sides, hiding themselves as they went, sought one another, hunted one another along the tangle of interwoven paths, which themselves were always faint, uncertain and variable. It was a ghastly kind of hide-and-seek played by blind men in a dark room — the forest. It was a matter of guessing right. For victory lay in hitting the right spot, in finding the one path that the human quarry would take through the maze of jungle tracks. The attacking side would vanish on either side of the trail, melting into the green walls, and there they would wait. If they had judged correctly the enemy would appear, suspecting nothing, in Indian file. This was the great moment for patience, the moment when the enemy had to be allowed to get thoroughly into the trap, for all the men were to be shot down at one blast, in a single volley like a firing squad. If a shot came too soon, if the trap were revealed, the prey would escape: they would fling themselves into the jungle and be seen no more. What is more, there would be the danger of falling into just the same kind of ambush as that which one had set and which had failed.

This hunt would often last for months. To win, it was necessary to march by night and day, to be physically and spiritually stronger than the adversary, and to possess a keener set of instincts. It was a game in which a man had to use all his powers to the ultimate degree, in an appallingly hostile world, a green hell of vegetation.

I saw this astonishing war in action, at the foot of the Chain of Annam. Below the mountains there rose the huge wooden palisades and the red earth towers of the Dakto post. Squatting there, naked except for a gee string, the Mois waited, with their baskets on their backs. The bare-bosomed women were smoking water pipes. They were going to celebrate the Moon Festival. There was a buffalo tied to a stake, and presently the warriors would kill it with their spears, according to the ritual. Some ancient sexless creatures with shaved heads were digging up the jars of chum that would be drunk at the feast. Other Mois, dressed as French soldiers, were standing guard.

Sergeant Belleau, in command of the post (220 pounds: a red peasant's face), gazed with astonishment, a proper gendarme's gaze, at this world in which he was the god. And in the most natural way in the world, talking like a philosophical policeman, he described his job to me — the war he was carrying on. "In the first place you have to understand that the jungle is neutral. It doesn't help anyone. It is always the strongest who wins. Any man who is wounded is done for. You can't pick him up and carry him. Almost every time you have to leave him behind. You only get to know the jungle little by little, and it is only little by little that you come to understand how terrible it is. You can starve to death there, with flowers all around you. You can die of thirst in spite of the enormous monsoon rains, because the water just goes straight down the cracks in the limestone. Everything rots, and your flesh rots first of all. You get fevers, and horrible great boils, and the least little scratch sets up an inflammation that can't be cured. But you have to keep going on across the mountains, one after another, all just the same, like the teeth of a saw. You can't stop because the enemy is following you and you are following him. You have to go faster than him and get on to his track so that he won't get on to yours. When things are very bad you have to cut your own path with a machete, and then you go along at one mile a day.

"As an enemy the Viet is really tough: he can run all night. He doesn't give a damn for death. He will wait for days on end in an ambush, hiding there in the jungle without moving, without coughing, without making the least sound. His fire discipline is terrific, and he will wait there with his finger on the trigger, not stirring until the whole column is just right and the political commissar bawls out Fire!

"We have to be as tough as he is. I've stripped my men right down. Every useless thing you carry is so much against you. In the forest you have to be close on naked and you have to travel light, relying on your own strength alone.

"I go out with weapons and ammunition — that's all. Each of my men carries his rations as well, in a hollow bamboo: rice, a little dried fish, salt, quinine, a few tablets of codeine terpine to prevent sneezing when we are laying an ambush. The food is ready cooked, so we don't have to make a fire. Dinner is just squatting down for a moment to swallow a few mouthfuls: and we bury anything that's left — that's most important. You wipe out any trace of having passed that way. If the grass is trodden down you straighten it up again, because any sign might mean the end for you.

"I have the Sedangs as allies. They are great big good-looking fellows with nothing on except paint and tattooing and magic charms. They're red, like copper. They go right out of their minds when they sacrifice a buffalo;

they hamstring it and bloat themselves with its blood and guts. They are real warriors. They fight against the next-door tribe, the Katai, who are on the side of the Viets. And just as I do with the Sedangs, the Viet officers take on the Katai and train them. It is a very tough war. Because here we are quite near one of the Reds' springboards, the Vietminh enclave of Quangngai and Quinhon on the Annam coast. On the other side of this Chain of Annam (it has not been thoroughly explored), there is the sea: the coast down there has the rice fields and the towns and the great mass of the population — civilization. The Communists' regular battalions are not sixty miles away.

"I hold out, thanks to my Sedangs. They are faithful and I can rely on them so long as I don't do anything against one of their taboos. There are so many of them that I run the risk of breaking one every day: I am very careful about it. I never carry on with a raid if a stag bells away on the right of the column. That is the worst possible omen, and my Sedangs would desert me if I didn't take notice of it. And without my savages I should be like a wandering babe. They show me the way just as the Katai do for the Viets. The most important thing is that I don't see in the same way as they do: they act as my eyes. I can't explain it, but somehow they discover all the invisible traps that the Katai set in the forest and along the tracks: all of them, from the pits that you fall into and stick yourself on a spike, to the little darts they fix in the ground. There are some three or four inches long that go through your sole, some a foot long that stab the calf of your leg, and some high enough to get you in the belly. They are all poisoned with datura or rotten meat. You can run yourself through at every bush you come to. These simple creatures have a good many other dangerous tricks too. You stumble against a branch, and a huge creeper that has been balanced in all the green stuff overhead comes crashing down on to your head. Or else a bush that had been bent in two straightens out in a flash and darts an arrow into your chest. But the most dangerous weapon of the lot is their crossbow: they can hit a man with absolute certainty at fifty yards. My Sedangs deal with all these traps for me. And they have magical cures to dose you with. Once I opened my foot on one of those darts: they put a kind of plaster made of herbs on the place, and I was able to walk.

"I love my Sedangs, and they have some kind of an affection for me, in spite of that fickleness you find in savages. The Viets tried to corrupt them, and it cost them their lives. This was a couple of months ago. One evening five Vietminh suddenly appeared in a Sedang village, bringing presents and talking about peace. The elders held a meeting and promised to deliver me up. And while the drums were beating for the feast they sent me a messenger offering me their guests' heads. They would show me which track the Vietminh were going to leave by and all I would have to do would be to kill them. But there was just one condition. Afterwards they would have to shift the village a day's march away, so that the Red punitive expeditions should not be able to find them in the enormous forest. Carrying off the huts and putting them up again was nothing; but the *rays*, the mountain fields, would be lost. Would I give them the same amount of rice that they would have harvested? I agreed and the bargain was struck.

"The ambush failed. One partisan fired too soon. The Viets flung themselves into the jungle, but they scattered. And one man alone in the jungle is finished: you only have to track him until he drops from exhaustion. You seem to be absolutely alone, and then you hear the thump of a tomtom, then another one answering it, and then another. They are calling one another in for the kill. The Sedangs tracked the Viets, but they waited until they had lost the last ounce of their strength before closing in and cutting their throats one after the other.

"Four of the Viets were finished off in the forest. The fifth was given to me as a present — a mark of respect. He was reduced to something like a skeleton, and he was raw all over. A captain. I had him taken care of, and he cut his belly open with a pointed bamboo in his cell. We cured him again, and then, because of his courage, I had him released. To be sure, my generosity was much the same as a death sentence. The Red committee of Quangngai, the people I gave him up to, will certainly have him executed. How could he possibly not be suspected once I had set him free? For the Viets are crazy about security. They'll kill one of their best men, a hero, absolutely devoted to the cause, rather than take the slightest risk. And at the same time they are wily and smooth talking, and they know how to seem very gentle — they can act any part when they are trying to indoctrinate the savages. It is a mixture you just can't understand.

"The strangest thing is that in spite of the way they are always trying to do the right thing, always trying to find the 'correct solution,' the Viets sometimes make the most appalling blunders. It happens when they think they have won. Then they show themselves as they really are — pitiless domineering rulers. That was what caused the rebellion of the Rhes.

"One day several hundred horsemen, under a whole forest of lances, came riding slowly up to my post. They rode naked, with their long black hair down their backs: they had their war paint on and they were carrying their shields. Their crossbows and some odd-looking weapons hung from their saddles. A grave old monkey-faced man stopped in front of me and addressed me solemnly. 'We are Rhe warriors. Our tribe lives on the other side of the mountain, where the forest thins out on the edge of the Annamese country — there where their fields and villages begin. For a long time we were under the Quangngai Vietminh. They promised us great things; but a little while ago their political commissars came and took away our best rice fields. During the night three thousand of our men gathered silently and at nine the next day they flung themselves upon Chilang and Vinay, which are the nearest Vietminh villages. The people there begged us to spare their lives. 'Give us our lives,' they said. 'We gave you your freedom.' We said to them, 'Is it freedom never to be able to enjoy yourself, never to drink out of the chum jar, but always to be obliged to work for you?' And we ran them through with our spears, hundreds of them, women and children too. A few days later a Vietminh battalion arrived. They shot our chiefs and burned our villages. What could we do against machine guns? We have hidden our families in the jungle and we have come to you. Give us rifles.'

"I appointed the naked old gentleman colonel, and now I have a Rhe army that I can make raids with as far as the outskirts of Quangngai. But a little while ago the town's committee sent me a letter. 'Enjoy your life while you may. We are getting ready. When everything is prepared we are going to invade your jungle in huge numbers: we shall take your posts and you will be shot.' It is not an empty threat. Still, I think I shall have time to finish my tour of duty and go off on leave. The Viets are desperately methodical and so they are also desperately slow."

In the forest, then, there was an infinitely complex struggle. The Vietminh had their successes and their failures, but they were making ground, even if it was only at a walking pace and at the speed of dialectic reasoning — two kinds of slowness. It was antlike labor, and its aim was the setting up of the Red psychological and political system. The corruption spread. After the first peddlers of the good word there appeared detachments consisting of a few soldiers, then small military units. At the slightest hitch the process stopped: the situation had to be analyzed; there had to be autocriticism; the error, the fault committed had to be discovered and corrected; a better approach, better tactics had to be worked out. Despite countless withdrawals and fresh starts, the advance was relentless. After these years of preparation all the Red divisions had to do was to appear. In the end it was to be Dienbienphu.

The sects

THE French had some curious allies in this war, but none more curious than the sects and certain autonomous bands such as the Binh Xuyen. The sects were of a religious nature (unlike the Binh Xuyen, who started as plain pirates, and who had no spiritual or ethical pretensions at any time) and they were of a remarkably recent origin: they were armed theocracies, and at one time they had belonged to the Vietminh front. They changed sides when the Red leaders of the Vietminh decided to massacre their chiefs. The most important sects were the Caodaists and the Hoahao; the Hoahao religion was a "revived Buddhism" preached by Huynh Pho So, a Living God who was killed by the Vietminh, but that of the Caodai was more eclectic by far.

The Caodaists (for I shall just speak of this sect in passing, having no room to deal with the matter exhaustively) were most uncommonly pious. I have never known a prelate with a more soothing appearance than the Caodaist pope, His Holiness Pham Cong Tac, when he received me in his little house within the holy city of Tayninh. He was a very small Annamese, very lively, very neat, with eyes that looked ecstatic and at the same time knowing. He had tiny, beautifully shaped hands and feet, and every time he sat down he took his charming little bare feet out of his sandals. He was dressed as a seer — a long white silk robe and a conical hat with a tassel on top.

"Here's to your health," said the pope, uncorking a bottle of lukewarm champagne at ten in the morning. He burst into a harsh peal of laughter: every few moments there was this high-strung cackle and he would choke with mirth, clapping his transparent hands and beating his feet on the ground. His gold teeth gleamed agreeably from the midst of all this cheerfulness.

"Here's to yours," I replied. We touched glasses. I ventured to observe that I had supposed wine and spirits forbidden in the Caodaist religion. This delighted the pope so much that the bobble on the end of his curious headgear trembled wildly. At last Pham Cong Tac, having recovered his priestly gravity, explained, "I have granted myself a dispensation, you see. It is in your honor." Once more he shook with merriment.

We talked for a long while. Except during his strange fits of choking laughter, the pope spoke in a vein of high theosophy. He told me about love. Caodaism was the religion of love between men. It was the sudden defensive reaction of enlightened spiritualism in the face of the onslaught

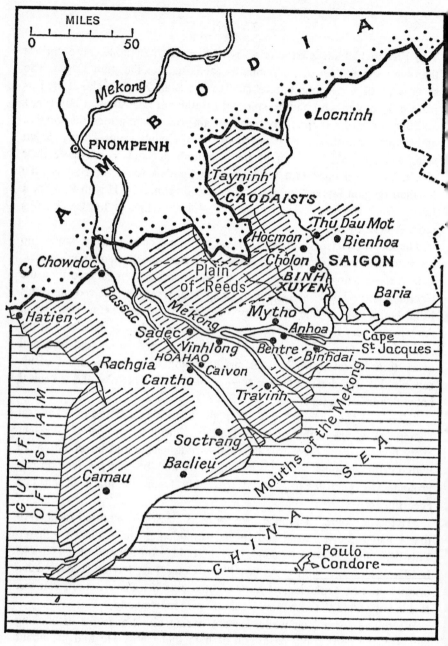

COCHINCHINA IN 1949

of Evil, of atheistical Communism. The religion's mission was to bring peace and brotherliness into this war-racked world. It forbade men to kill, steal, lie, commit adultery, get drunk, eat meat.

"Caodai is the Supreme Being," the pope told me. "Buddha, the Messiah, Mahomet and all the holy men and geniuses of mankind from Confucius to Victor Hugo were his forerunners. But when fire and terror were on the point of overwhelming the earth the time had come for him to make himself materially apparent and no longer to remain anonymous. During the year 1924 a mysterious spirit continually reappeared in the course of some spiritualist séances in Saigon. He said only that his name was Aaa. It was on the night of Christmas 1925 that he finally revealed his identity and stated that he was Caodai, the Supreme Being. He communicated this tremendous news in a message to Monsieur Le Van Trung, a former colonial councillor and a member of the Légion d'Honneur, who had made a fortune in business. This respectable figure was unfortunately leading a debauched and dissipated life. Yet it was to this sinner that Caodai said, 'Repent, and henceforward obey my law. Spread the truth that you know in all parts, and build a basilica to my glory.' "

The pope described the building of the famous temple of Tayninh and the religion's difficult beginnings — the French were suspicious and there was little money. Fortunately a very wealthy woman devoted her fortune to the cause. She was made an honorary female pope by Le Van Trung, who was himself the first pope. He died in office in 1935. "The Supreme Being chose me as successor," the pope went on. "I experienced persecution; I was sent to Sonla prison in Tonkin and then banished to Madagascar. But I was always full of faith. And I was right not to doubt, for now we have two million converts. You can say what you like, but I believe in quality. First-rate goods always make their way. We succeeded in the end because we had perfected a first-rate religion. After all, what other can compete with ours, since we have picked the best points out of each and put them all together . . ."

A few days later I discovered the other aspect of Caodaism, the sad one. I was riding in a jeep with a French lieutenant, the commander of a district. The bare horizon of the rice fields was suddenly barred by the dark shape of a wood.

"That's a bad place," said my companion. "It all belongs to *Tieudoi* 6."

Our car was running between the pale trunks of an abandoned rubber plantation. The narrow road was hemmed in by bushes. As we approached a corner the officer slowed down. "We are coming to the very spot. There is an ambush here at least once a week. The day before yesterday a patrol was cut to pieces: I had to come and bring in the dead."

Halfway around the bend I saw a villainous-looking crowd. I started, but the lieutenant said, "Those aren't Viets. It's a Caodaist column — there's no danger at all now."

We ran up along the convoy, which stretched over several miles. It was a human migration, primitive and at the same time absurdly modern. The Asia of ancient tradition was there, with its never-ending line of little carts that creaked along behind the slow zebu oxen. Each cart bore the usual mass of worn and wretched objects and people, submitting to fate. The rigid orderliness of the caravan and its dreary silence gave one the feeling that the whole was under the crushing weight of an all-powerful, pitilessly dominating will.

At the top of the unsteady pyramid that was piled up in each cart a motionless woman held aloft a yellow flag bearing a cogged wheel in the corner, the emblem of the Caodaist sect. The standard bearer sat among the sad odds and ends of poverty — children, old people, mothers nursing their babies, pigs, great jars, mats, a few bundles of clothes.

In a low voice the lieutenant told me, "It's a recuperation column. A flying brigade going back to its base after having made a sweep; and those are the people it has raided. They are either converted already or they will be presently, and from now on their function will be to cultivate rice for the brigade and pay it taxes."

The human booty was heavily guarded, so that the Viets should not get possession of them on the way. The Caodaist soldiers were marching in their strange fighting formation — the formation of war in Asia. Everything was suppleness and precaution, infinitely more so than in any French unit. It was the age-old insurance against surprise, brought up to date only by the weapons they were carrying.

Beside the last cart walked two men in overalls, wearing French caps dating from the First World War and pushing bicycles: they represented the column's security. Then at irregular intervals between the carts there were young fellows all hung about with weapons, marching with the elastic pace of the Annamese at war. They were dressed more or less like the Vietminh, in light cotton, but in colors ranging from black to pink. These were the regulars, the shock troops. In the middle of one group, guarded on every side, there was a "mortar soldier" and an "ammunition soldier," the first carrying the murderous tube and the second, behind him, with the mortar bombs hanging from his belt. All these troops wore a beret with the badge of the religion — the sword of the faith across the torch of purity, all enclosed in the circle of life. Farther along there were some human parcels, with everything tied and retied except their legs, which were free to march. They went along in the midst of bayonets, which perpetually goaded them. They were prisoners, the Vietminh of a murder committee — the rivals who had hitherto been in control of the *nha-qués* that the Caodai now owned.

The endless convoy moved forward at three or four miles an hour. All around it there were almost invisible shadows prowling through the bushes; they were the scouts who protected the convoy's flanks. Each of them had one grenade and nothing else. Their function was not to fight but to see, to detect the enemy, who might be lying in ambush. There were hundreds of these scouts, ranging over a depth of five hundred yards on either side, peering into every bush and every tuft of grass. Their lives had no value. They were merely auxiliaries, former Vietminh to whom the Caodaists were giving this chance of redeeming themselves, or else forcibly enlisted peasants who, if they survived and proved faithful, might become regulars.

At last the road was clear. A minute later we reached a band of perfectly ordinary *nha-qués,* some with carrying poles, some with buckets of night soil. Among them were men and women, and even children, hurrying along and gossiping in the most usual way in the world. But for all that they were intelligence agents who were scouting in front of the column, unrecognizable even to the Vietminh themselves.

During the whole time that we had moved up the length of the convoy I had not heard a word; I had not even seen any expression on a single face. Nothing but the tense masks and terrified eyes of so many automata. Once again I was in the presence of the extreme gravity of the Far East, the most overwhelming the world has to show.

The guerrilla war

GUERRILLA warfare is not merely one aspect of the art of fighting. It is in the first place a pitiless logic — the logic of the utter want of compassion. It is the mathematics of "persuasion," into which there enter precisely weighed doses of brainwashing and atrocity. It is a matter of arriving at "correct solutions" by means of dialectic reasoning, solutions that will allow one to dominate human beings completely and turn them into perfect tools for the cause. It requires a total dehumanization; all civilized society's feelings vanish; individuals no longer exist. The goal is the creation of the People, the politically worked-over mass that acts as the supporting basis for the guerrilla, the mass that is to be urged and drawn on to a higher fate and that is to be sacrificed to that fate.

The technique is founded upon cold-blooded cruelty — a cruelty that from this time on became part of the everyday life of the whole of Indochina. There was no getting away from it; it was in the air, and it even infected the French. In their counterguerrilla warfare they became skilled in its use, applying all its rules. They said that it was necessary, and to some degree this was true. But there was also a corrupting, catching delight in it — Asia's well-known sadism. In the end it was a sickness of the mind that infected even the most normal beings.

It was at Hocmon that I experienced guerrilla warfare as a commonplace event, as a matter of course. It was appalling, and yet everybody found it quite natural. There I knew an ordinary French couple who had grown used to these horrors and had acquired the habit, the taste for them, although they still remained "thoroughly decent people of our own kind." The Eastern education in cruelty had been superadded to their former schooling.

> O Saint Barbara, holy flower
> By Our Lord's almighty power,
> O Saint Barbara, shield us all,
> When lightning-strokes and thunder fall.

This was the prayer of the kneeling C children, aged four and two, while the Vietminh were firing mortars at their house. Madame C had told them it was a storm and made them pray to Saint Barbara, for Saint Barbara is very good against thunderbolts.

It happened almost in the suburbs of Saigon, just ten miles from the capital. Outwardly Hocmon was just one more little colonial town in Cochinchina, drowsing in the heat and the boredom. In fact it was an inferno of guerrilla and counterguerrilla activity. It was virtually besieged. Around the town there prowled the most important *tieudoi* of the powerful resistance leader Nguyen Binh. For the last two years the 13th Demi-Brigade* of the Foreign Legion had been vainly trying to thrust them back, but they had impregnable places of safety just at hand. On the one side the Plain of Reeds thrust out an arm as far as Hocmon, and on the other the Moi forest stretched out to Thuddaumot, a few miles away. Saigon was in easy reach, and there the hunted Vietminh leaders concealed themselves under a variety of disguises.

---

* A formation peculiar to the Foreign Legion consisting of two combat battalions: it is an autonomous unit with its own transport, signals and sappers, and it is commanded by a colonel.

The fighting for Hocmon was exceedingly fierce, for the little town occupied a vital strategic position: it commanded the main road from Pnompenh, which was squeezed into a narrow stretch of firm ground running between the marsh and the jungle.

I was staying with the administrative delegate C and his wife. C was a man of twenty-six, strongly built, short and powerful, with a rather doll-like face from which there peered sharp and indeed suspicious eyes. He was designedly unpolished and he was dressed very carelessly, in khaki; he shouted at people, but his language bore the mark of education and good manners. This very young man was carrying on his particular war in command of several hundred irregulars, alongside the Legion.

C lived in a bungalow on the edge of the town: an odd mixture of the Far West and the traditional magazine serial. Pistols and ammunition were lying about everywhere on the dusty furniture. The table in the dining room was splendidly laid, with a great deal of glass and china — chipped, I may add. The very ceremonious meal was good: we drank well. But the servants' hands were dirty.

Madame C apologized for them. "They are Vietminh prisoners. My husband wanted to try an experiment and he took them on as houseboys. To begin with I was frightened: I was continually thinking that they were going to cut our throats or poison us. They could easily do it — they are not watched. Now the idea of what they are never even crosses my mind. But I have never succeeded in training them."

"So I am eating a meal cooked and served by Nguyen Binh's soldiers?"

"Yes," replied Madame C, smiling.

The butler, a middle-aged man with a bony face, took the dishes around again with deferential gestures. He was a former political commissar. I asked C how many Frenchmen he had killed or caused to be killed earlier on. C shrugged. "I've no notion. It doesn't matter."

In the drawing room there were some grenades that had been forgotten in the chair where I was about to sit. C roared with laughter. "It's quite all right: the pins are still in."

Once more his wife was embarrassed. "Really," she cried, "these Vietminh houseboys are dreadfully careless. They might at least have tidied up."

So that was family life in Hocmon! The C's carried on their middle-class life in the midst of horrors. What a strange dichotomy! The C's had retained all the principles of old-fashioned France, but at the same time they had completely identified themselves with a life of violence, torture and bloodshed. Atrocity was a commonplace for them.

How little time had been needed for the transformation. It was only three years before that C, fresh from the Ecole Coloniale and newly married, had arrived in Indochina. He was offered Hocmon and he accepted without knowing anything about it. He settled in there with his better half and their little brood. Apparently it was as simple as that.

But it was not in fact quite so easy. You could feel a slight difference between the two of them. C was perfectly happy; she was not. C was deeply attached to Hocmon; she far less. But she loved him, and so she rose to the occasion.

Madame C was a calm, good-looking woman, with a rather buxom figure, regular features and a very white skin. At Saigon they had told me that she was "a real lady," and they had described the way she lived, always waiting for her husband as he carried on his murderous war. I was told, "She eats her heart out all through those never-ending hours. She knows that C is too rash, too desperately keen — the Viets will get him one day. She is living in the expectation of dreadful news, but she never shows it. She is always calm and collected and she does not turn a hair, even on those nights when the Viets attack Hocmon. She is never afraid for herself — only for him."

Once, they told me, the Viets attacked their house at dusk. C had not yet come home. She rallied the panicking irregulars and posted them at their action stations. The Viets opened up with machine guns and mortars. Madame C directed the defense until her husband, who heard firing from a great way off, had time to rush back to the house, from which he launched a counterattack.

I had been advised not to mention Madame C's exploits in front of her husband: his view was that women should not make themselves conspicuous. I contented myself with saying to my hostess, "But how can you stand the atmosphere of Hocmon?"

"I've grown used to it. You get used to anything, even if you are a person who had never left France — and I never had. I have got into the way of this life, but I don't feel passionately enthusiastic about it, as my husband does. I don't like the cruelty."

"Hocmon is rather strange, it's true," said C. "It arises from the fact that the Vietnamese are possessed by a kind of anarchic cruelty — cruelty primarily for its own sake. It is not merely that people are out of their wits with fear: so much has happened that their nerves are utterly flayed, and they are living in a state of sadistic exacerbation that takes any outlet it can. I noticed this unnatural state of affairs as soon as I came to Hocmon.

"This happened in 1946. At that time criminals were still beheaded with a sword. One day a killer, a man who had liquidated scores of outstanding figures, was captured and condemned to death. The execution took place in the main square, in the presence of the *nha-qués* who were there selling their vegetables as usual. When the time came for him to lay his head on the block the Vietminh, a huge dark thick-set peasant, cursed the French in the traditional manner. 'I hate you,' he said to me. 'May my blood be upon your head to the hundredth generation.' I expected a wave of compassion for him from the crowd, even perhaps of fury. Imagine my complete astonishment when the bystanders burst into hearty laughter, rolling about and holding their sides. For them the execution was a thoroughly amusing spectacle. During the days that followed it there were twice as many people in the market and dozens of young fellows had signed on with me as irregulars. That was my first lesson. I grasped that in Asia you have to be the strongest, the most formidable, in everything, even in cruelty. But it took me longer to learn my second lesson: it is that this cruelty has to be as exact as an equation. It is just as harmful to be cruel in a haphazard way, or mistakenly, as not to be cruel when it is called for. It all has to be worked out."

While he was speaking Madame C kept her eyes fixed on her husband. Then, letting herself go, she spoke her mind. "What you mean is that you are drunk with this atmosphere of danger and madness. You're an addict. You have to have it now." She turned to me. "Just beyond the garden there is a piece of waste land, covered with tall, thick brushwood. The Viets slip into these bushes to fire at the house whenever they choose. I don't know how many times I have asked my husband to have them cut down. He won't. He has to have these Vietminh machine-gun bursts."

C was vexed. He replied very warmly, "My wife will never understand the question of face. I don't want to lose the little I possess: I've spent years acquiring it. But if I have these thickets done away with the entire population of Hocmon will say that the Delegate is afraid, and that the Viets must really be strong for him to be taking all these precautions. On the other hand if I pay no attention to these bushes I am also paying no attention to the Viets. I show the whole town that I consider them a bunch of weak-kneed hooligans."

Madame C was put in her place. She withdrew, leaving us together. Yet most of what C told me after she had gone concerned a woman, Madame Thi Be: but she was the leader of a *tieudoi* and almost his equal . . .

The war in the mud

A MILE or so from Hocmon C showed me an imposing building made of brick — the home of the 13th Demi-Brigade. It was the Foreign Legion itself that had built it, and built it splendidly. At a parade the colonel had given the order, "Architects, three paces forward: engineers, three paces forward: artificers, masons, carpenters and plasterers, three paces forward." They took their three paces forward, they built, and they returned to their state of anonymity. Under its badge (a grenade) the Legion possesses every trade known to man.

It was perfectly well known that the colonel was mad. He was made entirely of bone and sinew; his eyes could flash lightning and he was capable of strange, disconcerting sarcasm. But he was much respected, for he was a splendid fighter, and his "eccentricities" were in the best line of tradition. They say that once he went to a reception stark naked, clad only in medals spread upon his bosom: he explained that the invitation was worded "Dress: decorations."

He agreed to see me. But I had scarcely come into his office before he sent for an enormous trumpet, at least six feet long. "Would you like to know about my secret weapons? To begin with, here is my Jericho trumpet. When I have it blown my legionaries know that the enemy's ranks are going to crumble, just like the walls of the city in the Bible. Now that I have let you into the secret you will be able to write a splendid article. I will not detain you any longer."

Fortunately I met an acquaintance, a fat, red-haired lieutenant who took me to his company's post and who, unlike his colonel, showed me all around the place. After having seen the trophies taken from the Vietminh and photographs of the corpses of "Viet bigwigs," I came to a very clean little room. On shelves there were things that might have been medical or surgical instruments. I thought I was in a sick bay. But with the utmost candor, as if it were the most natural thing in the world, the pleasant young officer said, "This is my own little intelligence section. I have all the equipment I need, you see — quite simple, quite cheap . . ."

He led me away, hoping that I had not understood. All I said was, "Just as well I'm not a mischief-maker, eh?"

Then we went to have a drink, brandy and soda served by legionaries. A few second lieutenants joined us, charming, handsome young men of about twenty, the age of pure faith. Everyone very naturally talked shop. But from what I heard it seemed to me that the 13th Demi-Brigade's work was a most wearisome routine. It consisted of perpetually crossing and recrossing the Plain of Reeds to destroy an indestructible enemy. Continual operations, with men killed and wounded.

One of these young officers had just come back from a patrol. Two hours earlier he had been worn out, covered with mud from head to foot. Now he was a pink cherub, kind and smiling. He was a well-bred young man, and in order to give me pleasure he told me about his expedition in detail.

"My objective was a Vietminh 'factory' on a little island in the Plain of Reeds. Usually I put my men into sampans and we go up the canals, whose banks are lined with water palms so that they hem you in like the walls of a prison. You can't see anything, but you can be seen. This time, so as not to be picked up, we went on foot through the shit, as we call it — the stinking marsh covered with reeds and lotus that stretches out forever.

"The approach lasted for hours, and all the time we were up to our waists in the muck. We had started at midnight: by dawn we had still not been seen. We were only a few hundred yards from the 'factory.' Then came the horn sounding the alarm. I looked through my field glasses. The little island was like an ant hill that has just been stirred up. I heard explosions and saw flames. I knew what that meant. The Viets were taking their heavy equipment away in boats and they were carrying out their scorched-earth policy with the rest. It always happens that way.

"It took us another half hour to get ashore, to struggle up on to the firm ground. There was nothing but destruction and emptiness. Some frantic buffaloes by the remains of the burning huts. We killed them. The stocks of rice had been soaked in gasoline and now they were only smouldering heaps. We found a little in the way of machinery, all smashed with hammers. But all the really valuable equipment, the lathes for making shells and the electric motors, had been carried off, in spite of its weight.

"We did not see a single man, either. There were certainly hundreds of Viets still there, but so hidden that there was not a hope of finding them. Some would have turned into bushes. Others would be right down under the mud, breathing through hollow bamboos. Most would be in carefully prepared burrows. It was like being surrounded by a crowd of ghosts: they would stay there for hours on end, waiting for us to go. To have unearthed them, we should have had to spend days there, searching everything. We couldn't do it. It would have been too dangerous. Besides the Legion needed us elsewhere for other assignments. If we go back there in a month's time everything will have been repaired. We will find the factory going at full blast. We have tried to destroy it a dozen times without really succeeding.

"I must have been on hundreds of operations here in the Plain of Reeds. It is unbelievably monotonous. There are the ambushes — the ones you set and above all the ones you fall into. Suddenly men you can't see, amphibious creatures in the water and the mud, start firing: you don't even know where the shots are coming from. Then there is the chasing. Sometimes it is we who are after the Viets and sometimes the other way about, but it is always the same weird business. Men sunk deep in the mud, the gluey mud, slowly forcing their legs through it to catch other men who are bogged down in just the same way. You only see their heads, and the Plain of Reeds is so flat that you might think they were dots stuck to its surface. When you come to the open space of a canal or an irrigation ditch you swim under the water, so as not to present a target: all that you see of a man is one hand holding up a tommy gun or the part of a mortar that must never get wet. Often some of my men are drowned.

"Our great weakness is the wounded. I don't know what the Viets do with theirs: they never seem worried by them. But as soon as one of my men is hit I have to call off whatever operation we are carrying out. To get him out through those everlasting marshes I need every man I have — eight to carry him and the rest as a guard. It all turns into a dangerous, slogging retreat. If there are a lot of Viets behind us it can turn very nasty, seeing that we have this dead weight — all the more so since at the best of times they get along faster than we do."

"So you don't kill many Viets?"

"We kill scores and scores of them. But there are always just as many left — in fact more. There's an inexhaustible supply. And then it's not always the real full-blown Viet that we kill. We only know afterwards, and not always then. Often they are just villagers, people's militia, half or even only a quarter Viet.

"Not long ago we got three hundred at one go. An informer guided our legionaries to a Viet meeting that was being held on the bank of the Saigon River. The meeting was camouflaged in a field of maize. But we knew where it was going on, and we charged straight for the spot. The Viets flung themselves into the river, sinking into the water and the mud of the submerged forest and wriggling in among the mangrove roots. But the Saigon River is a tidal stream and the tide was on the ebb. We only had to wait. Two hours later the first Viets, stark naked, were in sight. They tried very hard to bury themselves deeper, digging down in the drying mud with their hands. We shot them like so many rabbits. The water ebbed further and further, and as it retreated every yard of mud had its quarry in it. They were certainly Viets; but we were never quite sure what kind."

The war in the mountains

IT was drizzling. The Tonkin delta was smothered in cotton wool. An endless miserable rain drifted down, and the gray of the sky merged with the gray of the flooded land. But for all that the war still had to go on in this bare, soaked delta, in an aquariumlike world, in the mud, in the dirty water of the rice fields, the filth of the little ditches and the roads.

But for my part I was going to fly off toward the vast sunlit jungle, westward toward Sonla, Laichau and Laokay. I was at Bachmai, the Hanoi military airfield. There were about twenty ancient Junkers lined up, their outlines nibbled away by the mist. These poor old machines, which had been scrapped everywhere else in the world, represented the entirety of the French air strength in Tonkin. These were the planes that provided the air link with all the posts in Upper Tonkin and Upper Laos, posts set down in a jungle area half the size of France.

One of the strange sides of the Indochinese war was that this enormous stretch of jungle, still in French hands, was totally cut off from the Tonkin delta. It was separated from it by the Vietminh corridor of the lower Black River, which connected Ho Chi Minh's quadrilateral with Vinh and Thanhhoa in Red Annam. So these planes, these Junkers, had to leapfrog the corridor to reach the forest posts and to keep them going in the midst of their solitude. Day after day the patched-up old kites took off. In spite of the winter drizzle, in spite of the summer monsoon and its terrible storms, in spite of the wild disorder of the mountain chains and the jungle, they had to carry out the revictualling of these posts at the world's end, and carry it out completely. They had to circle heavily over the dropping zones among the clouds and the mountain peaks, releasing the colored parachutes that carried the precious cargo: because for the men down there on the ground life came from the sky. So the airlift could never stop for any length of time. The Junkers had to get through whatever the weather. There was no ground-to-air guidance whatever: the crews had to make their way as best they could. Often it meant a crash — a peak looming up out of the murk just too late. On this particular day there were parachutes and propellers arranged to make a funeral chapel in one of the hangars at Maomai: the altar was set up in front of a discarded plane. But the bodies were not there: they were lying shattered somewhere in the jungle on the Chinese border, at whatever undiscovered spot their Junker had crashed. Unhappily the plane was not only carrying supplies that day, but men too. A stick of twenty parachutists had been killed. It was the fifth disaster of the kind in a month.

Someone came to find me for the takeoff. I went across the airfield: it was bareness, penury itself. The smell of old army stores pervaded everything; everywhere there was the aftertaste of a neglected barracks. The men, surrounded by these decaying hangars and their heaps of old iron, displayed a kind of weariness, a kind of deliberate carelessness. And yet, so long as they did not look as though they were working, and so long as it amused them too, how arduously these mechanics, old sweats with a heavy accent, toiled over their engines. So did the pilots, slim young men with a horror of seeming earnest. They were all expert tinkerers: nothing was organized, and everyone shifted for himself.

At that time there were neither fighters nor bombers in Indochina. Nobody had ever asked for them, either. But it had amused the pilots to drop shells by hand through the doors of their Junkers on to any Viets they happened to see. Then they got tired of tossing them out and asked their mechanics to fix homemade bomb racks under the fuselage. The bomb racks usually worked, but one could never be quite sure of them — the bombs might still be there. Not that it mattered, for it increased the sporting side of things — landing was more fun.

As I walked out a single Junker was humming like a May bug in the middle of the dead airfield. It was the one that I was going to fly in. The crew told me that they were going to take off in spite of the zero visibility, which in theory prevents all flying. The plane was going whatever happened, because it was on an assignment with absolute priority. It was essential that the plane should land at Sonla to pick up five seriously wounded men who were slowly dying as they waited to be flown out. The pilot finished by saying, "Still, it's going to be a tough job to jab through."

I did not know what he meant, but I did not like to ask.

We were scarcely airborne before the dirty weather swallowed us up, the almost solid atmosphere. With its engines roaring and coughing wearily, the Junker went up and up in a steady, arduous climb. Then for two long hours it thrust on through the white night. I felt quite lost, but the unloaders, the soldiers who push out the packages that are to be parachuted, squatted cheerfully there on the metal floor, drinking wine.

Finally the Junker began to turn as though it were riding around a ring, searching for something I could not make out. Outside everything was as impenetrable as ever. Another passenger, an infantry officer huddled in a blanket, told me what was happening. "We are just about over Sonla now. To reach this point we have flown on a given bearing. The idea is that after a certain time — two hours and a quarter, I think it is — we should be directly over Nasan, the Sonla airfield. Now it's the moment to go in: you can't make an instrument approach, because there's nothing down there, and everything has to be done by instinct. The crew are trying to find a gap in the cloud so that they can get down that way, more or less in safety. If they can't find one then the only thing to do is to go down blind. But it's rough country down there, and you're just as likely to hit a mountain as to find yourself over a valley."

Suddenly the Junker dived. Through the clouds I saw a big hard dark patch that rushed up toward us. It was a mountaintop. In a split second the pilot pulled out of the dive and the crash just did not happen. At last we came out into a pallid light and found ourselves flying along a strange corridor, in the middle of a triangle of clear air between the cloud ceiling and the two steep sides of a gorge. It was so narrow that the plane's wingtips almost scraped the rock. But ten minutes later we came out of the tunnel and flew over so wild a tumble of mountains that it was almost impossible to believe that men could manage to live there, let alone make war.

A trough opened out before us: we landed. All I could see was a grassy strip in the middle of the jungle. And yet the war was already there — it had already reached this ridiculous airfield. It was first to be seen in the form of a shattered Junker, a heap of rusting metal on the edge of the field. And above all it was there in the form of an ambulance, an absurdly ancient vehicle with the red cross painted on it. The first to come out was a captain, a man with that utterly drained thinness of those who are about to die or who have just escaped from death. He hobbled towards the plane on crutches. Everything about him was stiff, dry, coldly feverish: the first thing that he did with his remnant of life was to exaggerate military formality. With precise, jerking movements this ghost in an officer's uniform saluted the crew of the Junker. The captain still had pieces of a dum-dum bullet in his body, a bullet that had hit him several days' march away; and for a whole fortnight he had been carried back on a litter along the jungle tracks, fevered and thirsty. It was Meo savages who carried him, and they made him smoke opium to soothe his pain.

Then four stretchers were brought out of the ambulance. Each one bore a heap of blankets and blood-stained bandages, with a head appearing from them, hollow-cheeked and far too calm. There was one Frenchman among these dying men, one legionary and two Thai partisans. They too had been carried vast distances through the jungle, but suffering had taken too much out of them and now they were indifferent, resigned. They did not even show any hope when they were loaded on to the plane, and yet in a few hours they would be operated upon in the Lanessan hospital at Hanoi. They would probably be saved. But how many other wounded, as far gone as that, had died in the forest while they were being carried?

The Junker took off again. I heard someone bawling my name, "Bodard! Bodard!" But it was not for me. The Bodard they were shouting to was a very cheerful red-faced fellow who had an upturned bottle of wine to his mouth. He was the driver of the army truck in which I was to travel to Sonla, some twenty miles away. He hurtled down the winding road, upsetting the little horses of a salt caravan and the Thai women bowed under the weight of their carrying poles. Every time he roared with laughter. He passed the bottle round among the other soldiers crammed into his truck, and even to me.

Poor fellow. I had no suspicion that one of us, one of these two Bodards, was to be killed a few days later. As it turned out it was the other Bodard, that young soldier who was so enchanted with life. He was to die stupidly as people nearly always did die in Indochina: a stupid death on that same road to the airstrip. The road was classified as safe, but all that was needed was a hidden guerrilla pulling on a string that set off a buried shell. He was killed; and he had only been in Indochina a few weeks.

But the Bodard who set me down at Sonla did not know that he was to die. We said "Good luck" to one another, and he went off to get something to eat. As far as I was concerned he had played his part. For he had brought me into the Asia of the legends, removed several centuries back in time.

From Sonla I meant to travel on through the country of the Black Thais and then through the country of the White Thais and so across the mountains to Laokay, on the Chinese frontier itself, a journey of some three hundred miles.

A jeep would take me as far as Laichau, at the end of the R.P. 41, that road which was to be the Vietminh's main supply route some years later, when they were besieging Dienbienphu, and which the French air force was to try so desperately and so vainly to cut by bombing. Beyond Laichau I should have to make my own way on horseback, riding for a week or two along the mountain tracks through the forest and the jungle.

It was a marvelous journey, and it took me through some splendid country. For example, I went through the land of the Meos, and they are perhaps the strangest people in Indochina: they themselves say that they were begotten by the Great Holy Dog, but the ethnologists maintain that they come from the far north, that they are indeed Eskimos. At all events they only reached Indochina recently, within the last century. They spread in a slow, secret migration from ridge to ridge, at such heights that there was no one there to stop them. Sometimes they settled down of their own volition for a few months or even years, stopping on the summits of some abrupt, almost inaccessible mountain. There they set enormous forest fires ablaze, burning whole mountainsides away, and they planted poppies in the

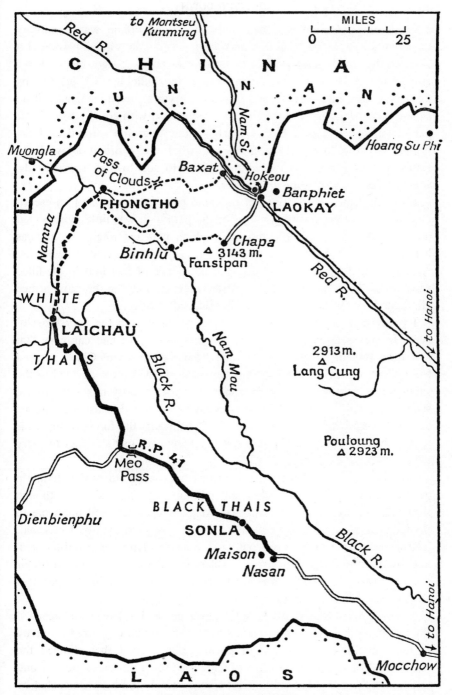

THE THAI COUNTRY

ashy clearings. Opium was their only crop, and opium was a military objective for both the Vietminh and the French. The Vietminh wanted it because they made huge profits by selling it in Hanoi, Saigon, Hong Kong and all the chief capitalist cities in Asia. Drug trafficking was justified by dialectic: the people were to make use of everything, even vice and evil, to ensure their triumph. And the French went after it with equal passion. The possession of the opium crop meant that the Vietminh were denied the opportunity of filling their coffers; and what was more it allowed the Expeditionary Force and the administration to add to their secret funds, which, officially, were absurdly meager.

Deo Van Long, the warlord of Laichau, gave me horses and an escort, and we traveled on towards Phongtho: the path — it was little more — led day after day over splendid mountains, high plateaus where the air was heavy with the scent of flowers — great sweeps of lilies, wild strawberries, roses and rhododendrons. We dropped thousands of feet into jungle-filled valleys with huge ferns and great twisted creepers like the thousand-armed Hindu god, and we rose again, climbing ridge after ridge.

I really had the impression that I was plunging into the very heart of Asia. It was as though frontiers no longer existed. We met caravans that had been traveling for weeks, coming from the depths of China or even from Tibet, following some ancient tea or musk road, now devoted to the smuggling of trumpery modern goods. We met almost unknown tribes, such as the naked, dwarfish Xas, who eat earth, rotted schist. Few things are more surprising than a glimpse of a Xa through the forest twilight, his grayish body wearing nothing but a string slung over one shoulder to carry the one thing he owns, a pipe.

There were many other tribes: and as we approached them the mountain people would freeze, motionless and without any expression, as though they had not seen us. Yet their gaze weighed upon us, and upon me in particular, with a frightening intensity. But this was not enmity, I was told, just curiosity. The only dangerous ones were the Hunis, the red-toothed, long-haired horsemen who thrust travelers through and through with their spears. But their country was right up on the frontier, in the pestilent marshes some two days' march away.

It was a marvelous journey; but I never got to Laokay. I had reached Phongtho, a day or two away, and another warlord had organized a convoy to take me there by an ancient paved Chinese road that climbed the shoulder of Fansipan by the Pass of Clouds at some ten thousand feet and so avoided the track that led through Chapa, which had been evacuated by the French and whose administrator had just been killed by the Vietminh.

And the day before I left an official telegram came through forbidding me to attempt the Pass of Clouds, for the road had been cut by a Chinese band that had crossed into Indochina.

So I went back, all the way across the mountains and the valleys, through the forest and the jungle to Laichau, to Sonla, to Hanoi, and there I looked for a plane that would take me to Laokay. For Laokay was a place that I had to see: it was the first important town that had been threatened since the Expeditionary Force had begun fighting in Indochina, and it was a fortress of great strategic importance. Laokay was the pivot of Upper Tonkin, the center for trade and smuggling, the chief market for opium, arms and information. It was the key to the Red River at the point where it made its way out of the high mountains of the most remote parts of Asia and flowed through the Tonkin jungle. Here there was a bridge across the Red River and there was not another until you reached Hanoi and the delta, nearly two hundred miles downstream. Still more important, it was a key to China, a gateway into Yunnan and thence to the high plateaus, the gorges and the wild mountains that ran down from Tibet, a gateway to the Burma road and to the high, narrow tracks that wound through the mountains to Lhasa and Chungking. It was the natural outlet for an enormous stretch of China, the tropical, primitive, almost unexplored China, that lies above the Asia of the deltas and the plains. It was in order to exploit these regions, which were said to be rich in metals, opium and rare woods, that the French built a railway, a marvel of acrobatics, as far as Kunming. But now it was China that had grown dangerous; and it was China, full of guerrillas, that threatened to spill out into Upper Tonkin. It was by way of Laokay that the armies of the warlord Lu Han had rushed down upon Hanoi in 1945. If Laokay should fall again the Chinese Communists, of whom there were a great many in Yunnan, would be in immediate contact with the Vietminh. An entire flank of Tonkin would collapse.

It was at Laokay that I first had the painful revelation that the war in Indochina might be lost. Up until then I had lived in a state of illusion. Like all the rest of the French I admitted that the Vietminh had an undoubted superiority in the treacherous art of guerrilla warfare, that murderous, bloody hide-and-seek. But I believed the soldiers of the Expeditionary Force when they added, "Ah, but if only the Viets would face us in a set battle, how we should crush them!" From now on I was by no means so sure that this was true.

For at Laokay I saw Giap's regiments attack the French army in force.

For the first time the Vietminh regulars, slipping out of their quadrilateral, launched a real offensive. And in the face of their attack the French officers changed their presumptuousness for fear, their complex of superiority for a complex of inferiority, and all this in a matter of days, even of hours. They fought with wonderful courage; yet at the same time they fought like men who were going to be beaten in time to come.

For my part, as I watched these extraordinary developments, I understood the full strength of the elements that were opposed to the Expeditionary Force — the hostility of the landscape and the climate, the mystique of Communism and the threatening weight of China. How strongly I felt the weakness of the French confronted with these men, these circumstances and these events!

That year Laokay held out and the general staff talked about a victory. But my chief impression was that the time was not yet ripe: the Vietminh were not yet ready and Mao Tse-tung was not officially in power on the frontier. During that spring of 1949 it was only a question of transitional fighting in the Tonkin jungle: the old Asia had not entirely vanished before the new, hard, pure, remorseless Asia. In a few months that would come about. What would happen then?

The war on the R.C. 4

In the Indochina of those days the only place where there was much bloodshed by soldiers killing other soldiers was the R.C. 4. Everywhere else it was guerrilla fighting and small-scale murder. To be sure I had seen the guerrilla war take on something of the appearance of a regular campaign at Laokay, but here it was different. Here Ho Chi Minh's regulars were at home, in their own quadrilateral, and this was the beginning of the real Red war that was to last for years, and which, creeping on from battlefield to battlefield, was to end nearly seven hundred miles away in the basin of Dienbienphu.

In this part of Tonkin, an almost uninhabitable jungle, the French strategy was to hold strong points such as Langson and Caobang, which were linked by the road, the R.C. 4. They therefore depended entirely on the road, whereas the Vietminh did not, for they were supplied by coolies coming through the jungle paths. So the Vietminh strategy was to cut the road. They already had whole regiments for this task, and presently they were to have whole divisions.

In the end the Vietminh did cut the R.C. 4 for good and all and the French had to rely on airlift; but in 1949 things had not reached that stage,

and I went up with a convoy bound for Caobang, at the far end of the
road.

The R.C. 4 was nothing but a shallow gash cut in the enormous
limestone cliff. I had the feeling that I was taking part in a Western that
had somehow been shifted into the tropics. On the one side the canyon fell
away to a ravine with a river at the bottom of it, and on the other the cliff
rose sheer, stretching up and up, smooth, with scarcely a tuft of anything
growing on it, up into the sky, overwhelming us.

By now the days of the traditional convoys of creaking carts were over.
The long, grinding, snorting, roaring train of vehicles that was slowly
moving along the R.C. 4 now was a procession of weapon carriers, scout
cars, light armored cars and jeeps. There were also scores and even
hundreds of trucks belonging to Chinese and Annamese traders, trucks
with thatched roofs and Chinese characters, looking strangely out of place
among all these steel monsters. But out of place or in place, they, together
with the army, made several miles of vehicles going in the direction of
Caobang.

The column had the appearance of a crawling animal, a caterpillar with
metallic bristles, for it was stuck all over with twinned machine guns,
automatic weapons, lethal tubes of every kind. Yet the thing had a human
life of its own, savage, overtense and on edge. All the soldiers had that
concentrated, uncomplaining look that is the usual sign of weariness and
battle. They belonged to every rank and to every race. In their studied
carelessness they could only be told one from another by the range of their
headgear, which ran from the broad-brimmed Australian hat to the white
kepi of the Legion.

I was in a signals car, in the middle of the convoy. The aerial waved
about overhead, and sometimes it caught on the rocks or the jungle growth.
The radio kept up a hideous roaring and whistling: sometimes voices
would emerge from this background. These were orders. "Attention there.
Attention. Suspicious signs ahead of the column. All vehicles keep to their
right intervals. Space yourselves out." My neighbor the radio sergeant sent
out a volley of call signals and shouted "Right: over" into his microphone.
Then he turned to me, shrugging his shoulders, and said, "This place isn't
really dangerous. We are coming up towards Pineapple Pass. This stretch is
quiet enough, although it looks so ugly. The cliffs over the road are too
steep even for the Viets, you see. They can't attack. And they can't aim at
us from the top because of the overhang. Every time their grenades drop
free of the road and go down into the ravine. All they can do is to blaze
away from the other side, from the top of that mountain on the far side of

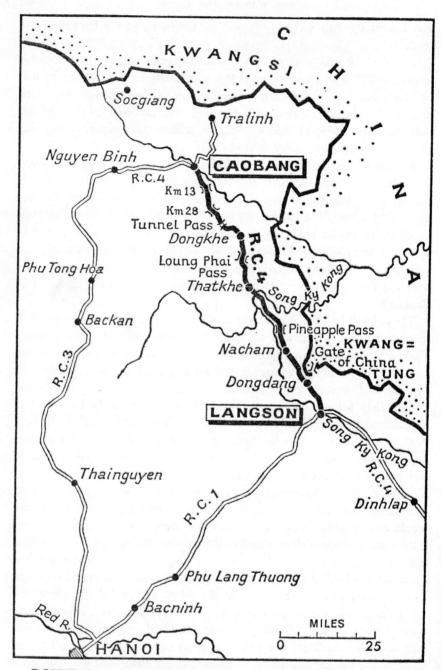

ROUTE COLONIALE 4, FROM LANGSON TO CAOBANG

the gorge. But it's too far off to be any use." The sergeant pointed out some jungle-covered hills away over beyond the chasm. "Once the Viets got the range on a convoy with mortars from down there and chewed it up. But the Legion has a post there now." The sergeant was a thin, sad man with running eyes, and he gave a mirthless laugh as he added, "It's after Thatkhe that we shall have to reckon up the butcher's bill." He lit a cigarette and went on in an unexpressive voice, "This road will get us all. The Viets shoot us like rabbits. I've been in six big ambushes already. Twice I've been in trucks that were burned out — look at my hand. Done rare."

That day I had left Langson at dawn with the convoy. I had been told that if all went well I should reach Caobang that evening. I had also been told that one convoy in two was attacked somewhere along the ninety miles of road. In the last attack twenty vehicles had gone up in flames.

Now we were coming up to the top of Pineapple Pass. On a grassy ridge there stood an important post. It was in the best story-book tradition, with the tricolor waving overhead. The legionaries of the garrison, fair-haired Germans, almost naked, were throwing buckets of water over one another to keep cool, and laughing as they did so. They broke off their play to make friendly signs. Everything was calm and beautiful, bathed in a peace that seemed to have been made to last forever. It was in fact the peace of watchful death.

The R.C. 4 ran downwards now in the midst of countless whitish peaks: there were hundreds, thousands of them, a kind of eruption coming up through the blanket of jungle. This was a riven, fissured stretch of country, full of caves, waterless and devoid of food. It was a desert that made even the Viets hesitate, it seemed. But the French dreaded it too.

At last I caught sight of a valley below us, all squared with rice fields. There were Tho peasants, dressed in blue, peacefully leading their stubborn buffaloes. The column pulled up at the bottom of the hollow, in the straggling village of Thatkhe: an hour's halt. This was safety — civilization itself. The warlike, metallic din of all the motors died away. There was a marvelous feeling of relaxation. The tense faces of a little while ago turned back into the mild, ordinary expressions of good-natured soldiers. There was a general rush towards the wood and corrugated-iron drinking booths where Annamese women with skin-tight tunics and oversharp eyes did their best to look seductive. With what astonishing avidity their eager hands grasped the filthy piasters! The sun beat down. The street stank. The wide gutters on either side overflowed with filth. A little girl was playing with a dead rat by way of a doll.

I went to the citadel of Thatkhe. It was only a barracks, and everyone was asleep. In the officers' mess there was a Foreign Legion major drinking an aperitif all by himself. He was the commanding officer. And he was anxious. He told me that the Viets had gathered two thousand men on the peaks surrounding the hollow and they had warned him that they were going to attack Thatkhe in two days.

"What is so tedious about it," the major explained, "is that sometimes they keep their word: and I only have two hundred legionaries."

I went back to the convoy. We were leaving. Already the huge caravan had resumed its wartime existence. Faces had turned back to masks. The soldiers were sitting in their places, extraordinarily grave, silent, thinking. I had the feeling that the convoy was not a thing, an object, but a being with a collective soul, a physiology and an awareness of its own. It was clear that every man there was turned in upon himself, with dread in the pit of his stomach; and it was clear that every tommy gun was ready to start into instant life.

Only the unmoved Chinese seemed unaffected by the solemnity of the moment. These were the drivers of the civilian trucks, which were piled up with every conceivable kind of merchandise, from joss sticks to cases of brandy. They ventured on to this mortal R.C. 4 because every load that reached Caobang was worth a fortune.

"Swine, that's what they are," said the radio sergeant. "They run no danger. It's never *their* trucks that are burned. They pay the Viets."

We were under way again. There was no more countryside to be seen. The jungle was so thick that it was a green fog. It even hid the shape of the mountains. The road zigzagged, a tunnel through the dense greenery. Suddenly, as we were going along under this heavy twilight, the sergeant said, "It gets worse and worse all the time. These last three months scarcely a single convoy has reached Caobang without dead and wounded. Every time, when you pick up the casualties after an engagement, they fill two or three trucks. What can we do about it? Even if a convoy is stiff with weapon carriers and armor it can't look after itself — it goes along sticking its neck out. So you have to put people all along the road: set up a whole network of posts and patrols. But even when you've occupied all the dangerous places and spread out all the men you can get hold of in the jungle, it's almost no use at all. The caravan stretches out forever and whatever you do the Viets attack it with thousands of men. I don't say that the CO hasn't tried everything imaginable. But as soon as he has found something good in the way of protection the Viets think up new tactics, a new way of getting in close and attacking. After a week or two they get around the French defense and there they are right up in the trucks, killing and looting."

The sergeant explained how impossible it was to protect a convoy, whatever one did or tried to do: and yet everything had been tried. The defense had begun in the simplest way. The army built a post wherever an ambush had taken place. They had to build a great many. For no sooner was one finished than the next ambush was laid just next to it, only a few hundred yards away: a new fort was set up on the spot. Presently both the money and the troops for fresh posts ran short. It was then that there began the practice of "sweeping" the road. This was carried out from one end of the R.C. 4 to the other. On a convoy day each post sent a patrol out as far as the next post to inspect the road, drive the Viets away from it and fill up the holes and cuttings they had made. It was a huge and very dangerous task, with small groups of men searching every yard of the road, fighting and carrying out repairs. The convoy would only leave when messages came in from every post announcing that the way was clear. Often it was not. The Viets only had to hide in the green walls on either side not to be seen. The convoys went on being shot to pieces, and often a "sweeping party" was destroyed as well, as a preliminary.

A more complex system was thought out. They took to sweeping the jungle too, for several hundred yards on either side of the highway. Twice a week, once for the up convoy and once for the down, the soldiers had to climb every peak that commanded the R.C. 4. And there were hundreds of these peaks. All of them had to be occupied for the whole time the convoy took to go by. Every time it meant hours of climbing, often cutting a path foot by foot. Every time the unknown paths by which the Viets might come had to be searched for: every cave had to be investigated. It was an unbelievable effort that took up whole battalions and that called for even more. There were not enough troops for this, either.

Merely to get one convoy through, the command was henceforward obliged to use all the effectives available in the entire frontier zone. Every time very large numbers of men had to be deployed. Everything had been very carefully studied and rehearsed, down to the last detail. Yet there was as much bloodshed as ever: perhaps even more. The Viets always had the advantage. It was absurd to imagine that it was possible to go through such a solid jungle and such ragged, tumbled mountains with a fine tooth comb. Trying to do so never stopped the Viet regulars from slipping through the network of French defenses in thousands whenever and wherever they chose, and massing on the sides of the R.C. 4; just as they had done before, they remained hidden behind the embankments until the convoy arrived,

and then they destroyed all or part of it. And more and more often now the
Viets were shooting up the sweeping parties, who had to fight blind in the
jungle.

Meanwhile we were traveling at about twelve miles an hour along the
R.C. 4: it was now no more than a narrow trail of patched-up, roughly
mended, blackened earth, a wretched kind of track that wound through the
overwhelming majesty of the forest.

In the green darkness I could not even see the soldiers who were supposed to be protecting us. I asked the radio sergeant whether the covering
force had in fact been posted there. It had. At dawn men had left all the
posts and they had climbed and marched for hours, taking up their positions in all the dangerous places. Perhaps during this taking up of positions
all over the countryside there had been skirmishes and men killed — I did
not know and I never shall know: that was mere everyday routine. At all
events the legionaries, the Colonial Infantry, the Asian partisans, the
North and Central African light infantrymen, all the ingredients of the
Expeditionary Force, had been waiting for us and were at that moment
protecting us with their weapons. And when we had gone by they would
leave their positions, march for hours and hours and then shut themselves
up in their posts. Perhaps they would not have fired a single shot: perhaps
they would have had to fight to save their lives or to guard the convoy.
They were the world's most extraordinary traffic police.

And they would start this labor all over again indefinitely: they could
not do anything else: for they too were prisoners of the R.C. 4.

But however hard I looked I could see nothing of this military deployment that was guarding us, except for a post from time to time. There was
nothing to be seen in the jungle, neither friend nor enemy.

Once more the metallic voice spoke from the radio. "Forty-One West
coming into sight. Take care when leaving the overhang of the river."

It seemed that there was a rapid stream flowing just by the road. But
that could not be seen, either.

"Here's a gun," said the sergeant, handing me a revolver. "It might come
in handy. We are reaching a really dangerous area." And he gave me some
advice, explaining how to look after oneself in an ambush. "Even if the
machine-gun bursts sweep the road and even if they start hitting the truck,
don't jump out, not as long as the thing will move. What you have to do is
to push on as fast as you can and as long as you can, without firing back.
Our drivers are used to it. You have to have real guts to drive your truck or
whatever straight into the fire of machine guns when you can't see them.
And in the big ambushes there are dozens of machine guns trained right

down the middle line of the road. What's really bad is when the cars in front of you begin to burn. They block the way for everything behind them. The rest of the convoy is paralyzed.

"But if we're blocked like that, what you have to do then is to get out fast, fast, before the Viets attack the trucks. You can't defend yourself inside — you get your throat cut at once. The most important thing of all is to regroup outside and make little knots of resistance among the Viets. I can't tell you what it's like. There's hand-to-hand fighting over hundreds of yards, sometimes for miles, on the road itself and the embankments. The battle is all in little unconnected bits, separate engagements. There are uncountable Viets everywhere. Yet nearly always there are parts of the convoy that hold out and that even counterattack. In other sections the Viets rush everything and wipe it out. How they howl! If there's no other hope at all, the last way out is to fling yourself into the jungle and hide as best you can. But if you run, above all you must run far and not stop in the bushes on the edge of the road, because the Viets mop up very thoroughly with their jungle knives."

We were beginning to rise to the Luong Phai Pass. This was the most blood-drenched area in the whole of Indochina. The road climbed the sheer mountainside like a winding ladder, turning in dizzy hairpin bends: and there was not one of these corners that had not been used for an ambush and which had not seen the most savage hand-to-hand fighting. The sergeant reeled off the monotonous litany. "Here there were ten men killed. Here a major and a captain were wounded. Here two weapon carriers and twenty trucks were burned. Here there was a very big ambush — we lost fifty men. Here . . ."

The litany went on and on: it was the litany of dread. I sensed the convoy's intense apprehension from the automatic head movements, all swinging together. Far away from here, right down in Cochinchina on the Camau road, I had seen men's eyes turn all together at the same second, staring, searching, first on the right and then on the left. But then there were only a score or two of them. Here on the R.C. 4 there were hundreds of us, perhaps a thousand, and we were all swinging our heads with the same automatic reflex. It was extraordinarily comic, and at the same time extraordinarily dramatic. And the weapons which bristled from every vehicle followed the heads and the eyes that were searching for the signs of danger.

One after another the turns wound up the greenish mountainside. The soldiers in the convoy knew the road by heart and instinctively they located the danger spots, even those from which an attack had not yet been launched but where an ambush was waiting for us now, perhaps. I imitated them. I stared where they stared. Like every other man in the convoy I said to myself, as we came nearer to one of these evil-looking places, that at that very spot and at that very moment there were thousands of Viets getting ready to leap out at us. I also told myself that the Viet regulars, well protected in the caves of this contorted range, were in the act of aiming their heavy machine guns at our crawling vehicles — desperately big, heavy and slow.

The climb lasted an hour and a half. At last we came to the pass itself. Over our heads there reared a peak and in its side there was a great pit, a kind of black crater. The Thos said that it brought bad luck: they called it the "roaring hole." The sergeant too believed that it was somehow diabolic. "Every time there's an ambush around here," he said, "that hole starts howling. A dreadful, wicked row. All the noise of the fighting gets into it and the echo comes back ten times louder. I know it's only an echo, but it's an evil thing — it frightens you."

We went over the pass. It was no more than a nick in the sharp ridge. Water trickled from a stone cobra's head: a spring. "That's the only good spring in this poisonous country; the only water that doesn't eat your guts out. So this is where we give the wounded a drink — and you want a drink when you're all burned up with fever."

We dropped again to the valley of Dongkhe, which was Thatkhe all over again. Here too there was a round plain, rice fields, placid Tho peasants, Vietnamese whores, legionaries and a citadel. Here too we had an hour's halt. Then once more we pushed on through the same tangle of jungles, mountains, ridges, gorges and passes. Still, throughout this splendid landscape, not a single man to be seen. From time to time, however, there was a post, and the mere sight of it was heart-warming, an immense relief. Then the fear-haunted journey began again.

The sergeant resumed his beadroll of ambushes. "Here's what we call the 'finger on the trigger' gorge. No need to tell you why. Here's the stretch called the 73/2's boulevard: that's the company of sappers who look after the sector. They spend all their time rebuilding the bridges, and then the Viets blow them up again immediately afterwards."

For a few miles there was order in the chaos: the landscape had taken on a geometrical regularity. This section of the R.C. 4 did in fact look almost like a boulevard. It followed the bottom of the gorge that might have been leveled with a plane, an enormous, very long, almost entirely straight natural trench several hundred yards wide. On either side this valley was flanked by strikingly regular limestone walls, both of the same height, and both rising sheer to heights of seven hundred to a thousand feet.

"This is where the great February ambush happened. Technically it was far and away the best — really scientific, with everything synchronized. And you can believe me when I say so, because I was there. To begin with the Viets paralyzed the convoy. Mines went off behind the armored cars at the head of the column, cutting them off from the trucks. Immediately after that a dozen unattackable machine guns in those limestone cliffs opened up, raking the whole line. Then came a hail of grenades. There were regulars lying close-packed along the embankment over the road and they dropped them just so, tossing a dozen at each vehicle. There were flames everywhere. Anywhere you looked there were burning trucks, and they completely blocked the road. All this only took a minute.

"Then there was a terrific shouting. It was the charge. Thousands of naked bodies leaped up from the sides of the road, just by us, and hurled themselves at the convoy. We were still inside. But before this tide broke over us we jumped out and forced our way through the current. Our idea was to climb the embankment and regroup in little fighting units. We shouted to one another to keep in touch, but the Viets shouted louder still. We could see mobs of Viets below us, furiously attacking our comrades who had not been able to follow us and regroup. They went under in a few seconds.

"The Viets were very methodical. Regulars went from truck to truck, gathering the weapons and the goods that had been left behind; then they set fire to the vehicles. Other regulars attacked the French who were still fighting on the embankments. Coolies with jungle knives finished off the wounded who had fallen onto the roadway or into the ditches. It was hand-to-hand fighting everywhere. There were hundreds of single combats, hundreds of pairs of men killing each other. In the middle of all this mess the political commissars very calmly supervised the work in hand, giving orders to the regulars and the coolies — orders that were carried out at once.

"The middle of the convoy was wiped out. The armored cars at the tail-end began firing their guns point blank into the trucks that the Viets had taken. There were Red officers hurrying about in the midst of the fighting calling out 'Where is the colonel? Where is the colonel?' in French. They meant Colonel Simon, the CO of the 3rd Etrangers, the man with a bullet in his head — it has been there for years; he got it long before the war in Indochina. He was in the convoy and Giap had ordered that he should be taken alive.

"I was in the part of the convoy that was destroyed. I found myself on the embankment together with a few legionaries, and we fought furiously for half an hour: then we were overwhelmed. I escaped into the forest and hid in some undergrowth about fifty yards from the road. Just next to me I heard some shots. It was the legionaries blowing their brains out — the Viets had discovered them. As for me, I was not discovered.

"I don't know how the whole nightmare ended. They say that Colonel Simon managed to gather a hundred of his men around him and form them up in squares that thrust back the waves of Viets with grenades for hours on end. Three hours later the reinforcements came up — the heavy armor. A few minutes before the sound of the tracks was heard the Viets had disengaged. At the very beginning, when they attacked, they had sounded the charge on a trumpet. Now there was another trumpet call for the retreat and they vanished into the junge in perfect order, unit by unit. Special formations of coolies carried off their killed and wounded, as well as all the loot they had taken.

"We remained on the battlefield. The road was a graveyard, a charnel-house. Nothing was left of the convoy but a heap of ripped-open bodies and blackened engines. It was already beginning to stink. The survivors gathered on the roadway: we cleared it and picked up the corpses and the wounded. And what was left of the convoy set off again.

"Afterwards one of my friends told me how he had saved himself by pretending to be dead. All around him the Viets were pillaging the trucks and finishing off the wounded. He flung himself down by a dead man whose head had been smashed: he rubbed the blood on his own body and smeared himself with the brain that lay there all by itself on the ground. Then he dragged the body over onto him, covering himself with it so it should look as though he had fallen first. The Viets searched him, took his shoes, his watch, his wallet. All the time their hands were about him he held himself stiff and stopped breathing, pretending even harder to be dead. At last the Viets moved on, still searching the bodies and killing the wounded. He says that there were some whites among them . . ."

While the sergeant talked we were climbing another pass. This one was called the Tunnel Pass, and indeed instead of climbing right up the ridge the road burrowed through a tunnel a hundred yards long.

"After there had been three or four ambushes just here, a post was built on top of that sheer mountain, directly over the mouth of the tunnel. Those zigzag steps lead up to it. But there's no water up there, not a single drop. So every day a fatigue party goes to get it at a spring hundreds of feet lower down. It takes hours. They carry buckets and tommy guns. The Viets often shoot at them, and sometimes they have to carry a body or a wounded man up with them as well as the water."

But we were getting nearer. Still more passes — passes that did not even have a name. There was one at the 28 kilometer stone and another at 13 kilometers. These too were ill-omened places. The convoy traveled on and on. At last, at five o'clock in the afternoon, it reached Caobang: it had not been attacked.

That night the whole convoy got drunk. It was a tradition: the military authorities allowed it. This time it was nothing extraordinary. But if there had been men killed and wounded the survivors would have drunk until they reached total oblivion — until they had lost all recollection, all awareness.

The dirty war

I saw every sort of guerrilla and counterguerrilla fighting. So often I wanted to ask a French officer, man to man, "Can you defend civilization while you let yourself slide toward everything most inimical to it — violence, deliberate cruelty, torture?"

But for months, for a year, I could find no one who would talk. The younger officers of the Expeditionary Force were aware that in France, in their own country, they were unpopular, even detested, and they bore the condemnation in silence. Some even took a strange pleasure in knowing themselves alone and misunderstood; and they kept on in their "dirty war" with even more stoicism and pride.

The older officers were more talkative; but their conversation was all shop and malicious gossip, which it would have been fatal to a journalist to repeat. Some, more intelligent, had their doubts about the conduct of the war, but they were too discreet to express them. Their superiors were tolerant of mediocrity, eccentricity, and even vice, but not of independent thinking or, worse, pessimism. The watchword of the high command (especially after Carpentier became commander in chief) was *"pas d'histoires."* And around the forbidden topic, the conspiracy of silence was absolute.

Both the Vietminh and the French, of course, showed me masses of pictures of atrocities committed by the other side.

I never, with my own eyes, saw any French atrocities. But I did see ugly things. Often I saw French patrols returning from abandoned villages, garlanded with chickens, and driving herds of pigs and water buffaloes.

One day I happened into an empty pagoda about twelve miles from Saigon, and found an old man there. The instant he saw me, his astonishing response was to take down his trousers and present me with his bare posterior. I learned later that a North African battalion had been recently stationed nearby. And village notables sometimes complained to me, "We know what war always is. We understand your soldiers taking our animals, our jewelry, our Buddhas; it is normal. We are resigned to their raping our wives and our daughters; war has always been like that. But we object to being treated in the same way, not only our sons, but ourselves, old men and dignitaries that we are." There again, they were talking about Moslem troops.

In a war of assassination, reprisals were not uncommon, and some were even ordered by the high command: collective sanctions for anti-French activities. I do not know whether hostages were ever taken and shot on orders from high up, but whole villages were burned and dynamited.

Sometimes it was for strategic reasons, when a "white zone" or no-man's-land had been decreed around some road or post, for its protection.

And there was the matter of interrogation, for which most intelligence officers had more or less standard electrical equipment. (Most of them had Vietnamese assistants for the actual work.) And I heard of one officer who would take his "clients" up in airplanes. He would throw two or three of them out into space, and say to the others, "Talk, or you'll get the same treatment."

It was an appalling picture: but French progressives and left-wing intellectuals were mistaken in comparing the Expeditionary Force with the S.S. or the Gestapo. They did not bring the practice of torture with them to Indochina; they met it there, for in that country, used in the manner laid down by Mao Tse-tung, it was an instrument of liberation.

One day, when I had been a year in Indochina, an officer broke the code of his caste by talking to me; but he made me swear not to repeat anything he said until the war had ended. "You know too much," he said. "You have seen too much already. It's better that you should understand the whole problem."

We had been on a raid on an assassination committee who had escaped us. Now, under a roof of woven reeds, surrounded by about twenty sleeping partisans, we lay on the low deck of a sampan, floating silently down a wide river in the tropic evening. I was remembering the Vietminh village we had taken by surprise: the straw huts by the stream, the ancestral tablets, the pictures of Ho Chi Minh, the jars of rice, and the stunned faces that watched us dash past, as we made for the "house of the people" where the assassination committee was likely to be. I remembered a young peasant woman with her baby in her arms. When we appeared before her, she groaned like an animal and collapsed, the embodiment of dread. And on her face I had time to see her animal anguish, from deep in her entrails — the age-old, atrocious anguish of war, torture, and death.

Violating all the conventions, I asked the officer, "Have you ever tortured?"

He replied very calmly, "I have ordered torture."

"Often?"

He remained impassive. "When it is necessary."

"When is that?"

"When I decide it is."

The sampan's roof was very low. We were stretched out side by side. It seemed to me we were the only sentient beings in the world. Around us the partisans slept in their black clothes. Beyond us there was nothing but the immensity of the sky, the night, the river.

It was then that the officer told me he would "talk." Lying there, he said in the same neutral tone, "I, a French officer, have come to the conclusion that torture, in the Indochinese war, is the most humane and the least wasteful method — the method which saves most lives. That is, if you know how to use it.

"I have changed a great deal. I was in the Resistance in France. When I got to Asia, I was revolted by what I saw. We are like the Boches I thought. We are applying the principles of the occupation of France: Order, Collaboration, Repression. I am an assassin like them. I thought of resigning my commission, but I hadn't the courage: it would have been casting a terrible slur on the French army.

"We French had come back to Indochina to fight a war of colonial reconquest. But very soon, almost in spite of ourselves, and certainly in spite of our second thoughts, our monstrous errors, and our basic incomprehension, we have become the only force which keeps the Vietnamese from falling into the Kafkaesque world of Asiatic Communism. And because of that we have millions of people with us, notables and nha-qués alike. No doubt they don't like us, and will want to get rid of us later. But in their hearts they have the anguish of knowing that only we can save them.

"We are not exactly disinterested crusaders, but it is true that we are here to defend human values. And it is true that, to defend them, we must degrade ourselves to inhumanity. For we are dealing with the Vietminh, for whom such things are simple and logical. The individual, the people, must be converted to the Good. Their thinking must be supervised, controlled, turned way from evil; and by means ranging from the 'mildness' of autocriticism to torture and execution. Whoever resists the Good, whoever will not 'progress,' whoever does not repent, is a criminal. He must be punished, corrected, and forced to repent. Even those condemned to death are obliged, before they are executed, to proclaim their joy in the just punishment that awaits them.

"It is inconceivable in France; it defeats the occidental mind. But think of the Christian middle ages, and the Inquisition. Then too, no man had the right to refuse the Good.

"And do not forget that in Asia torture is part of the code of civilization. Before there were political commissars, the good mandarin would punish the faults of a village by killing all the inhabitants and sowing the earth with salt.

"I thought at first that I could cling to the moral principles of the West, and that surely the only chance of winning was to attract the *nha-qués,* who had been crushed by a cruel world, by always being kind and just. It was not possible. Everything in Asia is torment — the way the Viets make war, the sadism everywhere, the fatigue, the climate, the feeling that one is constantly being betrayed, the haunting awareness of being surrounded by *nha-qués* who help the enemy by finishing off the wounded. And then there is inexorable necessity. For torture is a force; it is finally impossible not to use it against the Viets, who employ it constantly. It would weaken us fatally, and we would lose all the support of the population.

"I began by commanding a post. I forbade all brutality. And one day I discovered that my noncom had forced a Viet prisoner to talk. I gave him hell. And he answered, 'I had my suspicions, and I was right. This man has told me that two of our partisans were to open the gates at four A.M. tomorrow night, to a *tieudoi.*' What could I say? *'La question'* had saved our post and our garrison. And then the Viet who had been questioned reformed a few days later. I took him on as a partisan.

"I was telling you that torture saved human lives. It's true. It provides you with the information you need to finish off a few men you must kill — the real Viets, the cadres, the political commissars, the militant Communists, the heads of the committees, the professional assassins. Then gradually you can take the mass of the people in hand, without killing as many as you would in a regular military operation. I finally left my post, and my unit, and took over this commando. This way, I wage my kind of war. And I think my war is clean."

"Are you satisfied, then, with yourself?"

"No. I am morally finished. That is the price of the Indochinese War. I have seen so many Expeditionary Force officers go half insane. But at any rate, I am doing useful work, whereas they . . ."

"You mean their war is dirty?"

"No, I mean it's stupid. They're botching it."

The officer was silent. And then, as though he might never again have a chance to unburden his heart, he began again, with a sort of nervous haste.

"Take the central problem of torture. The Viets shed rivers of blood, and make innumerable 'examples.' But it's always for the same reasons, there are well-established criteria, and in every case there is a trial and a sentence. Each time, it is a political act, a 'correct solution.' A political commissar explains that 'the people have been injured by an enemy of the people.' The crime must be expiated, and the damage made good; but also the people must be instructed. They are taught to hate the guilty and to rejoice at their punishment, even if a husband or son is involved. Their misdeeds are to fill the people with such indignation that their revolutionary enthusiasm will be doubled, and they will work harder and fight harder, always harder, for there are no limits to what the people can do.

"This pitiless Red vigilance, which knows all, punishes all, exacts all, creates in each *nha-qué* the obsessive belief that the Party is omnipresent and omniscient. Not even an evil thought can be hidden from the Party. The individual's only chance, therefore, is to show zeal, to do all he is told, even if he must volunteer his life, like the coolies with their bangalores.

"On the other hand, the man whose attitude is 'correct' has nothing to fear. The discipline of Viet guerrillas, regulars and cadres is unbelievable. The great rule is that the soldier is the people's friend. In the villages he helps with the housework and the harvest, he smiles, he's polite, he plays with the children, he makes himself useful in every way he can. He never steals; any soldier who takes a handful of rice by force is promptly shot before the whole population.

"The Viet system eliminates all surprises. Every *nha-qué* knows what will happen to him as a result of his attitude, whether 'good' or 'not good.' But he does not know what the Expeditionary Force will do when it bursts into his village; perhaps they will burn down his house, perhaps they will give him medicine. Their punishments and rewards make no sense to him.

"What does a regular army, an occidental army, do about a population in which every individual is involved in the hostilities? The old international law, in which civilians who fight are treated as francs-tireurs, cannot be applied, or we would have to shoot millions of men, old people, women, and children. There is no 'official point of view.' Saigon insists on 'mildness,' and says that we are not making war but suppressing a revolt (though it seems to me the word suppression is even worse than the word war). The high command forbids flame-throwers and napalm, and recommends that tanks and artillery should be used with extreme moderation. But big set-piece operations in battalion strength are mounted in areas where there are only guerrillas and assassination committees. Useless and murderous. You attack a village; it turns out no Viets are there; but you have killed a crowd of *nha-qués;* and you find women and children lying on the ground torn to pieces by your shell bursts. And after that, they're supposed to love you!

"Sometimes the army is soft; sometimes its measures are draconian. Who knows what has decided them — faulty intelligence, an interpreter's lie, an officer's ill humor or his liver trouble, a misunderstood incident, or just pure chance?

"Discipline is poor. The high command has not managed to establish any general discipline; everything differs with each unit. Some are irreproachable, some are murderous. And I have known units in which the riflemen were scandalous thieves; and a few weeks later, with a new officer, they wouldn't take so much as a chicken. Some officers can get away with appalling atrocities, others are ferociously punished, if they have no friends in the high echelons.

"There are a lot of executions in the Expeditionary Force. They say that there are days when the execution ground near Saigon is a bloody horror.

"Rape carries the death penalty. But often a legionary is executed because some *nha-qué* woman yells rape when he hasn't paid her full price.

"Yet High Commissioner Pignon had to interfere several times to see that a certain sergeant was punished in Cambodia. The man used to amuse himself by shooting from his post at people passing by — shooting to kill. And in the end, he was merely transferred.

"There have to be reprisals, sometimes; but to control them the high command needs brains and an iron hand. Instead, they cling to a stupid 'legalism,' which is nothing but an impediment. For instance, if you catch a killer, or a political commissar, you have to turn him over to the regular courts, give him lawyers, see that he has every chance the law allows. Every such case takes months. And there's no hope of collecting evidence; half the time you can't even establish the man's identity or discover his real name. Then if he is sentenced at all, but not to death, he'll be back again soon with every intention of killing you, because nothing is easier, with the Annamese guards' complicity, than getting out of jail.

"So the Expeditionary Force becomes exasperated and imposes its own rough justice. You can imagine what that is.

"The Viets push us into atrocities, and our absurdity helps too. Yet we kill infinitely less than the Viets, and infinitely less than the Americans would. They wouldn't bother to go into details, they'd just bomb whole 'zones.' Liquidate the population and liquidate the problem. And at that, international opinion puts up much better with the most lethal wholesale hammering than with the torture of a single assassin.

"The Expeditionary Force does have one virtue. In spite of everything, in spite of cruelty and incoherence, the Force's war is on a human scale. I have seen real generosity and splendid impulses mixed right in with all the evil. I've seen medical officers going out under fire to pick up wounded Viets and carry them to an ambulance. And that is a rule: the Viets are cared for, operated on, and cured exactly like the French. The prisoners get fat in the camps; and instead of escaping they ask to become P.I.M.'s, battalion coolies. Only the cadres escape; the other Viets, even many of the regulars, prefer to stay with us.

"And how often I've seen soldiers risk their lives to go to the help of a village that called for it. They could just sit by not caring, but I've seen whole columns set out, often at night, to save *nha-qués* who meant nothing to them.

"And in the hamlets, right where they pillage, the soldiers play with the children — and quite often adopt them — and take rice to the old people. The doctors give them shots and bandage them. The officers palaver with the notables. There are real love stories. Never has there been such close contact between white and yellow people. It's a grisly war, and yet it's a sort of game that everyone plays. Hate is not really hate here, because it isn't alienation. There really is no wall, no absence, no quarantine; we really are not 'foreigners' because that means beings whose empty eyes will not see, beings whose existence one refuses to acknowledge. They chop us to pieces, but they don't push us away. In a way we are part of this country and these people, and in a happy, an almost luxuriating way. Even the tortures are part of this strange enchantment and this complicity. That's why the Expeditionary Force loves this 'dirty war' so much."

We talked on into the night, as the sampan glided quietly on down the river. The officer spoke mournfully of the high command's clumsy tactics, of poor training for jungle fighting, of too-heavy equipment and a want of mobility, of the army's enormous and absurd bureaucracy, of excellent

Intelligence and purblind staff interpretations, of the Commander in Chief's shortsighted optimism. As the sampan drew into the smelly dock of the little town which was the commando's base, the streets were quiet. A few lights flickered in the silence. Only a few whores dawdled in the alleys, a Chinese soup peddler, a dog or two. In one house, I could hear the click of mah-jongg pieces.

"The worst thing about this miserable Indochina," said the officer, shaking hands in farewell, "is that it gets under your skin." He walked off into the night. I was never to see him again. Meanwhile, the colonel was expecting me to dinner.

PART II

Saigon

T HE "happy war" of guerrilla fighting and torture went tirelessly on, day after day. Blood flowed steadily on the R.C. 4; the Expeditionary Force grew ossified in its heroism; the Viets held on until Mao Tse-tung's armies should reach the frontier; Monsieur Pignon, the French High Commissioner from 1948 to 1950, dreamed of "a great Vietnamese policy"; His Majesty Bao Dai returned to the land of his fathers.* Such was the news from Indochina during the years of 1948 and 1949.

* Bao Dai was educated in France, and had returned in 1932 at the age of eighteen to be crowned Emperor of Annam. In that court of mandarins, diviners, ancestor worship, and an ancient etiquette, tyrannized over by his mother, "the Tigress," a betel-chewing Annamese crone with a passion for gambling, the cosmopolitan young elegant was out of place. Not realizing how powerless he was, nor how lonely and frustrated, the Annamese Nationalists called him a traitor for his obedience to the French. It was at this time that his neurasthenia began, and his solitary hunts in the forest. It was on one of these hunts, in 1945, that the Japanese captured him. In exchange for his life he signed a proclamation announcing the independence of his country and the end of French rule. In the summer of that year, Ho Chi Minh sent an emissary to demand Bao Dai's abdication. Bao Dai agreed, to save his skin, and was given the derisory title of Ho's "supreme counselor." His wife and children were held as hostages in Annam, while Bao Dai, now called Citizen Vinh Thuy, was paraded by Ho at revolutionary meetings in Tonkin. To humiliate him, Ho would invite him to lunch with his own chauffeur. Doubtless he would have had him killed but for his fear of the superstitious populace (who believed Bao Dai to be a god) and of the Chinese warlord Lu Han, in Hanoi, who would have made Bao Dai's execution an excuse for "vengeance."

Bao Dai managed to calm the Reds' suspicions enough so that he was sent as their emissary to deal with Lu Han. Once there, he demanded protection, and an American plane flew him to Nanking to see the new U.S. Ambassador, General Marshall. In exchange for his help and compliance, the Americans offered him support, but with the reminder that "Vietnam was an artificial country" and that Tonkin really should be a southern province of China. Out of patriotism, Bao Dai refused any deal. Abandoned by all, he lived in miserable exile at Hong Kong; and went later to France.

His recall to the throne was due in large measure to Pignon, the MRP man who was appointed high commissioner in 1948. Pignon's first hope was to channel the active zeal of Nguyen Binh's Resistance into reforming the Saigon government, which he saw to be too reactionary, too corrupt and too bourgeois to be truly representative of the Vietnamese people. When this failed, Bao Dai was summoned, to "rule" over the republic of Vietnam, "a free state forming part of the Indochinese federation and of the French Union." The hope was of course that the little emperor would serve both as a puppet for the French and a rallying-point for the Vietnamese.

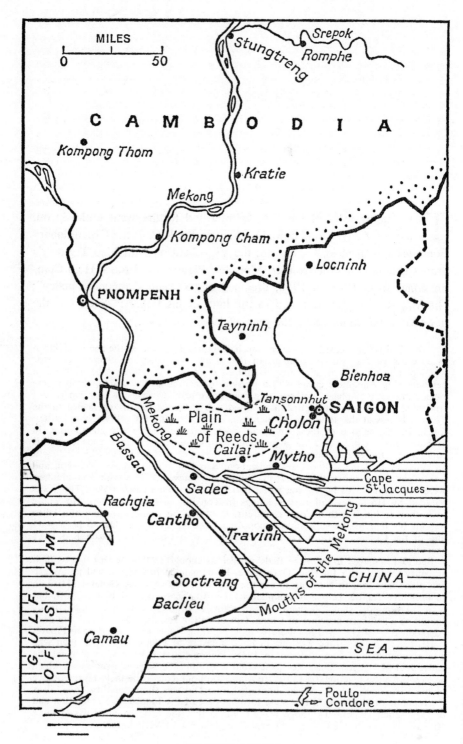

COCHINCHINA

But above all a great motor, a great driving power, revolved steadily, ceaselessly, efficiently, to the profit of one and all. And this engine that turned out the piasters without which there would have been no history, no events, no Indochinese war, was Saigon. It was Saigon's inhabitants, Saigon's two million piaster-worshipping inhabitants, who kept the war going and who in return derived a wonderful degree of prosperity from it. For, thanks to the piaster at seventeen francs, Saigon, with its Chinese suburb of Cholon, was the richest town on earth.

I will try to describe this motor.

First you must know that there were several Saigons. The one that counted, the big-money Saigon, was no bigger than a pocket handkerchief. This civilized Saigon had the appearance of an orderly and complacent middle-class city. Outwardly everything was so normal that I once heard an old French woman exclaim, "But who are all these Vietminh one has been hearing so much about these many years past?" And she was the wife of a man high up in the Saigon import-export business.

Coming to Saigon I found myself in a flat town, one that had been founded on mud. And within this Turkish bath there was nothing very remarkable to be seen. It was by no means a Shanghai or a Hong Kong. There was no splendor. Not even any sinful pride of the flesh. Saigon had no "City," no conglomeration of banks. It did not even possess a stock exchange. Not a single tall building broke the skyline. The port on the Saigon River was unpretentious, and it stank abominably. The famous Rue Catinat was nothing more than a commonplace street whose fashionable shops were some years behind Paris. The chief import-export houses were still content to put up with the corrugated-iron and wood constructions of their beginnings. The French lived in old-fashioned villas that dated from the high days of colonialism after the 1914 war. Air-conditioning was unknown. The electricity did not work well, because the company did not choose to spend any money on it. The telephone was even worse. People were thirsty in this uncomfortable atmosphere, and the shares of Brasseries et Glacières d'Indochine (beer and ice producers) multiplied in value ten times. The buses were exceedingly bad and the taxis had no meters. There were quite a lot of automobiles, but the possession of one meant a fairly high place on the social ladder, and the poor Europeans traveled in pedal rickshaws.

Everything had something of the air of a French provincial town. Ostentation was not at all the thing in Saigon. Society was pigeon-holed, labeled and devoted to a stay-at-home life and a meticulous set of conventions. Prin-

ciples were of great importance: some principles, that is to say. For in spite
of everything there was a fundamental immorality. The only thing that
counted was money, and it counted to a degree unknown in the rest of the
world. The French were in Saigon "to make piasters," and all means were
fair. But real money, big money, is a serious and indeed a moral thing. The
important houses were those in which the quest for profit was a religious
nature. There were still unbelievably unscrupulous firms in which business
was carried out beneath the austere portraits of the gentlemen of the board
of directors with stiff collars and eyeglasses — portraits hung in due form
in places of honor. These firms insisted upon great integrity and respectability in their employees — upon their having "the right attitude of mind."

This big-money Saigon was the one that carried weight in Paris, the one
that had its own lobby there. It was this Saigon that felt virtually in its own
house when it visited the high commissioner: and even more than the high
commissioner's office, this particular Saigon "owned" the Vietnamese
government. The great men of the regime had all been more or less its
employees, and to a very considerable extent they were still its men of
straw. His Excellency Nguyen De, the Emperor's principal private secretary, was a former comprador* in the Bank of Indochina. And as for
Huu†, the prime minister, he had been an official in another bank, the
Crédit Foncier.

These worthy, respectable people exercised their powers in providing
their firm's activities with legal form and in turning their business into a
methodical science. But in the shadows beneath this high capitalism there
existed a tormented world of the piaster, a world of go-betweens, touts and
penniless adventurers; and thanks to them Saigon had something of the
atmosphere of the Paris of John Law or the London of the South Sea
Bubble. The piaster was primarily a mental disease. Dealing in money
became a kind of mysticism, a hysteria, an end in itself, which liberated
every kind of appetite, and above all every excess of the imagination.

The Europeans of the "upper piaster," the smallest and the greatest,
were shut up in one district and its extensions. But next to this puritanical
and demented Saigon of the piaster machine there was the Asian Saigon, a
city of innumerable people in which the population had quadrupled in a
few years. All these men of Saigon were infected too. They were no longer
ruled by passion nor even by hatred: this ant heap of Vietnamese and

---

* The all-purpose go-between acting for a foreign firm in its relations with its
Asian customers or employees.

† Huu belonged to the Cochinchinese upper class. He became Bao Dai's prime
minister, although he loathed him.

Chinese was subjected to the rule of the almighty piaster, the poor man's piaster, the filthy piece of paper money hidden in dirty rags.

This was an unknown Saigon, an unhealthy, dangerous city, almost as remote as the other end of the world. The Europeans knew only that undesirable things happened there at the soldier and *nha-qué* level. For them this other Saigon (like the rest of Indochina) was a market which supplied their wants but which they did not go to see. The other Saigon was the unknown, the social abyss: yet there were degrees in the descent into this bottomless pit.

At the very top there were the bland Asian millionaires with their perpetual smiles. Many of them were Chinese compradors — every bank or important commercial house had one. They were much more than employees: they were the powers behind the throne of the piaster. It was they who made the junction between French capitalism and that Chinese capitalism which had the task of exploiting Indochina at the lower level, the level of the "natives." The two capitalisms were allied, and it was the compradors who made the alliance work. They were at the heart of market operations, of speculation, exchange and trade. Each possessed his own fortune, often amounting to tens of millions of piasters. Each had his own organization, his front men, his touts and even his own killers. His family was a tribe. He was often related to the great Chinese dynasties of Hong Kong and Singapore, who were said to dispose of the greatest resources in the world for playing the currency and raw material markets.

Many of them were patients of a doctor I knew in Cholon — a Frenchman who had gone Asiatic, with a Chinese and a Vietnamese wife, and a purely Chinese practice in his clinic near the Great Pagoda. "People think these big Chinese are calm and impassive," he said, "and how wrong they are! It's just a façade. Actually all the Chinese are neurotic, moonstruck, half-crazy, with their nerves in shreds. How could they be normal, when they spend their lives in a chaos of noises and lights, and always brooding, calculating, reasoning like madmen? Their mental tension is much higher than any New York businessman's; and they really think their 'odd little symptoms' are due to evil influences or even spirits. I have to be a bit of a sorcerer to cure them. The queerest thing is that all these crazy big shots can be so composed in public."

The activities of any comprador or any millionaire were limitless: so were his capacities. But everything that he did was secret; and everything invariably had an outward appearance of rectitude. He displayed this respectable aspect during the lavish, fifty-course banquets to which he invited his European "friends." There would be *kampés,* toasts drunk in

rice spirit, conventional jokes and speeches. The millionaire's senior wife
would be there, dried up and wrinkled, speechless, steeped in civility.

The French partners or employers did not wish to know anything; for
knowing nothing they would always be able to take their huge profits with
clear consciences, whatever might be done by others — and they could do
so without there ever being the slightest scandal or the slightest suspicion
of any irregularity. Furthermore the compradors would never say a word.
Mystery is the foundation of business in Asia. Any unnecessary word might
be literally fatal — there were so many hidden dangers! Especially so since
the Vietminh, the bandits and the police with whom they had dealings were
only too apt, in given circumstances, to say to them "Your nest egg is
altogether too big. Give us a little of it." There was an infinity of subtle,
diplomatic blackmail and counterblackmail, accompanied by kidnapping,
ransoms and murders. Generally speaking the big-time Chinese would give
in, pay up, and engage in fresh and profitable deals with his tormentors.

The Asian millionaire's piaster was omnipresent, continually at work,
but always under the surface. It was anonymous money and no one ever
knew its owner. There was no getting to the bottom of it — everything was
too complicated, too entangled — unless one could seize the man and say
"We shall slice you into little pieces if you don't tell us." Gangsters could
do this, but not the tax authorities. Besides, the big-time Chinese knew
other gangsters, other politicians, other armed men on whom he could call
for help: he also had his own weapons, his threats of commercial and
financial reprisals. Trade, underhand dealings, finance, kidnapping and
extortion were all carried on at the same time. This was the most real, the
most important Saigon: the most secret, too.

Far below this exceedingly discreet Asian uppercrust and yet far above
the abyss of total destitution there was the Saigon of the "compartments,"
a Saigon that still reflected the French wealth. This formed a first ring
around the Saigon of European money, a ring of decent poverty in which
there dwelt the "natives" who had done tolerably well. A compartment is a
roofed corridor, thirty feet long and six wide: this tunnel is the Asian form
of the middle-class shopkeeper's house. It stands at right angles to the
street and it is divided into an open shop at the pavement end, a general-
purpose room, and a courtyard. Real estate companies had run them up in
concrete by tens of thousands, hundreds of thousands, and let them out at
a very high rent.

The compartments stretched away forever, street after street, mile after
mile, all exactly the same, the same invariable cells arranged in exactly the
same order. Everywhere there were to be seen the same goods, the same

little trades, the same population of shopkeepers and craftsmen. It was peaceful, happy, crowded with life, rather smelly, and it looked as though it were the honest, incredibly diligent East of families working all together from dawn until darkest night. Here the squatting tailors, bare to the waist, would turn you out an admirable suit, made to measure in twenty-four hours. Here everything that business and hard work could do was done. The roads were properly drawn and there were even lamp posts and policemen in uniform. The people appeared to have names, identities and means of support — they could be vouched for. Every family seemed to be living in the public gaze — father, mother, grandparents, children, clerks and workmen were crowded together in the stall or the workroom that stood wide open to the street with neither walls nor glass to shut it off. But there were also the back rooms and the courtyards. Everything was double-faced.

The district swarmed with little opium dens, little brothels, massage houses, abortionists' shops. The police closed their eyes, partly because they were paid to close them and partly because they were by no means sure what was legal and what was not in these questions of morals and hygiene. The district also swarmed with murder committees, Vietminh tax officers, the headquarters of gangs, and arms dumps. Inextricably mixed with the poor Europeans, the white-collared civil servants, the informers on the French side, the "collaborationists" and the "traitors," there dwelt a whole world of killers, terrorists, gunmen, bomb throwers and illegal tax gatherers. But here the police could do nothing.

The best defense against the police lay precisely in this extraordinary uniformity of the people and the surroundings — these hundreds of thousands of men all much the same and these tens of thousands of exactly similar compartments. The murderer, like the bureaucrat, was dressed in a poor but very carefully pressed suit. His face was the same. How could anyone distinguish between all these yellow faces, between all these Annamese, when they were all so slim, correct and clean? Naturally they all, both honest citizens and assassins, had their French papers, all perfectly in order.

The compartments had been turned into one interconnecting maze. Everywhere holes had been driven from one compartment to another, hidden holes through the fragile Party walls. At the back the succession of courtyards formed a kind of hidden alley which communicated with other alleys of the same nature. So as soon as a man believed himself to be threatened by the police or by a patrol he had but to pass through a hole in the wall to escape into the alley — he would vanish into a neighboring compartment, from there into the infinity of compartments throughout the district and so disappear in the crowd. This underground also had its own watchmen and its own warning system. Raids and searches seldom yielded any result.

The Saigon of the compartments was the Saigon of the real full-time Vietminh. Here there were the well-organized, well-sheltered networks that profited to the utmost from civilization and city conditions in order to work over the Saigon of European wealth at their leisure. For the rich Saigon was just down the way, at the end of the street — sometimes the transition could not be felt. Generally speaking these technocrats dealt mildly with European Saigon so as to be able to draw off the piasters more easily; but sometimes Nguyen Binh would call for a dose of terrorism.

Out beyond the compartments there were the straw huts, a hopeless labyrinth, a shantytown of nearly two million wholly anonymous beings. There everything that went to make up Saigon, everything that formed the town, had practically vanished. There were no streets, no shops, no laws. The people had built their own cabins on the bare and stinking earth, on the mud, in the midst of the canals that wound in every direction — canals that were themselves densely populated, covered over with floating cities of sampans and barges crammed side by side in utter promiscuity: whole families, many generations together, lived perpetually upon the meager planks of a rotting lighter. How often I have seen these arroyos, forests of dead wood keeping thousands of people afloat from birth to death upon the thick, the almost solid water.

The whole population of these shantytowns was made up of rootless, displaced people. There was no steady work, no proper way of earning a living. In order to get by from one day to another the former nha-qués turned themselves into coolies, trishaw drivers, peddlers. There were also soothsayers, quacks, public letter-writers, outlaws, small-time pimps, small-time gangsters, a few laborers and a few men employed at pitiful wages. There was the crowd of beggars, cripples, men who were walking corpses, abandoned, eaten up by vile diseases. (The lepers lived in the cemetery, in little holes they dug between the tombstones.) There was the company of thieves. During the daytime these people came from their underworld and spread out in Saigon and Cholon in search of piasters: and in the evening they came back to bed down on their pallets. It was hard labor, utter exhaustion: a cheerful, half-naked colossus who drove a trishaw would become tubercular in three years. It was an immorality so deep and natural that it became ingenuous. What would a man not do for a few piasters? And of course there could be no question of virtue for the girls.

There all beings were in the natural course of events wholly anonymous. No birth certificates, no identity cards: there was scarcely so much as a distinct name, a known age. And there was the defense mechanism of giggling stupidly at every question, of being nothing, of being devoid of identity, personality, past, money. If you asked a coolie about his affairs or how much he earned, he would tremble and dart away; for the question implied that the questioner was the stronger and was about to impose himself upon the weaker man.

It was vast, wide-spreading wretchedness: yet not, at least by Asian standards, wretchedness to the last degree. For no one, or almost no one, actually died of starvation, whereas they did in many other Far Eastern cities. This state of affairs arose primarily from the minor profits of the war. The piaster prosperity reached out even as far as the shantytowns: it even touched the men at the very bottom, giving them their daily bowl of rice, as well as the escape of opium, whores and gambling.

It was not sad at all. It was cheerful. To get an idea of the intensity of that life you had but to see the avid happiness of a squatting ring of coolies pushing food into their mouths. To get an idea of the passion of that life you had but to watch the beggars gambling with their day's takings hour after hour through the night by the light of a candle, with rudimentary cards. Abandoned corpses were to be found often enough, but they worried nobody. From morning till night there was the sound of women chattering — gossips and procuresses. Sometimes the women would seize one another by the hair and scratch one another's faces in a hysterical quarrel, and the neighbors would watch, laughing. Or a couple of trishaw men might come noisily to blows, and lay into each other with their wooden-soled sandals. And what could be more delightful than the evening scene at the fountain? Laughing pigtailed girls in black cotton came with their buckets and flirted charmingly for hours on end with the young men of the neighborhood. It did not matter at all that the fountain was only a rusty tap, that the girls were whores and the boys pimps: it still had a wonderfully rustic simplicity.

Yet no tidal wave, no common impulse ever mounted from the depths of this Saigon of the shanties. It was the Asia of total selfishness, where each man fought for himself and where there was no compassion whatever. The inhabitant of the underworld was appallingly alone and to protect himself he had nothing but obedience, cunning, and (when he could manage it) treachery.

That was the basis of Saigon, a great mass of people who tried not to be stripped and who were stripped. The easiest means of doing so was gambling, a business farmed out by the state to the organization called the

Grand Monde, the biggest institution of its kind in the world; and into these gambling rooms a whole city came in order to ruin itself.

In addition to this there were three main organizations that squeezed the masses by mere brute force. The Vietminh. The Binh Xuyen. The police. They waged a three-sided war among themselves for the monopoly of the racket. These secret battles were full of tragicomedies; there were plenty of corpses, and there were gentlemen's agreements too.

In 1949 the struggle was unusually ferocious. The organizations were fighting for the control of the Grand Monde, the biggest piece of cake in Saigon. It was then that His Majesty Bao Dai entered the ring and intervened decisively in favor of his Binh Xuyen friends. This was direct official collusion and indeed it was alliance between the state, the government and the gangsters.

The prisoners of the piaster

MORE than three quarters of the French of Indochina — the civilians — all lived together in the Saigon of the piaster, one little corner of the immense city. There were about thirty thousand of them, and they lived in a kind of luxurious prison. But they were unaware of being prisoners. Indeed, they were happy. Their happiness consisted of pursuing money.

Besides, the money hunters' Saigon was well equipped. It had everything that was called for. In the first place, obviously, it had a district for "piaster turning." This was the port and the scruffy financial quarter, which was both official and unofficial, or black, and which lay behind the docks. Here, next to the Exchange Office, there stood the hundred-year-old import-export firms, the Bank of Indochina, and all the most respectable institutions — everything that was needed for carrying out a deal. It was here that there were to be found the Corsican bars where the alleged sailors came, carrying their smuggled gold. It was here that the powerful Chinese banks specializing in the financing of illegal operations had their headquarters, camouflaged as filthy little run-down booths. It was here that the stuffy little Rue Lefèvre acted as an exchange every morning, a speculator's fair, swarming with people.

There was also a district for living in — above all for sleeping in. This was on the "Plateau," a slightly less muddy piece of ground that rose a few feet above the rest of the city. There, all along the green shaded walks, stood the cumbrous villas of the "top people," the high civil servants and the chiefs of the banking and the import-export houses. At eight in the morning chauffeur-driven cars took these gentlemen off to their offices. The ladies, for their part, went to the very exclusive Sporting Club — no Vietnamese or Chinese were admitted as members, although there was no official rule against it.

And there was an administrative district. This was on the edge of the Plateau, and in it there stood all the buildings needed for the smooth running of society — the high commissioner's palace in its park; the somewhat less beautiful palace of the Vietnamese government; the red-brick cathedral; the prison with its watchtowers, next to the government palace; the long Sûreté building with iron bars all over it, a few paces from the cathedral; and the law courts a little farther on.

The Rue Catinat was Saigon's umbilical cord, linking all these necessary quarters. It began splendidly at the Plateau, among the fine houses and palaces, and it ended squalidly half a mile farther down at the port. The last stretch was the domain of the Corsican underworld. There one might see the dark, suspicious faces of the tough guys from the Isle of Beauty: their headquarters were the shiny bars, full of chrome and neon lighting, with their espresso machines, and roaring music. Endless mirrors reflected everything, from the manner of the boss's greeting (the true barometer of that particular world) to the long speculative stares of the habitual clients. Beyond the watchful, Junoesque cashier, beyond the doors that common mortals never entered, lay all the mysteries of the racket.

In the middle part of the Rue Catinat beat the heart of Saigon. This was where people came when they were neither speculating nor sleeping. Here, all mingled together, one might see the Saigon of the piaster, the Saigon of the high commissioner's office, the Saigon of the general staff, the ordinary Frenchman's Saigon (for that existed too), the Saigon of the adventurers, the Saigon of the bums — all the Saigons imaginable. The thirty thousand French of the town paced up and down these hallowed few hundred yards day after day; it was always, invariably, the same faces — the exercise yard of prisoners who were unaware that they were imprisoned.

Everybody came. The fashionable woman was to be seen next to the Marseilles whore. A general would bump into a legionary. A police inspector would gaze after one of his "customers" who had just come out of prison. Every passerby knew the squalid stories and the intimate secrets of all the others. But they did not greet one another: they carefully took no notice. There were complex rules of civility. You had to be of exactly the same social level to say good day and shake hands.

This everlasting promenade had its halts, the places where you had to stop. For it was in this stretch that all the holy places of Saigon were to be found: Monsieur Franchini's Hôtel Continental; the Pagoda tearoom; the

Bodega, a very ceremonious restaurant where the high financiers ate their discreet dinners; the Paix, smelling strongly of garlic and full of old Indochina hands; the shop called the Galérie de l'Eden, where the well-dressed women did their shopping; and Portail, the bookshop where the intellectuals bought the French papers from the sophisticated saleswomen, often the widows of officers.

What was really important were the café terraces and the aperitif. At noon and at seven o'clock in the evening all the French in Saigon, disregarding the risk of grenades, crammed and crowded themselves around the little tables. And all of them, in little associated groups, whispered among themselves with mysterious airs. It was then that the news of Saigon society was spread. The news items began with who had gone to bed with whom, and then in ascending order of importance went on to the state of the opium market, current bribery, hushed-up scandals, and above all the piaster, the omnipresent, haunting piaster. For hours on end they would talk over masterly strokes of business and the more brilliant shortcuts and subterfuges in the matter of transfers and speculation. The women would cry out in admiration; for them financial imagination was an integral part of virility.

This phenomenon of Saigon gossiping about Saigon, this scrutiny that took place twice a day, was called Radio-Catinat. But nowhere, in any group whatever, did anyone talk about the war. It was a subject that interested no one. The French-language papers of Saigon were there to provide reliable information upon the operations, upon the warfare that kept Saigon going in spite of its indifference. Occasionally there would be a wave of anxiety: but when that happened the authorities hurried forward with the necessary reassurances. The French drew the conclusion that it would go on for a long while yet; and they turned their minds back to business.

And yet the war was right there, immediately at hand. You could hear it. Sometimes as night fell over the city, people sitting at dinner or around the bridge table would listen for a moment to the thunder of artillery or the rattle of machine guns. There would always be an old inhabitant of Saigon there to make the diagnosis: "This evening it's going on over by Giadinh. No doubt they're attacking one of the posts in the outer ring." Then no one would pay any more attention to these commonplace noises. Men were fighting and dying, and just next to them people lived ordinary lives and amused themselves. But the French of Saigon felt no uneasiness about it. It was perfectly natural.

Indeed sometimes people would go to watch the war. The best place to see it was from the Majestic. This was a hotel, built in 1950, that rose on the bank of the Saigon River. It was a palatial affair, and Franchini had had it built for the dollar trade, the Americans and the foreigners. It was all very flashy and exceedingly expensive. On the sixth floor there was an enormous bar with a jazz pianist. This was where the snobs of Saigon gathered, together with jovial Americans remarkable for their patterned shirts, which they wore outside their trousers. And here whiskey had taken the place of the traditional imperialist brandy and soda.

The bar overhung the Saigon River, with all its anchored ships and its crowded docks, and it looked directly out onto a landscape that was already in Vietminh country. It was a few hundred yards away, no more. In the evening the contrast was extraordinarily pronounced: one could see the two worlds just below, side by side. On the one hand there was the huge expanse of Saigon, flooded with light; and over against it a great area of shadows, without so much as a gleam. You saw the riding lights of the ships, and beyond them nothing — everything was night. That dark stretch of stagnant water and marsh vegetation with villages scattered about in it was the battlefield of the "dirty war."

Once, a little before midnight, the people sitting on their high stools at the bar saw flames below them, apparently very close. In fact the fire was two or three miles away. No one was moved: it was perfectly common-place. Yet a Viet village had gone up in flames and forty *nha-qués* had been killed. And it was French sailors, recruits, who had gone out there, and had set fire to the place and had killed the people. A few days before they had arrived from France, quite free of hatred. Now they were out of control, thinking of nothing but revenging their comrades who had wandered out one cheerful evening, peacefully looking for fun in that apparently friendly village, and who had been sliced to death.

In this way the terra incognita of the Vietminh, of Asia and the war hemmed in the French of Saigon on all sides; and they were condemned to live an artificial life on a few square miles of artificial ground. The sensible thing to do was not to stir from this shelter, and most of the French remained quietly at home. The most they did was to go out to one or another of the "colonies" of civilized Saigon, little nondangerous patches set down in the dangerous suburbs. There was a golf links protected by barbed wire, for example. There was also a race track, where cheating was an official custom. One day an owner went to complain to the committee that the arrangements whereby his horse was to win had not been observed. The chairman of the committee, an aged, opium-smoking Corsican with splendid white hair and wrinkles, cried indignantly, "Here, sir, we are perfectly straight. If a special agreement has been made, it is invariably honored."

But the chief satellite was Cholon, two miles away, at the end of the huge, deserted Avenue Gallieni. It would really be more exact to call it a twin city, another center of civilization. Here it was the China of the old days, allied to European capitalism. Europeans did not live there, but they went to Cholon for its exotic flavor, for its sophisticated pleasures, for the Chinese cooking at the Palais de Jade and the Arc-en-Ciel, for the artistic opium rites, and for the love of the haughty taxi girls. A European financier might have a whispered exchange with an Asian millionaire in a restaurant: perhaps it would be to ask the Chinese to use his good offices in a negotiation for the favors of some dance-hall princess, but more often it would be a matter of some highly confidential business transaction.

There were also young men, small-time Europeans who went to look for their amusements in the districts of the compartments. It was dangerous, but cheaper. And then what a choice one had! Many connoisseurs preferred the little Vietnamese whores to the Chinese, those cerebral calculating machines. The simplest of the Annamese girls, as well as those who were painted and made-up, were so much more spontaneous! They made love better, too. An expert told me, "The most skillful girls and the most charming are those who were brought up first by the nuns and then by the Colonial Infantry. The nuns take in abandoned, naked female babies and turn them into good Catholic little girls, meek children who say their prayers and do their embroidery in the work room. When the time comes they have to be found places, and they are sent out as servants in respectable households. A few months later they are *congai** to the noncommissioned officers, and these gentlemen complete their education."

So the young men of Saigon went out looking for fun, not very far from the European quarter, into the dubious bars, the notorious dance halls, the whorehouse opium dens or the opium dens that were *not* whorehouses — these being for the real smokers, the puritans of the drug, who were utterly opposed to mixing their pleasures. Here, in surroundings of singularly impressive squalor, there was to be seen a whole nation of whoredom, bawds, wenches, detectives, informers — an extraordinary social phenomenon. But sometimes the spectacle was also accompanied by death.

In spite of these distractions there were some Europeans who could not bear being shut up in "their" Saigon forever; they felt a claustrophobic revulsion against the gilded monotony. So they would launch out onto the roads without having made any arrangements, without having paid the

* *Congai,* literally, means "girl."

Vietminh "toll." By doing so they entered into the war. And how often it would turn out disastrously, because these people did not obey the very strict rules of "how not to get killed in the country." These were the main points:

You were never to go and flirt in the woods and the rice paddies near the town. Nothing was more dangerous than lingering in a deserted pagoda or in the shade of the banyan trees. An American girl and her lover who had discovered a really lonely spot near Saigon were caught in one another's arms and hacked to pieces. Yet the pair had taken the precaution of having a third person with them to keep watch: he was murdered too.

You were never to go shooting in the nearby marshes. At all events you must never go back to the same place twice even if it was in the utter solitude of the virgin forest. Otherwise it was death. The first time the sportsmen would shoot some teal. The second time they would see a peaceful *nha-qué* in the reeds. The third time they would be mowed down by a burst from the Vietminh lying in ambush.

You were never to stop on any road, above all at twilight. Anyone immobile on the road was condemned, given over to the men in black: in a few minutes they would rise out of the landscape, close in and kill. Once I saw them emerge myself. As I was driving back from Mytho my car broke down, only a couple of miles from Saigon. I could see the suburbs in the distance. It was a quarter to six in the evening and there was still a great deal of traffic: I was not worried. But just a few minutes after I had come to a halt things stopped going by. Night was falling. Suddenly I noticed that I was in a place where the road narrowed, hemmed in by two coconut groves, already full of twilight. Two hundred yards ahead of me there were some partisans in a tower, and they were making violent signals in my direction. I decided to push my car as far as the tower, and I was trudging along, sweating, when I saw them open fire. The bullets whipped past me. I reached the tower and darted up the ladder, which was instantly pulled up. The partisans laughed, and told me that I had been within a few seconds of being kidnapped. They had been firing at a group of Vietminh creeping up behind me.

"The French close the road at half-past six," explained the head partisan. "But for their part the Viets close it at half-past five. So after half-past five no one travels along it, since the Viets attack anything that moves."

The last rule was that you were never to try to be clever. It was stupid to bawl out the man in charge of a post who warned you not to go on because there were mines and Viets ahead. You were never to lose your temper in a convoy that moved too slowly and try to get away in front. Almost all the civilians who got done in on the roads had ignored an order: they thought they were so bright that nothing unpleasant could ever happen to them. They would escape once, twice, ten times: but in the end they would get it.

But even if you did strictly obey the rules of how not to be killed you were still quite likely to be murdered on the roads. So the really careful people only moved by plane: there was the airfield of Tan Son Nhut, which allowed one to escape from the prison of Saigon in complete safety — it was a link with the rest of Indochina and the rest of the world. Once it had been a neglected stretch of fields, with all the dreariness of the colonies, but now it was a positive town of runways, hangars, towers and buildings, a complex protected by barbed wire, searchlights, soldiers and machine guns. It was Indochina's iron lung. Indeed, it became one of the world's most important traffic centers. The movement in and out was almost on the scale of Orly or the other great airfields. Almost every minute throughout the day a plane flew in or took off with a mosquitolike buzz. But Tan Son Nhut was closed at night.

Thanks to Tan Son Nhut the people of Saigon could leapfrog from point to point all over Indochina. Peering through the portholes they would see the peaceful countryside of rice fields and jungle — the lethal realm of the Vietminh. And when they reached a town all they reached was a miniature Saigon, a smaller prison with a few Europeans in it. Like the capital, every town was surrounded by a terra incognita: yet each town was also a center for the Pacification, with all that that implied. So there were deals to be made, piasters to be picked up.

But it was an unbelievable air fleet that came in and out of Tan Son Nhut. The planes were decrepit antiques ten or twenty years old, thread-bare, patched-up, infirm, flying by a miracle — the aerial equivalent of the Chinese buses. They were catchalls into which there were stuffed the *nha-qués,* their huge families and their weird baggage: most of this consisted of net bags of provisions and basins of strange victuals. The stench was appalling, because of the *nuoc mam,* that briny sauce made of rotten fish that the Annamese invariably carries with him in little pots. And in the right season there would also be durians, costly, delectable fruit carried as presents for the family: they are marvelously delicate and they have the property of smelling very strongly of old corpse and old cheese, both at the same time. But the dominant odor was that of air sickness. The Vietnamese had weak stomachs and they would vomit with a shattering din, the more discreet making use of paper bags, which would instantly burst. After a little while, particularly if the machine had gone through a storm, it would seem as though everything mortal in the body of the plane had expired. They were only air sick, but there would be no movement, no word spoken — nothing to be seen but huddled bodies. And the smell would grow steadily worse.

An advantage from the point of view of the companies was that the Vietnamese weigh very little: about a hundred and ten pounds each, on the average. So you could get a great many, perhaps forty, into a machine that was only made for twenty or twenty-five. In addition to the close-packed humanity there was the freight, those mysterious crates of the Indochinese war, prosperity and Pacification. There were no real timetables. The plane would take off only when it was full, when it was impossible to cram a single extra object into the wild mixture that filled the cabin and the baggage compartments. Every time one wondered whether it would manage to get off the ground. The takeoff was arduous, lengthy, but usually successful. Indeed, there were not a great many accidents.

Except for Air France the airlines were decidedly raffish; yet without them the Saigonese would never have been able to get out of Saigon. But they always came back to their prison: they always reappeared at the same unchanging Tan Son Nhut.

This airfield played an essential part in the social life of Saigon. The French who remained shut up in the city to make their daily piasters went out to greet those who arrived and those who left. It had a symbolic significance. Those who flew in were comforted on their return to prison, and those who flew out were congratulated on their release. It was a necessary, invariable ceremony. If any employee or underling did not go to welcome his boss he would get a black mark, if not the sack itself; so there was always a crowd of people, hundreds of parked cars and countless groups going through the motions of farewell and greeting. At the airport the standing of the travelers could be almost mathematically gauged by the number of people who had come out in their honor.

And thanks to the precise grading of ceremonies it was also the center of political and military life. Every time an important official took the plane or landed, the civil servants, the soldiers and the Vietnamese Excellencies would put on their best uniforms and stand in respectful rows. If it was for Bao Dai there would be the high commissioner and a many-starred general, a band, a review and speeches. The road from the airport to the city would be guarded by troops, one soldier every ten yards with his back to the traffic and the official cortège so that he could keep watch over the suburbs and the marshes from which the Vietminh might emerge. And all this would take place several times a month.

On the days when the French of Saigon did not go to Tan Son Nhut, they paced up and down like lions in the cage of their city — lions tamed by the piaster and quite used to captivity. So long as they stayed in the big-money Saigon, at least they were reasonably sure of being safe. Grenades did slaughter Frenchmen on the café terraces and in the crowds coming out of the cinema. Worse: from time to time there were hideous murders. Sometimes one would hear of a little boy being kidnapped as he left school; and his body would be found violated and maimed. But accidents of this kind were the price of the piaster, the risk that had to be run — the thousand-to-one risk.

The piaster was charming in itself, and there were enormous profits to be made in a country at war; but its charm was wonderfully enhanced by the fact that it was worth seventeen francs in Paris — seventeen francs once it had been transferred to France. And although the franc had remained fairly stable since the end of the Second World War, the piaster had depreciated by more than five times. This artificial pegging had been decided upon in 1945 by some financial counsellor or other without any particularly good reason. It was this man, more than any other individual whatsoever or any other circumstance, who lengthened the Indochinese war and rendered it corrupt. For it was he who gave this war its outstanding feature, that of profit: and the concrete form that this took was the transfer, the right to transmit Indochinese piasters to France to be changed into an absurdly high number of francs. Soon nothing else counted. The true order of rank in Indochina depended upon the ease or the difficulty with which a man could make money. His place in society was a function of the amount and the number of his transfers, the ease with which he could obtain them, and his ability to deal with the situation if the transfers were refused.

The entire system was bad; but it was kept up for reasons of state. The importance of the Exchange Office was not economic but political. It was an instrument of government. All the great secrets of Indochina at war, the Indochina of the palaces and the army staffs, led to these dusty, moth-eaten offices in the Rue Guynemer where sanction for transfers was given or refused.

It often happened that the director of the Exchange Office would receive an official note saying "It would be expedient if you were to grant His Majesty Bao Dai a transfer for fifty million piasters." The Emperor never reached a decision that the French wished him to reach without a preliminary transfer: his love of France was kept alive by continual watering. The same applied to other personalities of the Vietnamese political world, the importance of the transfer being proportionate to the importance of the bigwig. Every crisis in Vietnamese politics was accompanied by a wave of transfers. The French said, "You will have transfers if you do so and so." And generally the Vietnamese would reply, "Give us the transfers first, and then we shall see."

If the authorities really wanted to court a big man, to buy him entirely, they would first give him an export license, say for rice or rubber. It was a huge favor: it was the same as giving an enormous sum of money. The profit was then doubled by a transfer. Bao Dai and his immediate circle were very partial indeed to export licenses.

And then the secret funds, both for the administration and the army, had to be found somehow. Opium did a good deal, but there were also certain financial operations that passed through the Exchange Office.

But arranging these things, squaring them, in Indochina was not everything that had to be done: Paris also had to be stirred up in favor of the Indochinese war and the way in which it was carried on. That too was another reason of state. "I'm not blind," a highly placed young official said to me once. "I know all about the trading with the Viets; but I think it's in the interest of France. I'm in favor of active trade; and the Indochinese war is like a stiff breeze for the French economy, which is just getting under way again. The war costs the French state a billion* a day, but it brings in far more than that to the French, not just here but at home. There isn't even any erosion abroad, because everything — money, goods, equipment — stays in the France-Indochina circuit. So the profits wind up in France, finally, and are invested there. That's the kind of inflation you want."

And it seems that almost all the French political parties profited from transfers. Apparently they added to their wealth thanks to the piaster — the parties in favor with the approval and even the help of the Saigon authorities and those on the other side as best they could, by whatever means they could command. I have no proof, no certain evidence, but that was what the world in general said. The only virtually certain thing is that the Exchange Office in Saigon was sometimes required to grant certain transfers when the applicant was unknown, a person who was using a false name and when it was obvious that his documents were faked from beginning to end.

Naturally this system and this atmosphere bred an unusually active and populous underworld devoted to the piaster, to transfers, the black market, illegal and semilegal deals without number, gold trafficking (a gram of gold that cost 586 francs in Paris fetched 1300 in Saigon), and countless other

* Then 3 million U.S. dollars.

ways of making money. Naturally the Corsicans took a large part in these activities, and they were particularly eminent in the European prostitute trade; but they were outdone, far outdone, by the Chinese.

It was the Chinese who carried out the great majority of the deals, at least as far as big-time trafficking was concerned. Here no European could follow them or know what was really afoot. Everything was in the air, everything was calculation in its purest form, speculation that left no trace behind it. It was during those years that the great Chinese banks established themselves in Saigon. These were not official concerns, connected with the Chinese government. What I am talking about is the "secret society" kind of bank that is to be found in Asia, an organization that knows neither country nor frontiers. In Singapore these banks gamble on rubber. In Hong Kong on smuggled goods. They came to Saigon to make all they could out of the piaster. They had huge reserves and great technical ability: in comparison with them the local Chinese millionaires were mere schoolboys.

Nothing definite was known about these banks. They had no imposing head offices, no presidents, no employees; they kept no books, they quoted no capital. They scarcely went so far as to have names: and if they did, the names were false. Their operations were mysterious. All orders were given by secret radios. Nothing was ever written down. Settlements were made by contra accounts, by the complicated shifting of goods. Checks were unknown.

These banks were usually closely connected with still greater, still more anonymous organizations. Nobody apart from a very few belonging to the innermost circle ever knew who were the real chiefs. Yet these mysterious bosses, who were quite unaffected by any governments or laws, were the real governors of money in the Far East. Nobody knew, either, how far their tentacles extended. All over Asia they had relations, partners, informers, messengers, killers, male and female agents. They were wholly indifferent to the means they employed: they could cause a man thousands of miles away to disappear by the use of a prearranged code word. But the Chinese capitalists, the nameless men of Asia, preferred corruption and persuasion to murder. It was their belief that more was to be gained by coming to an understanding than by slitting throats.

In Saigon all that was known was that the Macao Organization had settled itself in. This was the most recent and the most formidable group in the Far East, and it specialized in gambling and foreign exchange. Its home town was Macao, that tiny Portuguese colony on the Pearl River, full of bells, convent walls and brothels, where there was to be found in its highest degree the Catholic civilization of grace and sin. There, over the last four centuries, a particular breed had come into being, the Macanese, made up of five per cent of Portuguese blood and ninety-five per cent Chinese, an uncommonly good proportion for enterprise and trafficking. Formerly Macao was a gambling hell ruled by a few gangs and heads of gangs, some being killers, others bankers, millionaire bankers, "big-time Chinese." When the flames of this particular hell were put out these gentlemen, still intimately allied, became the kings of the trade in gold.

From 1945 until 1950 Macao was the world's greatest center for gold trafficking. There was no airfield, but special seaplanes brought in the ingots, which then vanished into the unplumbed depths of neighboring China, then wholly plunged into civil war. (The Bank of Indochina possessed one of these machines.) The profits were immense. The whole thing was done with the complicity of the authorities and it was practically legal. An ugly little man by the name of Lobo, born in Timor and more of a mongrel than the Macanese since he possessed every strain of blood in Asia, had been promoted by his talents to the head of all the economic services in the colony, and he organized a prodigious racket. Officially, as a Portuguese civil servant, he sold licenses for importing gold at unbelievable rates. Afterwards, once the precious metal had arrived, he made no inquiries as to where it went. It traveled along the gold road that ran the fifty-odd miles between Macao and Canton, the main highway for smuggling on the grand scale, under the paid protection of a warlord.

But then, after gambling, gold too dried up in Macao. That was in 1948. The big Macanese, still in tight formation, moved their headquarters to the other side of the Pearl River, to Hong Kong. From Hong Kong they sent out intelligence agents in all directions and settled down to the quest for profitable opportunities for the exercise of their talents. Saigon appeared to suit their requirements. They moved in.

Their arrival was most remarkable. Everything had been arranged with unrivaled skill. The Macanese began by a discreet, universal, secret flood of "presents" with no strings attached; the undiscriminating flood reached all the authorities it could attain and all the organizations that owned machine guns. It was a flood such as Indochina had never known, homeland though it was of bribery and corruption. After that the Macanese won the friendship of the compradors who were in control of the market. In particular they made an alliance with the chief comprador of the main European bank, who put his army of touts and spies at their disposal. In a few weeks they were in business relations with the Vietnamese government, with messengers from the Vietminh and representatives of the sects, with the Corsican pimps, policemen, shady lawyers and highly experienced Frenchmen from Shanghai. They had made contact with the banking and import-export houses of the "straight piaster," and with all kinds of dubious little booths and bars. They were probably in touch with Monsieur Franchini, the proprietor of the best hotel, who also had interests in the Grand Monde — not in the gambling itself, which would have been too big for him, but in the dance hall there.

The first victory of the Macanese was the contract for running the Grand Monde, which they obtained thanks to the good will of Huu, the prime minister, and the Vietnamese authorities. It was a master stroke. Macao had not been the capital of gambling for some while, and now Saigon would take its place.

At the same time they steadily and patiently built up their "piaster line" across the world. This was trafficking on the highest, the most scientific plane. All that was known was that they had to have transfers to Paris. On the return voyage everything vanished, disappeared into an abstract circuit. The currency and the gold did not change place physically. The francs realized in France turned into the most varied currencies and commodities, passing through all the great exchanges and markets in the world — Switzerland, Tangiers, the United States, Hong Kong, Singapore. All the orders were given by coded telegram. The series of sales, purchases and bills falling due ended up in Saigon. One final settlement of accounts produced the piasters, great masses of piasters. The whole cycle, from Saigon back to Saigon by way of Paris and the rest of the world, took just a week. The Corsicans took two months. And how much more arduous and dangerous their way was, and how much less profitable!

Sometimes a French military radio operator would be approached in Saigon by respectable-looking Chinese. They would offer some thousands of piasters for a few minutes' work. He only had to promise complete silence and allow himself to be blindfolded. The zigzagging ride took a long time. At last the operator would end up in a small room with a modern transmitter in front of him. A smiling Chinese would hand him a coded text. All he had to do was to send it out. The journey back was the same — he traveled blindfolded in a car. If the Frenchman went on he would notice that every time he was taken to a different place with a different Chinese in it. But the messages were always coded in the same way.

The Macanese never appeared in any of these deals. They remained in the background, unknown, hardly to be made out at all. The only physical sign of their presence was the arrival of young, modern, well-dressed, very westernized Chinese at all the strategic points along the chain, beginning with Paris. They joined the universities as students. How could the police have anything against them?

In Saigon itself it was exceedingly difficult to get as far as the Macanese. The crucial moment for them was the actual obtaining of the transfers, which they either acquired legally through the Exchange Office or bought on the black market. But the Chinese had a standing very unlike that of the Corsicans! Their status as Chinese millionaires won them the confidence of the important banking and import-export circles: this allowed them to procure really respectable front men, and they chose them from highly considered business houses. And they made friends with the rising young financiers. The eligible young men would be studied for months without their knowledge. They would be tested. When one was selected they would say to him, "Stay with your firm, but work secretly for us. In exchange we will let you in on our deals."

No traces were left at any time. Thanks to these exceedingly careful precautions and to their remarkable technical ability the Macanese carried on their traffic for years without a single accident. The system was so well thought out that it was impossible for anything unforeseen to arise. It was in vain that the French authorities, rendered uneasy by these impenetrable refinements and suspecting that behind it all there might be the Vietminh or some foreign agency, set their traps to unmask the Macanese bosses and expell them.

All that the French police knew was that the managing committee of the Saigon Macanese met once a week at the Grand Hotel in Cholon, which was one of those Chinese establishments known to offer every kind of service, whatever pleasure or whatever business was concerned. But when the detectives appeared they found nothing but respectable Chinese feasting upon shark fins.

Yet there was a certain amount known about one of the Macanese chiefs. This was a Chinese of the old style, a plump, robe-wearing fifty-year-old, as gay as a lark and speaking nothing but Cantonese. He loved the old ways, and he practiced the forms of politeness of his childhood. At the splendid banquets to which he invited his French friends — his European agents and sometimes an important personality — he himself would rise to serve his guests. That is to say he would choose the most luscious morsels among the countless dishes, pick them up in his chopsticks and place them in the bowls of those he wished to honor. There was a continuous flow of merriment: there were innumerable toasts. Everyone drank to everyone

else, and to the everlasting Franco-Chinese friendship, and to the prosperity of trade.

These banquets were very like conspiracies. You arrived at a closed door
in a blind, dirty wall. You had to knock. A Chinese servant peered through
a judas hole and somehow recognized the guests, whom he led into a little
hidden, unsuspected room, elaborately luxurious, full of jade and artificial
flowers. This was the inner sanctum. This was peace itself. Here, in front of
the round banquet table with its beautifully decorated rice-grain bowls,
dishes, plates — the mass of porcelain that almost hid the dirty cloth (for
even among millionaires devoted to the utmost refinement a clean table-
cloth would be inconceivable: it would stifle both appetite and digestion) — was the sweetly smiling Monsieur Wu: for that was the name by
which the chief of the piaster Macanese was known. On seeing him you
would swear that he was the very embodiment of the oldest and most
venerable China, the China of ancient wisdom.

Yet I knew that this old-fashioned, this outwardly very civil character,
was extraordinarily up-to-date as far as business was concerned. He was
also most uncommonly hard. Sometimes, breaking off in the middle of a
compliment to one of his guests, he would begin to stamp with rage,
shouting furiously and uttering harsh, brutish noises. It was his way of
making his views known to his assistants, the young Chinese around him
dressed in the most elegant Western clothes and speaking the most perfect
English. When his paroxysm was over the good old gentleman would turn
back to the Europeans he was feasting and take up the compliment exactly
where he had left off and with just the same degree of benevolence.

This kindliness had an exact meaning. The feast was a rite, a ceremony.
It was the celebration of a common greed for money. It was the communion of the piaster. Decency required that love and friendship alone
should be mentioned; but among the Chinese there were no humane
feelings at all, nothing but self-interest. So in fact Monsieur Wu, as he
bowed and smiled to his guests, was really saying, "I am receiving you as
honorary members of my humble secret society. But from now on you are
under my rule. Woe betide you if you disobey." Clearly, no one disobeyed
the formidable Monsieur Wu.

It was he that the French police discovered at the end of their researches
into almost every kind of traffic. But they never had a shadow of a proof.
What is more, his identity was very far from certain. And again, was he
really the head of the Macanese piaster network? Was he not perhaps a
mere puppet, the real boss in Saigon being wholly unknown and unsuspected? An old inspector, a veteran of the French concession in Shanghai,

assured me that it was utterly useless to worry over such details. Curiosity of that kind was dangerous and pointless, for there was no possibility whatsoever of getting to the bottom of Chinese finance.

The delights of Cholon

YET these tough and pitiless Macanese suffered a resounding defeat. They lost the Grand Monde. The Binh Xuyen wrested it from them after a hidden, underground war. And in the long run this battle between the gangs was to have immeasurable consequences for Indochina. For it was to mean the triumph of Bay Vien and the setting up of official gangsterism with the approval of His Majesty Bao Dai. It was to end with a bandit's becoming the Saigon chief of police, with his gang as the force itself.

Things had not reached this stage yet. In 1948 it was still the hidden struggle between the Macanese and the Binh Xuyen. To begin with I will describe the battlefield. It was Cholon. And the stake that they were fighting for lay within Cholon — it was the notorious Grand Monde.

Cholon was a true Chinese city with all the proper traditions. It was a huge watertight club whose eight hundred thousand members devoted themselves to the practice of wisdom as it was understood in the ancient Chinese conception of life. Life's only aim was sensual enjoyment. So right conduct consisted of getting the necessary money for pleasure and a life full of delights, whatever the cost. Hundreds of thousands of men were reduced to crushing toil, disease and death so that a few tens of thousands of "big Chinese" should be able to devote themselves to a civilization consisting of good eating, an endless succession of banquets, *kampés,* opium, gambling and every conceivable form of eroticism, maintained by aphrodisiacs. Miraculously, this savage gluttony was not exhausting. On the contrary, it created an extraordinary vitality. Yet there was no such thing as a definitively gained advance: each single day every man began the life and death struggle all over again. Everything was dynamism, an energy directed at profiting, surviving and escaping. Cholon, therefore, was an arena in which anything at all was possible. But it was also, superficially, a place in which order reigned; for the daily battle had its exact rules, a hidden code of its own.

By day the town seemed asleep. The outward appearance was that of a poverty-stricken place, squalidly utilitarian, with warehouses, empty building lots, peeling walls and locked-up houses. The only living thing was the rice. It arrived in junks and sampans along the never-ending canals, thousands of tons of it every day. Cochinchina was so fertile that in reasonably peaceful times it could export two million tons of rice a year. The small-time Chinese, the poor relations, the agents and the money lenders who dealt with the *nha-qués,* bought up the grain in the provinces, and just as though there were no war being waged at all, they sent it to their chiefs, the big-time Chinese of Cholon.

So Cholon was the general center for rice — the rice exchange. During the daytime the millionaires, the masters of the trade, dozed behind their thick bars, with their tireless minds working out profitable ways of manipulating the market rates. Little opium lamps glowed perpetually at their bedsides. Meanwhile the laboring people were at their task, unloading, sifting, husking the rice. There were no machines. Human effort and human life were cheaper by far.

It was particularly in the afternoon that the town seemed so dead. But some way out, on the banks of the Chinese canal and the loop canal, there was a milling horde of the very poor. Here, where the land could scarcely be told from the water, since both were mud, a whole mass of people clung to life in sampans moored side by side in the stench and the floating rubbish. From time to time a splendid fat-bellied junk with rustling sails and rigging would thrust through this accumulation of creatures and things and tie up at the quay. Then began the endless to and fro of human beasts of burden. Puny, almost naked coolies carried sacks weighing two hundred and twenty pounds out of the hold on their backs. They worked with the age-old movements of the Chinese crushed under enormous burdens but carrying them in spite of everything. It was a positive art. They all had the same way of hoisting the load, throwing it onto their bowed shoulders and running forward, panting, uttering inarticulate cries to keep people from getting in their way and breaking their rhythm. They went by with strange hitches and jerks, continually thrusting up the load that threatened to make them fall. This ballet went on for ten or even twelve hours. There were women coolies, child coolies. Foremen, some of them armed with pistols, bawled and dealt out blows. No one fell.

At the end of the day, after the foremen, the super-foremen and the Vietminh and Binh Xuyen "tax gatherers" had taken their contributions, protection money or patriotic tax, the coolies had a few low-value coins left out of their pitiable wages. It would be enough to allow them to buy a few mouthfuls of food and above all to spend the rest of the night gambling, squatting there like animals. Some of them would go for dross, the dregs of opium, which was practically neat poison and which stunned them so that they fell unconscious in the middle of the indifferent crowd. These working conditions stirred no one's indignation. Besides, in comparison with the rest of Asia they were normal — indeed, they were quite good.

At twilight the big Chinese left his house. He said farewell to his number one wife, his concubines, his countless children, his countless relations and servants. He left the tribe in a house that was almost a fortress, strongly protected against the outside world and its perils. Alone, with his big, benign, almost anonymous Chinese face, he went out to begin his real day's work and live his real life. The market that he went to dealt in both business and pleasure — it was the whole of Cholon.

With the fall of darkness the town suddenly took on a totally different aspect. It was in the grip of the Chinese intensity of living, and there is nothing else in the world that can be compared to it. It is scientific excitement by every possible means, by noise and by light, by quantity, by vast numbers. Everything is priced, proffered, buyable, and yet at the same time mysterious. The huge Chinese characters in aggressive, blazing neon bring the swarming humanity out into the narrow streets, the light reflecting on their faces, intensely eager and yet expressionless, pressing on by every possible means of locomotion, on foot, in trishaws, in American cars, always an inexhaustible stream.

On sale, there were not only extraordinarily striped socks, tons of rice, and aphrodisiacs running the whole gamut from rhinoceros horn to tiger's liver, but also smiles, the singing of girls, civilities, reputations, little boys, maidenheads, lives and the service of murderers and kidnappers. There was neither morality nor immorality, nothing that brought sin to mind: for sin was a concept that had no meaning here.

Everything was on sale; and yet everything was hidden. All that appeared on the surface was the lovely girl in silk with a haughty, painted face, stepping out of a trishaw and vanishing into a doorway, going to see honorable customers whose offers she had deigned to accept. She would always take the utmost care of her face, her pride, her standing. For even in its extreme eagerness this wholly venal Chinese society had very complicated rules, rigid laws of convention and propriety, a whole art of orderly processes and a scrupulous division of labor that added still more to the voluptuous pleasure. And everything was arranged between insiders.

The only thing the Chinese displayed publicly in the street was their gluttony. There, belly was king. In China, after thousands of years of starvation, the customary greeting is "I hope that you will always have enough to eat." Cholon was scarcely menaced by famine — far from it. The entire city, right down to the pavements, was one vast display of food, an enormous cook shop. Around the thousands of soup merchants there squatted crowds of people shoveling the rice from their bowls into their mouths with chopsticks, a perpetual motion. The personification of good eating was the Chinese butcher, a cheerful, formidable creature, with his triple belly falling in modest folds over his obscene navel, singing the praises of his pink sides of bacon, his pressed duck reduced to paper thinness, his immense lacquered pigs, like so many barbarian gods.

But all other pleasures were enjoyed behind the shelter of walls, of guardians and precautions. Once it was dark all the leading Chinese would gather with their friends in little groups, in the thousands of small secret societies that lived the "good life."

The place of meeting was usually the "Chinese hotel," an institution in itself. In a remote, poor side street one went through a sort of hole in the wall and came out into a dirty, extraordinarily empty hall whose sole decoration was neon lights, mirrors and an array of spittoons. A Chinese in a singlet was the absolute judge of all who arrived, and his utter lack of expression was the most absolute refusal to those who were unknown. But to those who had the right to come in he bowed double, showing them to the deal staircase that led upstairs to the floors where the rumbling of the mah-jongg pieces drowned countless discreet little sounds.

The hotel was a factory that ran almost nonstop, all night and a great part of the day. It was a large building divided into little boxes, arranged next to one another and over one another in great numbers. But it did have an extraordinary aspect too, which was that in each of these cells the customers could satisfy absolutely any desires whatsoever. Nothing was impossible: you only had to ask. And no one would come and interrupt, ever.

Generally speaking the worthy Chinese took their ease informally. Wearing only their drawers, fanning their vast bellies, belching, they lay there in armchairs. Often they would carry out business deals involving millions of piasters. It was all very simple. Three or four half-naked businessmen, spitting out sunflower seeds and nudging one another, would murmur, "I've had a good idea. I'm going to put x million into it. What about you?" Yet it was these casual remarks between cronies that brought about all the strange economic phenomena of the "happy war," the bear and bull operations, hoarding, smuggling. Against conspiracy of this kind the authorities were powerless: their control measures only made the Chinese laugh.

Business was accompanied by every kind of Oriental pleasure. Above all, those concerned ate for hours on end — rare, marvelous dishes, of which every mouthful amounted to a coolie's wages for hundreds of days.

And to increase the delights of the table, poetical and amorous refinements were called for at the same time. The big Chinese had a whole tribe who specialized in attending to their amusements, a female army with exactly defined ranks and functions — massage women, singers, little flowers, courtesans and taxi girls.

Behold the massage woman. An old, toothless, immensely skillful woman with astonishing strength. She seizes the customers, pulls their bones out of joint, wrings them, makes them crack as though the place were a torture chamber, and the customers gurgle with satisfaction. Then the little flowers begin their work. They are dolls dressed in long silk or lamé sheaths, very young, very much made-up, with the face white and the cheeks red: under a wonderfully pure forehead their moist brown eyes are drawn out towards their temples. Delicacy is their calling, and all the most exquisite and accomplished feminine graces — they have studied for years to become so expert. Every evening their dressing calls for hours of care and meticulous attention. When they are on the job they are all wonderfully modest, splendidly adorned, eager, delightfully eager to foresee the slightest wish. Not the least hint of vulgarity. No sentimentality either. It is all art. Everything was laid down in the rules of the art — every movement, smile, word — rules dating back hundreds of years.

The little flowers had to know how to make themselves agreeable in every possible way. In the first place they had to charm the customer with informed, literate conversation, full of quotations and references to ancient legend. Their value rose with their intelligence, which was highly prized. But as they talked, cooing and smiling, they also made themselves useful. They made the satiated clients eat still more, feeding them by hand with carefully chosen morsels. They prepared the opium pipes for the smokers stretched out on their couches. They remained sweetly silent and attentive while the big Chinese gave themselves up to their passion for mah-jongg and poker for nights on end. It was when the Chinese were gambling that you could really see their cerebral quality — their cold, intense, inexorable concentration. The little flowers acted as croupiers, with their costly hands serving as rakes; and as they handled the huge wads of paper money they had a lofty, above-it-all expression. For face required that although they should ply their calling with great skill they should at the same time remain detached, superior. In actual fact they were fascinated by these men at grips with one another, by their total war, and by the heaps of money. Money and the merciless struggle for money was what all Chinese women understood and what they really loved.

The great diversion was listening to songs. The singers were the most expensive of the little flowers. They could be quite mature — it did not matter. They formed an aristocracy. The best known was an imposing woman of close on thirty with a face like a full moon and coils of black hair done up with tortoise-shell combs, large almond-shaped eyes and a small full round mouth. She was called Mademoiselle My. Her speciality was the recitative, the ancient chant. To begin with, her tiny fingers would draw sad sounds from a curious instrument something like a xylophone; then her pure and yet grating voice would rise in a lament for a princess who drowned herself for love — *"On the shore of a mere there died a golden lotus."* The guests were enchanted.

The little flowers would make love, if the big Chinese wanted them to. When singing, dancing, alcohol, mah-jongg and high eating had aroused their desires it was but right that they should be satisfied: nothing should be left unassuaged. But the best sort of people only asked the little flowers for the pleasure of their company, not for their bodies. When they had reached the time for those particular delights they sent for other girls, courtesans trained in all the sophistications of lechery.

Generally this staff of little flowers, singing girls and whores — so much livestock, from the old Oriental point of view — did not belong to the Chinese hotel. They were brought in from outside according to the customers' requirements. Each girl belonged to an old woman, her "god-mother" or "guardian," who had bought her as a baby from her coolie parents for a hundred piasters or thereabouts. This woman would invest considerable sums of money in giving the child a careful education. She would recoup a great deal of her outlay by selling the girl's virginity at the age of ten, selling it after long bargaining to a wealthy lover of such wares, which fetched a great deal of money — ten to fifteen thousand piasters. Maidenheads were very much in demand, for the elderly Chinese men were of the opinion that deflowering a virgin had an excellent physical effect, rejuvenating them and giving them back their vigor. When the girl was thirteen the woman would say, "I have spent a great deal of money on you: from now on you must work to pay me back." The new little flower would have to carry out all her requirements, obeying orders directed by an intelligent economic and erotic strategy. Her only chance of freedom was that some wealthy man would want her as a concubine, and would buy her.

Such was the state of prostitution at Cholon. Essentially it was a form of civilization, an established order of society, a philosophy of life and of the world. Everything was unchangeable, inside the community and secret. Above all there was that typically Chinese need to get together, to form private groups; and this was the same for the rich and for the poor. In their own houses the millionaires had their private clubs that were even more exclusive than the Chinese hotels, protected by guards, bullies, servants, locks and bars. It was said that inside the luxury reached fantastic heights. Everybody in Saigon had heard of the Huy Bon Hoa club, an artificial paradise beyond anything the rest of the world had to offer. Once a Frenchman was invited, and he came back two days later, exhausted and out of his wits with voluptuous delight.

In the ordinary course of events Europeans were excluded from these pleasures. To all intents and purposes the Chinese hotel was closed to them. It was not a flat refusal that they met with, but an emptiness. When they appeared they found nothing — there was nothing to be had. After an hour's negotiation they might succeed in being allowed one bottle of beer, but that would be the limit.

This exclusiveness, this dislike of outsiders, applied even to the little Chinese brothels for the poor. There was a whole district of them at the far end of Cholon, by a Catholic church. But filthy though they were, they too were clubs — family affairs in which everybody knew everybody else.

You went into the ordinary little narrow streets and on either side you saw compartments just like the countless others in Saigon. Indeed everything was rather more than ordinarily quiet and orderly. Each entrance had a panel devoted to the parents and the whole family. An imposing photograph showed the madam (now a shaven-headed dowager whose grin displayed black stumps of teeth) in her young days, with her husband and their offspring. Fifty other smaller photographs displayed the grandchildren. The far end of the room was entirely taken up by the huge altar and the ancestral tablets, together with Buddhas and the ritual halberds. Joss sticks burned slowly, filling the room with acrid smoke. A diploma bore witness to the fact that the proprietress was a worthy and religious woman and that in 1927 she had given a hundred piasters towards the building of a pagoda.

Yet these were bawdy houses. Besides, on the pavement there were the girls, sitting on stools in the classic attitude of the Chinese prostitute, one fat white leg tucked under their bottoms — a position of great antiquity that was meant to stir the passions of the customers. The said customers, however, did not satisfy their appetites at once. They remained in the hall with the photographs and the Buddhas. There everybody, the men, the whores, the madam, her husband, her children and the toddlers who were her grandchildren, gossiped until eleven o'clock. They ate: they smoked opium. It was still another exclusive community. To get into it you had to be known and to pay thirty-five piasters.

The rules of good behavior were very strict. It would be quite improper to want to make love before eleven o'clock — a barbarous, a European way of carrying on. A little before midnight the idlers went away and only a few regular customers were left. They had a rack for their own personal napkins, just as they might have had in a boarding house, napkins as dirty as can be imagined, but not for wiping their mouths. Lying with a wench cost fifty piasters. All the customers operated at the same time, in little boxlike rooms opening off a central corridor. These coops were only separated by frail, head-high bamboo screens. The furniture consisted of a mat-covered bench, a jug and a spittoon. The honorable assembly went on talking from one room to another. Only the conversation took a somewhat particular turn.

It was unusual for the French to come to these places, except for the police — as for them, they were treated with great respect and their palms were greased. It would be disastrous for a European to want to have one of the girls — it would discredit the house for a great while if he were to succeed. When an uninformed European wandered into this district all the bawds would do their utmost, their cunning utmost to send him away without any scenes or noise. There would be endless explanations — the girls were unwell, out of form, not in the right condition at all. And in the end the intruder would always go away.

Yet not far off, in other alleys, other quarters, there were hundreds and thousands of bars, dance halls and brothels where the girls rushed ferociously into the attack, seizing firmly upon their quarry. The prey was mostly made up of Frenchmen, soldiers of the Expeditionary Force, small operators in the piaster black market. But here it was a question of Annamese prostitution, westernized by French civilization.

For their part the Chinese in Cholon maintained their overweening pride, their racism and hatred of foreigners. They would not share their pleasures. They preserved their exclusiveness by a wonderfully polite and smiling conspiracy of silence. Cholon was still the age-old, self-regarding China: but it was also a China that had learned to make a profit out of the foreigners without dirtying its hands, by inventing the art of conventional relationships. Contact was absolutely necessary because of business. So banquets and feasts were organized: but they were imitations, facsimiles, and they gave no more than a hint, a foretaste of the real thing.

Cholon was the oldest, the most reactionary, the most exclusive China. There was nothing modern except the dance halls and their taxi girls. These were institutions that had been imported from Shanghai and Hong Kong, those extraordinary cities in which Chinese capitalism had expanded, but had necessarily grown less pure in doing so. These establishments were curious in the extreme, for Chinese eroticism had borrowed some ingredients from the West, such as "sex appeal" and jazz, but in doing so it had twisted and deformed them. It was difficult to tell whether one was in Paradise or the chamber of horrors. The ancient tortuous Oriental attitude to life was more present than ever. Europeans were allowed in: but still what they entered was a secret place, full of conventions that they did not understand.

The main dance halls in Cholon were the Paradis and the Arc-en-Ciel. Inside everything was dimly lit — a place under a spell, you might have said. Bizarre decorations on the walls, futuristic shapes mingled with plants or limbs. It might be the sea, or a forest, or a colossal fornication. In the midst of all this there were wandlike apparitions, the flower maidens, the wonderful taxi girls. They danced, some supple, others rigid, talkative or full of an affected scorn, glancing with unseeing eyes at the staring men. All of them wore the famous dress of these present days, that extraordinarily provocative garment which has a high, stiff collar, but which clings everywhere and which is slit up the side, showing an ivory leg. It is a dress that makes the body a silhouette, a single brush stroke. And in a way its shamelessness is both catlike and decent.

The customers were all men, nothing but men: but they were of every color, white, yellow and brown. The *taipan,* the "captain," moved about among the tables with his book of tickets, like a bus conductor. The idea was that the customer chose his girl — in one corner there was a group of waiting "taxis." But in fact there was a deal every time. The *taipan* had to have a quick mind. He only had a few seconds to estimate the standing of the "buyer," his wealth, his intentions and the amount of money he was willing to spend. On the basis of his calculations he suggested a girl, always taking into consideration the proprieties and the good of the house. And then from the point of view of yield there was the question of making an exact match between the girl's looks and the man's purse.

The ticket, which cost a hundred piasters, gave the right to one hour's dancing and conversation. But almost invariably the girl would manage to make the time very much shorter. She would put on a bored, haughty look, refuse to answer, and go away after a few minutes. For the taxi girl's strongest suit was virtue: her great art was to appear inaccessible. Her line was to give herself airs. In this way she got rid of the no-account customers altogether, and prompted the more eligible to produce both compliments and gifts. The queens of the game had three hundred dresses and a whole court of millionaires. They were quite appallingly touchy. A coarse gesture, a hand touching their bottom, and they would shriek, creating the most violent scenes. But they would also be exceedingly offended if they were not caressed at all, for such coldness would be an insult to their charms. Most of them claimed to have only one lover at a time. They had others in fact, but secretly: the girls who were known to be easy were despised by their competitors. The ideal role for the taxi girl was that of the coquette wooed by a yearning admirer. The pursuer had to show his open-handedness — and he was not to ask for anything until some time had passed. But often, if he was inexperienced, he would think that the great day had come, only to find himself sent empty away. What numbers of Frenchmen ruined themselves buying tickets! At last one evening they would buy the whole book so as to have the right to take the object of their passion out for the night. But as soon as the wench was in the open air she would vanish.

The little flowers were a tradition of the China of the old days. It was an old-fashioned pleasure, and one which depended upon the girl's entire submissiveness. She was a slave. There was harsh, squalid bargaining, but always with the procuress. With the taxi girls the young Chinese could nourish the illusion of romanticism. It was all the more pleasurable in that the result was known in advance, illusion or no illusion. True enough, the taxis were independent. But they were also terribly in need of money. They nearly always had someone depending on them — an old mother, a consumptive husband, children. They were usually girls from an educated background reduced to prostitution — even if it were a classy sort of prostitution — by the hard times, by adverse circumstances. In Saigon the mainstay of ruined families was the sale of their daughters. And this is a theme that is to be found in Chinese tales and legends going back for thousands of years.

Underlying it all there was a pitiless realism. The young Chinese were perfectly aware that it would be boorish to be in too much of a hurry. The taxi acquired face by playing the inaccessible princess. But the customers too acquired face by buying countless tickets and giving ostentatious presents. The one end and aim of these pretty gestures on the part of the wooer was to display his wealth and power. In the end, when the right moment came, the whole business would be settled. Besides, each girl had her market rating, in just the same way as dried fish. At Hong Kong or Manila the cost of each well-known taxi girl was common knowledge.

The taxis were very much in fashion. Their customers were the young men, rich men's sons who had been converted to the modern way of life. Every evening the fathers would go to the hotel or the club and strip to their drawers; their sons, wearing very elegant suits, would come to the dance hall.

A young man of an exceedingly rich family said to me, "Times have changed. The new generation is discovering love. My father is all in favor of our way. If he had brought me up according to the old ideas I should be an opium addict by now. In the good families it was the rule to get the boys used to taking it as soon as their adolescence began, so as to damp them down and prevent them ruining themselves with whores. Because opium works out cheaper than women. But although my father is an incurable smoker himself he broke with the tradition. He says that he would have grown even richer if it had not been for the opium. And he wants me to be a go-ahead, dynamic twentieth-century businessman."

It was in fact still the old generation that controlled Cholon. And to do so they had to be most exceptionally astute, for now, in the Chinese Cholon of rice and pleasure, a most formidable gang of Vietnamese pirates had set itself up. This was the Binh Xuyen organization, which had just seized the Grand Monde and which was about to turn it into its stronghold.

The battle of the Grand Monde

Has anyone ever heard of the battle of the Grand Monde? the battle in which the strong and peaceable Macanese Lam Giong was crushed by the small-time bandit Bay Vien, thanks to the support of His Majesty Bao Dai, a battle that was to modify the entire history of Saigon, Cochinchina and Vietnam?

No. So I shall describe the various stages of this war — the magnificence of the Grand Monde, the glory of Lam Giong, the satisfaction of the prime minister Huu; and then the engagement, with its bombs and its kidnappings; and the deus-ex-machina intervention of the Emperor.

As you came along the road from Saigon you found the Grand Monde at the outskirts of Cholon (in fact the Grand Monde company had several gambling houses, but this was the main establishment). The cheerful Rue des Marins was dominated by huge yellow walls, great thick walls built to hide and to shut in. There were chains that funneled the crowd towards two little entrances. You had to let yourself be searched. Two aged hags dressed in something that had been a uniform searched the women, cackling as they did so. It was young toughs in singlets and sandals, with cigarettes dangling, who dealt with the men, taking particular care of their pockets. These people were police auxiliaries, and they were making sure that the customers were not carrying revolvers or grenades. This was a formality that was practiced everywhere in Saigon, even at the cinemas. But here it was rougher.

Once you were past the outer barrier you found yourself in a great courtyard of beaten earth: it stank, the ground was greasy with filth, and gutters plowed their way across it. At night thousands of naked bulbs showed corrugated-iron buildings set down on bare cement. There were about fifty of them, and each contained four or five gaming tables. A whole nation of people, thousands and thousands of them, were packed into these hutches. It was the same crowd as those who thronged the streets and the canals. You saw coolies with their lean ribs protruding, poor men of distinction with little beards, peasant women with lacquered teeth, hordes of shopkeepers of every kind, houseboys, ladies of the town. There were a great many pregnant women and mothers with their babies on their back. And there were some old ladies of such antiquity that their hair, according to the custom of the country, had been cut very short — a crew cut — so that now they looked like old sexless grotesquely senile men. Little boys and little girls lovingly held hands: but their fingers would unclasp to seek some filthy note at the far bottom of a pocket — their stake. The whores were still in their streetwalking clothes; they were horribly made-up, with their eyes far too big, and the paper-thin cotton of their blouses and their skirts offering their bodies; but they were not working. Having just satisfied a customer they had hurried in to gamble with the fee.

The Grand Monde was a clip joint raised to the highest power, a grinding mill, all that was most squalidly simple and organized. It was mass-production gambling. The tables went on one after another forever. They were mere crudely painted planks, daubed with figures or characters. There were all the games from all over the world, a score of them and more — games with cards, dice, large balls, little balls, knuckle bones, and many other things. But the chief of them were *bat-quan* and *tai-xieu,* Chinese forms of gambling with extraordinarily involved combinations.

At each table a team of men and women croupiers worked at full speed with the same streamlined movements. The only human sound came from a woman croupier, always young and made-up, wearing a skin-tight Chinese dress. When she had shaken the big glass bell that held the *tai-xieu* dice she called out the results in the traditional harsh, modulated chant, almost a moan. The croupiers wore singlets: they were dried-up men, bony, melancholy, uncaring: their long clawlike arms raked in the notes. They unfolded the piasters one by one, for the players staked them folded in four, just as they carried them, according to the way of the poor. All these wretched people lost without a sign, without so much as a shudder.

Every few minutes you would see them search about among their rags and bring out still more folded notes.

Perched on a six-foot stool above each table there was a man who seemed to be dozing. This was the head of the table, and he was supervising the play. But he never intervened, for there was never any dispute or quarrel.

The exploitation reached its culminating point toward ten o'clock in the evening. Gong strokes and cymbals rang out in a kind of scruffy amphitheater, and great red lights came on: this was an Asian ceremony, all din and dazzle. Before a great wall of faces, a huge crowd turned to stone, a well-dressed person in a suit climbed onto a platform and began to speak. His mission was to proclaim the Beast — he announced the name of the creature that had won that day in the game called the Thirty-Six Beasts. Beside him another person, dressed as an aged scholar, gave a learned discourse on the reasons for this victory.

The business was carried out like this: every day the Grand Monde's thousands of touts made their way through every alley in every district of the town, crying, "Thirty-six beasts, thirty-six beasts!" Everywhere they handed out yellowish sheets covered with pictures and rhymes concerning the age-long history of the Middle Empire, the legends of the war of the Three Kingdoms, the great dramas of the Chinese theater and the ancient tales. Now all the occurrences in this fabulous past had happened under the signs of auspicious or inauspicious beasts, the instruments of fate, who numbered thirty-six. The game consisted of finding out what happening it was that was described, and of giving the name of the beast that, by its benign or malignant influence, had ruled the event.

Returning from their rounds the touts told the managers of the Grand Monde which beasts the people had betted on. So in the evening, during the ceremony at which the official result was given, the right beast, the Grand Monde's beast, was invariably the outsider that no one had thought of. For example, if all the bets had been placed on the Mouse it would be the Bat that was proclaimed. And the scholar on duty would give a long, reasoned explanation of why it was the Bat and why it could not have been any beast but the Bat. So every day all the stakes were pocketed by the Grand Monde.

At one point the Thirty-Six Beasts became the Forty Beasts. The Vietnamese government had grown concerned. The poorer people could no longer buy their rice — the shops had no customers. The Thirty-Six Beasts were taking all the money. The authorities put them down. This severity only lasted until the Grand Monde announced its intention of closing. A disaster of such dimensions would have hurt too many important people. So after a few days of negotiation a satisfactory solution was arrived at. The Thirty-Six Beasts were still forbidden, but a new game was authorized, that of the Forty Beasts.

As well as the low gambling hell, there was also a Grand Monde for the better sort. Beyond the great courtyard where the common people were robbed, beyond the Thirty-Six Beasts' amphitheater, very much apart, there stood a building at the far end of a dark alley, and this was for the rich man's gambling. It was a kind of yamen, and its inner walls were of painted wood. The decoration was that of commonplace Chinese luxury, with huge spittoons. Here too everything was reduced to the strict essentials; and here too there was neither noise nor excitement. It was elementary, utilitarian, but still it was at a much higher level — the electric bulbs had shades and the croupiers were in uniform. Above all, instead of the crowd there was space; and in Asia space is the most valuable, the most costly of commodities.

The building was made up of several rooms, and these grew smaller and smaller and more mysterious the farther you advanced. The wooden walls could be moved, so that the arrangements could be changed every day. The whole formed a continually shifting labyrinth that moved according to the circumstances — that is to say, according to the impenetrable decisions of the management.

Yet the first room was just like that of any ordinary casino. It was intended for anybody who happened to come along with a fair amount of money in his pocket. Money was not used here, but counters ranging up to a thousand piasters. There were only three or four tables, and at these the game was Asian roulette. The only difference was that because of a particular curve in the rim, the little ball skipped from hole to hole for minutes on end before coming to its final halt.

Most of the gamblers were perfectly happy to be there, without the slightest awkwardness or shame. They were Chinese millionaires, the dealers in every kind of traffic. They were Annamese dowagers covered with diamonds and jade. These ladies and gentlemen had nothing to fear from anyone, not even from the detectives who carefully noted the names and the stakes in little books, pretending to be working out their systems. For the Asians of the piaster and the government everything was allowed and indeed encouraged. No tax gatherer, no member of the fraud squad would come and ask them to explain where they got their money from. It was all part of the policy of prosperity.

Yet I knew one Excellency who was a positive hero of the gambling rooms. He was a wonderfully elegant, blasé old gentleman who bought his clothes in London and cultivated a remote, disillusioned smile, rather like Metternich. At the Grand Monde he was utterly terrified, and that was by no means because he had all his ministry's secret funds on him. But in his youth he had been one of the chief informers of the French police: he had insinuated himself into revolutionary networks and had denounced them. And now the Vietminh had decided to rub him out. How often, standing by the roulette table, he would mop the sweat, the cold sweat, off his brow and say to me, "Every time I come here I stake my life as well. It would be so easy to kill me while I am gambling! I should like to be able not to come, but I can't: I am not strong enough."

A few Frenchmen gambled too. But they were uneasy and they affected a false indifference. Most of them did not normally possess the means to be there or to take part in games where thousands and tens of thousands of piasters were at stake. The most uneasy were the civil servants: this was no place for honest civil servants. Furthermore they knew that everything they did would be in the police report the next day.

It is true that among the gamblers there were also to be seen men in the police and the intelligence service. They indulged their vice in front of their colleagues on duty. And in the end everything passed off very well.

After midnight the heavy gamblers, perhaps fifteen of them, moved on to a smaller room. There were no more Europeans left among them — the Europeans were not rich enough. Each counter was worth a fortune.

Anyone could go and humbly watch the Asian ladies and gentlemen sitting heavily there, unemotionally staking hundreds of thousands of piasters. But beyond there was no admittance. There were other partitions, other rooms where, amid all the silence and precautions imaginable, the most extraordinary sessions took place. It was so organized that even the detectives did not know what was going on. The money betted was in the form of checks: some of them reached a million piasters.

Still farther on, sheltered from everything, was the realm of the manager, "the man in the light blue Packard." He lived there alone with his bodyguard and his safes. In three years Monsieur Lam Giong had brought the Grand Monde to an incredible pitch of perfection. During all this time he had reigned peacefully over his gambling kingdom. He himself was a specialist who had been trained at Macao; he was a man in the prime of life, plump, smiling, pitiless: a true Chinese. And behind him there stood the whole of the Macao Organization.

Furthermore this wonderfully organized Grand Monde was one of the pillars of Vietnam. Every year the government once more awarded the contract to Monsieur Lam Giong. This was done in the most regular manner. There was a public invitation to tender for the contract and the competitors handed in their offers in sealed envelopes. The articles and conditions included rigorous stipulations. A daily royalty of four hundred thousand piasters had to be paid to the state. Lam Giong always won the day.

In fact beneath these outward appearances of legality the contract was put up for auction. It was so big a piece of business that everybody had a finger in it — it seems that a messenger from the Vietminh came to give Nguyen Binh's views on the matter. But in the days of the prime minister Huu it was always the Macao group that ended by winning hands down. In the first place the prime minister, a man who loved high finance and orderliness, certainly appreciated their great technical competence. And then the Macanese were also the most substantial group and the one that paid best from all points of view.

Monsieur Lam Giong poured out money to those who might do him harm, either legally or by way of hand grenades, and to those who might be useful to him. In any case they were the same people. In addition to the four hundred thousand piasters due every day to the state, Monsieur Lam Giong also spent the daily sum of one million piasters in semi-official expenses — protection money, marks of esteem. The chief figures of the government received part of this, and rumor had it that the prime minister Huu was the first in line. The imperial court and His Majesty Bao Dai had some, but less. So did the Vietminh, and a great deal, for true to their long-established principles they insisted upon getting as much as the state. The police insisted according to their rank and duties. The sects got some, above all the Binh Xuyen, who were the established protectors of Cholon. The machinery of the contributions was so well regulated that for years on end not a single grenade went off in the Grand Monde or any of its branches.

A most intensive exploitation was called for to meet these huge expenses. But Monsieur Lam Giong pushed the Grand Monde's turnover to astonishing heights. He possessed a boundless imagination and a wonderful art of pulling in the customers. He spent most of his time in his office, controlling the flow of money. He kept his accounts in his head and he stubbornly refused to buy an adding machine. "If I were to forget to press the rubbing-out button," he explained, "it might mean disaster. My ancient abacus is the most reliable of friends." On the other hand, half the room was taken up by an enormous triply armored safe, which yielded the money to begin the day and which received the winnings when the session was over.

There was an exact timetable. At eight in the morning the bodyguard searched the office. At a quarter past eight they withdrew, leaving Lam Giong alone with the safe. With his sausagelike fingers he twirled the combinations, opened the massive steel door and took out four or five pounds of piaster notes. For the next two hours he was busy, still alone — though armed men were not far away. Handling the enormous mass of paper money with his plump but nimble fingers he built up as many heaps of twenty thousand piasters as the establishment had gaming tables. When everything was ready the croupiers filed in, each receiving one of these heaps from Lam Giong. It was the croupier's bank. He was responsible for it. He was to prevent it from being broken whatever happened.

The Grand Monde had worked out an elaborate technique to deal with fortunate gamblers: among other things they forbade doubling systems, they would refuse to pay up; and they would expel winners. If in spite of everything a bank did break, Lam Giong, who had to produce another twenty thousand piasters, would explode into a violent rage, cursing his ill luck at being saddled with such miserably inefficient employees. But this was a very, very rare occurrence.

The play started at ten in the morning. Each time one of the tables had made a profit of twenty thousand piasters the croupier put that sum into a container that he locked and took to Lam Giong. A well-run table ought to bring in five or six of them a day. In view of the number of tables that meant that one box reached Lam Giong about every ten minutes. Each time he would open it, recount the notes, arrange them in a sheaf and put his mark upon it. At the end of the day all the croupiers came in to make their report. The day's profit amounted to some five hundred per cent.

At the beginning of 1950 all the Chinese of Cholon and Saigon admired and respected Monsieur Lam Giong. He reached his highest pinnacle at the moment of his eldest son's wedding. The parties were even more cheerful and splendid than those for the burial of a millionaire. For days on end Cholon rejoiced at his expense. He outdid himself in the banquets of acknowledgment — an old Chinese custom required that the bridegroom's father should show his gratitude to all those who had deigned to be present at the marriage by means of an astonishing feast. The crowd at the marriage was so vast that the banquet had to be divided into a series of celebrations: there was one for the relations, one for the Excellencies and the upper civil servants, one for the important merchants, one for the journalists and one for the police. At each the guests numbered more than a thousand. They were seated at little tables, each one of which was crowned by a sucking-pig glazed with burned sugar. The number of dishes and the delicacy of the food surpass description. Hidden in the napkins, by way of presents, there were Grand Monde counters and little balls of opium.

It was shortly after these splendors that the war of the Grand Monde suddenly began — a war in which Lam Giong and his team of Macanese were to be crushed. The first warning shot took the form of a grenade, but a grenade of the most dangerous kind, a real army grenade. It was tossed into the Cloche d'Or, a branch of the Grand Monde. Sixty gamblers around a table were blown to pieces. But the explosion was anonymous. It was not yet known what gang had gone into action against the Macanese.

Next there was a kidnapping. At first it seemed a perfectly commonplace affair. It was only an unknown old Chinese gentleman who was seized in the middle of the street at ten o'clock one morning, in Cholon. The old gentleman was in a trishaw. A car jammed the trishaw against the curb and two armed men leaped out. In a few seconds they had grasped the old gentleman, pushed him into their car and driven him off. Of course no one in the crowd had seen anything.

But soon Cholon was jerked out of its calm. It learned that the victim, the ordinary-looking old man, was in fact a Macanese, one of the chiefs of the international Asian consortium of gambling and foreign exchange who had been passing through Saigon. What was such a powerful man doing in a trishaw? And who had dared kidnap him? The police wanted to look into it, but the Grand Monde was violently opposed to any investigation. Officially the detectives did not know who the kidnappers were; but Monsieur Lam Giong knew and he was in the midst of his negotiations with them. An enormous ransom was insisted upon: and it was paid. After a few weeks the old gentleman was released. He kept his mouth wholly and entirely shut and hurried into the first plane for Hong Kong.

But now everyone in Cholon knew what had happened. It was known that the kidnapping had not been done by the Vietminh. It was the act of Bay Vien and his Binh Xuyen. Bay Vien had chosen this way of announcing his claim to the Grand Monde.

The former convict had become Bao Dai's favorite and His Majesty's tool for the total exploitation of the Grand Monde by the court. The spoils were to be shared. To be sure, the knowing Lam Giong had already allocated a very handsome share to Bao Dai in 1949, when His Majesty returned to Vietnam. But nevertheless the Macanese Grand Monde remained within the prime minister Huu's sphere of influence, and Bao Dai wanted it to be within his. The whole of Vietnamese policy in 1950 was concerned with the bitter struggle between the head of the state and the head of the government over the Grand Monde.

By means of his direct action Bay Vien had already horrified the Macanese. Now Bao Dai threw all his weight into the battle. Huu and the Macanese were finally and definitively overcome when tenders for the renewal of the gambling contract were called for. In the end Huu was forced to bow to Bao Dai's wishes; but he never forgave the Emperor. And in 1950 the Grand Monde was officially awarded to Bay Vien.

Lam Giong vanished from Saigon forever: but at least he had saved his skin. And Bay Vien even allowed the other Macanese — those who dealt in the piaster market, not the gambling branch — to continue their sly activities.

Outwardly the Grand Monde remained the same. But presently very little of Lam Giong's work was left. Instead of the model establishment, the abode of peace, of pure technical skill and of Monsieur Lam Giong's intelligence, it became a bandits' lair. Men with submachine guns were hidden everywhere, and at the slightest incident they came darting out. Behind its high sheltering walls the Grand Monde turned into a fortress, a separate realm. Bay Vien had to be able to defend it by force of arms, for he wholly refused to share its profits with any of the other organizations. The subsidies that Lam Giong had poured out in every direction were abolished. Bay Vien would not even pay the Vietminh's daily four hundred thousand piasters. And although he was forced to yield the state its dues, he did away with the private payments and all the sums provided for the members of the Saigon government and the police authorities. Bay Vien kept everything for himself — himself and his sleeping partners, the Emperor and the imperial cabinet. This two-handed monopoly of the Grand Monde was to have exceedingly important consequences for the history of Vietnam; it caused such jealousies that five years later it caused the fall of Bay Vien and then that of Bao Dai.

For the daily income of the Grand Monde remained enormous. Indeed the gains increased, for Bay Vien added little subsidiary enterprises to the main concern. In a discreet spot within the walls, for example, he built an opium-processing plant — in fact he controlled the wholesale trade in the drug throughout Saigon. The Grand Monde was also used for other rackets. Hideouts were set up for the smuggling of gold and cigarettes, and workshops for forging everything that needed to be forged. All this was untouchable. Neither the police nor the customs made their way into the Grand Monde or even thought of trying to do so. Even the Vietminh refrained from interfering with the Grand Monde and clashing with Bay Vien's armed gang, firmly dug in, secure in their control of vice, in their legality and in their armaments.

Nobody even dared talk about what Bay Vien was doing. For his touchiness was appalling, and so was his revenge. Nevertheless, a Vietnamese journalist once referred to some of Bay Vien's activities in an article. The next day he and his wife were kidnapped and taken to the Grand Monde. They were led to the torture chamber. Bay Vien himself showed them the collection of instruments and gave them an exceedingly detailed account of the function of each one of them. Finally he said, "I leave the choice to you. Which would you prefer?" And when the pair begged for mercy on their knees, Bay Vien patted them jovially on the head and said, "I will forgive you this time. But don't do it again, or I shall be quite merciless."

What a deathly silence descended upon the Grand Monde in full blast when Bay Vien appeared for his evening inspection, accompanied by his staff, his concubines and his bodyguards! He wore a general's uniform, for Bao Dai had given him that rank by decree. And when he could tear himself away from the Grand Monde or his operational headquarters at the nearby Pont en Y (the Y-shaped bridge which crossed the canal and the loop canal at Cholon), he was also one of the personalities who took part in all the official and patriotic ceremonies. The army bands played the Vietnamese national anthem when he appeared. The high commissioner and the leaders of the Expeditionary Force greeted him. French society, both the civilians and the military, made much of him. For the businessmen had long ago forgotten their prejudices against the sects and the "organizations," particularly the Binh Xuyen, who were growing so remarkably civilized. The Saigon upper crust asked Bay Vien to its cocktail parties. The hostesses smiled upon him, and their husbands joined him in establishing all kinds of trading companies. With his piasters Bay Vien was buying up all the buildings that were for sale in the town. People felt a need to help him to invest his money properly. Surrounded by all this prosperity Bay Vien even became the arbiter of taste, and his Jaguar, the only one in Saigon, took part in the rallies. He possessed a tiger which he played with as though it were a dog, and a python as thick as the trunk of a tree, which used to curl itself around him. And in the midst of all this he remained a fat, coarse, overweening rustic without a word of French — a potentate and yet at the same time a *nha-qué*. Even for Vietnam Bay Vien's story was something very out of the ordinary.

Yet this was the same Bay Vien that I had seen barely two years before, overwhelmed with distress and almost devoid of hope. He had just escaped from Nguyen Binh, but his best men had been killed and he himself was reduced to the last extremity. To begin with, the Binh Xuyen had belonged to the anti-French Vietminh front. But the Nambo Committee (the Vietminh committee of Cochinchina) disliked and distrusted them all and made up its mind to put an end to them by that usual Asiatic maneuver, a mass murder. The leaders were to be killed and the rank and file incorporated into the main Vietminh body.

Nguyen Binh, then the head and the legendary hero of the southern Resistance, knew for example that Bay Vien was keeping back the greater part of the taxes that he levied in Saigon in the name of the Vietminh. He also knew that Bay Vien had contacts with the French intelligence — indeed, one of his lieutenants, a certain Maurice Thien, was even a member of it. So Nguyen Binh sent Bay Vien an invitation to "come to the Plain of Reeds and have an open and friendly talk with me." The meeting took place. But this time (unlike the occasion upon which the Living God of the Hoahaos was murdered) the treachery had been prepared by both sides — and Nguyen Binh's failed.

Yet the trap had been cleverly laid. In the first place, under pretext of a coming French offensive, Nguyen Binh had moved his forces and had imperceptibly surrounded the mass of the Binh Xuyen army. The distrustful Bay Vien went to the rendezvous accompanied by two hundred of his best bodyguards, who had the order to rush in and kill Nguyen Binh at his first shout. Nevertheless Bay Vien went along into Nguyen Binh's tent: Nguyen Binh welcomed him with the words, "You have betrayed us, but I forgive you." The two men embraced. But the clasp was scarcely loosened before the killers came for Bay Vien. He had time to roar "Help!" and a furious struggle broke out in Nguyen Binh's headquarters. Bay Vien fled blindly across country and reached his oldest haunt, the village of Binh Xuyen near Cholon — in his distress he returned to the place where his gang had first been formed and from which it took its name. Bay Vien was safe, but more than a thousand of his soldiers, surrounded in the rice paddies by the Vietminh, had had their throats cut. He ordered terrible reprisals, for his murder committees in Saigon were still intact, and in one night they wiped out the rival murder committees of Nguyen Binh. For days on end the canals were charged with floating corpses, and nobody cared.

But Bay Vien was in a bad way, on the run and at his wits' end. It was then that Major Savani, a scarred, tough Corsican, the chief of intelligence in Cochinchina, took me with him to see him. Savani was going to offer the hunted Bay Vien the alliance of France.

The meeting place was somewhere in a landscape of mud and wretchedness on the outskirts of Cholon. We crossed the loop canal. A guerrilla fighter guided us along a path, a reddish line that wound through vacant lots. The ragged gutter dwellers watched us go by with a certain collusive air. These were the Binh Xuyen, and a few days earlier they would have cut us to pieces. One old man smoking the fag end of a cigarette winked at us. A little farther on a very well-dressed, slender Annamese, speaking perfect French, introduced himself. "I am Monsieur Bay Vien's secretary. I have been asked to take you to him." Now at regular intervals the path was lined with young fellows carrying submachine guns. We came to a village and went into the "communal house," where the lacquer of the ancestral tablets glowed blood-red in the dim light. Here there were some very westernized young men, among them the brothers Thai and San, the first, Bay Vien's political and the second his military adviser. They shook hands with us. A few yards away, in the darkest corner of the room, there was a man who had not stood up to greet us — a huge bulk in a spangled Annamese tunic and loose trousers. I noticed the great belly that swagged out in the middle of a black-wood armchair. The man seemed to be asleep, with his eyes closed. His formidable shoulders had collapsed, but his great head, which was also drooping, swung to and fro like a pendulum. It was Bay Vien, meditating upon his despair. Occasionally he would fan himself as though he were in a dream. Long silent moments passed slowly by. At last Bay Vien raised his eyelids and Major Savani said "Bay Vien, there's no other way out. You have only a few hours of life left if you don't sign with us."

Upon this the extraordinary human heap in the chair cried out, "I can't. I am not worthy of it. Just think of what I am — a criminal, a bandit chief!"

A few days later I saw Bay Vien alone. The agreement with the French had been signed. He had moved into the middle of Cholon, at 31 Rue de Canton. From the outside it was a perfectly ordinary shop, with its iron shutter down. I gave the password and made my way into a caravanserai — all leprous walls, worm-eaten staircases and endless corridors. I passed sentries on guard everywhere, with their fingers on the trigger and that shut-in, expressionless look of the real killer. At street level there was a whole crowd of women, children and old men, lying about on mats. It was obviously a hideout organized for underground work in the town, dating from that very recent period when the Binh Xuyen were killing the French.

I found Bay Vien right at the top of this curious dwelling, in an attic faintly lit by a round window. His chief lieutenants were all about him. A worm-eaten Buddha stood upon a table, and on it one of these gentlemen had hung his hat. There were revolvers lying here and there on the chairs. Strings of onions hung from the beams. A thoroughly martial atmosphere pervaded the confusion.

But Bay Vien himself was wholly and completely transformed. He was no longer in the slightest degree a weakened, despondent man, but rather an Asian Vautrin, the leader of a gang exerting all his strength in digging himself into his new racket. He was already in his working clothes, a khaki shirt and shorts. His head was exaggeratedly square, a block whose harshness was emphasized still more by his crew-cut hair. Everything about him was trim, sharp, exact, frighteningly massive. As he spoke to me about the investments that he would have to make his eyes sparkled like two little glowing coals in his smooth face. Each phrase had a metallic ring. All the time he spoke he sat there in an armchair — no longer an Asian armchair, but one of the latest styles from the Rue Catinat — and he thumped its arms with his ring-covered, clublike fists. "Why can't the French understand what I am? If they gave me the money and the arms I would liquidate every Vietminh in Saigon, without their having to stir a finger."

In the very first place he needed a decent headquarters, with the four or five sections that every proper regular army possessed. Then he would be able to get going and set about the task in hand. Was I aware that five million piasters had been put upon his head by Nguyen Binh himself? And with a little laugh Bay Vien ended, "I have had too much to do with the Vietminh to let myself be killed like any old son of a bitch. I am going to do the killing, not them."

The audience was over. I shook hands all round and withdrew. I had grasped the point that Bay Vien wanted Cholon for himself, and not in an underground manner as in the days when he had been with the Vietminh, but openly, as its official master. Now the French refused to give him the wealthy Chinese city and only granted him the dismal suburbs and stinking marshes as his area of activity. Once more he was about to set himself to conquering it.

At the height of the colonialist era, when he was no more than one twenty-year-old hooligan in a horde of others, his daring had already won him the esteem of the underworld. In those days there existed a wretched, down-at-heel gang, never more than one jump ahead of the police, which practiced the old-fashioned kind of banditry. This gang generally attacked poor, defenseless people and held them to ransom, cutting off little human samples which they posted to the family if there was too much in the way of bargaining. They were the pirates of Binh Xuyen. Bay Vien, having escaped from the island prison of Poulo Condore, became their chief. His genius enabled him to reorganize the primitive band of small-time thieves, using an entirely modern technique. Instead of squeezing the poor, Bay Vien milked the rich. Having terrified them by a few acts of terrorism he then offered himself as their guardian for a given yearly sum: this was the well-known protection money of Asia. As his go-between he picked a certain Maurice Thien, the son of a distinguished family, an unusually well-educated man who owned a stable of race horses. It was he who visited the big Chinese to sell them Monsieur Bay Vien's friendship. "He is an easygoing fellow," he would say. "Come to an understanding with him if you don't want ugly scenes."

In this way the new boss of the Binh Xuyen set up the Shanghai type of gangsterism in Saigon, a gangsterism that worked at the big-business level. All this called for bookkeeping, typewriters and telephones, an intelligence section and a whole network of agents. He bought his first submachine guns. He was in command of several hundred fanatical followers. Within the band there was cast-iron discipline. All professional errors were punished with death.

He was cunning enough to hide his frigid realism. He made himself an image: the knight errant, the righter of wrongs, the defender of the downtrodden people. "I am one of you. I too was born in the midst of poverty. It is for you that I rob the rich." At the same time he held himself out as a patriot and he sheltered nationalists on the run. He was the idol of the common people; he was the avenger; but he was also beginning to establish relations with the colonialist police.

He was already someone to be reckoned with in Cholon; but still his soaring genius was restrained by the law and order of the French, the scrupulous imperialist regime. But when French Indochina collapsed at the beginning of 1945 there was nothing left to stop him and he seized Cholon. At the time of the very first riots he robbed the gunsmiths' shops and the arsenals to equip his men and he got back his chief lieutenants, whom the Japanese had released from the prison island of Poulo Condore. For the first time he was lord of Cholon. The Vietminh were obliged to treat with him: they acknowledged his domain and they even appointed him a member of the Nambo Committee.

First there was Bay Vien, the hidden ruler of the Chinese city in the name of the Vietminh — Bay Vien, the inveterate and elusive foe of the returning French and their Expeditionary Force. But his inability to put up with any restraint was already evident, as well as his anarchy, his immense personal arrogance and pride, and his greed. And a huge lust for life, for every sensual delight. For the first time he became very wealthy — too rich by far for Nguyen Binh's taste. Everything in Bay Vien ran contrary to the bloody puritanism of Nguyen Binh. It was then that everything came to a climax, and Bay Vien escaped from the Plain of Reeds by a miracle. And by the stroke of a pen he changed sides.

Once more everything had to be begun all over again. The French had saved him, but at the same time they had forced him to relinquish Cholon, his fief and his prey. It was as though they had wrenched out his heart. At the darkest hour of his distress he had brooded on the splendor of suicide. Instead of killing himself he had come to terms with the imperialists, and he had done so at the cost of a two-fold shame — he was both the patriot who betrayed his cause, and the bandit who joined the side of law and order. From now on he wanted every last penny of the price of his betrayal. He was irrevocably bound to the French and he could not defy them openly; he had to start by reestablishing his underground control of Cholon, much as he had done in the days when he was their enemy.

In a few weeks he had already set up a Binh Xuyen military settlement at the far end of the Pont en Y. The filthy water was the frontier that he had been obliged to accept. But looking out of his office he could see the smoking factory chimneys of the distilleries and the rice-treating plants close at hand, as well as the whole tempting mass of Cholon, standing there ready to be taken.

For some months nothing more was heard of Bay Vien. The French staff was pleased with him. All around Saigon and in Saigon itself he kept rigorously to his word, waging a ferocious war against the Red *tieudoi*. With Bay Vien there were none of all those difficulties, the treachery and the blackmail, that were so usual with the other sects. The army looked upon the Binh Xuyen as reliable allies: the army therefore overlooked the protestations of the police. For the police asserted that Bay Vien had secretly retaken Cholon and that he was now more in command of the Chinese city than he had been in the days of the Vietminh.

It was true. At that time I was invited to the Pont en Y camp by a Binh Xuyen major whom I had met on the occasion of Bay Vien's submission, and a strange evening it was. As soon as I came into the neighborhood of the bridge I saw a great number of sentries. They were no longer the gallows-bird killers dressed in black, with villainous old hats and dangling cigarettes. Already they were uniformed automata. They pointed their weapons at me with a fanatical lack of emotion, and with the same weird indifference they let me through as soon as I had showed my signed pass, presenting arms with a rigid immobility. They seemed to me even more dangerous with this new discipline than they had before. The camp lay on the bank of the canal, lower than the bridge and under its last arch. There was all the filth, all the swarming life that you expect in Asia — rubbish, shacks, naked children, women paddling in the mud, pigs. But in the middle of all this dirt a sudden barbed-wire hedge outlined an area of cleanliness — Bay Vien's new military stronghold. There were a score of brand-new buildings, serving both as quarters for the staff and barracks, and they were almost too perfectly cleaned and swept. The most remarkable thing about them was their extraordinary number of maps, filing cabinets and indicators. Bay Vien's quarters were in the middle — a plain wooden bungalow. But judging from the names and the notice boards he already had as many departments as a French commanding general. It was really quite pathetic, Bay Vien's longing to transform his gang into a respectable army.

The first thing I saw was some prisoners being unloaded from a truck. They, for their part, had not improved: they were skin and bone, almost as though they had been stripped of living force. The soldiers were not at all rough, but treated them with a terrible scrupulousness. The Binh Xuyen major who had come to welcome me was delighted at the sight. "They were a Vietminh murder committee who were going to kill one of our intelligence agents," he told me.

The next thing I saw was the Binh Xuyen war memorial, a stately column, certainly the most expensive piece of undertaker's ware in Saigon, upon which there were hundreds of names. And the major who had been so pleased at seeing the prisoners proudly showed me the inscription: *To our martyrs, our heroes who died in the fighting against the French oppressor.*

The major then led me to his own quarters. I was received in a room filled with countless photographs. They were all pictures of the Resistance. One was a photograph of Giap reviewing the troops and it was signed by Giap himself. Elsewhere, all over the room, there were French posts being stormed and burned. All these were earlier exploits of the Binh Xuyen.

Yet just next to these photographs, in the most conspicuous place, there hung a most appreciative mention in dispatches, ornamented with the French colors, which had just been awarded to the Binh Xuyen troops for their loyalty by a French general.

We arrived in the midst of a little party. Some of Bay Vien's officers and some well-heeled merchants from Cholon (many of the top men in the piaster racket had already come over to the Binh Xuyen) were tirelessly drinking brandy and soda. Among all this cheerfulness an Annamese in civilian clothes put on the gramophone and at once there arose a sad and moving song. All the guests took it up. They had suddenly grown serious, you might almost have said inspired. The Annamese said to me, "It is a song of the Resistance. Think of the patriots in the maquis who are singing it at this very moment. They are in the swamps. They are in the forward posts, right up against the French guns. It is a terrible life. All through the long hours of the night they think of their wives and the children they have not seen for years — no news of them, either. And sometimes they think about the Saigon bourgeois who live in luxury, with money and with their family round them. They, the resistants, have none of these things: all they have is their youth and maybe death. So they sing to keep up their spirits and their fury."

He was telling me of the glories of the Resistance right in the head-quarters of these Binh Xuyen who had just betrayed it. Furthermore he himself was one of those back-line bourgeois profiteers he had just de-nounced. Immediately afterwards he brought his face very close to mine and asked whether I had any good contacts in the Exchange Office or with the high commissioner's people. For if I had we might be able to do some business together and make a great deal of money.

The evening warmed up more and more. There was an immense amount of laughter. The gramophone poured out jazz. The toasts came one after another, all very hearty. Everyone in turn went out onto the balcony, to be sick. But darkness had come on, and I noticed that the Binh Xuyen major had vanished. A quarter of an hour later he reappeared. He had taken off his French uniform and was in mufti — a cream-colored suit and a straw hat. He asked me whether I should like to go with him on a tour of inspection that he was to make in Cholon. We set off in an unidentified jeep, which carried neither pennant nor badge.

For hours we moved about through the lowest slums; but ours was a professional tour. We began by plunging into filthy, dark, stinking alleys. We went into squalid little booths: under the light of oil lamps rough-skinned coolies were gambling away their rice money, squatting around coarsely painted planks. Elsewhere we saw opium smokers, utterly dried-up and wholly self-absorbed, sprawling promiscuously on dirty benches. There were often several layers of bunks with their human contents — an opium dormitory, a kind of morgue. In the intensity of their vice these gamblers and these smokers were virtually dead. What life there was in the place was brought in by the whores. They laughed. Yet by the age of twenty these girls had already lost their teeth and had been brought down to the lowest possible human condition.

Everywhere we appeared there was an immediate respectful silence. The woman of the place would come cringing forward with greasy tumblers and a bottle of brandy by way of compliment. And every time a young fellow would slide up to the officer and whisper a brief report. He was a Binh Xuyen agent. They were scattered everywhere: they literally sprang out of the ground. After one of them had made his report it was decided to punish an overrapacious policeman. The oppressed bawd thanked the major on her knees.

This tour through wretchedness and vice seemed to me to go on forever. What I saw on every side was an infinity of poor people, all under the total "protection" of the Binh Xuyen.

Afterwards we went into the region of more costly pleasures. But throughout this quarter too, in the dance halls with their taxi girls, the well-run opium dens, the top brothels and the Chinese hotels, there appeared the little rat-faced Binh Xuyen agent with his whispering. But here he came up to us more discreetly and he wore a suit — he even talked a little pidgin French. We visited dozens of joints in this way, and when we said good-bye to one another at about four in the morning the Binh Xuyen major said, "You see how Bay Vien maintains order in Cholon and what trouble he takes to look after the people."

But from his camp by the bridge Bay Vien had not merely regained his monopoly of vice in Cholon. He had also taken up all his former rackets once more, including kidnapping and protection money. He levied all sorts of contributions and patriotic taxes. He dominated trade. Not a single sack of rice came into Cholon now without paying dues to the Binh Xuyen: Bay Vien had set up toll gates on all the roads and canals. It was intensive exploitation.

Bay Vien's chief financial adviser was a Chinese gnome with a devilish imagination. He was unspeakably fertile in ideas for extorting money. It was this dwarf who put it into Bay Vien's mind to cause equity to reign between debtors and creditors. To accomplish this Bay Vien used his authority to buy all difficult bills at a very low price, and then it was the Binh Xuyen killers who went to require the debtors to produce both capital and interest to the last penny.

The little creature also persuaded Bay Vien to play his part in promoting social peace. The Binh Xuyen went to see the bosses and said to them, "If you don't want strikes, pay such-and-such a sum. Upon receipt we shall see to it that your coolies behave properly." In this way there appeared Binh

Xuyen's "trade union leaders" who carried revolvers and ensured that the men worked according to the bosses' wishes.

The gnome was rarely to be seen. He possessed a whole set of names. His connection with Bay Vien dated back for twenty years. At the beginning he had been a wealthy, thriving Chinese businessman and he had taken Bay Vien on his chauffeur. But both men fell on hard times and they met again in the prison of Poulo Condore. When they were let out the relative positions had changed: it was Bay Vien who had become the leader.

But never did the two friends, the proud Bay Vien and the subtle dwarf, work so well as they worked in 1948. The wealth of Cholon allowed Bay Vien to gather excellent troops and to gather them rapidly: they amounted to some five thousand extraordinarily well-armed men. With this praetorian guard he could squeeze Cholon even harder. And then the piaster brought such a degree of prosperity that even Bay Vien could not manage to squeeze Cholon dry. The wealthy Chinese merchants lavished gifts and flattery upon him, recouping their loss by raising their prices. In the end gangsterism acted as one more form of economic stimulus.

It was at this time that Bay Vien began to turn into a respectable character. People started to consult him when there were governmental crises. The French army had a high opinion of his worth. The French banks, the import-export trade and Monsieur Franchini treated him as a serious client. In order to deal with so much business Bay Vien formed a little brain trust to help him. In addition to the Vietnamese and Chinese there were some half-castes among these adventurers, and even a few Frenchmen.

The brothers Tai and San, a foxy pair of Vietnamese who had long since been cast off by their respectable family, still looked after the important political and military questions. Tai, the political expert, was a weakly, saccharine, lying creature with a gloss of education. San, the soldier, was tougher and more silent. These two were Bay Vien's closest advisers, his ears and his eyes. Their importance derived from the fact that Bay Vien was subject to a curious shyness — he felt exceedingly awkward in good company. He went into society occasionally, as grave and composed as a lord, but without ever uttering a word. What he really liked was staying in his camp by the bridge, in the midst of his innumerable concubines, his wild animals and his soldiers. There he lived in the utmost informality. He always made the really important decisions himself, but it was Tai and San who moved about outside the camp, carrying out negotiations and gathering information.

Besides these two were five or six others who belonged to the inner circle. Vinh, a thick-witted brute, acted as commanding general. The soldiers loved him dearly. He was one of Bay Vien's earliest companions. Adorned now with boots, belts and a helmet, he played the part of the loud-mouthed faithful old soldier. The ministry of the interior — everything to do with the rackets, gangsterism and the lower reaches of the police — was entrusted jointly to Maurice Thien and the half-caste Sanmarcelli. But they had a disagreeable inclination to murder one another. Maurice Thien came to a bad end — a bullet in the head when he was at the barber's. And it was a Binh Xuyen bullet. Fashionable affairs were the concern of Jacques Long, Bay Vien's aide-de-camp, his favorite and his white-haired boy.

Inside the gang every man worked with the knowledge that Bay Vien would never desert him. He was capable of astonishing efforts to save one of his own people. In return he insisted upon unwavering loyalty. He was merciless in punishing anyone who strayed out of line, working secretly on his own account. He would excuse mistakes, but never unfaithfulness or egoism. He did not spare even Jacques Long, though indeed he was very fond of him. But the good-looking Jacques had put his hand into the till and then had lied. He was completely disgraced. For a long while he was shut up in a cell.

Bay Vien loved his men. He wanted them to love him. But he knew that at any moment he might be betrayed. Calm and smiling, he would listen like an indulgent father to the reports of his lieutenants; but if a doubt came to his mind, he would burst out in rage. Once they brought him two of his officers, who had been approached by the Vietminh. He began by groaning. "You? You? How can it be you, two of my oldest comrades . . ?" And because of his pain and his disappointment he ordered them to be put to death by means of extraordinarily refined forms of torture.

He was still capable of handsome gestures, of unselfishness and magnanimity, but the richer he grew the more insatiable became his greed and his ambition. Above all he was attacked by a morbid touchiness. How far away was the time when in his simplicity he could state, "I am a pirate." From now on he was hag-ridden by the need for social standing, for respectability.

And then there came this extraordinary consecration — the sudden favor and the eager friendship of Bao Dai. It all happened in a flash at Dalat, where all the Excellencies and all the warlords had been summoned by His Majesty, so that a chief might be provided for the Vietnamese army — which in any case did not exist. The imperial cabinet put forward the name of Bay Vien. It was so unexpected that it gave rise to an appalling error. Giao, Bao Dai's man at Hué, was not aware of His Majesty's new intentions. Speaking to a very well-dressed man whom he did not know in the hall of the Langbien Hotel he impetuously exclaimed, "What a crying shame to tolerate the presence of that Bay Vien among us — an ex-convict and gangster." Unhappily the man was a Binh Xuyen delegate. As soon as he had been told, Bay Vien came running, foaming at the mouth and waving an immense revolver. Giao had just time to take shelter in the Emperor's villa, and there he remained shut up for some days — indeed he stayed there until Bao Dai had arranged a reconciliation between the two men in the name of the nation's welfare.

Bao Dai did not quite dare appoint him chief of the general staff in 1949, because the French high command would not have stood for it. But it was then that he caused the Grand Monde to be given to Bay Vien. Now the conquest of Cholon was complete: and from now on he could not be touched. Instead of being a mere tolerated gangster he was one of the pillars of nationalist Vietnam. Every time Bao Dai appointed a government he required, as a necessary foregoing condition, that it should never do anything against Bay Vien. And in any case Bay Vien existed no more, for the ex-convict had assumed the respectable name of General Le Van Vien.

Five years later he accomplished the highest point of his ambition. Thanks once more to Bao Dai he became the official head of all the police forces and of all the security services in the state of Vietnam. The Binh Xuyen, once hunted down by the police, had turned into superpolicemen. The will of the gang became the law, not only in Cholon but throughout the whole immensity of Saigon. The gang took over the Sûreté building in the Rue Catinat and all the police stations, and they built up a civilization and a social order founded upon vice. One of Bay Vien's first acts as chief of police was to build a palace of prostitution in which an army of whores was guarded by an army of Binh Xuyen.

This was Bay Vien's highest point: then came the crash. And his fall had incalculable consequences — the collapse of Bao Dai, the end of the predominating French influence in Saigon, the setting up of the pro-American regime of Ngo Dinh Diem.

But at the moment of which we are speaking — in 1950 — Bay Vien had only reached the Grand Monde and the possession and the legitimate exploitation of Cholon. This was the time of rejoicing in his domain, thanks to the friendship of Bao Dai. Furthermore the Binh Xuyen were graduating from heroic gangsterism to the civilized version. They gave up some practices that caused too much comment, such as kidnapping and armed assault. But they would not allow any political or commercial deal to be carried on without their participation. Instead of remaining bandits and no more, they now became shareholders.

This was also the period of softening, of slow decomposition from within. Bay Vien lived like a pasha. He had never been farther than Poulo Condore, but now he made a discreet journey to Paris, where his new Corsican friends gave him good advice about investing his surplus millions. His lieutenants displayed an ostentatious luxury. Tai, the political adviser, had himself built a chateau with flights of steps, balustrades, statues, a peristyle and fountains of colored water. There were neon lights everywhere, and they were on all the time, even at midday. There were always four huge American cars waiting for him outside the front door.

A warlord of Bay Vien's kind can never have enough. But in 1950 he still had to wait for his hour to strike. He withdrew from the public gaze, and at the same time he accumulated wealth and grew stronger. He left the forefront of the stage to the Vietminh and the police, who were beginning their death struggle in Saigon.

In 1948 the furious Bay Vien had ordered his men to massacre all the Vietminh. Since then he had grown calmer. He had confined himself to a rigorous observation of his agreement with the French army, and to the pursuit of his own interests. So wherever the Binh Xuyen were absent in the huge expanse of the city, the Vietminh built themselves up again. And all at once these Viets, who had been carrying out a kind of de facto coexistence with the imperialists and the capitalists, burst out in a ferocious terrorist offensive. This was the battle of Saigon, the war for the possession of the city. And to oppose them they found only the police.

Sitting in the Grand Monde or in his camp by the bridge, Bay Vien calmly let them kill one another. The Vietminh and the police were implacable enemies each of the other; and both were implacable future enemies of Bay Vien. So during 1950, while the hand grenades rained down upon Saigon, Bay Vien washed his hands of the whole business and stood aside.

The time of the grenades

THE people of Saigon had long been used to grenades. In the summer of 1949 the explosions greatly increased in number, but nevertheless prosperity and the good life went on. Anyhow the piaster fever left little time for sentimentality — it was just too bad about the victims, people said; but after all they only amounted to a few dozen French, not counting the soldiers.

Besides, people still went on believing that the Viets did not really mean to exterminate the piaster-French. The bombs were of poor quality. Often they did not go off at all. The throwers were recruited at random and they were not genuine Viets. You would have said that this bombing was primarily a sort of demonstration: the French of the Rue Catinat could not see what it was all about and they did not try to explain it.

They found it all the easier to put up with seeing that for a long while the grenade fodder was Vietnamese. There were great slaughters in the Asian districts. The grenades were thrown into the thick of the crowd, into the people massed around the Chinese soup sellers, among the children coming out of school: the coolies and the *nha-qués,* the *congai* and the *nho.* The survivors let the murderers go; they did not make so much as a single motion, as though they were terrified of doing anything at all; and when the police arrived and asked questions nobody knew anything. As for the bomb throwers, they were nearly always poor creatures, wretched youths picked out of the crowd in order to kill the crowd. But nowhere, either among the murdered common people or among the boys recruited by chance for the murdering, was there the slightest protest, the slightest rebellion.

Up until 1949 the bombing was not war. It was only psychological warfare. Hand grenades were a means of keeping the population's morale in order: they also acted as tax demands. They were the result of an analysis of the situation; they were necessary to the right political atmosphere of the capital; they formed part of the balance in Saigon. Unconsciously the population accepted this necessity. That was why they were so relatively unconcerned. That was why they were resigned to the powerlessness of the police — for the result of this want of power was grenades that killed quite a lot of people, but not too many.

This state of balance lasted for a long while, but in the autumn of 1949 the grenades increased to an intolerable extent. Suddenly the French of the piaster discovered that their comparative immunity no longer existed. They discovered that from now on *they* were the targets, that the grenades were aimed directly at them. All the places where the top people gathered, the good restaurants, the fashionable bars, the cinemas, the night clubs, were continually attacked. The Rue Catinat in Saigon and the Rue des Marins in Cholon were the chief haunts of the grenade throwers. Every night the explosions, coming one after another like a stick of bombs, formed the background of the city's noise. Each outburst lasted only a few seconds: each grenade was a sharp bang, a few shrieks from those who had been hit, one or two flying shadows, and then several minutes later the klaxon of an ambulance and a police car. And never, even in the European quarters, was a grenade thrower arrested.

The protection of the town began in the Rue des Marins, at Cholon, in an eating place where the Chinese proprietor cooked steak and chips for the poor Europeans. After the tenth grenade the worthy owner of this cook shop, having carefully weighed the advantages and disadvantages, decided to make an exceptional outlay. This was all the more meritorious since he was at the same time defying the Viets. He enclosed his establishment with a thick iron curtain. A fat bouncer guarded the door, letting in none but reliable customers. They dined in peace: and in a cage.

Now the better part of Saigon took on the look of a prison. It surrounded itself with wire netting: shops, bars and dance halls swathed themselves in veils of metal. Thoroughly protected, the French listened to the explosions as they ate and drank. Some nights they might count up to close on a hundred. The worst time was in the twilight, just after sunset.

People made it a point of honor to flock to the terraces of the cafés for their aperitif as though nothing had happened. For on the terraces there was no wire netting. Both the owners and the customers would have thought themselves dishonored if, in these holy places of the French presence, they had taken the slightest precaution. The top people went on sitting around the little iron tables on the pavements, sipping their drinks as though the danger did not exist. Above all, it was incorrect to watch the little *nho,* the shoeshine boys or peanut vendors, who might at any moment throw a bomb of some kind.

Strangely enough, bombings were most unusual at the terrace of the Continental, Franchini's place. But they were commonplace at the Pagoda tearoom, although it had protective netting — not that it was often in position. The customers, instead of giving up their cakes and five o'clock tea, adapted themselves to the situation. Every time there was an explosion everybody, in one movement, plunged to the ground — the plump young owner, the cashier, the tea-drinking ladies and the little Annamese gentlemen who preferred chocolate, the slow-moving, offhand waiters. After the bang they got up again. Those who remained on the ground were the dead and wounded. Then the police would arrive, and an ambulance to take away the dead and dying. As soon as that was over the waiters, hurrying for once, wiped up the pools of blood with their floor cloths and rearranged the furniture. An hour later there would be fresh customers sitting where the victims had lain in their agony. And the ladies of Saigon, once more gathered over the teacups, sweating in their open-necked dresses, returned to the gossip that really mattered to them — the coming dance at the Sports Club.

Yet in time the Saigonese were forced to acknowledge the facts. The Viets were no longer playing fair. They no longer had any respect for the piaster. What they were carrying out was a full-scale offensive against the seventeen-franc piaster and everything that it implied — transfers, returns and splendid profits. And that was something that the French of Saigon could not forgive them.

The French population, wronged, injured and threatened, began to hate the Viets. They did not even have the comfort of being able to revenge themselves: the Viets did what they chose when they chose. There had been a tacit understanding, a silent complicity; and then without warning the Viets, at their own convenience, switched from this to the blood bath. The whole mass of the Asiatic people were with them, actively or passively, assuring them of impunity. The furious victims cried, "Oh, if only we could get our hands on one of these bomb throwers!"

One day they did at last make a capture, and not merely of one bomb thrower but of two. This happened in front of the café-restaurant de la Paix, the place where all the old Indochina hands met one another — not the top people of Saigon, but those of the middle reaches of the piaster. These worthy people were still active, but they were coarse, fat, purple-faced and common: you would be quite at home there only if you had a swagging belly and a passionate attachment to garlic. The boss was shaped like a barrel, round and short. Everything there was very informal; but still, the women did have diamonds. One evening the well-fed, contented diners saw two Annamese passing along the street, both on the same bicycle — two thin street arabs. One pedaled: the other threw a grenade. A few people were slightly injured. "Stop them! Stop them!" bawled the whole restaurant. The thinner men darted out in pursuit. The bomb throwers only had fifty yards' start. They lost their heads. The one at the pedals stood up to pedal faster: the thrower crouched over the frame. The street was full of shouting. All the French in the district joined the pack. After two hundred yards the "terrorists" began to wobble. They were caught and hurled down just by the Bodega, another restaurant — a very fashionable one. Its customers, all people of high standing, rushed out to join in the kill. The two Annamese vanished under a heap of men battering and kicking them. Hysterical women shrieked that they should be killed out of hand, finished off at once, or the stinking police might let them go. But the cops suddenly appeared. They plucked the two "killers" from under several cubic yards of Frenchmen, and I saw two thin little boys, children of less than fifteen.

Later they told the police that they had been picked up down at the port by a Vietnamese who said to them, "This evening you will toss this grenade into the café-restaurant de la Paix." He showed them how to take the pin out and he gave them twenty piasters. He added that he would be on the spot; and that the Vietminh would kill them if they did not throw the bomb.

A few other terrorists were arrested too. It made no difference. The grenades went on exploding everywhere. One cinema had a bomb going off in its auditorium almost every week. The customers were searched at the entrance, but it still went on. At last they found it was the operator, who dropped a grenade from time to time out of the slit in his box.

Those were the days when French women discovered that the houseboy was the leader of a murder committee. And the bep, the cook, of a high civil servant was found to be directing a resistance network from his post at the kitchen stove. You could no longer be sure of anything. All the Vietnamese withdrew behind a veil of silence.

Every week the situation grew worse. In the autumn Nguyen Binh sent real killers into Saigon. And these carried out their work scientifically, using real high-fragmentation grenades. Now there were horrible butcheries right by the Rue Catinat, particularly in the dance halls where the soldiers found their girls. At the Paprika a jukebox turned up loud and pouring noise into the warm night prevented one from hearing the explosions. One could not understand why all of a sudden there were whores and soldiers flat on the ground, like so many skittles that had been knocked over. The whole joint had been cleaned out by grenades. No ambulance appeared. Private cars carried the wounded away. I took a prostitute and two dying sailors. Bubbles of air were coming out of one sailor's perforated lungs. The fat, painted girl poured dark blood onto the seat. The houseman at the military hospital did not want to take my cargo — it was not the right place. Still, after some argument I persuaded him to take them in.

That was the time of the grenades in Saigon. And still every week saw things getting worse. Presently the murders began — a whole plan drawn up for a complete revolution. The battle of Saigon was beginning.

For the Legion and the paras and for the places where they took their ease, Giadinh and Dakao, nothing was changed: nor was it changed for the tough guys of the slums. It was only that the game had grown a little hotter. But the French of the piaster grew more and more appalled, and they continually asked, "What can Nguyen Binh possibly want? What are the Vietminh after? Have they no respect for anything any more?"

But to find a reply to that question one had to look beyond Saigon. For without its being thoroughly realized, the war in Indochina had reached a critical stage at the beginning of 1950. Each side was about to throw in everything it possessed in an all-out struggle. It was possible, at this period, that everything might come to a head very rapidly, that everything might be finally decided, one way or the other. And it was for this reason that for a while the Vietminh were going to do without the advantages of capitalist Saigon as neutral ground. They were going to try to conquer the capital. And it was only later, when they realized that the Indochinese war would go on for several more years, that they loosened their grip, giving Saigon back its role of the headquarters of the piaster — a metropolis that worked for the profit of one and all. And this time it was to last as long as the piaster at seventeen francs continued to exist, almost until Dienbienphu.

There were many other things that lasted too — corruption, for example, and the extraordinary Press Club. This was not a place of calm repose for journalists so much as a cheap and appallingly noisy canteen for angry young men, "intellectuals," strange wrecks, dubious and sometimes very amusing characters who could tell one a great deal, some of it true.

One man I met there proved the soundness of the statement that it is easy to be too clever by half, particularly if you happen to be honest. He quite astonished me by his shrewdness and his profound knowledge of the Viets. But a few days later they liquidated him. He was by no means one of the dubious characters; he was an honorable and decorated engineer in the highways department, plump, busy, thriving, the perfect bourgeois — but one who knew his way about just a little too well.

A few weeks before his death we lunched together at the club. The good soul was in a state of high delight. I asked him the reason for his sunny temper and his success. For here too (as it so often happened in the Press Club) there was some mystery, since his roads were always beautifully maintained, even in the heart of the Red area. (Indeed the public works were one of the most curious aspects of this war: for again and again, in terribly dangerous regions where the soldiers would not go without every weapon they possessed and unending precautions, I would suddenly catch sight of a notice by the side of the road saying "Caution: works ahead." Nothing could be more peaceful. A stretch of road with hundreds of coolies, huge tubs with tar boiling in them, an ancient steamroller. Teams of men and women bringing stones in little baskets. Even a foreman, some huge tattooed European or half-caste with vast muscles and a brutish face. bawling at the laborers as though this were still the good old days. In the evening they would all go away, leaving their scanty tools — picks, shovels and wheelbarrows. Out of mere conscientiousness they would sometimes push the steamroller as far as a watchtower, so that it should be under the illusory protection of a few partisans. The next day everything would be untouched.) I said to my guest, "How do you manage to be so peaceful? Is it simply because the Viets analyze the situation and come to the conclusion that they need good lines of communication too?"

He burst into a satisfied laugh. "No such thing. You have to pay them for everything, even their neutrality. So I came to an agreement with them — a proper formal agreement, solemnly sealed and signed after lengthy negotiations and after all the clauses had been carefully weighed. It was agreed that every month I should pay them a sum of money, and in addition to that certain quantities of iron, cement, concrete and even powder. The stipulations in the contract have been scrupulously observed on both sides. Everything runs perfectly."

"But isn't that collaboration with the enemy?"

The engineer was even more amused. "No, no. It's just knowing your way about. The authorities just must have good roads — they never stop telling me that the outcome of the war and the well-being of trade depend on them. It's up to me to use my wits. How could I manage without my little arrangements? My Europeans would be killed, my coolies would clear out and all the equipment would vanish in one night, including the two-ton roller. So I choose the lesser evil." He winked an eye. "The high-ups have a very good idea of what I'm doing, even if they don't choose to know anything about it officially. But I'm not green — I wasn't born yesterday. So I give the French information, just a few little tips. In this way I am covered on both sides. My system is perfect."

"So what it amounts to is that you deceive the Viets too. But surely they'll get wise to it and kill you?"

The engineer was so sure of his artfulness that it quite touched one's heart. "I'm not out of my mind. I like being alive and I like keeping my head on my shoulders — but believe me, it's very firmly attached. The whole thing is to make your compromises balance. When I give this to the Viets, I tell that to the French. I take care of what I give and what I tell. So everybody's happy. I see you don't believe me. All right, then, I'll show you: you shall see with your own eyes what I can do. I invite you to come to a big party I'm giving soon. I'm giving it at night, in a quarry some thirty miles out of Saigon. There will be oxen and pigs roasted over huge fires that will blaze up into the darkness, and we'll eat and drink until dawn. It is to reward my work people for all their efforts. I shall have my technicians there and my white foremen, my Annamese office workers, and my coolies too, hundreds of them. There will be a whole crowd. Some French bigwigs — an administrator and some officers — will be there to honor the affair. But when they and their escorts have gone, the *canbo* and the political commissars of the district will come, discreetly dressed as *nha-qués*. You will be able to talk to them and drink with them. It'll be terrific."

Then this man with a bloated face and a paterfamilias belly made this strange profession of faith. "For my part I don't give a damn for the piaster; nor for politics. I am a builder of bridges: I keep up the great colonial tradition. Nothing stops me, not even the war or the Vietminh. Doing so I respect myself, and I am thoroughly happy."

It was the language of Kipling's heroes — a language oddly adapted to a time when, in order to carry out one's duty, one had to know how to betray. Essentially he was yet another man caught in the toils of Asia and urged on by the passion of gambling. Whether he knew it or not he was staking his life.

The feast he had promised me never took place. The Viets wiped him out first. He had a decent, obscure funeral, at which his vile murderers were held up to obloquy: it was indignantly said that the savages had killed him without any reason. And then nobody spoke of him any more. In official eyes he had been an "imprudent" member of the service, and it was better not to refer to him again.

But things were changing, hardening. Presently the intelligentsia and the eccentrics vanished; and in the end, after a long decadence, even the Press Club closed its doors. In its place there was to be a Press Camp, set up by de Lattre at Hanoi, the capital of the front. But this was a grave establishment, something between a monastery and a barracks, designed for real war correspondents.

When the full-blown war came Saigon still remained cheerful. There was still the piaster, there was still love; but it was never quite the same as it had been before. The officers coming back from the fighting still went out in search of fun; but it was the champagne that counted even more than the girls — the first happiness was that of forgetting.

But those days had not yet come. In 1949, at the time of Bao Dai's return, the only thing that haunted the minds of the working masses of Saigon was the grenades. Nobody worried about the Chinese or about Giap. And yet, though no one knew it, the hard times were beginning. It was a race against the clock: could the French smother the Vietminh before Giap was able to launch his great offensive? This rivalry, this competition full of the strangest vicissitudes and the most complex intrigues, was to last a year: it was to last until the decision — until the race came to an end in the first French disaster.

PART III

The Illusion of Victory

I N the autumn of 1949 Mao Tse-tung's armies reached the frontier; and
no one knew that this was to seal the fate of Indochina. How people
cherished illusions in those days! That was the time when they believed
in the "good" Chinese Communists, and when even General Alessandri,
that swarthy little man who was in command in Tonkin, said to me, "I am
glad the Chinese Communists are settling in next to us. That will bring a
little order into things."

General Alessandri was one of those old Asia hands who thought that
the Chinese, with their anarchistic leaven going back over the centuries,
could never really be Communists. "They are far too individualist for
that," said these experts on the Far East.

And so the China of the Kuomintang collapsed like a house of cards.
The divisions under Lin Piao,* the Red Napoleon, joined hands with the
divisions under Giap. From this time on six hundred million Chinese were
our enemies' allies, the allies of Ho Chi Minh and the Tongbo Committee.† But was there anyone who had the faintest notion of what the near
future was to bring — the crushing of the Expeditionary Force under the
continually increasing weight of Asia? There were very few leading figures
who had even the slightest idea of what this dangerous proximity meant.
High Commissioner Pignon was uneasy; indeed, he was very worried. But
most of the civil and military leaders firmly said, "China will always be
China. Even if she goes Red she will still be a huge mass of weakness, a
huge mass of corruption. We will buy Mao's 'comrades' just as we bought
Chiang Kai-shek's Nationalists a few years ago. And even if the Chinese
Communists do have evil intentions, they will never be capable of helping
the Vietminh systematically, adequately and in time. What does Mao
signify? In Indochina victory is within our reach: we have only to grasp
it!"

* Lin Piao was one of the best-known Communist generals. It was he who won
the great victories that destroyed the armies of the Kuomintang.
† The supreme Vietminh committee.

The power of blindness! Optimism brimmed over. Everything was going so well that in Paris the government wanted to have some of the French units brought home, for that would have a most desirable effect upon French public opinion and upon the voters. It would be a token of the war's being almost over, almost won. In Indochina the generals provisionally agreed.

Furthermore it was true that from the monsoon of 1949 to the monsoon of 1950 practically all the news was good. The Pacification of Cochinchina had been completed. The whole of the Tonkin delta had been won back. The Vietminh were hungry, so hungry that they adopted the slogan "A grain of rice is worth a drop of blood." The Americans, those "quiet men," those zealous anticolonialists who a little while before had been so hostile to the idea of a French-run Indochina, were henceforward to give massive quantities of dollars and equipment: and so the war was becoming more and more of a good deal. Lastly, the Korean War had broken out, turning the Chinese into the enemies of the entire civilized world — and the Viets were tarred with the same brush.

The Expeditionary Force had so clear a conscience that it calmly hushed up its bloody setbacks, for there were some. The R.C. 4 was cut, and Caobang had to be made into a hedgehog fortress, with its supplies flown in by air. But here again it was all happening in the jungles of Upper Tonkin, far from everything; and nobody, or almost nobody, knew anything about it. The high command lied, but it lied for the sake of the good cause and in order not to endanger a triumph that was so near at hand.

Giap might break his year's silence and proclaim that now he had a real army of shock troops and that he was about to launch a general counter-offensive, overwhelming the entire frontier and wiping out all the French; but he was only taken for a braggart. And yet *it was known:* it was perfectly well known that he had increased the number of his regulars in training camps in China and that he had provided them with formidable weapons. From this time on the jungle was swarming with Viet soldiers; they had immense fire power; they possessed the equipment to destroy the hopelessly isolated French fortified posts. The army intelligence reckoned that the Viets had more than thirty battalions grouped about the R.C. 4, with guns, mortars and bazookas. For their part the French had only fifteen, and far from strengthening the force covering the frontier, they were steadily depleting it.

A strange year! In the midst of success the French were traveling towards a destiny that was logical, relentless, foreseeable — and no one foresaw it. It was the period of happy illusions. On the surface all was calm: but in these days of the eleventh hour everything underneath it was going badly — never had there been so plunging a descent into military byzantinism. The highest officers hid from one another, outwitted one another in squalid quarrels and bitter rivalries. Everything was planned and carried out in an appalling lack of order and in the midst of an unbelievable muddle of conflicting rank and command. Added to this were the intrigues, the underhand scheming, that originated in all quarters and above all in Paris. The Revers affair* brought into sharp relief everything that was dubious and unsavory in the Paris ministries and ministers' waiting rooms, and in the general staff of the army both in France and in Indochina. And it left behind a legacy of inconsistencies, rivalries, uncertainties, ignorance — sometimes voluntary, sometimes not — calculating, selfish pessimism, and above all a stupid, complacent optimism. This was the maze that was at last to lead to a final reckoning, in the harsh mountains of Dongkhe.

At least it was colorful. The extraordinary cast of characters included Nguyen Binh, foredoomed to kill himself; the upright General Chanson, who was to be blown to pieces; the neurasthenic voluptuary Bao Dai; Nguyen De, the power behind his impotent throne; General Carpentier, the Commander in Chief, shut up in his air-conditioned room; Tam, whom they called the Tiger of Cailay; the worthy General Alessandri, who rather fancied himself as Indochina's Joan of Arc; the excellent, ever-active, conscientious Pignon; Monsignor Le Huu-tu, that medieval bishop; the big boss Huu, who was frightened of grenades and schoolboys; General Revers, coming as an official plotter; Colonel Constans, in command of the frontier zone, who never took a plane because his heart was not very strong; and Charton, the legionaries' hero. Also there, although their heavy, boding presence remained unseen, were Ho Chi Minh and Giap, buried deep in the jungle, getting their armies ready.

And at the end of it all the humiliation — the appalling, stupefying, unbelievable defeat on the Chinese frontier. Later, after the defeat, it was thought that a recovery was possible. But in fact there was to be no getting over it, right up until Dienbienphu. For a new Asia had been discovered, one in which nobody had believed. From now on it was known that this Asia did indeed exist, that it was formidable, and that in the long run it was too strong for an Expeditionary Force that was so isolated, so far from everything. People had been sick with arrogance; now, at least unconsciously, people were sick with fear.

* See p. 230.

The Long March

I WENT to see the coming of the Chinese tide, that avalanche of hundreds of thousands of men. For in the autumn of 1949 Mao's four great Peoples' Armies were on the point of reaching the frontiers of Tonkin. Would their impetus carry them on? Would they invade Indochina? Or would they at last come to a stop, thus putting an end to the Long March that had been going on for twenty years?

For it was more than twenty years since the epic of Chinese Communism had begun. It had been the most astonishing of human adventures: in the early days who could ever have supposed that Mao would win? He had started off so wretchedly, with such feeble resources; and against him there had been such enemies, such immensely superior strength — the power of the Kuomintang, the Japanese, the Americans, either one after another or all at the same time. And yet Mao, the rebellious peasant, alone, suspected on every hand, even at Moscow, had finished by conquering the enormous expanse of China. Would he not snap up Indochina, a mere mouthful for him?

During the oppressive monsoon days of the preceding months I had been looking into the story of Mao on the spot. In Hong Kong how imperfectly the phlegmatic expressions of the British hid their anxious waiting! But above all I had been into China itself, to doomed Canton and beyond, to the battlefield upon which the Nationalist defeat was consummated. And I had come to understand that Maoism was utter inhumanity, with force of will, hatred and deceit carried to their highest pitch. To form any idea of this unheard-of, this furiously systematic dynamism one had to come into direct and immediate contact with it. In a modern, civilized world it was something that went far beyond the imagination.

What passionate intensity! It had begun when Chiang Kai-shek had drowned the Chinese revolution in blood, the revolution that had brought the urban masses out into the streets in memory of the October Days and the Great Afternoon. Malraux has described the slaughter, the executions, the decimation of the proletariat, the men flung into the white-hot fireboxes of railway engines, the mutilated bodies scattered about the roads. It was then that an unknown little agitator by the name of Mao, a deviationist, proclaimed that the revolution would triumph in China only if it were Chinese, and that the real China was the China of the peasants. He loudly insisted that with the support of the Communist Party hundreds of millions of peasants would rise with the force of a tornado.

The beginnings were appalling. Those were the days when Mao was young, long-haired, pitiless in establishing the reign of virtue and of terror. In southern China, in the mountains of Kiangsi, he set up the Peasants' and Soldiers' Republic of Juling. It took Chiang Kai-shek four years to overthrow it. But even when it fell before the assault of a million mercenaries, that was not the end, for there now began the Long March, a desperate, fantastic undertaking, a journey from the south and then back again that lasted for twenty years, a journey of thousands upon thousands of miles.

The outward journey was a flight. On August 16, 1934 a hundred thousand men, women and children broke through the Nationalist lines that were tightening around Juling. They had to cross the whole of China, in spite of the countless armies of the Kuomintang and the warlords, to take refuge in Yenan, far to the north, a country of yellow loess, bare, treeless, as cold as Siberia. In Yenan there was a secondary Red base which would be their haven if they could reach it. To escape from the pack of their pursuers the hunted column was obliged to plunge into the desolate regions on the Tibetan frontiers, fighting as it forged on among mountain ranges, appalling chasms, unfordable torrents, deep ravines, forests and fever-ridden swamps. The Long March lasted for eighteen months at a little more than thirty miles a day. The Communists escaped ten armies; they crossed eighteen mountain chains and twenty-four great rivers; they took sixty-two towns on their way. By the time they reached Yenan there were no more than thirty thousand left. Yet it was they who conquered the whole of China in just over ten years.

For in Yenan, Mao invented the "people's war." He lived in a cave, and at night he worked by the light of a primitive oil lamp. He was older now and he had performed his autocriticism: violence was not enough; what was needed was persuasion, too, to win the people's heart. All the passions must be acted upon. In the name of patriotism he called the entire nation to arms, launching it against a fresh enemy, one still more dangerous than the Kuomintang: for the Japanese had invaded China. Chiang Kai-shek was also fighting them, but he did so in the most classic fashion — he brought up regular armies against the regular armies of the Mikado, and they were always beaten. But Mao confronted the formidable Japanese military machine with the people. With Communism as his guide he filled the people with inspiration, organized them and made them into a whole. He was a brilliant theoretician on the subject of war fought by the masses, and it was he who set down the four rules of guerrilla fighting on a huge scale: "When the enemy advances in force I retreat. When he stops and pitches camp I harass him. When he tries to avoid battle I attack him. When he withdraws I pursue him and destroy him."

Gradually the Japanese divisions were reduced to impotence. They no longer had any objectives: the unfathomable vastness of China perpetually closed over them. Millions of men and women, tens of millions, were cruelly put to death by the Japanese soldiers or died in huge numbers from starvation, pestilence, wretchedness, all the miseries of war. But that was of little importance, and even the suffering was valuable, since it brought into being the people's will and transformed them into the People. Atrocities were suffered and atrocities were perpetrated, and at the same time the Red guerrillas multiplied prodigiously, swarming all over the country. The Japanese soldiers, unable to kill all the Chinese in China, began to wear out. As they chased the uncatchable guerrillas, hidden in the mass of the people and in the landscape, they themselves became vulnerable. In the end, after years of battles and murders, the proud, splendid armies of the Mikado became a prey for Mao's ghostlike fighters.

Then how rapidly things moved! Once more the Long March began, the return journey towards that south from which Mao and his hunted partisans had escaped twenty years before. But this part of the Long March was a triumphant last act. It was all over in a few months. Throughout the war against the Japanese Mao had observed an armistice with Chiang Kai-shek so that the whole of China could fight the common enemy. But after Hiroshima and the collapse of Japan the credit for the victory, in the eyes of the world, had gone to the Generalissimo. Had not America, filled with admiration, wanted to turn the China of the Kuomintang into the fifth of the world's great powers? America did not choose to see that the trial had been too severe for the bourgeois nationalism of the Kuomintang, which had stooped to every sort of compromise and dishonesty, had yielded to every temptation, and had been brought down to the lowest pitch of decadence. America did not know that for the whole of Chinese youth and for all the uncountable Chinese working class the obscure Communist Mao was the hero, the incarnation of the Resistance. Furthermore at the time of the Japanese defeat Mao, in addition to all the troops of his People's formations, had a million real soldiers, a million fanatics. But who was aware of all this? Nobody, not even Stalin, who gave Mao cautious advice. "Take your time. Wait for your hour to come. You are still too weak to take up arms again and conquer the country." And Stalin treated with Chiang Kai-shek.

Yet everything was accomplished with astonishing speed. Mao took no notice of anyone — no notice of Stalin, no notice of America nor of the whole of the rest of the world, nor of the Kuomintang: the time for striking, for finishing it all, had come. As Mao saw it, the vainglorious Chiang Kai-shek's China was nothing but an immense mass of weakness, a corrupt mass in which nothing was left but gross sensual delight and inflation. And that was so in spite of his numerous armies, his merciless police and his administration, in spite of the whole machinery of the state, the American alliance and American aid. The Communists, on the other hand, had been brought to an even greater purity by their ordeals. The balance of power had imperceptibly changed. And Mao knew the extent of his own strength.

This was a great turning-point in history — one of those moments when the lightning strikes. Mao's analysis had been correct. After all these long drawn-out years, after so many tragic, desperate efforts, so many trials, so much death and blood, he struck the final blow with ludicrous ease. To the whole world's amazement the Red divisions that had been formed from the guerrilla bands smashed the huge, magnificently equipped armies of Chiang Kai-shek in Manchuria. Mao had only to reach out his hand to gather China.

Now it was the second Long March, no longer a rout but a victorious procession, no longer a journey from south to north but from north to south; and throughout its two thousand miles it was the triumphant occupation of the whole enormous country, the China of six hundred million people. Everything surrendered, everything capitulated. They entered Peking, the ancient and splendid capital in which the conquerors proclaimed the foundation of the People's Republic of China and where Mao became the Red Emperor, the successor of so many Sons of Heaven over the centuries. They entered Shanghai, the fabulous great metropolis of capitalism and imperialism, which Mao was going to reeducate and turn into a people's city. Lastly, in the summer of 1949, they entered Canton, that city of the old, traditional China in which everything was carried to extremes, pleasure and distress, refinement and debasement, in the midst of an unbelievable seething mass of people, goods and corpses. This was where, in former days, the revolution had been proclaimed; and it was here that it had been vilely betrayed and crushed. Twenty years later Mao arrived as its avenger.

But there was virtually no resistance. The people burst into a delirious joy: there was a tidal wave of flags with the five red stars — a huge upsurge of wild delight. The uncountable people had never seemed so numerous. Men and women came out in the millions to follow the soldiers in mad demonstrations of happiness, and then they hurried off into the halls — any kind of hall, cinema, barn, stable — to be present at the first political meetings. There unknown political commissars, thin, clean-shaven, wearing overalls, preached the gospel according to Mao. These were beings of a kind that had never been seen before, Chinese of a new species, devoured by an inward fire, marvelously simple. All the enemies of the people, all the reactionaries, even the warlords and the employers of sweated labor, begged to be forgiven. It was only the last of the Kuomintang troops that fled before the final inexorable Long March of the Communists.

I had seen them, the pursuers and the pursued, the second only a little way ahead of the first, not far from Canton. What prodigious lines of soldiers! They all marched as though they were in a dream, marching by day and by night without a pause, the Communists hurrying in for the kill and the last of the Nationalists still trying to get away. Now, a month later and six hundred miles farther south, I was going to see them all again. For both the first and the second were about to run into the Indochinese frontier. What was going to happen?

I was afraid. For what could those few French battalions on the frontier, who already found it hard enough to deal with the Viets, do against these armed hordes if things were to turn ugly? The total strength of the Expeditionary Force only amounted to a frail screen in comparison with the numbers that were about to appear, the tens of thousands, the hundreds of thousands and even possibly the millions of men whose intentions were unknown but who could brush everything aside as though it were a trifle if they chose, if Mao were to say to them, "Go on. Liberating China is not enough. All oppressed Asia must be liberated too."

My anxiety was very great because I knew what Maoism was — the most implacable mysticism of modern times. It was the boundless pride of the Chinese race, kept down for close on a hundred years, that was longing for a complete revenge. It was not enough to expel all the imperialists, all the colonialists, all the exploiters and all the whites from the soil of China; they were also to be punished, because they were evil itself. They had to be destroyed — or rather they had to be brought to repentance and to virtue, to good as opposed to evil — wherever they were, wherever man existed anywhere in the world.

So it was a crusade. And it was only just beginning. China's mission was to conquer the world so as to ensure the everlasting triumph of good over evil — that evil which, like original sin, is to be found in every man and every nation, even the purest. Evil was intolerable, and Maoism was to attack it until it was rooted out all over the globe, rooted out of all men right down to the very last. But victory was certain. It could not elude the people, since "new things are unconquerable because they are new." The masses, "blowing across the earth like a hurricane" would bring down the whole of the worm-eaten structure of the past and build up, on completely fresh foundations, the splendid monuments of socialism.

It was madness. For as Mao saw it what did it matter that half the population of the earth perished, if that were necessary? What did an atomic cataclysm signify? Afterwards, for the survivors, it would be the golden age, the paradise in which "the east wind would blow harder than the west" and in which yellow would dominate white.

I was afraid. For the first source of infection to be cleaned up was that very Indochina where the Expeditionary Force was fighting for what China hated. Wiping out the Expeditionary Force would be simple. Mao's soldiers had but to go on marching a few more hundred miles after so many thousands and tens of thousands. That was what ideology required. But was it the "correct solution"?

In that autumn of 1949 Indochina's only chance was that Mao, in his meticulously reasoned insanity, might have concluded that the time was not yet ripe for his Red China to throw aside the mask. Might it not be better to take advantage of universal ignorance, the ingenuous simplicity of the rest of the world, to purge the submissive but still essentially petit-bourgeois China without hindrance — a China that also had as yet no suspicion of what Maoism really was? To begin with it was necessary that twenty or thirty million Chinese should be physically liquidated in a scientific manner and that hundreds of millions of others should be completely reeducated — that is to say tortured in their bodies, their souls and their minds — before Maoism, firmly established, could take on the whole world, making use of all the means at its disposal, in the name of virtue.

That was the most hopeful supposition. If it were right perhaps the Long March might come to a halt at the Indochinese frontier. But at best this could only be a pause of a few weeks, a few months, a few years — it could only be a respite. And in the meantime Mao would have so many indirect ways of bringing pressure to bear on the Indochinese war and of making it deadly for the French!

But in high places, the authorities were very far from realizing this messianic attitude. Precautions were only taken against what were termed "technical incidents." It was the Nationalists who were feared, not the Communists. The authorities were afraid that the wreckage of the Kuomintang, flooding down into Indochina, would say "no" and refuse to let the French disarm them. For if they were to set themselves up in a series of anti-Communist maquis in the mountains of Tonkin Mao's Communists might very well come and get them. That would mean a hopeless tangle of Mao's divisions, the remnants of Chiang Kai-shek's armies, the Vietminh and the Expeditionary Force, all around the R.C. 4 and its surrounding jungles, with everybody more or less the enemy of everybody else.

So perhaps a catastrophe was on the point of bursting out in the midst of the general staff's mild torpor. In any case their comfort had already been upset by the arrival of Father Maillot, the bearer of an exceedingly disturbing message from the famous General Pai Shung-si.

This Father Maillot was a missionary, a gentleman missionary, a real swashbuckling Templar, and he was a great friend of the tiger-hearted Pai Shung-si, the battle-worn veteran, the master of Kwangsi and, which was more important, the owner of an army of several hundred thousand men which was said to be the most modern and the best disciplined in anti-Communist China. He detested Chiang Kai-shek, but from time to time, when he was paid, he brought him his soldiers. He even dreamed of taking his place. A year before he had remained neutral while a decisive battle was being fought out a few miles away between Chiang Kai-shek and Lin Piao: he deliberately allowed the annihilation of the Generalissimo's last divisions.

A few months after this, Pai Shung-si was in fact the only ruler left in Kuomintang China — a China that diminished week by week, day by day, like the ass's skin in the tale. Chiang Kai-shek had already fled to Formosa. The warlord of Kwangsi had no competitor: his was the last great Nationalist army on the mainland. He was very pleased and he proclaimed that he would at last be able to wipe out the Red hordes. His troops did indeed resist behind the Blue River and they did stand before Canton: then came the day when they did not stand any longer. It turned into a panic-stricken rout — three hundred thousand men flying southwards, in the direction of their native Kwangsi. But they were unable to make a stand even in their own province. So that meant that a great many men were coming towards Tonkin — a very great many, seeing that the Communists just behind them were even more numerous.

It was at this moment that Father Maillot became Pai Shung-si's envoy. When he arrived at Hanoi for the first time after a long and dangerous journey on muleback he was beaming with delight. He was so sure that the French would be pleased with him! For in the immense sealed letter that he presented to them the warlord, in the most civil terms, offered his alliance — his soldiers would fight in Tonkin at the side of the Expeditionary Force against every kind of Red without distinction — Chinese or Vietminh. The suggestion was put forward as a boon, a favor that could not possibly be declined.

Poor Father Maillot. He was not nearly as welcome as he had supposed. In the end he was sent back to Kwangsi with no as his message. Then he passed to and fro, continually traveling on foot, by plane, on horseback, carrying letters that grew more and more disagreeable. Pai Shung-si's civilities became ultimatums: if the French persisted in their refusal his soldiers would enter Indochina by force.

The complications were beginning. The Communists also uttered threats: in his turn Lin Piao warned the French that if they did not disarm Pai Shung-si's army in Indochina he would come and do so himself with his troops. So the French were being blackmailed on both sides, and they could do nothing about it. The Asian forces were too great. The French were no longer in control of events. They were arguing from weakness. Everything depended on the innumerable Chinese of every kind and upon the real intentions that lay behind the threatening words. The French solution was to cling meticulously to international law and to its most scrupulous application. Their only hope was that when it came to the point the Nationalists would let themselves be interned and that the Communists would come to a halt at the frontier — the final halt at the end of the twenty-year-old Long March. Pignon and Carpentier* staked their all on international law: but on these remote Asian borders how much did international law count for?

But in spite of Father Maillot, General Pai Shung-si, Marshal Lin Piao and all the hosts of Chinese advancing upon Tonkin, nobody in Saigon or Hanoi really thoroughly believed in any danger: there was only a marked uneasiness. Nobody knew anything of what was happening on the other side of the frontier, in those mountains and jungles of southern China that were the scene of this huge death agony. It seemed that Lin Piao's columns had launched a savage, exhausting drive to cut off and destroy Pai Shung-si's multitudes before they could reach Indochina, the land of the imperialists. Curious "imperialists"! All they wanted was that the Communists should kill all the Nationalists who were fleeing towards Tonkin.

But the weeks went by and still nothing was known. Still nobody knew how many Chinese would appear — a few hundred, a few thousand, hundreds of thousands? No one had any idea. If there were huge numbers of them and if they refused to obey there would never be enough men on the frontier to take away their arms and intern them. And what would

* General Carpentier, Commander in Chief of the French Expeditionary Force in Indochina from 1949 to the end of 1950.

happen if they fought their way in and the Communists followed them? But no one wanted even to think about such a supposition.

In spite of this confusion the administrative machinery did begin to turn. A civil and military commission was convened in Saigon. Since the authorities would be forced to give the Nationalists asylum it was necessary to consider how they should be lodged and fed. This called for the setting up of a whole organization. The army did not want its stock of supplies to be touched and asserted that the entire business of looking after the refugees belonged to the high commissioner's officer. No agreement was reached. As he closed the session the high civil servant representing Monsieur Pignon stated in his shrill little authoritarian voice, "There is no sort of hurry. It is not tomorrow that we are concerned with. With the Chinese everything drags along: it is always slower than you expect."

Meanwhile the frontier battalions took up their positions at the chief crossing points. Three groups had been formed. It was a pretty little deployment, and General Alessandri was very pleased with it. It looked exceedingly well — there was the Legion, there were parachute troops, colonial infantry, Moroccan goumiers, a few guns, a few blockhouses and even a few spotting planes, which circled perpetually overhead.

Alessandri and his staff continually told the officers and the soldiers, "There is nothing whatever to worry about. If fifty Nationalists appear at the frontier that will be the outside figure."

On December 8, fifty thousand Nationalists were sighted one day's march away. General Carpentier took the trouble to go and see his troops on the frontier. As usual he seemed full of confidence. But as usual deep down he had his doubts: he was afraid of a hitch. That was why he let himself go to the extent of saying to the officers entrusted with stopping the yellow wave, "It may be an avalanche. Perhaps there will be a million Chinese. Two million Chinese. We don't know. If that happens, we shall need reinforcements."

Then General Carpentier, having reflected, added mildly, "Perhaps I will be able to send you a company."

The wait at Monkay

IN the Autumn, some months before this conversation, I went to Monkay, the last village in Indochina, to meet the Chinese tide.

After an unspeakably uncomfortable, gay and smelly voyage along the coast I reached Monkay. I stood on the top of a little rise, ten yards from the frontier. Two legionaries were on guard there continually, one squatting

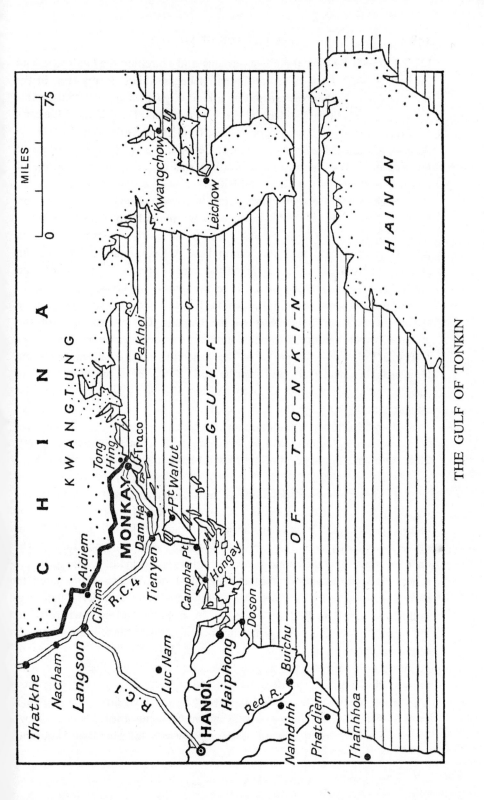

THE GULF OF TONKIN

behind a machine gun, the other standing and searching the landscape with his field glasses. I too stared at China. It began almost at my feet, in the middle of a river that was crossed by a kind of gangway — its official name was the International Bridge. The other side was Tong Hing, Monkay's Chinese twin (the crossing points at the frontiers are arranged that way in Asia — a river, a bridge, two towns). Beyond, the yellow-green stripes of the rice fields rose in steps. The horizon was closed in tight by a line of mountains, the Hundred Thousand Hills.

How clear and sharp everything was, how calm — made to last forever. Coolies, heavily loaded with burdens, went to and fro across the International Bridge, with no formalities. On the other side, opposite the French post, waved the sun flag of the Nationalists. A Kuomintang soldier was on guard. The usual sort of crowd filled the narrow streets of Tong Hing, and the shops were open. Nowhere did I see any signs of the crisis.

Yet for the first time in Indochina I was truly overwhelmed with a feeling of powerlessness. Next to me Captain G, in command of the garrison, which amounted to one company, was even more oppressed than I. For a long while he gazed at the peaceful, pastel-hued range of the Hundred Thousand Hills, and then he said, "Don't be deceived by the way people and things do not seem to alter at all. Don't be taken in by the appearance of those worthy people of Tong Hing, who look just the same, or by those splendid quiet mountains. In a few days or weeks that apparently unchanging country will be swarming with Chinese soldiers of every kind. And with my handful of men I shall have to say to them, 'Be so kind as to behave properly.' "

This officer was also something of an intelligence agent, of course. He regularly sent his Asian spies into China, and it so happened that one of them had just come back from the neighborhood of Kweiling, a great way off, with a ghastly tale. The retreat of Pai Shung-si's army had turned into an utter rout, and the panic-stricken soldiers were fighting among themselves. In some battalions the soldiers killed the officers who wanted to surrender, in others they killed those who would not surrender. There was nothing to eat. The Red guerrillas lay in ambush, and everywhere there appeared Mao Tse-tung's agents, his propagandists. Some were impaled; others succeeded in having the officers impaled by their men. Villages were going up in flames and the people fleeing into the jungle. There were dead bodies all along the tracks — slaughtered soldiers and starved peasants. This whole mob was being thrust forward by the final drive of Lin Piao's armies, which had started out a year ago in Manchuria for this last killing. Three huge Red columns were advancing towards the Hundred Thousand

Hills: they too were exceedingly hungry, but they were keeping perfect order.

Another agent returned from Nanning, where Pai Shung-si and his staff had taken refuge, some hundred and twenty miles from the frontier. He said that Pai Shung-si had tried to sell himself to the Communists, but in vain — they did not choose to give him any money. The warlord had then cabled to Washington to insist upon having the millions of dollars that Congress had allotted to the Nationalists. "They belong to me," he declared. "Chiang Kai-shek is a mere deserter who has taken shelter in his island of Formosa. I swear to fight on until the last."

Meanwhile a discreet exodus began among the people of Monkay. A man had arrived from Pakhoi, a picturesque, wretchedly poor, medieval Chinese port of a hundred thousand inhabitants, crowded with junks that were used for all purposes — trade, smuggling, fishing, piracy. It was close at hand, a few days' march away. This man reported that Pai Shung-si and his troops had not yet been altogether destroyed. Far from it: the warlord, surrounded by fifty thousand loyal soldiers, had dug himself in at Pakhoi. Lin Piao's columns were advancing fast — there was going to be a battle. After it, everything would bear down on Monkay. And what would happen then?

The well-to-do slipped quietly away towards the south. The only one to remain true was Vong A Sang. He was the chief of the two hundred thousand Nungs who lived along the coast, a separate race that had sprung up from the Chinese pirates who had settled there, multiplied and thrived. Vong A Sang himself had begun life as a brigand. But in the bloody spring of 1944 he saved some Frenchmen who were being hunted by the Japanese, and this was the beginning of his good fortune. Except for the time when he let the garrison of Monkay be massacred by his uncle's band because of his dutiful feelings for the old gentleman, he had been unswervingly loyal to the French. He so believed in France that he refused to be either a Kuomintang or a Vietminh general — and both offers had been made to him at about the same time. His emblem, his people's emblem, was the French flag surcharged with a junk. Furthermore he brought his subjects in on the side of the Expeditionary Force in a total war. He ordered all his men of military age to enlist. In the last phase there were thirty thousand Nungs busy fighting, some formed into partisan units called "umbrella handles," others adding to the "jaundice" of the French battalions, and still others put in to stiffen the Vietnamese army. The high command thoroughly trusted the Nungs. These descendants of the Chinese pirates were bigger and stronger than the Annamese, whom they hated and despised — the Nungs never gave any quarter. No people in Indochina committed themselves so much to the side of the French. (The result was a general migration after Dienbienphu: the Nungs left the sea, the coast and their homes for exile in the south and utter poverty.) But at this time, in the autumn of 1949, Vong A Sang was still full of faith in the strength of the French, and in his own. I went to see him in his yamen. He was a big-bellied Hercules with a strangler's hands and a beaming, prosperous face. Nodding mysteriously he said to me, "The Communists will never attack Monkay. They know that the Nungs are invincible." His confidence, however, did not prevent him from sending some particularly valuable possessions away to Haiphong that very day.

But Vong A Sang was right. At the beginning of December the exodus suddenly stopped. Monkay had learned that a gentleman's agreement had been reached between Lin Piao's armies and Pai Shung-si at Pakhoi. The warlord renounced heroism and last-ditchery and every kind of hostile act in China and Indochina. In return the Communists allowed him to carry out an amicable Dunkirk in the direction of the great island of Hainan, which commanded the Gulf of Tonkin. They halted to give Pai Shung-si's troops time to embark in thousands of junks. They carried their kindness very far, even to the extent of lending their own boats and allowing him to crush a premature Red rising in the town. For his part Pai Shung-si preferred a plane as his way of getting out. General Chennault, the well-known American condottiere of the air, the former ace of the Flying Tigers, organized an airlift for him with his CAT, his special missions force. In a shuttle service that went on day and night Chennault's planes flew out Pai Shung-si, his wives, his possessions, his staff, and his Iron Guard of five thousand men.

Monkay went back to sleep, and then suddenly there arrived a top secret telegram from the high command — the alarm warning for the whole frontier. The danger point was close to Langson. Thousands and perhaps tens of thousands had accumulated there in spite of Pai Shung-si's escape. These wanted to force their way into Indochina, and there were several Communist divisions just behind them. There might be an explosion at any moment.

I got a jeep and an authorization and at dawn the next day I was racing along the R.C. 4 towards Tienyen, on the road to Langson. I was in Tienyen that afternoon, a Tienyen filled with happiness, overflowing with congratulations. All the military leaders in Indochina were sending one another joyful telegrams. They also told the troops how pleased they were, as though they had just won a great victory. Even before I had got out of my jeep a colonel caught sight of me and shouted, "You're too late. It's all over. The first convoy of prisoners will be here in an hour. We've already bagged thirty thousand Nationalists near Langson. I always told you so — these Asiatics are still afraid of us: they give way every time we get angry."

Just then a scout car turned off the R.C. 4 in a cloud of dust. It came from Langson, ahead of a huge column of marching Chinese, the ones who were being interned. A lieutenant in battle dress was sprawling over the wheel: he told me about the capture. His version sounded quite different. "So they're hanging out flags. All right: but it's a miracle that it did not turn into a disaster. The slightest touch would have been enough. And every one of those Chinese, the Nationalists and the Communists, were armed and they were in a very ugly mood. All the time it was going on I hummed the old Legion song to myself:

> *The general said there was nobody there,*
> *So go up and look in it, said he.*
> *But of course it was five times as full as a fair,*
> *With grenades and machine guns so free.*

"The alert was given on December 9. The garrison of Chima, a tiny little post perched up on the frontier, signaled that there was a huge mass of people piling up on the Chinese territory opposite, a few hundred yards away. To begin with nobody knew whether they were Nationalists or Communists. This crowd did not move: it could hardly be seen, hiding in the ravines and the few straw huts of a wretched jungle village called Ai Diem. Then there was rifle fire and machine-gun bursts, all the noise of nearby fighting. The crowd that was standing there was a Nationalist army, and the Communists were attacking them in the rear.

"During the morning of the eleventh white flags were seen waving all over this mob, as if they formed part of it. It was rags that the Chinese kept waving on the end of long poles. A little later a group of men advanced towards Chima, Kuomintang generals and colonels: their uniforms were torn to ribbons, but they were still very proud and haughty. We received them.

"The talks went on all day long in that rough, lost little fort. It was extremely dramatic. Several times everything was on the point of being broken off. At some stages the Chinese wept, begging us to accept their proposals. But most of the time their voices were ice cold, very hard and unemotional, and threatening. Occasionally one would burst out in a fury and wave his arms, shouting like a maniac. They would not yield; they insisted that their soldiers should enter Tonkin with their weapons, as allies. The answer was that if they tried it there would be fighting. The conference went on and on. Communication was very difficult. Bad English was the language we used, and we had to speak through interpreters. Afterwards we learned that the chief delegate, General Ho Shan-pen, spoke perfectly adequate French.

"As the hours went by the situation grew uglier. What we could see over there in China was no longer the disorderly swarming mass of a routed army. Now the Nationalist troops were in a dense, compact body, right on the frontier itself. Behind them the battle was going on furiously. The Communists were continually driving in upon them, thrusting them harder. It was like a boil on the point of bursting. And by way of opposition, on the French side there was still only the few soldiers of the Chima garrison: they were dug in behind the bamboo barricade, all around the mess where the discussions were going on.

"Night began to fall. It was then that the French spokesman suddenly observed, 'You can no longer pass if we do not wish it. At this very moment our shock battalions are occupying the ridges that command the frontier.'

"Then the Chinese gave in. They signed some kind of a surrender document. They were quite overcome: they said that France had dishonored herself forever and then left it at that. The disarmament was to take place the next day.

"At dawn the peaks above Chima were in fact held by legionaries and Moroccans. They were lying there on the ground, by their weapons: half a mile behind them the guns and the armored cars were in position. You would have thought they had been getting ready for a battle.

"We knew the slightest incident could send everything sky high. And there were no less than four sides in this extraordinary business. We French only amounted to a few hundred, and we were strung out along this ill-defined frontier, with Chinese Nationalists, Chinese Communists and Vietminh all gravitating towards it in their thousands. So as to avoid total and disastrous confusion each French detachment was ordered to fly a flag. But just over the way in China the muddle seemed to be getting worse. There was not only firing now, but other sounds of war — bugle calls. Was it the Nationalists gathering to cross over or the Communists sounding the charge?

"Still, it all began quite well. We had prepared a corridor where the Nationalists were to come forward in groups of five hundred. After a long wait the first appeared at about nine in the morning: the generals and their staffs. The soldiers came, each carrying something wrapped in old rags at arm's length. It was their rifles; and they set them down one by one on the pile with a kind of gesture of renouncement. You could see that several of them were hiding revolvers and daggers in their padded uniforms. But there was no time for serious searching. We might have found some astonishing things if there had been!

"It went on fast and smoothly. Every quarter of an hour there arrived a fresh batch of men, or rather creatures, for there were some weird objects in that crowd. Next to sad, grave officers you would see evil-looking bandits and wretched beings with disgusting wounds. And mixed up with them there were all the people who get swept along in a flight of this kind — old men, women and children. The legionaries in charge were cheerful and very good tempered, and everything ran like a conveyor belt. The heaps of weapons became enormous. As soon as the Chinese were disarmed little escorts marched them to the rear at bayonet point, to a small plain half a mile back, a kind of natural receiving point. To get there they had to march through the mud, stumbling as they went: there was no expression on their faces: they were like a laborious line of ants. Then in this plain they crowded together and lay there, countless uncaring specters, waiting for whatever should happen to them.

"It was a dismal sight. Every defeat is a wretched thing to watch. And what made it worse was the horrible weather, the gray drizzle, the dampness that swelled your flesh, the wind that cut to the bone and the cloud that covered the mountainside. The only people to have any fun were the legionaries in charge of the disarming. The men in the covering units up on their peaks waited for it to end and ate their rations, churning out their perpetual infantry songs, and chewing over the perennial question: 'What'll you do your first hour in France, have a decent meal or a girl?'

"But after ten o'clock it was no longer possible to control the Chinese. They suddenly began flooding in from everywhere in huge masses, panic-stricken mobs coming by every track and path and down the mountainside. As they ran they shouted 'The Communists are coming. Hurry! Hurry!' Women were thrust aside, flung into the rice field. A legionary saved one who was stuck in the mud, struggling in the midst of her baskets and poles, and this amused all the fugitives — they stopped running for a moment to laugh. There were now a great many peasants carrying huge burdens in the crowd.

"And the flood was growing every minute. We were on the point of being overwhelmed by the everlasting, unimaginably big crowd. And what if the Reds arrived in the middle of all this mess, what could we do? And the Reds were getting closer and closer: they were only a few hundred yards away now. The battle was coming very near. Men with wounds only an hour or two old dragged themselves up to our post. This was nearly the end. The Nationalist rear guard had fought a last battle so that the mass of the refugees should have time to get into Indochina; now they had reached the end of their strength and they were going to cross too.

"And indeed exactly at noon there appeared a well-organized detachment in the midst of the fugitives, disciplined, in blue uniforms, armed to the teeth. We thought they were Communists, but not at all — they were the personal regiment of the Tupan of Lungchow, a Kwangsi warlord. We wanted to disarm them. The Tupan refused. 'I have signed no agreement,' he said. 'I am not bound by it. You leave us alone. In any case the Communists are just behind us. You have more important things to do — you will have to take care of them any minute now.' This was the real old China, this blackmail in the middle of a disaster, making the most of the catastrophe and these extraordinary circumstances. There was a feverishly hurried parley. Neither side would yield. After a few minutes of rage, after a tense, wicked silence, it was the Tupan who gave way. His regiment's weapons made still another heap.

"There had been no time to spare. Machine-gun bursts were plowing up the ground all around. The Communists were firing at us. We could not see them in the dreary light, but they had occupied the whole frontier and they had even overflowed into Indochina. Now it was headlong flight among the refugees. The women were shrieking. Order had to be restored with blows. The Reds went on firing: an NCO of the Legion went down, a Nationalist soldier was killed and three others wounded. We were ordered to return the fire and we let fly with our guns, armor and automatic weapons — everything we had. The Communists drew back as fast as they could. Just as well. We had asked for planes, but it was drizzling even more now and they could not take off.

"The next day was quiet. An agent told us that the Reds had even withdrawn from the village of Ai Diem. In any case the Nationalists, three or four hundred of them, mostly wounded, were still turning up. But during the day of December fifteenth there was a fresh alert.

"At three o'clock in the afternoon we heard a strange kind of shouting coming from Ai Diem, the dead-looking hamlet. About thirty men emerged from it and ran towards us like maniacs: then suddenly they rushed back again. We saw others setting up machine-gun batteries opposite us, and we on our side pointed our guns at them. But what was going on? We thought they were Nationalists who had cut their way through China as far as Ai

Diem but who dared not come up to us. The officer in command of our detachment decided to go towards them and make signs for them to come. This was Colonel Charton, a blunt little man completely in the tradition of the Legion, a high-ranking tough guy who knew his way about — up to every kind of caper and every kind of party. In short, a crack soldier who gave himself no airs. The genuine, heartily kind and heartily pitiless mercenary: rather vulgar on purpose: subtle, fair, not apt to worry about moral problems. Not a warrior but a real fighting man — toughness, quickness, wit and indestructibility in a half-pint version. He went off with his Annamese interpreter and two or three of his favorite legionaries. Fifty yards from the frontier he was surrounded by fifty bellowing maniacs with tommy guns and grenades with the pins out in their hands. They were dressed like the Nationalists, but without the Kuomintang sun on their caps. They closed around our people, waving their arms incomprehensibly. They took hold of the interpreter and in just one second they had robbed him of his hat and his waterproof. The poor devil shot back to the Chima post at full speed shouting "The Communists! The Communists!" And indeed it was the Communists.

"Their leader, a huge man from north China who looked even bigger in his padded uniform, was in a wild, strange kind of fury. He leaped about, clenching his fists and roaring. All at once he seized Colonel Charton by the arm and tried to pull him towards Ai Diem and the Chinese interior. The legionaries grabbed him and pulled him free. But the tension was greater than ever. Each side was aiming point blank at the other, with their fingers on the trigger. If one man fired, fighting would break out everywhere. It was war or peace with Mao's China that was at stake at that moment.

"They stood there with their fingers tight on their triggers: but nobody fired. The giant launched into a speech. He could not be understood. He was talking a completely unknown Chinese dialect from Manchuria or the far north. Charton's great anxiety was that the French troops could not see him: he was hidden by a fold in the ground. So while the huge Communist was spouting his fiery oration Charton very casually moved foot by foot towards the frontier. The Chinese, carried away by his flood of words, followed without noticing it. Suddenly he and his men found themselves right in the trap, immediately under the guns of the French detachment's armor, beneath the ridges where Charton's battalions were only waiting for him to raise his hand — the signal for retaliation.

"Seeing this, the Reds calmed down a little. Charton was far more at his ease now, and he went on with the conversation. Interpreters were found, three of them, so that the French could be turned into Cantonese, the Cantonese into Mandarin and the Mandarin into the giant's dialect. Hercules started roaring again and insisted that all the Nationalists who had crossed the frontier should be delivered up to him — he had been chasing them for such a long time, and he wanted to have them all shot. In a completely neutral, impersonal voice Charton merely replied, 'This is France. No foreigner can give orders here.' Once more the big man flew into a rage, and he brought up his rifle as though to shoot Charton through the chest. But the legionaries had come flocking around and they too were extremely angry. They were all in favor of liquidating this maniac and his escort. It would have been easy. A few orders in a language the Communists did not understand, French or German, and they would have been wiped out in a few seconds, before they had even had time to see where their death was coming from.

"Charton called out to his men 'Control yourselves.' But the furious legionaries went on growling in a threatening manner. Suddenly the big man, as though he realized that his life was in great danger, turned very polite. 'At least be so good as to let me know your honorable name.' 'Charton.' The Chinese tried to repeat the name, but he could not manage it. Then Charton gave him his photograph, an old one that showed him with General Monclar, the 'Father of the Legion.' At once the Communist's eyes sparkled with joy — he had the document that would allow him to explain to his superiors why he had not been able to exterminate all the Nationalists. At all events he said thank you, shook hands and went back into China. During these civilities the legionaries held up their clenched fists, laughing and shouting. What might have been a tragedy ended as a farce.

"During the days that followed everything was completely quiet. The officers and men grew bored. The villagers of Ai Diem told us that all the Communist soldiers had gone. We decided to go into China to repay the visit. No one mentioned it to the high command, of course.

"We went, just a few of us, unarmed, with only a few pistols well hidden in inner pockets. The people had come back to Ai Diem. And in the filthy village we also saw chickens and buffaloes wandering at large — a sure sign that there were no Chinese soldiers in the neighborhood. An inquisitive crowd gathered around us. They were not very welcoming. Some of the Chinese smiled awkwardly: others stared at us with hatred. They were obviously carrying weapons under their coats. It was best not to linger. We patted a few filthy children so as not to look too foolish and turned back. A corporal pissed on Chinese ground just before he passed the frontier stone. 'That'll be something else to tell the kids later on,' he observed.

"We had had this childish urge to go into China. And we had done it. We wanted to show the Communists that they did not frighten us. But fundamentally we had gone over because, maybe without admitting it to ourselves, we were afraid of them.

"At all events we had won a victory! This victory over the Nationalists. At last I was ordered to convoy them. I have brought them to you. Go and have a look at them — they're only a few miles back."

All this had happened a day or two earlier and now, at Tienyen, all that remained for me to do was to go and have a look at the "losers" on the way to their camps. First there came the ambulances, each one a self-contained world of indifference. The Arab drivers' utter indifference was equalled by that of the wounded. I opened one of the doors. The stench was appalling. Rawness everywhere, the color of decaying meat — pus dribbling through loathsome dressings made of mud and grass. These wretched people had not yet been attended to, for want of nurses. They were still in the same state as when they had fled through China, most of them dragging themselves on their stumps, with their bellies torn open or their faces ripped off. Even now not a single one of them groaned. What would have been the use? Everything that the most resolute will could do had been done as they dragged themselves like obstinate mutilated insects as far as the frontier. From now on all that was left to them was resignation: whatever happened to them now was in the hands of fate. They were as silent as a docile herd: they uttered no sound. An Algerian driver told me that he had never had such an undemanding load — two men had died in his ambulance without anyone noticing.

But the first marching column was said to be on its way, and I went to meet it. It was resting in a village. Once again I met this indifference, an even greater indifference, perhaps. The Chinese had not yet been given anything to eat, so now they were yielding up big silver coins and even Maria Theresa thalers, which they took out of bottle money boxes slung around their waists to buy fritters from roadside peddlers. It was done with no complaint, no joy, no emotion of any kind. And then, when the whistle blew, these people formed up again and set off, marching on and on, as they had already marched thousands and thousands of miles over the days, weeks and months before. The girls were as hard, distant and inaccessible as the men. For there were a great many Chinese women auxiliaries with pigtails and the regulation toothbrush just protruding from their breast pockets.

After this first convoy there came others, an endless train. Already the concentration-camp atmosphere pervaded everything — the manner of obeying and the manner of giving orders. I saw the gloomy discipline of the prisoners and I saw the fatuous airs of the soldiers of the Expeditionary Force as they strutted up and down the ranks with their haughty tommy guns and harsh words of command. There was a kind of odious boasting elation everywhere, particularly in the officers' messes and the staffs — the high places. I heard exceedingly unpleasant details. It seems that at an important post which was used as a sorting point the garrison ransacked the Chinese, beating them up, threatening them, searching them, taking everything they possessed, money, jewels, anything at all. The man in command of the post set aside the particularly rare and valuable weapons for himself. And he received telegrams from all over Tonkin, all over Indochina, from his friends and superiors saying "I am coming. I am going to pick out a souvenir from your collection. Have you a good-looking rifle?"

It was just as though the Expeditionary Force were for the first time enjoying the feeling of having some vanquished opponents at their mercy. For anyone would have supposed that these Nationalists who were going to be shut up had been conquered by the Expeditionary Force, not by the Communists. Anyone would have supposed that it was these Kuomintang soldiers who were the enemies, and by no means Mao Tse-tung's Communists.

Meanwhile the Chinese in our power passed Tienyen. Their march brought them to their first resting place, the mine head of an abandoned coal pit on the shore of the Bay of Along. A kind of ornamental arch had been put up at the entrance: beyond it there was nothing but the bare black earth. The authorities thought that good enough for those Chinese, who had laid down their arms and who were no longer to be feared. And anyhow quite soon the authorities began to treat them better — their sick and wounded were cared for, they were dressed and fed. Everything was all right. Nobody's conscience pricked him: far from it.

"Gentle" China

Two months later, in February 1950, the whole immense length of the Indochinese frontier, from Nuong Sing in Laos to Monkay on the Gulf of Tonkin, was occupied by Red China. This was the sweetly reasonable, "gentle" China.

But there had been weeks filled with danger before this point. There had had to be a real war against seven or eight thousand Nationalists at Nacham, between Langson and Caobang, in that region where the R.C. 4 was already the scene of the huge and murderous Vietminh ambushes. It was right in the middle of the Vietminh quadrilateral, with Giap's regiments all around. The leader of these Chinese was Vu Hong-khan, a Vietnamese belonging to the Kuomintang. When the Nacham garrison wanted to disarm his men he cried, "If you want our weapons come and get them!" And he and all his followers forced their way across the frontier and vanished into the landscape. At Langson, the headquarters of the frontier zone, there was wild anxiety. The town was almost stripped of men and it seemed that Vu Hong-khan was marching towards it — that he was about to attack. In all haste that valuable fighting-machine Colonel Charton was recalled from Chima with his shock troops of the Legion. They were installed at the approaches to the town. And to receive the Chinese, Charton prepared a particularly choice ambush stretching along two miles of the R.C. 4. But only a thousand appeared, and they surrendered.

Vu Hong-khan and his six thousand loyal followers had thrust their way into the most impenetrable jungle in the huge, terrifying limestone ranges that lay between the R.C. 4 and the delta. Their intention was certainly to come out onto the plain right next to Hanoi. Charton was ordered to go after them and destroy them at any cost. In his turn he, together with his legionaries and his Moroccans, pushed into that impossible region, where men could not live and where the French never went. For several days the column groped through the green vastness. Patrols were continually sent out to climb peaks, but they discovered nothing. The agents, the spies of every kind, knew nothing. The spotting planes, skimming the ridges and the mountaintops, saw nothing.

It was heartbreaking. Then suddenly, at about five o'clock one afternoon, a Chinese leaped to his feet in the bushes a few yards from a French lieutenant: no doubt it was some drowsing sentry starting up from his sleep. The officer was of English origin; with British impassivity and in Shakespeare's tongue he said to the Chinese, "As you see, the French troops are here. Go and look for your comrades and tell them to surrender prettily." "O.K.," said the soldier. Five minutes after he had vanished there was a tremendous burst of mortar and machine-gun fire. The Chinese had entrenched themselves in a hollow. They were raking the legionaries strung out along a track with the fire of their automatic weapons. It was an ugly position: the battle was very tough. Fortunately Charton had brought guns with him, and the 105-mm shells exploded in the jungle where Vu Hong-khan's men were thought to be. The calculations must have been right, for the cries of the wounded and the dying were heard. But night was coming on. The French felt that there were too few of them to maintain contact. They called for planes, and under the cover of rockets they broke off without loss.

That was December 31. At midnight the Legion celebrated the New Year. From the ridge upon which they were camping they began to shell the Chinese again with their 105's. At dawn the next day a patrol went out to reconnoiter the place where the fighting had been. No one was there any more, but corpses were lying about and there were some hastily dug common graves. Joss sticks were still burning. More than a hundred Nationalists had been killed.

There were clashes on the following days, and still more Chinese were killed by artillery fire and by the planes. On January 6 a Moroccan troop called for assistance: Vu Hong-khan's six thousand men were in front of them. The Chinese wanted to surrender, but there were not enough Moroccans to disarm them. The capitulation took place near Lucnam, at the edge of the jungle and the delta — the Chinese had traveled as far as that.

Later one of the survivors said to me, "We could not resist any longer. We had had nothing to eat for several days and we had no strength left. Since our crossing into Indochina we had lost more than two thousand in killed and wounded. But for all that, if it had only been the French, even with their guns and their planes, we should never have been taken and we should have carved ourselves out a splendid fief somewhere in Tonkin. But there were Viets everywhere, on every track, harassing us, following us, killing our men, driving us out of our minds. What we hoped was that they would also attack the columns of the Expeditionary Force just behind us. But they never fired a single shot at them. They were diabolically cunning. They camouflaged themselves as the legionaries came near and managed to remain unseen — the legionaries were not to suspect that they were in the jungle at all. But at the same time they thrust us back towards the French, making us an easy prey. That was how we were beaten: the Viets made use of the French and the French never knew it."

The epic of Vu Hong-khan and his Chinese was one of the best-guarded secrets of the Indochinese war. At the time nothing whatever leaked out. The high command gave the strictest orders and smothered the whole story. It was essential that it should not be known, for it was too clear a proof of the weakness of the frontier. After all, a few thousand fleeing Chinese had upset the whole mechanism of the R.C. 4 for close on two weeks. And although it had all ended well that was only because the Viets had wanted it to do so — it was because General Giap and Ho Chi Minh, analyzing the situation, had established priorities in the liquidations to be carried out — the Kuomintang and everything to do with it first and only then the Expeditionary Force.

At that period, therefore, the two opposing sides had the same enemy. The danger was not yet over. For if Vu Hong-khan's little band had almost managed to establish itself in Tonkin, what might not whole divisions do? Now there was the threat of Lu Han, the formidable warlord of Yunnan. Every time it seemed that the Nationalists were finished it became apparent that this was not the case. The collapse of an entity like China was something unimaginably vast.

Nature had made Yunnan a fortress. For the Red armies it was even farther off than Tonkin, behind which it lay — a wild corner of Asia at the foot of the Himalayas. And how hard it was to get there! For it was a huge plateau six to eight thousand feet high with precipitous edges and enormous gashes cutting one part off from another. It was all fever-ridden jungle, half-savage tribes, unexplored country: and yet tales of its fabulous wealth had always lent it a strange fascination. How many adventurers had dreamed of its opium and its precious ores!

The high-standing mass of Yunnan dominated the Asia of the deltas. The huge rivers that were the wealth of the laborious Asian masses farther down their course flowed out of Yunnan through a number of fever-haunted gorges. So its strategic importance was of the first order. It was there that the Burma Road of the Second World War came out, a road that had been built on the sides of the highest mountain ranges in the world by tens of thousands, hundreds of thousands of coolies, of whom a great many died. It was there that the Americans built their great airfields from which the Flying Fortresses took off to bomb the Japanese bases, roads and towns.

If he chose, Lu Han could hold out in his lair for weeks and months in a war along the Indochinese frontier — a war that would be terribly dangerous for the French. And it seemed that he did indeed intend to do so. At least that was what he told me.

For I went to Kunming, to his capital, by means of the airlift that brought out the tin. One good thing about the East is that trade always has its finger in every pie, however disastrous: and where there is trade there are possibilities. The one thought of the big Indochinese business houses, the banks, the import-export trade and their compradors was to get out as much as possible of the eminently desirable, eminently profitable and costly

Yunnanese tin before events made it impracticable. The profit was so high that it paid the big companies to charter all the planes available on the market. All the free-lance pilots were there, shuttling endlessly through storms, over wild, tormented country; the outward journey empty and the return loaded with ingots and perhaps a secret store of a few pounds of opium — but that was the very private perquisite of the crew.

My interview with Lu Han lasted three hours. It took place in his palace: there were armed guards everywhere. He received me in an immense, imposing drawing room, hung with portraits of naked women. He had pale green eyes in a too-smooth face with strangely receding lines, as though it had been carved by some craftsman out of a jungle wood that was too hard for him. He had the highly cultivated impassivity of the real warlord, the one who can do anything, give any order, without ever showing the slightest emotion. His voice was colorless and weary, expressionless. But his strength of will seemed unshakable. He told me of his total loyalty to Chiang Kai-shek and of his hatred for the Reds. He solemnly declared that he would not merely hold out in Yunnan — he would turn it into a stronghold from which he would launch the reconquest of China.

But what was one to believe? What was he really getting ready to do behind this screen of words? It was a terrible choice that he had to make — a choice between what he dreaded and what he hated. He loathed Chiang Kai-shek with all the strength of his primitive soul and all his hellish wounded pride. There was no possible atonement. By an unspeakable piece of treachery the Generalissimo had reduced him to the status of a puppet and had made him his prisoner. The soldiers who moved about while we were talking were loyal to Lu Han: they were his private bodyguard. But they were all he had. And in Kunming there were two Kuomintang divisions who had been there for years, to keep watch over him, to ensure that he remained powerless, and to destroy him if necessary. They had got into Kunming in 1945, when Lu Han had been stupid enough to send his troops into Tonkin for the splendid booty — troops that he never saw again — and they had stayed there ever since.*

But what could that deeply rooted, sour hatred do against his anguished dread of the advancing Communists? He had been the most savage killer of the Reds: he had put thousands, tens of thousands of them to death with the most elaborate tortures. There was a price on his head. Above all he was on Mao Tse-tung's black list, the list of the great criminals whom the

* See page 12.

people could never forgive. So it seemed that in spite of himself Lu Han was condemned to play Chiang Kai-shek's game.

At least that was the impression I took away with me. But how easy it is to be mistaken in Asia, and how far the resources of Chinese ingenuity can surpass anything that one works out for oneself! In the last analysis hatred is the ruling emotion in the Far East: hatred overcomes fear of every kind. One day Lu Han, the warlord, the feudal millionaire, the exploiter, the torturer, the very type of the enemy of the people, wired Mao: "I REPENT MOST HUMBLY. BE SO KIND AS TO RECEIVE MY SUBMISSION." The next day Mao's reply arrived. "I BELIEVE IN YOUR REMORSE. I ACCEPT YOUR SURRENDER." For the Communists, the people's interests, what is termed "the correct solution," must come before everything else; and in the immediate future Lu Han's coming over was most uncommonly useful.

From that time on everything developed very quickly. Lu Han, governor of Yunnan, this time in the name of the People's Republic, slaked his thirst for revenge. He raised the people and hurled them against the two Kuomintang divisions that had been the instrument of his humiliation. They fled. And the triumphant governor had but to welcome the Red troops when they made their very peaceful entry.

Poor Lu Han! Much later, after the war in Indochina, I met him again in Peking. They told me he was someone inportant, a deputy minister for sport. In fact the whole thing was a mockery. The person I was shown was a terrified old man, a wretched creature who recited his lesson and who did not even dare remember that he had seen me before. His shirt was threadbare. His voice quavered. Nothing whatever was left of the pitiless warlord: there was only a man, a poor frightened man who desperately assured me of his good fortune.

And yet what services he had rendered the Communists at the end of 1950 and the beginning of 1951! For it was he, Lu Han and his passionate hatred and revenge, that had won precious time for the Red army — several months at the least. Without him and his extraordinary conversion the Communists would never have been able to establish themselves so quickly and so firmly and so entirely on the whole of the Indochinese frontier. And how valuable it was, that time which was saved thanks to Lu Han! It was that very saving which allowed Mao's China to set about its new objective at once, without the loss of a day — the forming and the building-up of the Vietminh army. The result was to be the death of many and many a Frenchman on the R.C. 4 less than a year later.

But at the beginning of 1950 how happy the liquidation of the Kuomintang made the French high command! For at last this was indeed the end.

Now it was just a question of gathering in a few thousand more Nationalists, laggards who appeared in little groups here and there along the
frontier. A great many of them turned up at Laichau. But how were they
to be taken through the Vietminh corridor of the Red River, which cut
Tonkin in two? No elaborate organization was set up — they were left to
themselves, with little planes to guide them in their march through the
dangerous zone. The Viets did not attack them, as though the watchword
was "No trouble over the Chinese Nationalists." The only thing that
counted for the Viets was to be rid of them forever, and they relied on the
French to take them out of circulation for a very long while.

That is what happened. The authorities were determined to send all the
Chinese refugees — between thirty and forty thousand of them — as far
away as possible. Only the Kuomintang generals were allowed a more
agreeable kind of internment — they had the delights of an urban life,
particularly in Saigon, where they engaged in various rackets. As for the
main body, they were shipped away beyond Cochinchina to an island in the
Gulf of Siam, the island of Phuquoc. Billions of francs were needed to feed
all these people (for as it always happens, in the end the French army did
what had to be done: but did it in its own particular manner, which is both
parsimonious and at the same time exceedingly costly). Almost a whole battalion was needed to guard them. Later there was very nearly a general rebellion. The Chinese shared the island with the Viets, according to a strange
modus vivendi that they worked out themselves. On this island they built
themselves up again both politically and militarily, drilling with wooden
rifles and hiding the real ones. In the end the French guard force was virtually imprisoned by the prisoners — they no longer went outside their own
lines. This state of affairs went on for years, in the midst of the most disagreeable complications.

All that needed to be done was to send these men to Formosa, a solution
that they ardently desired and incessantly clamored for. But at the beginning there was an overriding desire not to vex Mao Tse-tung, not to irritate
him in any way. Later, when all illusions about Red China had vanished,
the authorities were still afraid of Chinese reactions and Chinese anger. It
was only a little before the end of the Indochinese war that, shaking with
alarm, they made up their minds to send these "prisoners" off to Chiang
Kai-shek: neither the Chinese nor the Vietminh Communists even bothered
to utter a serious protest. So the authorities had been trembling all these
years for nothing; they had misused these men and poured out money all in
vain.

But in 1950 there was little thought for the poor Nationalists or their fate. The high command had much more important things to occupy its mind. To begin with there was its own delight. And there was its own relief too, for after all it had been more than a little scared of the Chinese Communists. But they had behaved so well! Their correctness allowed all sorts of hopes to spring up. The thing to do was to win them over completely, to make friends of them. There was even a great plan for negotiating with Mao Tse-tung, for inducing him to abandon the Viets and allowing them to be crushed by the Expeditionary Force. Against compensation, of course. But had not General Alessandri said again and again that one could always come to an understanding with the Chinese?

In the gaiety of their hearts Carpentier and Alessandri sent reports to Paris, promising the final victory for the near future. The French government was charmed. It was much concerned with the coming elections — could not a first detachment of the Expeditionary Force be sent home before the voting to prove to the electors that the Indochinese war was over and even that it had been won? The generals in Saigon and Hanoi replied, "Very well. But it would be better to wait for a little while."

Back to Monkay

FOR my part I went back to Monkay. I wanted some firsthand experience of this "gentle" China in which they all had so much confidence.

Once more I stood on the little hill from which I had looked out over the China that was awaiting its destiny. Now its fate had been accomplished. What I saw on the other side at present was the people's "joy." Under its banners the whole of Tong Hing was a bunch of red flowers. Day and night reechoed with the firecrackers of rejoicing. Loudspeakers unendingly poured out impassioned speeches.

Captain G was at my side again. He was browner, more wiry and wrinkled than ever, and he was still just as amused. As though it were a great joke he showed me some men who had left the patriotic rejoicings and who were splashing about naked in the water of the International River. "They are guerrilla fighters," he told me. "They are always bathing there. A fortnight ago I had a report that some unknown men were peacefully swimming about in the frontier stream. I made inquiries: they were Communists. That is how we learned that they had arrived, for we never saw them enter Tong Hing."

The occupation had been so discreet, he told me, that nothing had been noticed at all until the first red flag went up. It was a masterpiece of the Chinese way of carrying things out in three separate stages. In the first place Tong Hing's Nationalist soldiers, every sort from the commanding colonel's bodyguard to the ragged militia men, went aboard junks by night and vanished. Then the town's most prominent citizens informed the guerrillas of the Hundred Thousand Hills that they could make their solemn entry without the risk of any disagreeable clashes. Following this good advice, they triumphantly marched in: the vacuum between the two regimes only lasted a quarter of an hour. Lin Piao's regulars were still several days' march away. When they in their turn took possession of Tong Hing it was an even greater triumph, a prodigious display.

"A little later the Red authorities sent me a message saying they would like to establish friendly relations with the French. My pleasure, alas, was quite spoiled by my shame. Obeying my orders, I had closed the international bridge and refused entry to a band of Nationalists who had appeared from God knows where. They begged to be let in, and then they tried to force their way through: both in vain. The wretched men stayed there clinging to the bars and calling out until the Communists arrived and seized them. It seems that they were shot."

But on the whole things were going very well from Captain G's point of view. Even trade, on which he raised a little private tax for his secret funds, had started up again. Monsieur Chong, Monkay's millionaire, was once more sending his French goods into China.

"A little while ago," said the captain, "he reported to me that he was delivering huge quantities of gasoline — thousands of gallons. That could only mean one thing: the Red army was getting ready to invade Hainan, still held by the Nationalists. But that great island commands the entrance to the Gulf of Tonkin and it threatens all the lines of communication by sea between Saigon and Hanoi. Hainan in the hands of the Communists would be very dangerous for the Expeditionary Force in Tonkin — they are down at the bottom of a blind alley and they might be cut off from everything. I brooded over it. To go on letting the gasoline through meant helping them to capture Hainan, and that was a crime. But stopping it meant cutting off the flow of money into my secret funds, which just have to be well fed at this juncture: so that too would be an error. In the end, when I had thoroughly turned it over in my head I said to Monsieur Chong, 'As a good businessman, you must carry out your bargain.'

"Presently the Chinese bank of the International River was covered with two-hundred-liter barrels. Three or four hundred motor-driven junks were tied up close by — an invasion fleet, a little armada. It was obvious that the expedition was about to leave. And then suddenly there was a catastrophe. A huge fire broke out in the gasoline. A cloud of black smoke whirled up into the sky. Men shouted and escaped as well as they could — some were burned, no doubt. The flames ran towards the junks, but how could their crews maneuver them? The shells and bombs that had been piled up there were exploding in every direction. You would have thought the place was being bombarded. Most of the junks did at last get away, but the town was in danger.

"Of course I had had some well-timed detonators hidden in Monsieur Chong's wares: but what I had not known was that explosives had been stacked among all the gasoline barrels. In fact the stroke was almost too successful.

"Houses began to burn. The Communists had no pumps. I offered ours: they were accepted. Tong Hing was saved, thanks to the intervention of the French. For some days the political commissars overwhelmed me with smiles. I don't think they have ever suspected what really happened."

Some days later Captain G said to me, "You can leave when you like. Everything is going to be quiet here for some months. The people over the way are too busy to give any trouble. All my agents say the same thing — the Chinese have set to work to build up the Viets."

He told me that a few weeks after they reached the frontier, behaving so correctly, the Chinese had launched their plan of help for Ho Chi Minh. It was done with all the unremitting method of the Asians, with incredible assiduity, orderliness and zeal. There were huge camps where, under the supervision of thousands of Chinese officers and NCO's, Giap's troops were turned into real wartime units. Battalions, regiments and divisions would come out of these camps, very thoroughly trained and equipped, ready for battle. There was no difficulty about arming them — the Chinese only had to give the Viets the rifles, machine guns and mortars they had taken from the Nationalists: all this materiel was of very good quality and the great mass of it was American. That was not all. Coolies were already carrying off heavy loads to build up stocks of food and ammunition in secret dumps, camouflaged and guarded, just inside Chinese territory but still very near the R.C. 4. Elsewhere, in the mountains of Kwangtung and Kwangsi, hordes of men, women and children were digging the earth with their hands to make roads that would come out at strategic points on the frontier. It was an all-out effort. How much time would it take? A few months, in Captain G's opinion. In their own way, although they moved with two different kinds of slowness, the pace of a walking man and that of dialectic advance, the Asian Communists went fast, very fast.

"All Indochina is hoodwinked because these Chinese have 'behaved properly,' pulling up short at the frontier," he said. "Peking has devised a 'correct solution': Peking has come to a decision. The first objective is to expel the French from Indochina. The tactics have been decided upon, too. An attack by Mao's army is unnecessary and it would be clumsy. The Viets are perfectly adequate, so long as they are well trained and well driven.

"The whole thing is decided, I tell you. The Chinese will pitilessly carry out what they have decided, as they have decided it and at the decided time. And they will go on until the end, until they have accomplished what they intended — our defeat and our expulsion. We shall never capture a single one of Mao's soldiers; and yet in the end it will be the Chinese who beat us, the Viets being no more than their tools.

"From now on the Indochinese war is above all a Chinese war. But they don't choose to know that in Saigon. For if it were known, imagine what would have to be done — imagine how people would have to prepare their minds for doing it. In the first place they would have to think everything out all over again.

"Hurry back to Saigon. For while Tonkin is being lulled into a false sense of security, Cochinchina will come to the boil. The enemy needs to pin the Expeditionary Force down far to the south so that he can get on with his preparations here."

The battle of Saigon

I WAS back in Cochinchina. And everything was happening as the Monkay captain had foretold. Scarcely had the People's China settled down peacefully next to Tonkin than the battle of Saigon began — a great battle of terrorism, murder and torture. Nothing was spared.

The worthy Frenchmen of the banks, the import-export trade and the administration did not understand. Why should they suspect that this outbreak was the direct consequence of an event that had taken place a thousand miles away — the arrival of the Chinese on the frontier? Nobody had taken any notice of it: nobody had thought about it.

Saigon was a city in which the piaster was no longer a shield. It was an extraordinary spectacle, this city in the process of liquefaction, with ever-present fear, with the police disarmed and the French detectives ordered not to show themselves.

To tell the truth, a deliquescence of such a kind would never have been possible without Vietnamese independence, the "Pignon Independence." Having long sulked in the mountains, Bao Dai had recently set his seal upon this independence by coming to Saigon. Along the three miles from the airport to the town the procession traveled between two hedges of heavily armed policemen, one every five yards, with his back to the road so as to face the squalid plots and the reed huts from which danger might come. A dreary ceremony took place at the inevitable town hall, with the inevitable Vietnamese and French notables. Not a scrap of color in the streets, in spite of the order to hang out flags. Not a moving creature either, nothing but an emptiness and a silence that meant contempt. Yet trucks brought in a crowd of "enthusiastic demonstrators" at five piasters a head. The sects were kind enough to display their good will. A few Hoahao warriors marched by, wearing enormous green helmets shaped like chamberpots. The Caodaists were represented by the "nation" of the faithful, men and women all in step, waving the lumps of bread that had just been issued to them. Trucks took all these people away again. Bao Dai, having displayed his boredom, returned to Dalat.

Meanwhile, His Majesty was in need of a head of government. He was tired of General Xuan, the soldier educated at the Ecole Polytechnique who led the provisional government. Xuan was an agreeable, smooth, flattering creature, a mild old gentleman who might well have loved the quiet delights of angling. He was always happy to do a good turn; and with a cheerfulness that was almost dignified, so well was it assumed, he helped the Emperor to conceal certain delicate love affairs under the appearance of jaunts in the country. But at the same time he intrigued against him with everybody, even with the French ministers, to whom he wrote, "Bao Dai won't work." So Bao Dai, now that it was a question of the first real government of the time of independence, chose someone else. It amused him to pick Nguyen Phan-long.

Nguyen Phan-long was a spiritualist somewhat given to Caodaism, one who had been involved in terrible struggles around the holy basket in which the Caodaists received communications from the other world: he had been granted some messages of unusual splendor from Victor Hugo, in verse — though indeed he was always suspected of having made them up himself. A very odd character: a needy journalist, highly literate, with a touch of something like genius, writing the best kind of imitation French. For the last thirty years he had belonged to every shade of opinion, and he had practiced every kind of vice, too — but pleasantly. He smoked opium, he drank far too much, he was a passionate gambler, he was debauched, and he was overburdened with wives and children. In his own way he was rather a great man. He was ugly enough to make you shudder, his face having been much disarranged by an old wound, and he was cross-grained and bitter because of all the wretchedness of the past and the insults he had suffered; but his effrontery reached truly sublime heights. It was said that he offered his services to the French in 1945: they thought his price too high and scorned him. In his vexation he then became the mouthpiece of that half-bourgeois, half-crypto and wholly business-loving nationalism that gave Saigon its real color. For years he savaged the colonialists in his newspaper, spoiling their breakfast as they sat at the Pagoda. It was not that he really hated them — he was both entirely Vietnamese and entirely French, a state of affairs that provided him with a very complicated personality. But he wanted his revenge.

So what unspeakable delight it was for him, the scorned outcast, to be in power! He profited by the situation to the full, without the slightest shame — but that was perfectly usual. Straightaway he took for himself the four "profitable" ministries, those which had copious secret funds. One evening a French journalist suddenly came upon him in his office when he thought he was alone. He was squatting in front of a wide-open safe with his big head deep inside. And his hands were incessantly feeling, smoothing, petting the great wads of money in a kind of happy bewilderment, the very height of sensual ecstasy. It was now he who was the giver-out, he who had begged and cadged so long!

But the most important thing now was the implementation of independence. And it was to this Nguyen Phan-long whom they had so humiliated that the French were obliged to hand over their services, even those they valued most, such as the criminal investigation department and the police (though they still kept a secondary investigation department under Monsieur Perrier for the "protection" of the Expeditionary Force). But the Sûreté building itself, at the top of the Rue Catinat, a few yards from the cathedral, was transferred to the Vietnamese. For the whole of Vietnam this building was the symbol of French "oppression": at all events, countless nationalists had been taken there by the French police, both long ago and in the very recent past. And Nguyen Phan-long practiced the doctrine of the "outstretched hand," basing himself on the supposition that the Vietminh were primarily nationalists and that an understanding with them was quite certain. On his orders harshness was replaced by the mildest possible treatment. Thus, as head of the Vietnamese investigation department, he appointed a scholarly lawyer who insisted upon gentleness. This man's first action was to order the release of all those held on suspicion or with a charge against them, and to empty all the prisons. He forbade the rougher kind of questioning and all the little ways of inducing suspects to talk. Now the way for a policeman to show his zeal was to know nothing and to arrest nobody; and they were all the more zealous since they were afraid for their lives — they were no longer allowed to carry weapons, for persuasion was to take the place of tommy guns and revolvers.

Poor Nguyen Phan-long! The profoundly experienced schemer, the profligate rake devoid of illusions, was astonishingly simple-minded. For he was sincere, just as all the fat bourgeois of Cochinchina were sincere. These worthy Asian profiteers were convinced that Nguyen Binh, the Resistance, the Nambo Committee, Ho Chi Minh and Giap and the Tongbo Committee were all going to fall into their arms at the first hint of welcome! Yet these gentlemen really should have known the Vietminh and their implacability. But the capitalist bourgeoisie is fated, in Vietnam as elsewhere, not to see the glaring reality in front of their noses — the reality that bangs into them every day of the week. There was also vanity involved and a kind of delight in getting their own back: it affected all these collaborators with the French; for all collaboration has its own lacerating thorns. They were convinced that in the twinkling of an eye they were going to outdo the high commissioner's office and the Expeditionary Force a thousand times over: in a matter of days they would resolve all problems and put an end to the war by means of a universal reconciliation. How could their advice, their pleas, possibly fail? Besides, these wealthy men had an overwhelming desire to enjoy their money, their privileges and their position in peace — and they were quite sure they were going to keep it all. A minister, a rich landowner who had not dared set foot on his estate for years, said to me, "It's all going to be brought to an end: and I shall get back my rice fields, my *nha-qués* and my rents."

But the euphoria of the first days of independence was shattered at the very beginning of 1950. Nguyen Phan-long had had peace proposals taken to Nguyen Binh. The reply was stunning. A few days later the Voice of the Nambo, Nguyen Binh's radio station, roared out that this independence was still, was more than ever, a betrayal. The reckoning day was coming and all the ministers of the regime, all the civil servants and all the profiteers would have to answer for their deeds and pay the penalty. The settlement was very near at hand, and it would take place during the offensive that was about to deliver Saigon to the Vietminh.

This was Nguyen Binh's great moment. To all intents and purposes Saigon was as it were offered to the Vietminh, and Nguyen Binh decided to make the most of his opportunity. He was acting on Ho Chi Minh's orders, but this was also his dream, his life's ambition. He was carried away by passion. He staked everything he possessed. In the final reckoning, a year later, he paid for his defeat with his life; for he was to lose — to lose through having wanted too much and for having gone too far.

But things had not reached that stage yet. In January 1950 he was very nearly triumphant — victory was almost in his grasp. How brilliantly he managed to exploit the situation in those few weeks, profiting by Nguyen Phan-long's illusions to corrupt everything and to install his own men secretly everywhere! All at once Nguyen Phan-long realized that he no longer had a police force, nor an administration, nor anything else. The men were still physically there, as good state employees were required to be; but instead of obeying him they were obeying Nguyen Binh. He had thrown away his weapons and delivered himself up, having first tied his own hands and feet. In a few days he passed, like all the other bourgeois, from silly optimism to abject terror.

That was how the battle of Saigon began. It was not even an armed rising, for in that case the French tanks and soldiers would have crushed it. And the whole point was that the Expeditionary Force should not be able to interfere, should have no pretext for doing so. The intention was that the French should find themselves faced with an accomplished fact, a state of affairs that they could not prevent — an increasingly Vietminh Saigon, a wholly Vietminh Saigon, and lastly an officially Vietminh Saigon.

There were known tactics for bringing this about — total revolutionary struggle, continually increasing terrorism and agitation carried to the point at which the Saigon of the piaster should drop like a ripe fruit. Every hour and every minute the city was to become more and more Communist, a de facto Red town. The power of the Vietminh was to work like a quicksand, drawing everything inexorably down. On the one hand the whole organization had to be dismantled, and on the other built up again. Finally the Resistance, the hidden force, was to rise nearer and nearer to the surface until at last it alone was the master. Such was the plan: the taming of two or three million men — or their liberation, whichever you prefer.

January, February and March were devoted to getting everything into position and to taking up action stations. Then came the attack.

Saigon in the hands of the Vietminh

ON April 28, 1950 I was peacefully walking down the Rue Catinat at about eight o'clock in the morning, with the intention of breakfasting at the Pagoda. At the corner of the Rue d'Espagne I collided with some French detectives, recognizable by their shirts worn outside their trousers and their little moustaches (the hep-heroic was the style favored by the police in Indochina). One of them called out to me, "Blood on the front page." And indeed I had almost trodden in a drying pool of it. "It was Bazin," said the detective. "What's left of him has been taken off to the hospital. As full of holes as a sieve. He's dying at this minute."

It had been a perfect assassination, a trained killer's job. At about seven-twenty a well-dressed Annamese with a briefcase in his hand was strolling up and down outside the place where Bazin lived. Bazin came out at half-past, as he did every day, to go to his office. He was a few steps from his car. On seeing him the killer faded into a doorway and took an automatic out of his briefcase. When Bazin was within a yard he calmly squeezed the trigger. He lowered the weapon, still firing, following Bazin in his collapse. Three or four other armed Vietnamese were keeping watch twenty yards away. The crowd in the street had fled. As soon as it was over the killers vanished in a fast car.

This Bazin had been the head of the French Sûreté's shock force. It was he who carried on the war against the Vietminh Sûreté's shock force in Saigon. I had been in his office a week before. "I am fighting for my life," he said to me. "Every day the Vietminh radio says 'Bazin, you are going to die.' I'm on the top of the black list, the people who are to be wiped out. My killers have already arrived in Saigon. I've only a few days to get them, otherwise . . ."

He was a little narrow-shouldered man with a ferrety face. His trade was repression, and he was very good at it indeed. He was a disturbing figure, this detective who had become too much part of his calling, so that neither cruelty nor pity counted for him any more, but only the smooth running of the service. He was completely unfeeling and completely honest, and his memory never let him down: he knew all the thousands of yellow-faced strongarm men of Saigon. One part of his life was devoted to building up perfect files: another to interrogating, to extracting information. The rest of the time he spent in making use of what he had learned. This he did amidst exploding grenades and pistol shots in the lowest quarters of the town, around the irrigation canals, in the fantastic surroundings of the Saigon of the gangsters.

Bazin was always calm; he was rather humorous and he had an iron nerve. Yet his world was an evil and a bloody one. He died the death that was ordained for him. And he was mourned by his subordinates, the Vietnamese whom he had trained for the most sinister tasks. They swore to revenge him.

When I saw Bazin he already knew that the game was lost. "They are giving me up to the Viets with my hands tied. My hands are tied just when the Viets are going to take over Saigon. The whole town is riddled with Viet cells. They are everywhere. They kill anyone they choose and they make everyone pay taxes. You can't name a single place that hasn't got its Vietminh agent. Clean through it all there is a clandestine administration running parallel with the official one. It is set up in the government and in the ministries, and in every district, every street and every house. There are thousands of networks giving their daily orders and carrying out their propaganda, spying and tax gathering almost openly. But you know all that.

"What is new is that the Nambo Committee has drawn up battle orders for Saigon, hundreds of pages, with chapters and sections and subsections. It is very long. Everything is foreseen. It has directives for all the kinds of network — the political committees, the economic committees, the committees for working up zeal and enthusiasm, the security squads. From now on it is no longer a question of exploiting the city, but of capturing it by means of a people's campaign.

"Murder used to be just a form of persuasion. A few hundred murder committees were plenty to keep the people under control — to keep them frightened. But now Nguyen Binh is carrying the war into Saigon and he counts on murder to win it.

"It is Nguyen Binh who gives the orders at the top level. But for working out the details of this patriotic liquidation campaign he has set up a special organization only five miles out of the town. Its headquarters is in the village of Tan Nhut and the head man is Tran Van-tra. It is in fact a huge ministry of death."

Bazin told me how the Vietminh had created the unit called Battalion 905 to fight the battle of assassination all through the huge city: its members were members of a suicide squad and professional killers as well. Their work was concerned with shadowing, gathering secret information, setting up Vietminh cells, blackmail and murders of the second category, presenting tax demands, throwing grenades, arranging strikes and riots: they were established throughout the whole area thanks to their hideouts and their extensive connections — they held meetings and received orders in every part of Saigon. It was through them that the Vietminh brought its weight to bear on the whole city. Battalion 905's main task was to see to the ordinary, small-time traitors, the commonplace people's enemies — the sort that were liquidated without reference higher up. For the fine work, the precise killing, of those who had been formally condemned to death, the outstanding enemies put on the black list by Nguyen Binh and the Nambo Committee, very highly specialized killers were brought in. The Vietminh shock security force was the instrument used for these important liquidations; and it was commanded by Le Van-linh. It consisted of a few hundred carefully selected men, pumped full of fanaticism, and trained to

kill scientifically by German deserters in a special camp in the Plain of
Reeds. This shock force had its base outside Saigon. Its killers were only
sent into the city for clearly defined tasks. They arrived in the most
ordinary, peaceful way one by one, coming on foot or in Chinese buses,
dressed as *nha-qués* or clerks. They carried nothing — no weapons, no
papers: and if they chanced to be questioned during their journey they gave
any name that came to their minds. How could it be checked, seeing that
there were no such things as birth certificates in the country, and that
identity scarcely existed?

Each killer was told only the address to which he was to go. It might be
anywhere at all, a straw hut or a rich merchant's house or a minister's
office. There he would find a leader, companions, orders, automatics and
tommy guns. The whole job had been prepared for the killers. They were
given files and exact plans. The victims' daily program had been noted hour
by hour: drawings of the relevant places had been made. Relations had
been established among the condemned man's servants and employees. At
the last moment a car was stolen and disguised. When the men of the shock
force arrived all they had to do was to add the last touch.

To begin with there was a rehearsal. Then came the performance itself.
The murder team always consisted of four or five men. The job was done
either openly in the street or else in the victim's house, and in that case the
killers slipped in with the complicity of the servants. One minute was
enough. After it was over the killers always stayed a few days in some
particularly secret hideout: then they left Saigon just as they had come.

From time to time one branch or another of this murder organization
had been destroyed, but never more. And it was always built up again at
once. The division of labor and the sealing-off of the various sections had
been carried to a high point. So when Bazin's men made a capture, questioning was virtually useless, for the man knew so little. And even that little
had no value. For the action group and the network that he belonged to
would be dissolved immediately only to be repaired a few days later. The
Viet organization was never disrupted: if a few links were broken they
were always repaired at once.

"How can we win?" Bazin had said to me. "We are surrounded by
corruption, impotence, cowardice, complicity, and betrayal."

After Bazin's death Nguyen Binh was the law giver in Saigon. It was a
law that was to last two months: for the city belonged to the Vietminh —
or very nearly.

The bourgeois, both yellow and white, hid themselves. They realized
there was no possible defense for them now that the police were de-

moralized, the civil service reduced to a mere shadow and the French authorities compelled to watch a disaster they could not stop, for since independence they were forbidden to intervene in Saigon. And as the machinery of government fell to pieces all the Vietminh of the Saigon underground swarmed out into the open: they were innumerable; they came from everywhere; and they did whatever they chose.

Now crowds carrying red flags flooded through the heart of the town, roaring "Long live Ho Chi Minh." Speakers climbed onto the roofs of cars and harangued the people, urging them to violent action. One day the crowd set fire to the great central market. The flames destroyed the stalls and the buildings, leaving nothing but a blackened shell. Nobody dared react or make any move at all. This seemed to be the end.

Nguyen Binh increased the atmosphere of dread. There were riots, one after another; and they were called "revolutionary days." Each had its own name. One was the Fortnight of Revenge. Another the Day for Acclaiming the People's Democracies. Another was Ho Chi Minh's Day. Every time the Vietminh radio gave out the watchword in violent, threatening terms. Every time it ordered a general strike. The men from the Vietminh cells went into every hut and cabin, ordering the shopkeepers to close and the people to come out into the streets: and woe betide the man who did not obey.

On the morning of the appointed day the town would seem stone dead. The Annamese shops were locked. The French avoided going out. The streets were empty except for a few nervous police. There were also groups of young men and women who had come on their bicycles: they were scattered about the city, and they waited, often lying down on the pavement. These were the members of the shock teams, and their job was to stir up the masses. Suddenly, at the given time to within a second, their groups all formed up again and they all flooded at the same moment into the emptiness, starting the riot. Within a few minutes a human tidal wave broke over the city, a Red fury: for an enormous host of people mysteriously appeared, rising up from everywhere. Before the authorities knew what was going on the demonstration would be at its height — flags, tremendous noise, speeches. Meanwhile all the rest of the town would be rigid with terror.

Each time it seemed as though the people were going to carry everything before them. But that was not the "correct solution." As quickly as the crowd had gathered, and in the same way, with orders from the same men, it dispersed. But that very evening the whole town, the entire population, would have to carry out its autocriticism, a term implying confession of error, expression of regret and determination to adhere more exactly to the true doctrine for the future. From the cells the agents went out to threaten the lukewarm, the people who had not obeyed properly or who had tried to cheat — for example, the tradesmen who had not shut their shops completely but had left a door ajar so that customers could slip in quietly.

Bombs exploded everywhere. Every night the army's outer posts were probed: tracer bullets blazed like fireworks in the sky and one went to sleep to the sound of mortar fire. Nguyen Binh's radio, Voice of Nambo, announced worse disruption. It said that food supplies for Saigon were going to be cut off for four months: everyone should build up a reserve of a hundred pounds of rice and two of salt. The speaker also stated with grim delight that the punishment of the traitors and torturers had begun — the execution teams had moved into the city and they were about their work.

After this came the endless reading of the endless list of those who had been condemned; and often, after a name, there was the observation "He has paid the penalty." The Vietminh also announced the prices put on various heads. Bao Dai's was quoted at ten thousand piasters, a ridiculously small sum that was a mark of contempt.

I remember Perrier, the former head of all the criminal investigation departments who was still the chief of the little French Sûreté. Reactionary himself, he had always been the generous and tolerant patron of any deadbeat revolutionary or "intellectual" who might wash up at the Press Club. He was numbered on the Vietminh list of traitors. Every time anything happened he arrived in a jeep with a radio aerial, together with two assistants armed to the teeth with grenades and tommy guns. He looked finer than ever, a splendid figure, blue-eyed, elegant, though somewhat touched by age, or at least by fatigue. A sheriff in the best kind of Western, you would have said. But the frank, piercing look, the manly voice, the carelessness were all put on. Every time I met him he said, "Now So-and-so has been killed. My turn is coming close. There's nothing, nothing whatever, that you can do against killers like this. They will get me whenever they want to."

Yet they never touched Perrier. No doubt Nguyen Binh did not consider him dangerous. Not that Nguyen Binh had any respect left for anyone: he was even setting about the capitalists — he had Ewans and Lebas liquidated, and they were the kings of tobacco in Indochina, owners of important factories. At nightfall, between Cholon and Saigon, a whistle stopped their car, and killers disguised as policemen opened fire. The Viets

certainly decided upon this killing to please the workers, who had griev-
ances against both men.

But it was above all the Vietnamese Excellencies who were nearly dead
with fear: most of them no longer went out but stayed in their houses
surrounded by bodyguards. Those who were forced to leave their shelter
had their cars armored. A very fat, very simple-minded young man, the
head of the Vietnamese information agency, himself stuck thick sheets of
rubber all over his Buick. He must have been in an extraordinary state of
funk to have labored so, using his very own hands!

In the midst of this deliquescence there came the shattering news that
Nguyen Binh had also launched his great offensive right across the whole
of Cochinchina. This one was a military offensive. Scores of French posts
were surrounded: whole towns, Travinh, Soctrang and Cantho were
threatened. Nguyen Binh had managed to bring together eight thousand
regulars. It was this army that he was hurling against the French forces
scattered along the bends of the Mekong in a decisive battle for the south.

It was a tragic situation — Cochinchina in the midst of war: Saigon in a
state of utter chaos. Even Monsieur Pignon's famous weapon, prosperity
for all, had jammed. In a few days prices had doubled. If that went on,
what would be the point of making piasters?

The degree of anarchy in Saigon was so great that the school children,
rising in revolt, very nearly took the town. All the boys and girls in the
secondary schools declared that they too were Vietminh fighters. The
educational establishments became Red citadels in which the teachers no
longer dared hold classes but where the pupils held meetings, carrying out
sessions of autocriticism and learning how to "acquire enthusiasm." One
day all these young people went in procession to the palace of the
Vietnamese government. The worthy Huu was now minister of the interior.
Unctuous, solemn and fatherly, he went out alone to meet them, without
any protection: were not these boys and girls the children of the best
bourgeois families? He preached obedience and good behavior in Confu-
cian terms; but they received him with stones and catcalls, and in spite of
his fatness he had to run for it as fast as he could. The children roared and
bawled. There were not even any policemen to put them down.

This time it was really too much, for all the rules of traditional morality
had been mocked and swept aside. Huu, the honorable ancestor, had been
insulted; and in his person all parents had been insulted too. If filial
obedience no longer existed the whole of Vietnamese society must crumble.
The time had come for the defense of the ancient ways.

The middle classes of Saigon, the governing bourgeoisie who had made advances to Nguyen Binh, suddenly realized that their own skins were at stake and that wealth itself was threatened. As soon as they discovered this they grew very savage. There was no longer any question of the slightest "gentleness"; no question of the Vietminh's nationalism. Now it was to be repression with blood and torture, a hundred times crueler than the French of earlier days.

It all developed very fast. Nguyen Phan-long, that crooked genius who had shown himself such a simpleton as prime minister, was replaced by Father Huu, a veteran of the old school. And what came to power with Huu was money, the landowners, the confederation of the rich. Possessors who fear for their possessions are cruel, and nowhere are they crueler than in Asia.

Huu gave press conferences. His eyes were so deeply buried in his flesh that you could not see them. He clapped his tiny hands together to emphasize his more pompous remarks; after thoughtful silences he burst into giggles, choking and gurgling. He was a mandarin of the capitalist era.

And it was in a gasping, coughing burst of merriment that he announced an astonishing piece of news: he had just appointed the *doc phu** Tam head of the Vietnamese Sûreté. This was the man who had hitherto been scorned and reviled by the whole of bourgeois Saigon as the "Tiger of Cailay," the "Executioner."

It was Tam who was to win the battle of Saigon in a few weeks, and with ridiculous ease. He destroyed all Nguyen Binh's networks, those organizations that the French had struggled against so furiously for so many years; and the work was so well done that the Vietminh never really won a foothold in Saigon again. But to accomplish this Tam used the traditional methods of Asia; and they are so cheerfully horrible that they are hard to describe.

The Tiger of Cailay

A FEW days later I was in the Sûreté building in the Rue Catinat, in Tam's enormous office. He was a little dried-up, gnarled creature who could scarcely be seen behind his imposing desk — his chair was not high enough. What a benign and yet awkward air he had, with old-fashioned spectacles riding on his nose, his ancient wrinkles, his stammer and his long, drooping arms that were so strangely joined to his tiny body. He smiled at me — the good-natured grin of a rough, unpolished *nha-qué.*

* *Doc phu:* a title in the mandarin hierarchy equivalent to head of a province.

As it happened we were old acquaintances. I knew that this was the way he had smiled all his life: it was the cheerful smile with which he wiped men out in the name of law and order. Tam was primarily an instrument for putting down, for crushing. His was a fatherly kind of repression, carried out with strength and cunning, with devilish boldness and with the pleasure that boldness confers. He devoted himself entirely to his cleansing task, and his conscience was perfectly clear.

That was how he became the Tiger of Cailay — Cailay being a little town at the far end of the Plain of Reeds. In 1940, when he was no more than a simple administrative delegate, that was where he crushed the bands of the first Red peasants' rising. Before this meeting in the Rue Catinat he had often told me of his exploit. "I only had twenty militia men. There were thousands of rebellious nha-qués marching on Cailay with their machetes. And their hatred. I went to meet them with my men, but the sight of my little band sent the crowd into a fury. I told the soldiers to go away. Walking forward alone, I began to talk to the mob as cheerfully as I could, chatting first with this fellow, then with that. After a while I said, 'Let's have a game,' and I brought a camera out of my pocket — they had no idea of what it was. I took several shots, as though I were playing. Later I was able to identify all the ringleaders perfectly easily and have them arrested and punished."

It seems that Tam did the punishing with his own hands, shooting the principal rebels with a revolver.

"At least I did learn about Communism and how to detect its presence," he told me. "I discovered that where people no longer went to the pagodas and where the notables dared not send in denunciations, Communism was already in control, and what had to be done was to apply the red-hot iron at once."

He was pitiless to others and he found it natural that his enemies should be pitiless to him. How cheerfully, with what satisfaction, he told me about the tortures he had undergone at the hands of the Kempetai in 1945. The water torture. The bastinado. The fan — the Japanese police had tied him to a big electric fan and had spun him like a whipping top, using their belts. After ten times around he fainted, and they sponged his face with cold water to bring him to so that they could begin again.

"Yet the Japanese could make fine gestures," said Tam. "They understood magnanimity. Once I said to them, "You people make a cult of friendship. I owe the French everything. So why do you blame me for being loyal to them?" After that they never once tortured me again."

Later Tam was the prisoner of the Vietminh in the Saigon central prison (this was during the first months of 1945, before the town was retaken by the French troops). All the arrested bourgeois truckled to their jailers, all except Tam, who said, "I am in the hands of my worst enemies: but I shall not bow down to them." They wrenched off one of his fingers. They killed two of his sons. Tam told me of this last incident as though it were a mere fact, an occurrence that had nothing to do with him. Yet he loved his children.

In the days of d'Argenlieu and then of Bollaert, Tam was a minister in the government of Cochinchina. When the other Vietnamese Excellencies set the Vietminh prisoners free they did so in the course of moving ceremonies. Not so Tam: he reviled them, bawling, "I know perfectly well that you're only a lot of scum and that you will go straight back to the Communists. But I don't give a damn. And I am letting you out for the very good reason that I despise you and that I do not fear you in the very least."

The Tam that I met once again in the Sûreté in the Rue Catinat looked more than ever like a minor clerk: he was even more filled with zeal and delight. "The position is clear. Against me, I have the Red security force with its seventeen posts and its connections everywhere, all working at full blast. On my side, counting the things I can really rely on, I only have this office we are sitting in at this moment. My Sûreté is rotten through and through and my informers are too frightened to give any information. For years the French let their agents go bad without even noticing it — they were betrayed inside the very Sûreté itself. I am alone: but that is of no importance. Straightaway I saw that there were cells throughout this building — that the place had been organized. So I am doing what has to be done about my detectives and my stool pigeons: that alone will entirely change the conditions of the battle in Saigon. For as soon as I have proper tools to work with — a purged Sûreté and informers whose confidence has come back and who give solid, worthwhile information — trust me, I shall make good use of them. I shall smash the Vietminh in Saigon in three months. The French could do nothing: everything they touched was faked. But for me it will be easy, since there will be no faking any more."

Tam told me how he was going to set about it. In the first place he would have to build up a little reliable Sûreté inside the huge contaminated organization. For that he was turning to the men who had been with the murdered Bazin, above all to Mai Huu-xuan. There was no one who inspired more dread than this Xuan: he had a toadlike head, both smooth and swollen; his face had no expression of any kind; and he was far too polite. He was intelligent and cruel, with a cold, unmoved, skillful cruelty that he exercised with none of Tam's delight in the confrontation of man with man, executioner with victim. Compared with Xuan, Tam was humane. All the Vietnamese, Vietminh or not, shuddered at the idea of falling into Xuan's hands. But he was also an exceedingly able policeman: Bazin had found him in the gutter long ago and had trained him up lovingly; and to the French technique Xuan had added all the instincts of Asia.

Mai Huu-xuan's job was to screen all the members of the Sûreté. He told Tam that his secretary (a secretary provided by the Sûreté) was a Vietminh, and that all his most secret orders were therefore known to the Nambo Committee within a few hours. Tam summoned the man; and in circumstances of this kind Tam could be frightening. He leaped up, seized the fellow, and roared at him (when he spoke Vietnamese he bellowed like a wild animal, although in French he had a little gentle voice), shouting "You are a Communist: I have the proofs. Confess." The secretary said, "Yes." His hovel was searched and they discovered the carbon copies of all the secret notes, bundles of them. He had been sending information to Nguyen Binh every day for years. He was executed that evening, after he had told all he knew.

"The Sûreté has already been cleaned up pretty well," Tam told me a week later. "They are afraid of me now. Next I have to make myself feared in Saigon — more feared than the Viets. All the professional informers have taken to working for them, and I am up against a wall of silence. But once they start thinking that I am the more dangerous of the two then I shall very soon know everything — they will tell *me* everything. I am going to be unpleasant."

Presently quantities of dead bodies were found lying about in the streets. They were full of stab wounds and on their backs they had a notice with the reasons for their condemnation. This was the Vietminh's usual way of dealing with the execution of "traitors": but the wording of the notice was unusual. It read, "So-and-so is a Communist murderer executed for his crimes." Every time the men were members of the Battalion 905 suicide squad, captured shortly before by Tam's forces.

"Things are going better," Tam told me. "The informers are beginning to work again."

I observed that he did not take enough precautions for his own safety. Anyone at all, coming into his office, could shoot him as he sat there behind his paper-covered desk. Shaking his head Tam mildly replied, "Oh yes, yes, I take care all right. As you speak there is a pistol trained on you. Look, there it is, in front of me, solidly fixed under the desk. It is always loaded. I need only make the very smallest movement for the bullet to go through the chair you are sitting in. It is all taken care of."

One day Tam was obviously in a hurry. As soon as our talk was over he got up. I shall always remember the greedy way he rubbed his hands in little nervous jerks, over and over again. Still rubbing them he said to me, with a kind of joyful excitement, "I must beg you to excuse me. But my men next door are questioning a Viet who was arrested yesterday. He doesn't want to talk. I really must go and see to it."

I often went back to see Tam. Our relations were always as affable as could be. Sometimes a high-ranking member of the Sûreté interrupted us to murmur something in Vietnamese into his ear. What furious roarings if the news was bad! But generally Tam would make a little gesture whose meaning was perfectly clear — prison, the question chamber, execution: a whole vocabulary.

And in July, exactly at the end of the three months, Tam's victory was complete. For his Vietminh opposite number, his Communist equivalent, that Le Van-linh who was at the head of the Red Sûreté as he was at the head of the White, was captured and in his power. And Le Van-linh's whole organization was decimated.

A man came to see Tam and said to him, "I want sixty thousand piasters. In exchange I will give you the address of the villa where Le Van-linh is staying at this very moment."

Tam replied, "I shall keep you in prison until I know whether what you say is true or not. I must have the address at once. If it is the right one you shall have the money: if not, you die."

The man did not waver. "I am not lying. The villa is in the Rue des Frères-Louis. But wait until night time before you do anything. Le Van-linh is often out during the day."

That afternoon Tam borrowed the sixty thousand piasters from Perrier, the head of the French Sûreté. He did not have enough money himself because as usual the prime minister, who was also minister of the interior, kept all the secret funds for himself. Perrier was very doubtful. It seemed to him that it was a great deal for such an uncertain business. But Tam insisted. "It is serious. I know the smell of these things, and it smells right to me." In the end Perrier let himself be swayed and he produced the money.

In the evening the villa was surrounded and rushed. It was a complete surprise. There was no defense. Le Van-linh was in bed and he was still asleep when he was taken, together with three killers. The Vietminh had completely transformed the place: behind a bookcase there was a little room that served as an arsenal — it contained the automatics and the tommy guns that had been used in the most recent attacks. Another room was full of the files of people who were to be executed: the way each one spent his time was already noted hour by hour. The biggest file was on Tam himself. The top specialist, the ace killer, was to arrive from the Plain of Reeds to deal with him in the next few days. The police also found a wealthy Chinese, kidnapped and imprisoned in a coal hole. The Viets had been asking a ransom of a million piasters for him. The Chinese "spontaneously" handed over a hundred thousand to his liberators the police, and that settled the difficulty of the informer's reward.

The next day Mai Huu-xuan carried out massive arrests, sweeping in forty killers. Ten days later the whole financial committee was taken in another villa, this time in the Boulevard Luro. The head of it, Van Sang, a former killer whose present task was the raising of money by all available means, was tattooed from head to foot with inscriptions such as "In life love is of no account: the people's struggle alone is worthy of a man." And once more a hundred Vietminh of the shock forces were taken.

From that time on there was a tidal wave of detectives in Saigon. The "special agent" became a conventional type, and he was to be seen everywhere, with his disagreeable face, his felt hat and his tommy gun. But the tidal wave of informers mounted still higher. A fifth of the population sold intelligence. That made four hundred thousand informers of every age, sex and religion. From now on it was little more than a game for Tam's Sûreté to arrest the fresh killers the Nambo Committee sent in — for it went on for some time before giving up completely.

The police gang

THE Vietminh had lost the battle of Saigon. Somewhere in the Plain of Reeds the Nambo Committee performed its autocriticism. It acknowledged its mistakes. It condemned pure, absolute terrorism as an error, a blameworthy temptation, a facile and "incorrect" solution, and a form of deviation. For it was impossible to seize a town with a population of more than two million solely by means of assassination. A new Party line was drawn up. The Vietminh were to leave the glory of the victory to Tam and his police and, in the most profound secrecy, to return to the profitable exploitation of a Saigon at the height of its economic prosperity. So there were to be no more murders or grenades. The vital thing was the careful restoration of the Red economic networks as well as those concerned with intelligence and military spying. The most suitable men were sent to Mao

Tse-tung's China, to the specialized schools that turned out "scientific" agents.

The Vietminh did not disappear from Saigon, but they remained there under the surface, like submarines. They had been taught such a lesson that even in the cities such as Hanoi or Hué where it would have been easier for them to be active they subsided into quietness. From this time until the end of the Indochinese war, calm reigned in the towns: the Viets devoted themselves to underground work of a purely utilitarian kind, remaining out of sight.

Meanwhile the enormous Red Saigon (with the exception of Cholon, which still belonged to Bay Vien and his Binh Xuyen) became a police-dominated city, and it did so with unbelievable speed. This would not have been possible if the people of the capital had been Vietminh at heart. But they had no deep convictions: they merely bowed to the stronger side. Tam had smashed the Viet organization that had been in command and now the mass of the people naturally came over to the victorious gang, that of the police.

As the Vietminh gave up the idea of conquering Saigon a new state within a state came into being — that of the police. Even Tam was outstripped. Or rather he chose another road, that of public, official, consecrated splendor — he became minister of the interior, governor of Tonkin, head of the government. But sitting in these high places he had no more real power than he had possessed when he was a cop; and with Tam vanishing into clouds of glory the Vietnamese police turned itself into a powerful ruling organization — it became Mai Huu-xuan's gang.

Bay Vien was one of the lords of Saigon. From now on the other was Mai Huu-xuan, proud, lecherous and grasping to the point of derangement; but he was still as frigid, still as calm as ever. Now that the Vietminh in the city had been dealt with, a remorseless gang war arose between the former convict, Bao Dai's present favorite, and Bazin's former pupil, the present king of the police. For years it was a hidden, underground struggle: much later, when Diem came to power, it ended in an appalling bloodbath.

But for three or four years Saigon was to have the outward appearance of peace. Bay Vien in command at the Grand Monde, Mai Huu-xuan sitting in the Sûreté, and the Vietminh going through their autocriticism in the Plain of Reeds — all this brought back the balance of the piaster that was so favorable to business and prosperity of every kind; and so there was widespread satisfaction and contentment.

This seemed to be the reign of harmony. Almost everywhere in the town the system of condominium operated, a triumvirate, a form of coexistence.

In every group of huts, in every alley, there were to be found a few informers working for Mai Huu-xuan, a few working for the Binh Xuyen, and at least one working for the Vietminh, to say nothing of those who were paid by the French. To be sure, there were still bodies full of holes lying about here and there, particularly in the more remote districts. But they were much rarer. Generally speaking all the people who made a trade of small-scale intelligence worked on the principle of live and let live, and they even combined to provide their respective employers with what they wanted. Once more the sale of hot tips became a profitable and well-organized business: and often the French paid very highly for what the other organizations had rejected.

The only people who were not altogether happy were the French police: their pride had been deeply wounded by the success of Tam and his men where they had so miserably failed. At great length the French detectives explained to me that the art of being a policeman was essentially one of delicacy and analysis, in which each case must be carefully unraveled, like a cocoon: one must inch forward subtly, gliding like a serpent, to carry things through to perfection and to extract the greatest possible yield. "Tam's people are not real policemen," they told me. "They don't know how to work over a man and suck out every last thing he knows. All they know how to do is to arrest huge numbers and beat them up until they are dead. Mere bunglers. They spoil everything. And then, really, the way they go on, it's scarcely humane."

Tam did not in fact kill everybody. Indeed he did not know what to do with his excess of prisoners, for they could not all be shot in attempting to escape. He did not care to hand them over to the Vietnamese courts. The judges, whose dread was of a more lasting kind than that of the other Saigonese, still went on with their wholesale acquittals. One aged judge, in answer to Tam's reproaches, observed, "I have nine children. Who will feed them if the Vietminh kill me because of my sentences?"

So Tam passed his terrorists on to the French military courts. The difficulty was to bring their crimes within the jurisdiction of the courts martial. This was solved thanks to the existence of a state of war — not the war against the Viets, who were only rebels and against whom there was no acknowledged war, but the war against the Japanese. After the peace treaty with Japan was signed another excuse had to be found. Fortunately the legal experts discovered that the much earlier agreement ending hostilities with Germany did not mention Indochina and therefore did not apply there. Thus it was Germany that allowed the French military courts to sit in judgment on the Vietminh captured by Tam.

One of these French army judges told me about the Vietminh killers, the men of the shock forces upon whom he passed sentence. "I have never known one of them repudiate the Vietminh. The men they bring in front of me are pale, sick looking, puffy faced, with all the marks of prison on them. In the dock they behave as they have been taught to behave, for the Vietminh regulations foresee this likelihood. According to their orders they deny everything, not so much for themselves as out of a last desperate loyalty expressed in negation. They do not bother to put up a defense, as though they were no longer concerned with their fate — as though they were already beyond material things. They stand like lumps in front of me, uncaring, occasionally uttering a few broken phrases in a dead voice — they don't remember: they did not do what I say they did. Some don't even listen to my questions. They come to life again for just one moment at the very end of the interrogation and ask me if it is seventy-six or eighty-three. For earlier, in the training camps of the Plain of Reeds, they have been told that those are the two articles of the French code of military procedure that will apply to them. And they know that there is an essential difference between seventy-six and eighty-three — that seventy-six is death and eighty-three imprisonment and consequently life.

"Curiously enough only the important leaders talk; though indeed they talk a very great deal. But it is not out of repentance in the least, nor to beg for mercy — merely to explain, out of pride in explanation. They take a sort of last delight in giving me all the names, all the details, all the secrets. It is very likely that none of it has any importance any more and that it already belongs to the past, for the whole organization has changed since then. At all events, these confessions have never been of the slightest use to us. These big Vietminh, these political commissars and officers, are all educated men. They speak French, though they pretend not to understand it. But once, when I gave the sign for the interpreter to question him, one particularly bloody killer got up and declared, 'I am a supporter of the French Union: I therefore demand that the hearing should be in French.' On another occasion, as I gave the death sentence, the condemned man remembered his French and shouted 'For all that, long live France!'

"These Vietminh die splendidly. It is more than courage: it is the highest possible form of detachment. Those who are condemned to death are kept in the little island of Poulo Condore, the old penal settlement. Once I had to go there. When I arrived there were twenty-two men waiting to be executed. They were shut up in special cells. When I went into the prison they all began singing their patriotic songs together. They already knew that a squad of legionaries had disembarked with me to shoot them.

"I had them stopped for the roll call. Then I said that eleven reprieves had been granted and eleven refused. So there were eleven of them who were to be executed at once. I went to the office for the usual formalities. I handed out cigarettes: I let them write letters. All this time the men who were about to die were laughing, not in order to insult me, but as though the whole thing amused them. Then for their last minutes they started their singing again.

"The sergeant major of the Legion in charge of the firing squad came and complained bitterly. He was really extremely vexed. 'I cannot understand,' he said, 'how they can have put an old soldier like me — twenty years of service and the military medal — to so much trouble just to shoot this little batch of Vietminh. Anyone at all could look after that. When I was sent I thought it was to mop up at least two or three hundred of them.'

"One of the condemned men was a Catholic. He asked to confess. A Vietnamese priest gave him absolution in the next-door room. When he came back his comrades made fun of him. Yet this Catholic was as courageous as the other Vietminh: though he did not sing, whereas they did, right up to their last seconds. There were no curses, not a word, only these Vietminh songs that still went on under the firing.

"These men were executed in groups of three. In theory they should have been kneeling and blindfolded. They asked me to let them die standing with their eyes open. I gave permission. Everything passed off very quickly. They fell whilst they were still singing. I told myself that I didn't have to feel any remorse, because these were murderers condemned for utterly appalling crimes."

The Red defeat in Cochinchina

THE summer of 1950, after the battle of Saigon, was a unique period in the Indochinese war: it was the time when the victory seemed to be in reach, as if you only had to stretch out your hand for it. It was the brief moment when the French believed that they were about to win the race against the clock. They were in complete control of the deltas of Cochinchina and Tonkin, and Giap's army was not yet ready in spite of Mao Tse-tung's massive aid. In Saigon and Hanoi the authorities were certain that the Vietminh jungle troops could not last out much longer in their quadrilateral. They were about to collapse for want of supplies, since everything they lived on — the men, the rice and the money of the deltas — eluded them, having definitively passed under the control of the French. And against that even the mighty People's China could do nothing.

Period of illusions! Yet still it is true that the picture of the Indochina of those days was that of Red distress, for two good little French generals, Chanson in the south and Alessandri in the north, were carrying out a genuine Pacification. In Cochinchina Chanson methodically crushed Nguyen Binh, who, having been defeated in Saigon, was now waging full-scale war among the rice fields in a last savage burst of energy. In Tonkin Alessandri set about the occupation of almost the whole of the delta. He accomplished this without meeting any great resistance, by means of a series of methodical, careful, well-prepared operations: he even took the bishoprics of Phatdiem and Buichu, far to the south, almost in Annam, with their million Catholics. And the result of these victories was indeed the strangling of the Vietminh, foretold by the French. To be convinced of this one had but to listen to Ho Chi Minh's radio, which now launched the famous watchword "A grain of rice is worth a drop of blood." The radio voices continually urged the people to make every sacrifice, to deny themselves everything and to save with the utmost rigor: speaking to the patriots they perpetually reiterated, "Refrain from eating, so that our soldiers may be fed." And the only reward in all these desperate appeals was the promise of victory and of the great offensive in which Giap would sweep away all the French, the whole of the Expeditionary Force and every vestige of colonialism.

But in those days who believed it? It was just words. For what the people could see were French victories, solid, undeniable victories. And they were won at the very gates of Saigon and Hanoi.

Let us begin the account of these fortunate events with Cochinchina. It was there that Nguyen Binh, pressed harder and harder since the battle of Saigon had gone against him, staked his all. He attacked the French army in the open country, throwing in everything he possessed in a massive assault. His plan consisted of a surprise attack, a general offensive all along the line; and he counted on the terror of the detachments, the little units of the Expeditionary Force that the Pacification had scattered all over the countryside, in the face of this sudden, unbelievable avalanche of Vietminh. Nguyen Binh knew that the French command believed the army of the Resistance to be at the end of its tether, quite exhausted by so many years of warfare. In fact it had never been so strong, so well manned, so well equipped and so determined. Secretly, patiently, and with an incredible perseverance, Nguyen Binh had increased the number of his battalions and his regiments, in spite of all his losses. He had found ways of giving them better weapons. And once more, with the magic words "Let us crush the French for good and all. Then as free men we can come to an understanding between ourselves," he managed to do away with all the discouragement, the contention, the countless factors that eat away a Resistance movement from within, as well as the opposition between the Nationalists and the Communists inside the Vietminh.

Over several weeks Nguyen Binh gathered all his regular units and made them carry out complicated maneuvers in order to mislead the French; for it was essential that the French should not suspect anything. Then all at once there came the sudden rush of thousands of Viets clothed in black, well armed, well disciplined, fanatical. Throughout whole provinces they leaped from the coconut palms or the mangrove trees in front of the French posts and villages dozing in the heat of the season before the monsoon and drowsy with the daily round.

It was a huge risk to exchange guerrilla fighting for a pitched battle. Nguyen Binh accepted it to the full, fighting three battles at once. He first attacked on one front, then on a more important front, and lastly on a front that was wholly essential, in a series of strikes, each harder than the last, each more unexpected, in different places and at a continually accelerating rhythm, in order to overwhelm the French before they had had time to realize what was happening to them. After a feint against the big market town of Travinh, after an attack upon the populous city of Soctrang, there came the great offensive against Cantho, the Pearl of the Mekong, the rice capital, the strong point of the whole of western Cochinchina. If Cantho fell Nguyen Binh would be master of virtually all Cochinchina and its wealth.

The fighting was extremely savage. While the regulars were flinging themselves at their objectives, a whole nation of *nha-qués* emerged from the night and the paddy fields to cut the R.C. 16, the only road by which reinforcements and supplies could reach the French who were being attacked along the Mekong and the Bassac.

For Nguyen Binh the stake was enormous — his entire life's work and indeed his life itself. If he lost, he lost everything, since he had kept nothing back and possessed no reserves of any kind. And in all likelihood the Tongbo Committee and Ho Chi Minh would call him to account: he would be liquidated by the "justice of the people."

And Nguyen Binh did lose. Once again it was proved that a Resistance that comes out into the open, that attacks a real army as though it were itself an army, signs its own death warrant.

At the beginning, to be sure, the fighting was indecisive. On the first day countless French posts were surrounded on all sides, scores of guard towers were taken, and innumerable roads and bridges were cut. Nguyen Binh's regulars even carried the fighting into the suburbs of the towns. The Vietminh fought with furious dash and heroism, and with every kind of ruse and cruelty. They used strange sorts of camouflage, astonishing forms of protection — for example, huge globes made of dried grass: nothing was seen but these strawlike balls rolling along, but inside there were Vietminh soldiers who were coming in to attack. Another form of armor for the Red soldiers was the people's flesh, the bodies of the mass. The political commissars forced the villagers into the pagodas, which were hung about with red flags: that kept the French airmen busy, for they shot up the pagodas instead of machine gunning the rice fields all around, where the regulars were carefully hidden, waiting their moment to rush in to the attack.

But none of it was any use against the French superiority in materiel. The French planes machine gunned the Vietminh troop concentrations, parachutists were dropped over the most threatened posts, the amphibious "crabs" worked their way through the network of canals and paddy fields and roared out of the mud and the reeds at twenty miles an hour in the rear of the Vietminh.

For the first time in this Indochinese war dawn broke on the desolate sight of a real battlefield, where the abandoned bodies lay in the hundreds beside their weapons. Usually the Viets stripped thier dead, leaving them entirely naked, without the least sign by which they could be identified. This time they were too hard pressed to do so. Next to the few French dead, lying there in their battle dress, what layers of Vietminh regulars, heaped up one upon another, in their black uniforms!

The hand-to-hand fighting had lasted all night. One French company, completely surrounded, had dug itself in behind whatever came to hand in the village where it was making its stand — in this case it was sacks of rice. They were firing their last rounds of ammunition when the amphibious crabs of the First Cavalry Regiment of the Legion appeared. The legionaries, coming in behind the Viets on their machines, mowed them down in long ranks with their twinned machine guns firing at point-blank range.

And there were so many other butcheries! At the end of ten days of fighting those regulars who were still alive suddenly renounced the "European war": they hid their weapons in the mud of the irrigation canals, abandoned their uniforms for the disguise of simple *nha-qués* and fled in little groups towards the hiding place in the Plain of Reeds from which they had set out with such dash for their offensive. The French columns pursued these fugitives, but they caught very few. Yet for all that, how many men had fallen because of the pride of Nguyen Binh! His army was utterly cut to pieces.

In fact, the Resistance in Cochinchina never recovered from this defeat: never again was it dangerous to the French from the military point of view. The whole of Nguyen Binh's splendid organization fell to pieces. He even had to disband the six regiments that he had built up with such tenacity and delight: never again did a Vietminh unit in the south go beyond the battalion level. He had to break up the general staff that he had so proudly settled close to Saigon in the days of his power. Together with his headquarters, his guard and the whole of the Nambo Committee, he had to move farther off, always farther off, for fear of being picked up in a French sweep. The little hunted band plunged deeper and deeper into the most dreary solitudes, the most inaccessible regions of the Plain of Reeds, far over towards the Cambodian frontier. And then even the Plain of Reeds was no longer safe. At last they were forced to hide on the edge of the great Moi forest, where the huge Indochinese jungle begins. And their presence was often reported in the mangrove swamps of Camau Point.

When it was all over nothing remained of the military resistance in Cochinchina except for a few patches here and there. And Nguyen Binh's fury was powerless: he could not halt the process and his rage only brought him nearer to his end. The defeated Nguyen Binh had not only to bear his own reproaches but the suspicions of the Communists as well, and the murmuring of the men of the Resistance, who said to him, "What have you done with us?" Lastly he felt himself dominated, in the confrontation of man to man, by his adversary, General Chanson, who had succeeded General Boyer de La Tour as commissioner in Cochinchina.

General Chanson was not a very imposing conqueror to look at — a small man with an invalid's shyness, and fine, sad eyes: exquisite manners. He would often remain silent, seeing nothing, with his head down, thinking. But in fact he was a strong man, with the strength of a clear-thinking mind: a Polytechnicien, an intellectual, an intelligent and even a sensitive logician, and immensely dynamic. When he had an idea he utterly changed — beamed with joy. You forgot that he was ugly. He became charming, seductive, enthusiastic, and he talked, he talked on and on: he was gentle and yet inflexible; he was brilliantly persuasive. He did not care for the simple old soldier's way of saying "This is an order." These words, uttered in harsh, clipped, implacable voice, never came from him unless he came up against a particular kind of stupidity, a particular kind of coarseness, a particular kind of hasty, shortsighted "soldier's" view of the war. He would very much rather convince. Again and again he said to me, "I believe that one should always explain." And he tirelessly explained to his superiors, to Pignon, to Carpentier, and also to those under him, until he had gained his point. He even explained to the journalists, and he would have done so even more if he had not been afraid of Carpentier's touchiness — for Carpentier was always very insistent upon his rights as commander in chief. And so when Chanson won his victories he took care to stay in the background.

For Chanson was steadily successful. He fought his war as though he were playing a game of chess. And when they spoke about him in the Expeditionary Force they said, "He's a good chief: you know where you are with him. And he's sound."

But let there be no mistake: Chanson was no humanitarian — it merely seemed to him that the best way of putting an end to the cruel Nguyen Binh and his Viets was to behave humanely. Most of his brother generals were quite happy to wage the traditional kind of war; but for his part he had the notion — a rare one among career soldiers — that the primary function of an army was to beat the enemy. So this spindly little man (with great powers of resistance under his apparent weakness) passionately set himself to accomplish this end with everything he possessed, his brains, his nervous energy, and above all his honesty, the honesty of a good technician, a kind of craftsman's modesty in which what comes first is the work, and by no means the satisfaction of vanity nor the honors or intrigues that make generals famous. So, as a mathematician, he worked out the situation in Cochinchina as though it were an equation. He was the first French general I ever saw analyze the "people's war" as it really was.

I first met him in an artillery convoy on a road near Mytho. He asked me into his jeep: how small he seemed in the midst of all this martial display, and how kind — too kind. All these guns and all these soldiers seemed huge in comparison. The landscape was horrible: everything had been burned. But it was he himself who pointed out the devastation to me. And in a harsh, strangely moved, strangely resolute voice he said, "I have punished the regiment that carried out these atrocities. I won't have this kind of thing. For we shall lose if we set about the traditional kind of colonial reconquest. Fire and sword tactics won't succeed here. There is no precedent for what we are up against. We have the 'new men' of Asian Communism opposite us — insect soldiers, huge crowds with a collective brain. So we have to rethink the whole thing from every point of view, psychological, political, economic and strategic."

In fact Chanson was carrying on with the Pacification. But with him it was no longer the old Pacification in which everything was hopelessly muddled, everything, including the "dirty war," the "war for fun," the war for the honor of the thing and the war of the piaster, all being fought at the same time. He made it systematic, basing it upon four essential rules.

In the first place, what counted was the mass of the people. The aim of the war was to wrest them from the Vietminh. "The only possible victory is that they should prefer us," was his perpetual refrain. The piaster was not enough to accomplish this, nor counterguerrilla nor counterterror. Force was often wrong. It was the *nha-qués'* hearts that had to be won, and atrocities and reprisals should no longer be anything but an exceptional technique. What mattered most of all was to have an Expeditionary Force that always behaved correctly, one that knew how to think, one that would act only after having thought, and one that would take a great deal of trouble intelligently. Then the people, reassured, would say, "Are not these good French soldiers, who are always so cheerful and who spend such quantities of money, better than the austere Communists who insist upon having everything we possess, even our lives?"

But — and this was the second rule — this "gentleness," that is to say this just and efficient violence that won the people over, must be continuous: there must never be a single pause. Tireless patience was essential, the daily repetition of the same movements and the same activities. It was not enough that a few officers or NCO's should be immensely gifted for this kind of work and become the kings or the gods of various odd corners of the country. The whole of the Expeditionary Force everywhere, at every moment of the day, must take care of the people, without giving the Viets a second's respite. Otherwise they would build themselves up again; they would draw the masses after them and they would come out on top just when it was thought they had been destroyed.

Communism was human activity pushed to the highest point, pushed beyond what would be thought believable. To overcome it one had to have the same degree of passionate eagerness and subtlety.

The background of Chanson's Cochinchina was the perpetual, detailed confrontation of two collective wills engaged in stealing men from one another — that of the Vietminh and that of the Expeditionary Force. This had already been the theory of the French before Chanson, but it had been botched. With him it was put into practice.

Then came the third rule. To this "militant kindness" Chanson added a purely military strategy of Pacification. He laid down one main operational axis, a slow, steady advance all along the Mekong to cut what was left of Vietminh Cochinchina in two. His intention was to make a solid barrier between the rice-holding Viets of Camau Point and the riceless Viets of the Moi forest. In the place of Nguyen Binh's huge organization in which the Plain of Reeds and Saigon acted as hinges, there would be no more than two Red blocks cut off from one another and therefore powerless, each being at the opposite end of Cochinchina.

The fourth rule was the most daring. It was opposed by everybody, by the Vietnam government, Bao Dai, Saigon, the banks, the import-export trade, all those concerned with the piaster, by the sects, the fence sitters, the nationalists and the Vietminh. It was the "rice war": the most formidable for the Reds but also the most disagreeable and irksome for countless interested parties. What a chorus of protests, above all from the worthy Saigon French, when it was first proposed! Pignon and Carpentier wavered, but Chanson forced them to accept his decision. He proclaimed the blockade of the region beyond the Bassac, the whole immense western part of Cochinchina, that wonderful granary: not a single ton of rice could move out of it any more without a permit. From now onwards the smuggling and the shady deals that supplied the Viets in the forest, the Viets to the north of Saigon, and those on the edge of Cochinchina were stopped — though not entirely, of course. Very soon the Viets began to feel the pinch. What is more, the decree meant the stopping of the long-distance convoys, the slow, slow plodding that eventually brought Ho Chi Minh and his soldiers their food as they trained in the jungles of Tonkin on the Chinese frontier, a thousand miles away.

This blockade was the first act in the economic war, and it was a severe blow for all the Viets, for Nguyen Binh's followers and for Ho Chi Minh's. It would have been very nearly a death sentence if it had been carried out completely and if other steps of the same kind had been taken. But nothing more was done, because of the piaster, prosperity and the holy interests of commerce.

At all events, throughout Cochinchina there reigned if not peace then something very like it. The country took on a new aspect, one that was almost without fear: there was life everywhere, houses were rebuilt, the paddy fields were cultivated once more; fat babies abounded, and in the over-crowded schools you could hear the children droning out their lessons; merchants and their wares, their now plentiful wares, came to even the most remote country districts; the civil servants underwent a transformation — they became more self-confident, and now they were bold enough to realize something of the extent of their powers.

The military posts were quiet, even those which had been almost continually surrounded in earlier days. Henceforward their officers came to

Saigon to drink. They were low in spirit. They were bored. "Where are the good old days when we were attacked every night, often by bands of several hundred? For the last six weeks there has not been so much as a probe. All we kill is time. Everything is splendid — too splendid. A village has suddenly sprung up all by itself next to the post, and the *nha-qués* who live there tell us everything — they warn us of what the Viets are getting ready to do and they denounce them."

The death of Nguyen Binh

AT the end of it all, in 1951, a year later, came the execution of Nguyen Binh on Giap's orders.

One autumn day in the charming kingdom of Cambodia a patrol of the Cambodian light infantry surprised a little band of Vietminh in the midst of the jungle. There was a clash. The Viets escaped, leaving a body behind them. The sergeant major in charge of the patrol described the corpse in his report: "It was the body of a middle-sized man, dressed in a singlet and blue gabardine trousers: his feet were bare. On his wrist he had a Movado watch. His face was mostly hidden by large sunglasses of the American type. Punch marks on the holster of his Colt formed the word Binh."

The Cambodians, pursuing the fleeing Viets, captured one of their officers. He revealed that the body of the man in gabardine trousers was that of Nguyen Binh, a lieutenant general and the commander in chief of the Vietminh troops in Cochinchina. And he gave some strange details: in the fight itself Nguyen Binh had been only slightly wounded, but a political commissar had ordered him to be finished off with two shots in the head. A man had blown in his skull with a pistol and then they had all fled.

To make more certain that it really was Nguyen Binh the French command had a hand cut off the body and sent to Saigon. There the fingerprints proved that it was his. So the dead man was indeed Nguyen Binh. But who killed him, and how?

A notebook told the whole story of the end of Nguyen Binh. It was found beside him, having fallen out of his trouser pocket. It was only a very ordinary little notebook — the sort of thing a schoolboy might have. But it was in this that Nguyen Binh made his entries day by day for his distant wife, to justify himself to her. It was the diary of a man who knew that he was going to his death, and who asked himself with the whole of his being whether he should accept his fate. He described his last struggles of conscience and his march in full awareness towards his own murder, his cooperation in being put to death.

His real spiritual and physical end had begun several months earlier. At the close of 1950 Nguyen Binh was still officially in command in Cochinchina: in fact he was a sick man, nothing but a fever-ridden bag of bones. It was when he was at his worst that there appeared Le Duan and his team of political commissars. They came from Tonkin. Giap and the Tongbo Committee had sent them, and they were all gloomy, pitiless Communists, dialectical machines. Their mission was to take complete charge of the Nambo Committee, which lay under the accusation of deviationism, to purge it, and to bring it back into the right way of thinking.

From that time on Nguyen Binh understood that it was no use struggling any more: he had reached the point of no return, the time when the unvarying process of dialectic called for his liquidation. What he was being asked for now was a last patriotic sacrifice: they wanted him to make his own disappearance easier.

It would arouse the indignation of the people to have Nguyen Binh killed in Cochinchina. So Giap asked him to leave everything and travel towards the distant north, where the Tongbo Committee had its being. Le Duan gave Nguyen Binh a letter from Giap: "My dear comrade," he wrote, "you will have an escort of thirty men. I am entrusting you with a task that is of the first importance for us all. You will reconnoiter a fresh line of communication towards Tonkin through the Cambodian provinces of Kompong Cham, Kratie and Stungstreng." Nguyen Binh knew that he would be executed in the course of this journey, and that its sole motive was his death. Giap knew that he knew.

Sorrowfully Nguyen Binh explained in his diary. "The doctor is very anxious about my condition and he tells me that I cannot travel far. I ought to rest for months before setting out. Once I have left I will go under very quickly, for I shall have no medicine — not even a medical orderly to look after me. I can scarcely walk, and yet I must face thousands of miles of the most deadly jungle! But how could I stay in Cochinchina long enough to get better? What a humiliation it would be to beg for a delay! And then I would be a nuisance to everybody. All the time I should be asking my last remaining friends and their wives for help. No: I will not do it. Nor shall I take shelter with my family. No. All those solutions are impossible. I leave with a firm mind, though my body is cruelly shaken. I reflect upon my duty. I am going away so that my fame shall no longer irk these men whom it so offends. If I were to stay they would say that I was malingering and that I did not have the courage to overcome my individualistic feelings — they would accuse me of putting my family before the Revolution. So I go. I am resolved to walk steadily along the path that has been drawn for me, wherever it may lead: but the few friends who understand me and who know how seriously ill I am are unable to keep back their tears."

One obsessive thought continually recurs in these hastily scribbled notes — he has sacrificed his own people, all the Vietminh nationalists, to the war, and now it is his turn to be sacrificed. For otherwise it would be cowardice — dishonor. All that was left for him was to obey and fade out of the living world during this long march, leaving it to fate and to Giap to see to the details of his end.

Nguyen Binh made up his mind in full awareness: he was too well acquainted with the Communist world, its dialectic, its concept of truth and its laws. On another page he wrote, "My health would have justified a delay. What would have been the point? I had reached the stage where the only alternatives were to yield and do what was asked of me, thus ensuring my own destruction and the victory of the Party, or else to resist, going over to Bao Dai. But if I had changed sides I could never have persuaded myself that I had not been a traitor. It would have been treachery towards my comrades in the Resistance, the living and the dead; and the next day they would have become my enemies. I belong to their side, and on their side I stay: for a battle fought together for years supplies the place of conviction."

And that is how it happened that a little later a wornout, hungry band pushed its way slowly through the hell of thick jungle, near to death; advancing, to be sure, but with such terrible slowness. Sometimes they stopped for a day, too exhausted to go on. Sometimes, too, they paused in the faint hope of finding something in the way of food — anything at all to eat. Endless negotiations were needed before the savage Mois, the cunning, distrustful inhabitants of the great forest, would sell them a little inferior rice, sticky rice that had to be eaten without salt. Once and once only the Mois agreed to let them have a calf. But then from the midst of the wretched band of thirty Vietminh there arose a true Red, an unswerving Party member, who called attention to the rule that forebade the killing and eating of such livestock (it came under the heading of sabotage of production, for it prevented the calf from providing much more meat later by growing into a bullock).

Usually they had to be satisfied with bamboo shoots and berries that made their stomachs burn: but above all it was the bad water (and in the jungle all water is bad) that rotted their guts and everything else inside them. And in the general putrescence of the jungle every wound went bad: the most dangerous were those which were imperceptibly inflicted by the leeches. Sometimes there were so many of these creatures that they covered the track in their thousands, a red, living carpet that undulated revoltingly under their bare feet.

It was all the more horrible since this was the rainy season. The whole spongy countryside was water or miasma, and there was no possible shelter. Yet in spite of everything the Viet detachment thrust on. They swam the swollen rivers. They dragged what little baggage they had in pushcarts whose axles were always breaking. At last, at the end of two months of this, they were close to the frontier of Laos. But that made no difference: before them there still stretched the unending forest.

Nguyen Binh wrote it all down daily, in his scrupulous way, in the diary that was also his testament. For he had fewer illusions than ever now. Giap had sent him into the jungle — sheer jungle, one of the worst stretches in Indochina, where there was no hope of help nor the least Vietminh post or influence — so that he should die of natural causes without the awkwardness of a killing that would have to look as though it had been carried out by the French or their partisans.

The situation within the band was curious. In theory he was in command, but the real leaders were Le Duan's two political commissars: and Le Duan had chosen all the men. Nguyen Binh was rather their prisoner than their chief — already the condemned man. But he had achieved a kind of serenity. It was often he who volunteered to do the cooking: it was he who took charge of the party's first aid, dressing the poisoned wounds and treating the fevers as well as he could. He himself was growing sicker and sicker, but he had no preferential treatment — a footing of complete equality.

The last words in his diary are dated September 21, 1951. Nguyen Binh wrote, "All night I was unable to get to sleep. I hardly get up before I feel weary. We have only enough rice left for one meal. I am one of those who do not eat today so that the other sick men may have our share. Yet we are getting ready to move on."

The group had passed the night at the Moi hamlet of Romphe, a cluster of miserable straw huts on stilts. At five in the morning a hand woke Nguyen Binh: it was time to go. Then they told him to wait a little. The Mois had agreed to supply some rice but they would not produce it until somewhat later in the day. Nguyen Binh lit a lamp and sat down to write the last words he was ever to write. At eight o'clock, climbing down the ladder of the hut, he joined the other Vietminh in a clearing beside the village. He talked to the members of the band, who were all vaguely uneasy. The wait was drawing out too long. It was almost noon. Yet they could not plunge into the protecting forest with empty stomachs merely because of an uncertain, perhaps imaginary danger. It would be suicide. Far better to wait a little longer.

Yet it was indeed betrayal. The Moi had sent a messenger to warn Sergeant Major Sang Saroun, who was some thirty miles away with his twenty-five Cambodian soldiers. The promise of rice was only a ruse to make the Viets wait. For while they were lying there on the grass of the clearing, losing hours, Sang Saroun's detachment was coming nearer and nearer, marching at full speed. To go faster they waded up to their middles in the great river Srepok; then, not to be seen, they cut their way with jungle knives through the spiny undergrowth. At about one o'clock they were before Romphe: suddenly they appeared from the jungle. Everything was over in a few minutes. The Viets had no sentinels out: they were too exhausted to bother with keeping watch or organizing a defense. That was why the Cambodians had been able to reach them without being seen or heard.

Although they were drowsing, in a moment the Viets were up and had run to fling themselves into the forest. But Nguyen Binh had been deeply asleep, and he understood too late. Shots were fired: he was wounded and he could scarcely move. In the midst of the confusion two men in black rushed at him, aiming their Colts — two men of his own band, two Vietminh killers. They had been given their orders long before: they were to kill him if there was any danger of his falling into the hands of the French. Their job done, they fled into the jungle.

That was how the tragedy that Giap had so eagerly desired and so carefully worked out reached its consummation.

So Nguyen Binh was dead at last. But as it happened, a few weeks earlier, by a stroke of chance that was full of meaning, the other great figure of Cochinchina, the man who had beaten him, General Chanson, had also been killed. He had met his end in a commonplace outrage, murdered by an ordinary grenade.

To die murdered was usual enough in Cochinchina. But in this case the circumstances were very strange. It happened in the middle of an official ceremony, in the heart of the town of Sadek. The general had come for an inspection: the procession, very much aware of rank and due precedence, came out into a broad esplanade, and the troops presented arms. A band played the "Marseillaise." On the pavement the other side of the open space a huge crowd shouted "Long live France!" Sadek's demonstrative welcome was very much in line with the new feeling in Cochinchina, where everybody thought the French had won. All at once a young Vietnamese came out of the cheering crowd and ran towards Chanson. But he was dressed in a French uniform, and so nobody stopped him. Everyone thought he was a soldier. When he was within a few yards of the general he began to jerk his trousers in a most extraordinary way, at the same time skipping about. The result of these odd movements was a huge explosion. The troops were still rigidly presenting arms, but Chanson lay in his death throes on the bloody tarmac, among three or four Vietnamese who had been wounded even more atrociously. The most horrible mess of all was the murderer, whose shattered limbs jerked for a few moments before they lay still.

It was the typical act of a "death volunteer" who, to make sure of success, had blown himself up with the others. The inquiry showed that in his pocket he had had a grenade with its pin out and the lever precariously wedged by a spoon — the least jerk was enough to dislodge it. That was why the ludicrous gesture of a man clawing at his trousers had meant death, both for him and for Chanson.

The killer's name was Trinh Van-minh. On his body, or rather on the remaining pieces of it that could be gathered together, there was found his photograph. It was that of a very well-dressed, very elegant man sitting at a big desk. And they realized that this suicidal assassin was by no means a Vietminh but a killer sent by the Caodaists to carry out their sentence upon Chanson, who had refused them weapons. And it was Trinh Minh-the himself, the bloodiest member of the sect, who had said to Trinh Van-minh, "I have entrusted this mission to you because you are my friend, and I want to keep the honor of such a deed for a man I love."

So both Nguyen Binh and Chanson, the two adversaries in the great battle of Cochinchina in 1950, had been liquidated within a few weeks of one another. Both had been killed because their day had passed, because the one had lost too badly and the other had won too well. From this time onwards Cochinchina no longer meant the fighting between the French and the Vietminh: it was no longer merely their battlefield.

In the first place it was a Cochinchina without a Resistance. The whole of the Resistance had died with Nguyen Binh. From now on there was nothing left in the south but a weak, purged Communist Party in which Le Duan was the mere agent of the Tongbo Committee, Ho Chi Minh and Giap. Discipline within the Party must come first — that was the watchword for the future. And sometimes I wonder whether the Tongbo Committee, having made use of the Resistance when that served its purpose, had not preferred that it should be crushed rather than that it should be victorious — whether it did not bring about this defeat on purpose. It all happened as though Cochinchina, having played its part, had been sacrificed because of its impurity when the right moment came: for it collapsed just as the new war began a thousand miles away — the real, huge-scale Communist war fought by Giap in Tonkin with Mao Tse-tung's support. This was to be the decisive war: at least according to the Tongbo Committee is was to be decisive. For years on end Giap's battalions were to be engaged in incessant fighting, and during all this time the propaganda in the south amounted to no more than this — "Maintain the Party but do not stir. Just do your utmost to improve Communist thinking and wait until the people's armies from Tonkin reach you and liberate you."

Nguyen Binh was no longer necessary in this plan: he was an encumbrance. And it was perfectly natural that death should be his reward.

To a certain degree almost the same applied to Chanson. He too was an encumbrance — not for the French, but for their allies.

The situation was plain enough. Suddenly, in this Cochinchina where there had been so much fighting, there was no war any more. The Resistance had vanished and the Expeditionary Force was moving more and more up into Tonkin to hold the terrible Giap. So in the south there was a military vacuum; but there were those who profited by this vacuum, those who did well out of the situation, and they grew increasingly avid and demanding: there were the "organizations" of every kind, there was the Saigon government, the various police forces, the gangs, the sects, and a little later the Vietnamese army, which also turned into a sort of feudal domain. France came to terms with all of them: she had an overwhelming need of their help because she had no more forces of her own to hold the south. So this Cochinchinese world settled down happily with its own balance of power and its own customs. But Chanson was still there: he was too much inclined to keep things straight, in order, and he was a nuisance.

And things had reached the point at which it was possible for the sects to kill a French general with impunity. The French could not even take their revenge: there was no question of it. The French army merely brooded upon its impotent hatred for Trinh Minh-the, whom it considered the real murderer. Silence closed again over Chanson's tomb, as indeed it closed over the whole of Cochinchina.

At least Chanson had pacified, or almost pacified, Cochinchina. The country stayed out of the news for years on end. Both for the French and the Viets it was now Tonkin that counted for everything. But in 1950 there was optimism in Tonkin too. Another good general was doing for the north what Chanson had done for the south — he was taking all the "profitable country," that of the rice fields and the swarming towns and villages. Were not the Viets about to be decisively beaten there too?

The prophet

IN 1950 the Viets were at bay; they were in a desperate state not only because of Nguyen Binh's defeat but even more because of the loss of the Tonkin delta. A certain General Alessandri had seized it almost without being noticed, without meeting resistance, and without any headlines.

He was a general endowed with common sense: indeed he was a prodigy of common sense. This was so rare a quality in the army that although he was of humble origin and devoid of influential connections he had a brilliant and successful career. But in the long run his common sense became a dangerous kind of mysticism; then everything took a turn for the bad. For his common sense told him that the Chinese were utterly incapable of being Communists.

In 1945, when the Japanese attacked the French, he had led a column of troops from his base at Tong through the jungles and had escaped into Kuomintang China. After the Japanese surrender Alessandri came into his own: he was promoted, appointed commander in chief of the French forces in China, interim governor-general of Indochina and chief of the French delegation to the second Dalat conference. D'Argenlieu, Leclerc, Sainteny and all the important people de Gaulle had entrusted with the making of a new Indochina recognized him as the specialist on Asia. Then, having served his purpose, he was set aside for a while, his collaboration with Pétain's Decoux being more clearly remembered than his column. But with the coming of Pignon and his civil administrators Alessandri was needed again: at first he found it impossible to get moving in Indochina, for General Blaizot was commander in chief, and he preferred a quiet war, with no interference from the top. There were also difficulties with other officers (Alessandri did not belong to the army's inner circle), and he spent a great deal of his first year merely telling Pignon his views.

What he described was the emptiness, the stupidity of everything that had been done so far — want of understanding everywhere, inefficiency, no general view, no valid military conception of the whole, a ridiculous scattering of effort throughout the length and breadth of Indochina. He, Alessandri, knew the right answer and the right answer was to strike in Tonkin. In his eloquence he compared the Vietminh to an octopus — the whole of Indochina was enveloped in its tentacles, to be sure; but its head was in Tonkin. That was where the stab must come.

Who was better qualified to destroy the Red hydra than he? All that was needed was that he should be appointed commander in chief: Pignon agreed. But when Blaizot left, Paris preferred a well-thought-of, comfortable general with everything that could be asked for in the way of stars, experience and good contacts — General Carpentier. But although Carpentier was better known than Alessandri, he knew nothing about Indochina.

Alessandri wanted to retire: but many times in the future he was to wish this and yet stay. He said, "I don't want to be left in charge of winding up a bankrupt concern." But with honeyed words Pignon dissuaded him. "The French government appoints you commander of the armed forces and high commissioner of the Republic in Tonkin. The government believes in your plan and wants you to carry it out. You will have full civil and military powers for doing so. All that is needed is that you should come to an understanding with me — which we can take for granted — and with Carpentier. But he's full of good will and he relies upon you — he will let you follow your own line entirely. That is what he has told me and that is what he will tell you."

And indeed, as soon as Carpentier, with his big foxy face and his sagging great body, landed in Indochina, he overwhelmed the highly strung little Alessandri with an old soldier's deep-voiced, convincing promises. "For my part I know nothing at all about this country. No, don't protest — I know my own ignorance. But you understand it through and through. So go off to Tonkin: you won't have any sort of trouble from me. Indeed, I thank you beforehand for all that you are going to do."

So that was how I found him at Hanoi in 1950. Once more these were splendid days for him. For he was utterly determined to succeed in what he thought he had very nearly accomplished in 1945 — the saving of Indochina. This sturdy little man sharp-eyed, lean and wizened as a prune, looked upon himself as Joan of Arc, but he did not say so: he jealously kept all his thoughts to himself. A strange character, intoxicated with self-confidence and with distrust. This arose from his past, of course; and the most important factor in that past was the Alessandri column. It was that episode that gave him his extraordinary opinion of himself. When all the generals of that time had been such miserable failures had he not succeeded in waging the warfare of the jungles and the rice fields? He had led his men and had fought battles in the most appalling conditions. And if he had done this against the formidable Japanese why should he not do it on a far larger scale against the Viets, the Chinese, anybody at all? To be sure, it was all one — the whole of the high command was incompetent and inept: he alone possessed genius.

With his inferiority complex he could be a difficult chief, particularly if he was opposed with any degree of obstinacy. So those about him took care not to rub him the wrong way: they obeyed without hesitation. When things were like this he was very likable, by no means a tyrant; both the civilians and the soldiers got along with him very well and they were glad that he was there, for after all he did have a reputation for ability and intelligence, and it was known that he was determined to act.

Who remembers him nowadays? Yet nobody, not even de Lattre, was so daring in Indochina. Alessandri alone was willing to run the risk of a great Asian war. Perhaps it might have been a disaster. But however that may be, in the end he was not allowed to have his way. Nothing was done. And the disaster was not avoided.

Did Alessandri's common sense border upon genius or upon madness? That is where the question lies. In any case, at the beginning of 1950 there were as yet no doubts or reservations about him. He was given a free hand and he made the most of it: he seized the whole of the Tonkin delta.

The conquest of the Tonkin delta

"IT's all up here," they said in Hanoi, speaking admiringly of Alessandri. Up here meant in his head. Working twelve, fourteen, sixteen hours a day, his head produced operational plans, all masterpieces of logic and precision. He turned out a score of them in a few months. To do this he shut himself up, either in the dilapidated old general staff building or in the brand-new high commissioner's office. He brought them forth enveloped in mystery; he had a mania for security, not only because of the Viets but even more because of the outside world, where he saw intrigue and plotting on every hand.

In the first place he turned his mind to the delta and he decided to occupy the whole of it. That was the common-sense solution; and none of the "great minds" such as Salan, Valluy or Beauffre who had been concerned with Indochina had accepted it. It was too commonplace for them. All of them, as though they dreaded the human ant hill, the great dense Asian mass, had preferred the more brilliant strategy of envelopment to that of occupation. Instead of taking the delta their idea was to set up posts all around it, to stifle it from afar, to cut it off both from China and from the divisions that Giap was building up in his quadrilateral. As a consequence of this immense "shutting-in" the millions of nha-qués would fall into the utmost depths of poverty and they would no longer be of the least use to the Vietminh — on the contrary, they would be a burden. And all this would happen automatically: no one would have to trouble with the uncounted masses living in the dismal rice fields of Tonkin.

This is how it came about that the French settled themselves along the R.C. 4, on the Chinese frontier, in the chaos of jungle-covered mountains. This was how the delta was voluntarily given up, with only a few towns and a few lines of communication, particularly the main Haiphong-Hanoi road, being retained. The whole French system was reduced to two thin parallel strips, two roads, the R.C. 4 lost in the jungle and the powerless R.C. 7 running along the delta. We know the results of this high strategy — on the one hand the bloody drama of the R.C. 4, more murderous day by day, where the French, far from isolating and separating the enemy, were already in fact his prisoners; and on the other the intensive exploitation of the delta by the Vietminh. What actually happened was the exact opposite of what had been expected. No situation could have been more favorable to Ho Chi Minh and Giap, who were left in peace to form their army in their quadrilateral, while the Expeditionary Force was pinned down on the R.C. 4 or remained idle in the delta.

This state of affairs lasted until Alessandri came. He was the first general with character enough to say "It's absurd!" And having made this observation, the Corsican moved into action at once. He set about the steady, unremitting occupation of the delta. He did the obvious thing: he began by taking what was nearest at hand — provinces, rice fields, people. He did not possess enough troops to carry out the whole thing at one go — considerably less than twenty battalions. So he took the delta section by section in a series of almost peaceful operations carried out with from three to five battalions. As soon as one was over another began. Every time, the French-held territory grew. The whole conquest was executed in a few months of unceasing movement. The operations had charming names: Pomone, Diane and Ondine to seize the opening of the delta, where the Black River runs into the Red, where the first paddy fields lie squeezed between the Bavi and the Tamdao mountains, and where the key positions of Vietri, Vinhyen and Hunghoa command the plain, the rivers and the mountain ranges; then came Parasols, Bastille and Canigou to disengage Hanoi on the north and to provide the city with a cover against an attack by the Chinese or Giap's regulars — for it was there, in the jungle on the Chinese frontier, that the two great traditional roads of conquest emerged; and after those came Diabolo and Foudre, directed at the heart of the delta, far from the European towns, the region of extreme poverty, of extreme crowding with its fifteen hundred wretched *nha-qués* to the square kilometer, the true Asia with its obscure hordes, and all protected from the outside world by an inextricable tangle of irrigation ditches, canals and filthy rivers. Obviously it was also a Red region and one that was difficult to supervise because of the great numbers of people and water courses, and because of the absence of roads — there was little more than a series of precarious dikes.

There was nothing picturesque about it. All the operations were much the same. The French columns appeared, joined hands, took their objectives, mopped up, built forts and recruited partisans. Sometimes the column might be accompanied by a group of LCT's, those flat-bottomed craft that could make their way up the shallow, muddy rivers: more rarely there might be a parachute drop. Day after day the troops deployed, concentrated their forces, advanced along the dikes, waded across the rice fields, pushed through the bamboo fences of the hamlets, marched into the villages and the towns. And then they began again somewhere else, but still in a countryside that was just as flat, just as water-logged, just as empty in spite of the multitude of people — the inhabitants made their appearance only gradually, but when they did appear they were uncountable. It went on endlessly.

It was as though the color of Alessandri's personality had come off onto his delta battalions. They carried out their work systematically, modestly, with great patience and tenacity. There were no swashbuckling heroes, no lordly gestures — attitudes of that kind would meet with strong disapproval in Hanoi. Here there were only sound, tough soldiers who carried on without making any fuss. This was the last time that I was ever to see an Expeditionary Force in Indochina whose heroism was devoid of conscious dash and without any sort of pretentiousness whatsoever.

And then these soldiers would put up with anything. They had no tanks, not many guns or trucks, and what materiel they had was poor worn-out stuff. But Alessandri was just as pleased that their means were so limited, for this forced his men to fight all over the countryside, to go on foot, to fight in the same way as the Vietminh. They had no complexes; they were not demanding; they were not afraid of physical effort, nor of contact with the enemy; and that was the old way, the way the country had been conquered a hundred years before, the man-to-man kind of war. All this allowed the little general shut up in his office to work out the most complex, demanding operations and the most subtle maneuvers — they would be carried out.

In this way Alessandri took the whole delta without making any noise about it — in Saigon the fact was hardly known, even by the journalists. Of course, as a respectful subordinate he gave an account of his activities to

Carpentier: but as it had been agreed, the commander in chief did not interfere at all. The only thing that he did not want was to send any reinforcements whatever, not even so much as a company. For the moment Alessandri could do without them very well: when he was pressed he scraped the bottom of the barrel and made out as best he could.

To tell the truth, the Viets did not cause a great deal of difficulty in this delta campaign: the real Viets, the regulars, were elsewhere, either in the quadrilateral or with Giap in the Chinese training camps. The remaining guerrillas scarcely attempted resistance — a few skirmishes and above all sabotage. Once more than six hundred mines exploded all together on the Hanoi-Haiphong line, destroying two hundred rails. Another time a commando got into the military airfield of Bachmai, burned three planes and damaged three others. On still another occasion false electricians hid explosives in twenty-two transformers just outside Hanoi: seven were knocked out and part of the city had its light cut off. But all this was not very far-reaching: the usual precautions were taken, the number of patrols and watchtowers was increased and searchlights were set up. And that was enough.

It all ran along easily, without a hitch: too easily, perhaps. The Vietminh tactic was to avoid combat — scarcely a thousand were killed. They simply sank into the people and were lost in the mass. Ho Chi Minh's orders were to stay without being noticed, to vanish into the crowd in order to supervise it and to work upon it in spite of everything — in spite of the presence of the French and above all in spite of the revenge of the Vietnamese Nationalists.

For Alessandri was Pignon's friend and they shared the same opinions: the only way of uncovering the Vietminh agents and of destroying them was to turn them over to men like themselves, to people of the same race. And Tonkin was not like the easy-going, wealthy Cochinchina, impregnated with French liberalism, where the big businessmen, rolling in piasters, nourished their foolish illusions. Here everything was hard: not only the Communism but the nationalism too. And blood called out for blood. So the little general found men ready to his hand, very able men who were set on partly by money, but far more by the idea of revenge.

It was a settlement of accounts. Throughout the delta the Nationalists hated the Vietminh even more than they hated the French — and that was saying a great deal. They killed the Viets because the Viets had killed them. In Tonkin Ho Chi Minh had not stretched out his hand to the Nationalists: he had ordered them to be massacred. For he had no need of "gentleness" here, of assimilation and advance by successive purges; he vas already strong enough, and what he wanted was "purity" straightaway, a solidly Communist Party. It had been appalling. Thousands, maybe tens of thousands of men had been liquidated in 1945, 1946 and later — always in spectacular numbers, as though the Communists wanted to destroy not only their bodies but even their memory. The intention was that horror and dread should extinguish the last trace of respect for them among the masses: their execution had to be both shameful and terrifying. That was the reason for the mass executions of hundreds at once, the fields of prisoners buried alive, the harrows dragged over men buried up to the neck.

It was a calculated annihilation directed at wiping out a dangerous rival; for these were the heroes of former years, and their names were famous. They had fought against the colonial regime in all its splendor for twenty years with their bombs and their conspiracies, holding out in almost hopeless conditions, hunted by the police like animals, betrayed to the law, sent to the penal settlement of Poulo Condore or to the gallows. It was they who had brought about the rising of Yenbay. But for Ho Chi Minh this past of theirs was a heinous fault — it was their condemnation. For these men had fought without an ideal, merely out of pride. They were not Marxists but reactionaries, outstanding men imbued with the moral order of Confucianism and the mandarin tradition: they did not arise from the people and they did not love the people. Instead of basing themselves upon the masses in their struggle, they formed what amounted to secret societies of the traditional Asian kind. In their powerlessness these organizations had sold themselves to foreigners. The Dong Minh Hoi* had been useful to the Japanese; and above all there had been the Vietnam Quoc Dan Dang, which was the tool of the Kuomintang. In 1945 its agents had arrived in Tonkin, in trucks belonging to the armies of Lu Han and Chiang Kai-shek — they even had a police force and some military units. Killing the French was still their aim. But they were even more concerned with killing the Vietminh, those newcomers to the Revolution who had stolen the power from them. We know how it ended — how the Kuomintang Chinese had to leave, how Ho Chi Minh allowed Leclerc's soldiers to come and how the Expeditionary Force let the Vietminh wipe out the Nationalists, with all their hatred of the French and their xenophobia. It had meant their extermination — or very nearly.

Those who had survived had now overcome their former loathing and were working with the French. Nguyen Huu-tri, the governor of Tonkin

* The Dong Minh Hoi was a clandestine political party that carried on its struggle against the French with the help of the Japanese.

appointed by Bao Dai, was one of them. Alessandri and he were "like two fingers on one hand." Alessandri handed over all his conquests in the delta, and Tri "pacified" them. To do this he hunted the Viets savagely. But above all he brought the people back to their obedience and to the traditional ways. It was all rather like a White terror. It was primarily a "counterorganization" of the masses, organization along the lines of the moral order taking the place of the Viets' organization for revolution. Militia forces and self-defense units were set up in the villages: rifles were handed out. And of course all the prominent citizens with their hair done up in the traditional bun and wearing silk robes were appointed as the leaders. Almost all of them accepted.

Alessandri was charmed. Since the population was pacifying itself he no longer had to scatter his forces in the outlying posts. He kept his battalions as shock troops and he aimed at striking the Viets, the real Viets, farther off, in their lairs.

It was at this period that Nguyen Huu-tri said to me, "Everything looks solid. But it is not: not yet. The very grave fact is that two or three years ago the Viets slaughtered all the veterans of the Revolution and of the fighting for independence who were not Communists. They knew very well what they were doing. For now there is only a handful of us Nationalists to stiffen and lead this huge mass of people, and it is not enough. The Viets are still everywhere, and we are not. The people are on the edge of turning against them, but they are hesitating because they are still afraid. And if once there is a single French defeat everything will fall to pieces."

So since nationalism was not enough, Alessandri played another card, that of Catholicism. And in Tonkin there were more than a million Catholics, fanatical Catholics — but their fanaticism was of a strange and complicated kind.

The ferocious Monsignor Le Huu-tu

ALESSANDRI named one of his operations Anthracite. Did he intend to associate the black of clericalism and the black of coal? For this was the occupation of the bishoprics of Phatdiem and Buichu, those extraordinary theocracies. It was indeed a very special operation.

The piaster certainly played its part in the winning over of the Catholics. A captain in the parachute troops of the Expeditionary Force, a Vietnamese called Vy, dropped from the skies to promise the cash. For this contact he was disguised as a *nha-qué,* but he brought a letter from His Majesty Bao Dai. A few weeks later he dropped again, in uniform this time

nd with two hundred other paras, all Vietnamese too, in front of the holy
ity of Phatdiem. Bishop Le Huu-tu had him discreetly warned that he was
ompelled to defend his neutrality. The Catholic militia was therefore
drawn up in order of battle behind a canal, and after the usual summons —
hat is to say, after they had shouted "Look out!" — they fired a few shots
ver the canal in the direction of the invaders. When the invaders had
etaliated with one or two bursts into the air, Monsignor Le Huu-tu was
ompelled to acknowledge his defeat and to sign an armistice.

To tell the truth everything was very dark and turbid in the bishoprics —
ar more so than this little act might lead one to believe. Phatdiem and
Buichu were a "sect" at the far end of the delta, facing Communist Annam.
Here you could behold religion with all its urge for power and domination. It
vas a geometrical world belonging wholly to the faith, one in which the
and, the men and everything else had been created by the priests as God
reated the earth. In the last century nothing existed but marshes, a
ermanent flood where the reddish waters of the estuaries merged imper-
eptibly with the tidal flow from the sea. But in this region of mud and
rine missionaries dug canals, bringing into existence a checkerboard of
reen islands and attracting a population, which they christened in bulk.
Later the clergy became entirely Vietnamese, and then very quickly there
rew up still another feudal domain, an ecclesiastical fief in the name of the
Lord.

The very landscape was clerical. Every main square on the board had a
ast church that out-topped and overwhelmed everything — the paddy
ields, the men, their hovels and their miserable villages. Each square, with
ts church in the middle, was a parish; the curé was the lord and the
arishioners his serfs. For the good of their bodies and souls the peasants
vere dominated by an army of little Asian priests with fat faces and shining
assocks; and there was no counting the Annamese nuns.

Over this Christian landscape, this Christian people, there ruled the
ontiffs Le Huu-tu and Pham ngoc Chi. Most of all Le Huu-tu, the white-
lad Trappist bishop of Phatdiem, bone thin in his pride and fanaticism.
When he was prior of the monastery at Chauson in the nearby Chiné range
he gave his monks such penances that they died of them, and he tortured
himself by flagellation. At Phatdiem, Le Huu-tu was as it were the inquisitor
of the faith — a faith without love and without charity: nothing but a cruel
discipline. The cathedral of Phatdiem was frightening: a huge baroque
nass, a forest of superstitions. It was from this place, in the midst of all the
ncense and all the chanting, that the wrinkled, arrogant Le Huu-tu,
educed to little more than a pair of burning eyes, ruled over his people —

a people continually on their knees or marching in processions. He was an Old Testament prophet. Compared with him, Monsignor Chi, the bishop of Buichu, seemed a plump, benign, smooth being: he was in fact quite as authoritarian, but in an insidious, hypocritical manner.

What relentless, eager tenacity these two bishops displayed, and how passionately they desired to set themselves up as absolute rulers in the name of God — a god who allowed the use of any means whatever. Thus in 1946 Le Huu-tu agreed to be Ho Chi Minh's Supreme Adviser. This he did out of hatred for the French, who earlier on had wished to hold him in check, and also because Ho Chi Minh agreed that he should have full temporal powers, allowing him to carve out whole Catholic states in the middle of the state of Vietnam. And so the bishops had their taxes and their treasuries, their law courts and their executioners, and above all their militia, which was under the command of Father Quinh. In 1949, therefore, the bishoprics were complete theocracies under the control of the Vietnamese clergy: the only foreign priest was a Belgian factotum of Le Huu-tu's.

But beneath the surface everything was going bad. The Vietminh were showing themselves more and more, spreading the spirit of atheism, carrying out propaganda against "superstition," against the priests, and against God. As the faithful went to prayer, simultaneously the Communist loudspeakers called the people to huge political meetings. But very soon Le Huu-tu had his loudspeakers and his radio too. When "bad Christians" started to worship the pictures of Stalin, Thorez and Mao Tse-tung he punished them most severely. To counteract the Vietminh organizations he set up the Catholic Association for National Safety, and presently it included the whole of the population, the curés being God's political commissars, opposing the political commissars who were His enemies. There were also the Vietnamese Catholic League, the Catholic Guard, and countless associations of Catholic peasants, Catholic mothers, Catholic maidens, Catholic fighters and so on. The whole of the clergy went into battle with their own weapons, making full use of confession to combat autocriticism, Holy Communion to oppose Communist enthusiasm, and prayer against emulation and all the other Red techniques. It was brainwashing in the name of Christ as against brainwashing in the name of the People. Somtimes all this took place at huge gatherings, which were called missions. And then, by way of helping Providence, Le Huu-tu furnished himself with hand grenades, rifles and pistols. Each side took to killing the other from time to time. And above all the Vietminh sent in men of its special force to murder the ferocious bishop, who nevertheless still bore the title of Ho Chi Minh's Chief Adviser. It was a very well-organized attempt, and it only failed by a hair's breadth.

Yet this curious state of balance lasted until the time Alessandri set about taking the delta. It was then that the Vietminh sent troops to occupy the bishoprics, which formed Tonkin's door to Communist north Annam — a door that the French must not control. The Vietminh resigned themselves to the temporary loss of the Tonkin delta, but not more.

In this crisis the bishops turned to prayer — vast solemn processions wound through all the villages — and to double-dealing. In the first place they told the Vietminh not to come and they told the French to stay away, proclaiming their revolutionary faith to the one and asking the other for money and arms. Then they called upon both the Viets and the French for help at the same time. The French, thanks to their paratroops, arrived first, and so Le Huu-tu signed with them, or rather with Bao Dai. But the following days were filled with remorse, hesitation, and all treason's temptations. From his cathedral pulpit Le Huu-tu thundered against the colonialists, and the faithful shouted "traitors!" at Captain Vy's paras. But secretly the bishops said to the French, "Because of you the Viets are going to carry out reprisals: they will slaughter us all. You must give us the submachine guns you promised immediately." An LCT brought a full cargo, and they had scarcely been issued to the militia before Le Huu-tu, his calm restored, said privately to his canons, "Now I have what I need for dealing with the French." He then had a long interview with a messenger from Ho Chi Minh. His Lordship was getting ready for an about turn: his underlying notion was to get the French and the Viets to kill each other off so that he should be rid of both of them. But the French intelligence service was aware of these maneuvers, and the next day the embarrassed Le Huu-tu was obliged to excuse himself: he had spoken too hastily, he said. In the end it was not the French who were attacked, but the Viet delegate who was murdered. This happened during a procession. At a given moment Le Huu-tu and his canons drew to one side; there was a burst of automatic fire and the delegate, also a part of the procession, fell to the ground.

Now, from sermon to sermon, his Lordship treated the colonialists more and more gently: their representative with him was a very Catholic colonel of a good Breton family, who was strongly in favor of the Prince-Bishop. Thus Le Huu-tu kept all that he had gained under the Viets and in addition he acquired a great many piasters and a great many weapons. The rule of the bishops was even more all-embracing than ever: indeed, they set about the forcible conversion of a great number of pagans who were living in their dioceses. It seems that in the bishopric of Buichu a certain number of obstinate heathens were beheaded. At all events a Catholic terror raged for several months.

This did not prevent the resumption of contacts with the Vietminh. The bishoprics even became the great region for smuggling contraband into the Red provinces of Thanhhoa and Vinh. What is more, Le Huu-tu and Chi utterly refused to obey the governor of Tonkin, and they held him up as an object of execration to their Catholic followers. From time to time they turned once more to extreme nationalism and insulted the French. In the months and years to come there were to be many more betrayals and disasters in the bishoprics. And in after days de Lattre hated the bishops: he was always convinced that it was because of their faithlessness, because without giving warning they let the Viets advance, that his son Bernard was killed at the Rock of Ninhbinh.

But in spite of everything this coming-over of the bishops of Phatdiem and Buichu, however full it may have been of dubious motives and plotting, did thrust the whole of Catholic Tonkin into the war on the French side. It was now quite certainly a religious crusade, even though the curés in their prudence may have preferred to speak of the struggle of the spiritual against the materialistic, Godless world. For this compact bloc of the two bishoprics drew in all the other Christian communities that were scattered throughout the delta. Whenever a cross was to be seen rising above the palms in the midst of the dark green of the Buddhist villages, there was a "Christendom." It was a ferociously different community from the others, ferociously folded in upon itself in its burning faith, the faith that dominated its entire life. And the whole drama of the Vietnamese Catholics lay in this difference: they had the pride of being the chosen of God and yet at the same time the humiliation of being rejected by the whole nation. For as the mass of the people saw it the Catholics were still the turncoats, the men who had earlier denied their race and had allowed the French of the nineteenth century to carry out their conquest. So gradually they had acquired the "convert's complex," the need to cry out to the other Vietnamese, "We are quite as patriotic as you: indeed, we are even more so." And that was why, in 1945, the Catholics had flung themselves into revolutionary nationalism, had carried it to extremes, and had collaborated with Ho Chi Minh.

But inevitably the moment came when Catholicism was riddled with Communist cells, when it was eaten away from within and without. Ho Chi

Minh had even wanted to set up a national church, separated from Rome. Then the Catholics had to make their choice: was the faith to come first or the country? And the Catholics who had so ardently desired not to be the tools of the French became their tools once more.

This brought in close to a fifth of the population of Tonkin against the huge Vietminh organization: it also brought in a mysticism that was as hard and relentless as all Ho Chi Minh's dialectic. It should not be forgotten that it was the Spaniards from the Philippines who brought the Truth to Tonkin: this unbelievable Catholicism of another era, another world, which could so easily turn into the Catholicism of total warfare, receiving and inflicting martyrdom with an impartial hand.

That is what happened around 1949. Throughout the whole delta every Christian community formed its own army, its militia, and turned its village into a fortress, with the curé in command. In time to come, how often did I not hear French officers say, "These Catholics are swine, even worse than the other Vietnamese — there's not a single trick they don't play on us. But with them, when the crunch comes, when the Viets attack, it's not like with the others: you can rely on the Catholics absolutely then — it's the steadiness of a holy war."

Thus the "Christendoms" gradually became human supporting points for the French in the midst of the swarming delta. It was an immense advantage: but it was also to prove a disadvantage. For here again the Expeditionary Force was basing itself upon a minority, and this had the effect of keeping at a distance — of rejecting — the greater part of the population.

The rice war

IN May 1950 the French were certainly coping with the Tonkin delta. As the Expeditionary Force spread, so also did money and goods. And, as Alessandri put it, "When the economy goes well, everything goes well." The little general was exceedingly proud of the peace and the prosperity that he had brought. Alone with his aide-de-camp, in an ordinary jeep flying his flag, he went without an escort to see what he had accomplished in the regions that had been the most disaffected and the most unsure. He traveled along the roads, the tracks, and even along those Red River dikes that had served as almost impregnable entrenchments for the Viets. Now there was life everywhere, activity, masses of people: it was a real resurrection of that countryside in which there had been nothing but hostile desolation. This was Asia enjoying itself — people crowding cheerfully into the marketplaces, villagers gossiping in front of their huts, long lines of women walking along the dikes all in step to balance their carrying poles. But above all in the paddy fields the millions of *nha-qués* gathered their harvest in peace.

Everywhere there flew either the French or the Vietnamese flag. There was not merely abundance, but it also seemed as though the mass of the people had it to themselves — as though they were not having to share with the Viets. Of course one could not tell for sure. The gray, dreary landscape of the delta gave nothing away, any more than the faces of the millions of *nha-qués*. But Giap's divisions were doomed in the long run if supplies did not come in from the delta.

This was Pacification. In any case there was practically no fighting in the delta during the months that marked the monsoon. The earth was as waterlogged as the sky, and in their dripping grayness they could scarcely be told apart. The ground was a flat liquid surface, and all over it one could just make out bent figures, the little saturated forms of men and women whose black hair and ragged clothing stuck to their skin and even to their bones.

Work in the fields — the works of peace, as people say. And yet it was not so: nothing was wholly true in Asia. For a war was going on, the most secret, the most immediately decisive of wars. This was the height of the rice war. If the Vietminh lost it, in a very little while they would lose everything else, including their lives.

Rice counts for everything in Asia. In 1945, when it ran short in Tonkin, a million *nha-qués* died of starvation. Their bodies strewed the Hanoi streets, and requisitioned trishaws picked them up every morning. Every village had its own charnel house.

For the Viets, too, rice counted for everything: more than everything. It was not merely food. Earlier, with the formula "rice or guns," it had allowed them to buy their first weapons; now rice, in itself, was the whole of Ho Chi Minh's economy — I mean his entire economic system. In the first place it was his currency. The kilo of rice became the official monetary unit after the Ho Chi Minh piaster had been abandoned. Taxes were paid in kilos of rice; so was the "patriotic loan." Even the budget was worked out in kilos of rice — income and expenditure were calculated in these terms. The pay of the soldiers and the civil servants was in kind, that is to say in kilos of rice. The kilo of rice was the standard for everything that was bought or sold. If the rice were to fail, it would mean not only famine but the total collapse of Ho Chi Minh's war.

So all through their fighting against the Expeditionary Force the Viets were obsessed with rice and the desire to possess it. The obsession produced strange results: it had a continual influence upon the war, and at times it was almost the predominant factor. Thus, in order to be able to go on with the full-scale war at all, they were forced to break it off at regular intervals to conduct the rice war.

These hostilities had their own rules. During the first phase, while the *nha-qués* were gathering the harvest, there was a lull: both sides let them work in peace, merely keeping an eye on them. But scarcely were the last sheaves in before the rice war broke out in all its fury, with both the French and the Vietminh rushing in from all sides to snatch the harvest from the peasants.

In order to gain possession of the rice the first essential was to have a complete hold over the population. The Viets threw in everything they had. To begin with their regulars and their semiregulars spread all over the countryside in large and small units. Their first task was to wrest control of the largest possible area and population from the Expeditionary Force for the necessary space of time. The tactics were fitted to the local circumstances. Where the French posts were slow witted the Vietminh soldiers slipped into village after village, taking care to arouse no suspicions. Where the posts were more wide awake the Viets organized ambushes, so that the French should be frightened and shut themselves up in their fortifications. But sometimes the French high command mounted large-scale operations and sent in whole battalions to hunt down the Red detachments. When this happened the Vietminh had orders to resist, and then the fighting might be very heavy indeed: the rice war could take on the appearance of the full-scale war, for as usual there were plenty of Viets available.

Behind the Communist army the whole of the Red political and economic system worked at full blast to secure the grain. All the Vietminh of every kind were mobilized for this — soldiers, guerrilla fighters, the whole membership of the Party, the most important political commissars, Ho Chi Minh with his even more frequent exhortations, and all the people's organizations. The one and only goal was rice, the greatest possible quantity of rice. That was the function of the taxes, the loans, the contributions, everything that could reduce the peasants to the very lowest level of subsistence and leave them with only just enough to prevent them from dying of hunger. The technique used was that of "persuasion": the people had to give "willingly, happily, for love of their country," and give all they had. There was the obsessional reiteration of the word "country." Running parallel with the fighting against the French there were immense people's festivities — political meetings, Stakhanovist competitions, ceremonies at which heroes were rewarded and traitors punished, and above all great patriotic campaigns such as "President Ho Chi Minh's campaign for rice" or "the soldier's rice-bowl campaign." And then there were Ho Chi Minh's unceasing appeals, perpetually coming over the loudspeakers, endlessly elaborated by the local leaders and endlessly analyzed by the masses: "I ask every family to give me ten kilos of rice. Of course I am not asking this of the poor. On the other hand, the rich who are willing to give me more will certainly be welcome. I shall write personally to all my fellow countrymen who help me most in the villages and the provinces. Forward to victory!" And then the poor gave in spite of everything and the rich gave too, so as not to be looked upon as reactionaries and so as to have certificates that might one day save their lives.

While the Vietminh army was doing its utmost to protect this intensive collection the French army exerted all its powers to hinder it and to get possession of the rice on its own account, on the principle that whatever the French bought was denied to the enemy. The advantage that the French possessed was that they could pay in piasters, the good Bank of Indochina piasters.

This was not enough. It was too formless, too patchy. For a long while the Viets had the rice they needed. Everything changed when at last both Saigon and Hanoi grasped that the only way of beating the Viets was by waging the rice war. In Cochinchina this led to the blockade of the region beyond the Bassac — the blockade so fiercely resisted by the exporters. One of them told me, "They are trying to ruin French business under the pretext of war." But above all it was Alessandri who inflicted their most terrible defeat on the Viets, almost without fighting, by definitively occupying the Tonkin delta. The soldiers of the People's Army and the political commissars went to ground and hid; and the yield of rice for the Vietminh dropped by almost half.

Half the population of Tonkin was under the effective supervision of the French posts. And so the remainder, all the rest of the people, no longer felt the same zeal for giving. More than any other, the Asian masses do not possess deep feelings: a whole mechanism is required to bring them into artificial existence. Formerly it was the Confucianism of the mandarins. Now it was the political commissars' dialectic. The whole Vietminh organization was used to urge on and animate the people. But the nha-qué was Red only when he was in a Red iron lung. If the system weakened all the Vietminh's hold disappeared. Thus, soon after the Red military cover disappeared from the delta the political network withered away. And when the nha-qués no longer had the militants to stir them up and keep them on the right road they once more became what they had been, just ordinary men. They realized that they did not like having no more than sixty kilos of rice a month as all that remained to them from their whole harvest, and they began to cheat.

In 1950 the Viets were in a state of the utmost apprehension about their rice supplies. Something very close to famine was afflicting the quadrilateral: full-scale rations could only be maintained for the shock troops, for Giap's army. For the rest, the ordinary fighting men, the civil servants and the Party officers, there was a starvation allowance of one bowl of rice a day. And Ho Chi Minh himself gave the lead.

Later one of Ho Chi Minh's ministers said to me, speaking of those days, "It was dreadful. I was ill with hunger, and for months on end I was very weak. Not only rice was lacking but everything — there was no salt left, no medicines, no clothes. What quantities of men died in those days among the terrible mountains! Morale was affected from top to bottom. The French had us by the throat. We told one another that we could not hold out much longer unless we broke their grip. As we prepared to fight we reflected that it was our last chance and that we had to win within a few months or perish utterly."

Ho Chi Minh's radio acknowledged this extreme shortage, saying that even more austerity was needed, even greater privations. There was rivalry to see who could eat the least. And the whole of the propaganda, the political commissars' continual "correct solution," was to save, to save even more. Lastly there came the supreme appeal — "Go without, so that we can build up the stocks needed for the great counteroffensive." In all these trials — the delta escaping from their grasp, the nha-qués growing lukewarm, the rice impossible to find — the Viet called upon their own people for the utmost sacrifice in the name of victory.

So the Viets were almost at the end of their tether: they admitted it themselves. Their only way out was a general offensive — in their language it was a general counteroffensive — in which Giap's army should really come to grips with the French army for the first time. But that was the solution that they themselves had chosen — double or nothing.

But who on the French side could possibly imagine that Giap might win? They remembered how Nguyen Binh, at bay in Cochinchina, had also tried to save himself by a "general counteroffensive," and how it had only ensured his total defeat. The whole Expeditionary Force, with the exception of a few units on the R.C. 4, thought that it would be the same for Giap, only more so. For the defeat of the Tongbo Committee would be the Vietminh's death knell, and that at last would be the end of the war in Indochina.

The French were all the more confident since from now on "morality" was on their side, and with it all America's support. It was not they who had changed but the rest of the world — there had been aggression in Korea; Mao's flag was flying on the frontier of Tonkin; the whole of Asia was in arms and there was the threat of a worldwide war. The Expeditionary Force was still fighting the Vietminh in the same way and with the same intentions; but in a few weeks its "colonialist" war had become a war fought by the free world against Communism. Formerly the French had had the feeling of being outcasts; and even among the fighting men, many of them had something of a bad conscience about what they were doing — about waging the "dirty war." Now they were being hailed as the soldiers of civilization. And the dollars and the American supplies were not far off.

The star-spangled alliance

JUNE 1950. American materiel began to flow into Indochina. It started on a very small scale with the delivery of a few old Dakotas (DC-3's). At Saigon's Tan Son Nhut airfield American military pilots handed them over to French pilots. No ceremonies, no speeches. Standing opposite one another the pilots of the two countries saluted; then soldiers appeared, carrying pots of paint, and they painted the red, white and blue rings of France over the white star of the American Air Force.

A few weeks later the first vessel, a Liberty ship called the *Steelrover,* docked at Saigon; this was in the port itself, in full view of the whole city. Her cargo was military supplies. This was a date of the very first importance — America was with the French. The Viets too were aware of what it meant, and on their radio they said they would blow up the *Steelrover.* Because of this the French took the most elaborate precautions: they dragged the fifty miles of the Saigon River (a little while before, the *Saint-Loup Pervia,* an ordinary trading vessel, had been mined there). On the appointed day the *Steelrover* steamed slowly up through the muddy, winding channel in the midst of the labyrinthine mangroves, surrounded by a remarkable escort — a mine-sweeper in front, guard boats all around, planes above, and both banks lined with troops. Precautions in the port itself were even stricter. When the *Steelrover* had tied up and the jeeps, already in their gray-green warpaint, were being unloaded, there was a policeman with a revolver and a Moroccan with a submachine gun for every coolie. I went on board and I looked at the crew — healthy, broad-shouldered, coarse, well-fed sailors stripped to the waist, with peaked caps on their heads. The captain was a huge man with an Irish name, and his red hair blazed in the sun. He offered me a drink — a Negro brought whiskey — and very cheerfully told me that he had little notion of why he was there in Saigon and that he did not give a damn. I gazed at all these big tattooed uncaring men and I realized that America had really swung into action and that she was backing the Expeditionary Force for good and all.

The change was plain to see and it was unbelievable. America was no longer calling for the expulsion of the Expeditionary Force but for alliance with it. The whole American machine had put itself into reverse, for now instead of rejecting France the United States was helping her. American generals, senators and journalists poured in to gauge the efficacity of the Expeditionary Force and to increase it. American money was allotted to Indochina — military aid, economic aid. This was the beginning of that great flow of dollars which meant that in the end the Indochinese war cost France almost nothing: indeed, it has even been said that she made a profit out of it. The notorious billion francs a day (and later it was to be well over a billion) was paid to an ever-increasing extent by the taxpayers of the New World.

After such vicissitudes this was a most remarkable recovery. Roosevelt had pronounced anathemas upon the French in Indochina. And at Potsdam Truman had once more taken up the doctrine of anticolonialism. The idea had been that Chiang Kai-shek, having turned out the Red Ho Chi Minh, was to have Indochina. Yet there had been a time when Uncle Sam's countless special agents had nevertheless tried to play the Ho Chi Minh card. The best known and the most conspicuous was a certain Major Patti. It was he and his assistants who had enthroned Ho Chi Minh at Hanoi during the summer of 1945. Standing by his side during those huge demonstrations, they gave him their countenance and their authority, while hundreds of French, who were virtually prisoners and who were suffering every kind of humiliation, might very well have been slaughtered.

At that time the American course of action, perfectly conscious and deliberately pursued, was aimed at preventing France from returning. This was done at all levels, from the "high politics" of refusing the ships to carry Leclerc's armored divisions to the ugly little meannesses at Hanoi. The Americans were largely responsible for the atmosphere in Hanoi in 1945, when their special agents were kings of the castle and the French were men who should be knocked on the head — and who were knocked on the head. Patti was all powerful and Sainteny was shut up in a house which he was forbidden to leave.

All this came to nothing. For the Americans it was a double fiasco: in

Tonkin, Chiang Kai-shek came to pieces in their hands, and then they began to have doubts about Ho Chi Minh as an alternative solution. Bao Dai had turned them down. The State Department and the Pentagon realized that Ho Chi Minh, instead of being the unadulterated Nationalist described in the reports from Patti and the special agents, might very well be a Communist. So after a few weeks Uncle Ho was dropped, and all recollection of the incident faded from the American memory. It is nevertheless a fact that it was the United States that helped Ho Chi Minh to settle himself in — and this at the decisive moment of the Vietminh seizure of power. It was largely America who "made" Ho Chi Minh.

During the years that followed these terrible disappointments the American attitude was strangely embarrassed and awkward. It was as though the Americans did not know what to do and therefore resigned themselves to letting the French carry on, still maintaining their puritanical disapproval, however. It went bitterly against the grain: they were fundamentally opposed to it, and they were only waiting for the chance to back nationalism once more and to give it their total support, but with this change — since Ho Chi Minh was a Communist, the right patriotic Nationalist had to be found, the one who would beat Ho Chi Minh and his Communism far better than the repressive French. All the Americans in Saigon, those in the embassy, those in the military mission and the special services and the USIS, to say nothing of the American journalists, were ill with Francophobia, virtuously ill at the spectacle of the French setting up "colonialism" once more. They had such a wonderfully deep and sincere belief in the essential evil of it all. And they were so sure that America would do so much better than France and they themselves so much better than the French. How many times did not some American say to me, "You Frenchmen are corrupt, and you still believe in Machiavellism. That's your only answer in Indochina — wretched Machiavellism. It's not only revolting but completely out of date as well." How passionately they all longed for a real Vietnam, a friend of America, instead of this Vietnam given over as a prey to the French. In such a Vietnam they would be able to use all the "expansionist" theories they had learned at college and in the Protestant churches: expansion, that is, of the domain of the American spirit and the American way of life. It was more and more of a Pilgrim's Progress crusade against French "Machiavellism"; a crusade based on priggishness, schoolmarm's morality and frigid anger. More and more every day they behaved like frustrated righters of wrong.

By the beginning of 1950 a state of exasperation reigned between the French and Americans in Saigon — a mutual hatred. Each side saw very little of the other: there was hardly any social interchange. In the midst of the French Saigon of the piaster and the Expeditionary Force the Americans were shut away with their dollars, their luxury, their parties, their intrigues and their particular functions — for each of them had an exactly defined job. Their numbers continually grew: they were very rich and very bitter, and they bought the most splendid houses for their agencies and their dwellings, setting themselves up as little blocks of resistance, living apart, devoting themselves to work and taking such care of their health that they reached the point of eating and drinking nothing but what came from the States, including water. But in spite of their puritanism they let themselves go in the evenings at cocktail parties where too much drink disappeared and where there were some very odd forms of amusement.

All the Americans in Saigon were against their ambassador, Heath, who was accused of being too passive: but his second-in-command, Gullion, was a great upholder of Americanism. Heath on the one hand was a cautious, wrinkled fifty-year-old and very small as well, with a long, frozen fish's face; and Gullion, on the other, was a fine, dark young fellow, something of a coxcomb and a member of the new generation, full of go, full of angry indignation. I noticed this inner rage of his one day when I was at his house, standing at a cold buffet; speaking to a Frenchman I made the commonplace remark that I did not much care for eating in the American way, on my feet. But Gullion had heard and he rushed over to me and shouted, "Do you know that in no matter what little American town there are more lovers of Beethoven and Bach than in the whole of Paris?"

But when the French set about manufacturing Vietnamese Independence this Americanism sprang most energetically to life. It had begun in Hong Kong where every day the United States consulate had advised Bao Dai (on the point of accepting Pignon's proposals): "Don't yield. Don't weaken. Refuse." And when Bao Dai accepted nevertheless, shutting himself away in Dalat with his neurasthenia and his debauchery, there was a kind of explosion of outbidding in Saigon: Americans of every kind whispered to Vietnamese of every kind, "Ask for more. Don't give in. Don't let yourselves be swayed by the French: they have just been waiting for their moment and they are trying to get out of their difficulties by disguising their colonial problem as anti-Communism." It worked one hundred per cent against the French. By every means, and above all by the use of dollars, the Americans built themselves up a following. The secret services for their part went further: they gave arms to Bacut the Hoahao, to Trinh Minh-the Caodaist, and to all the leaders within the sects who went on hating the French and killing them in the name of nationalism.

The campaign reached its height when the unbelievable Nguyen Phan-long was at the head of the government. It was then that there was talk of an American-inspired plan for replacing the Expeditionary Force by a national army of two hundred thousand men, trained and led by Americans or even by Japanese. Meanwhile Nguyen Phan-long, during those very weeks when his Saigon was sinking under the tide of anarchy, no longer wanted Vietnam to be a state associated with France — he wanted dominion status. And even that was not his underlying wish. He really wanted America to take the place of France — the regime of the Philippines rather than that of the French Union.

This was not America's official policy: but it was not far from it. More and more one had the feeling that the fate of the French in Indochina was going to be that of the Dutch in Indonesia — eviction by Yankee puritanism. And as the Expeditionary Force carried out the Pacification, so it worked against itself, for the moment would come when the Americans would reflect "There is no longer any need for a French military force: let's carry things through and do away with it."

So in Indochina the French were in the strangest position: for if they were to overcome the Vietminh they would thereby all the more certainly condemn themselves to another defeat. They were advancing steadily towards a deadlock when, in a few weeks, everything suddenly changed. For these were the weeks of the great American fear: the invasion of Korea saved French Indochina. For the moment realism swept puritanism to one side. In the high places of Washington only one thing counted now — that there should be a French army on the southern flank of the terrible Red China. So Washington gave France her head in Indochina: but this same France, with an army chiefly made up of mercenaries, herself became Ameria's mercenary for an Indochinese war waged within the framework of the overall American strategy for Asia. For although the United States provided the Expeditionary Force with materiel it was not really because of the Vietminh: it was primarily against Mao's China. There was a tacit understanding. The French would bar the way, with their persons, to the invasion of southeast Asia by Communism. And the Americans would pay them, providing the means to continue the war indefinitely.

During the months and the years to come this understanding was observed by the one side and the other, in a way that was both straight and devious. It was an odd state of affairs.

On the military level the Americans behaved well. After a very slow start they supplied such a vast quantity of materiel that the Expeditionary Force was unable to use it all — though this was very much later. To be sure, the American officers also tried to supervise strategy; but after a few fruitless brushes with a high command that was ferociously attached to its prerogatives they decided to leave it entirely to the French. In the end all the experts of the Military Aid Advisory Group kept in the background, resigning themselves to letting this Indochinese war be fought in the French way.

For the Americans the Expeditionary Force was no more than a temporary expedient. Yet they did their best to believe in it, however little confidence they may really have had; for the most practical solution was to make use of it as it stood.

Nevertheless the two-faced attitude was obvious. All the Americans, very patiently this time, very systematically and very discreetly too, were preparing an alternative solution. For after all it might happen that one day the French would draw in their horns and abandon the pushing back of the Reds — that they might either come to terms with them or be beaten. If this were to happen there could be no question of the American troops taking over in the jungle: Korea was enough for them. But if the Expeditionary Force were to fail or if it were no longer to suit, might it not be possible to build up an anti-French political system, with America playing her well-known part of defender of all forms of independence and nationalism? No doubt that would work quite as well; perhaps better.

Endlessly the Liberty ships brought to Saigon everything that was needed for the Expeditionary Force to wage an energetic French war. And endlessly too, fresh "quiet Americans" appeared in Saigon and all the rest of Indochina. The agencies multiplied: the staffs grew enormously. Everything increased tenfold. All the organizations that were already there swelled prodigiously, and even more were added to their number, in particular the huge machinery of the economic aid. Saigon swarmed with American civil servants, technicians and agents: there were hundreds of them, close on a thousand.

Every month the invasion increased. When the Americans had bought all the handsome buildings they had others, even more splendid, run up for them. The old French Saigon of villas and bungalows was put in the shade by the American constructions, which had the air of small skyscrapers. The Stars and Stripes flew in almost every street.

Not only the Americans' embassy but their main offices were guarded by Marines. Heath was terrified of being assassinated. To set his mind at rest Tam's police thought up the idea of manufacturing a plot against him, a plot that would naturally allow them to carry out all sorts of spectacular arrests and interrogations. But this proof of the authorities' watchfulness did not set Heath's mind at rest at all: its only effect was to make him far more nervous, and he insisted upon being protected by real American service-men, strapping great heavyweights — and they were flown in at once.

In theory this superabundant American activity was in no way hostile to France — far from it. The official pronouncements perpetually played up Franco-American friendship. In fact what was going on was an immense undermining operation. Thus the country was inundated with a flood of goods "made in USA": it was the whole gamut of Yankee civilization, from DDT to canned cheese. And to each parcel was sewn a huge label with the crossed flags of Vietnam and the United States and the words "A gift from the people of America to the people of Vietnam."

It was the experts of the Economic Aid Mission who carried out the free distributions. They traveled all through Indochina telling the crowds, "The French are your exploiters, but the Americans are your friends." Nothing diminished their zeal, not even the fact that their presents, instead of being gratefully used by the recipients, were instantly sold again on the black market. Most of the time the *nha-qués* had no idea of what they were for. Many of them tried the DDT as a fertilizer; and finding that it did not answer they gave up looking for any reasonable use for it. The cheese was particularly unsuccessful. At first the people thought it was a special kind of latherless soap; but on being told that it was meant to eat they were unable to conceal their disgust.

The more these disappointments mounted up, the more eager the Americans became. How ardently, in spite of their racial prejudices, they tried to love the Vietnamese. They visited them; they invited them to dinner. Every day their wives gathered to give English lessons to the more deserving neophytes. Protestant missionaries, uncommonly well supplied with dollars, took part in this crusade. They carried brassieres to the Moi ladies of the high plateaus. They had their own planes. One of them organized miracles, causing the voice of God to be heard from the heavens by means of a radio floating on a parachute.

The Economic Aid Mission's masterpiece was the Abode of Happiness, a brand-new prefabricated model village, set up near Hanoi so that the wretched *nha-qués* might learn what a decent life was like. But all through the following years, alas, the Vietminh attacked and destroyed it, and I do not know how many times the Americans had to build it up again.

The more obstacles the Americans met the more they loathed the French: no longer openly, as they had in the days before the "alliance," but covertly, and perhaps with even greater force. The disappointments were due to French sabotage: the Americans held them responsible for every-thing. I remember one day an American woman was unable to restrain herself and in my presence bitterly lamented the colonialists' wickedness, which prevented her husband from teaching the villagers to brush their teeth. All the Americans were convinced of this wickedness.

Underlying the alliance there was secret war. At the higher levels, in Washington for example or at Heath's embassy, there was straight dealing — with the slight exception that an American influence was being built up parallel to the French influence, one which might replace it from one day to the next if that were decided upon. But that was only in reference to the uncertain future. For the moment the action was merely indirect: the orders from above were that the economic and political machine set up in Saigon should not work all out, as it would have to do to abolish the moral and physical presence of the French. So what indignation there was in all the countless American agencies and offices in Saigon, what fury, what bitterness, what cries of impotence against the high-ups who understood nothing, and against the French, who went on being kings of the castle! Naturally all these little Americans, eaten up by their consciences and carried away by zeal, went beyond their orders and joyfully did everything they could think of against the French. By way of counteracting the vile French Machiavellism they set up one of their own, moral, full of the Bible, God and whiskey. Yet they were unhappy: they lived in a high state of nervous tension, their imaginations brimming with detectives, spies, French or French-paid agents provocateurs, who shadowed them, watched them, and who were capable of any excess. Was there a single American who did not believe that there were all sorts of men at his heels, lurking in the shadows and undoing all that he had accomplished — even perhaps threatening his life? In order to defend themselves the Americans bought still more people, but as they did so they became even more distrustful of everybody around them. They set up immense filing systems, with cards for everyone. They were suspicious of everything: the French were only friendly in order to carry out the most sinister schemes; and there were these Vietnamese gentlemen who might be anything — maybe French police informers, maybe disguised Vietminh.

It is quite true that the French thwarted Yankee evangelism in countless ways. All their "allies' " underhand dealings and ceaseless machinations vexed them. Their revenge was to make them come unstuck. But they were much less passionately eager about this than the Americans supposed, for the French thought the Americans too clumsy to be very dangerous. As a French military intelligence officer said to me, "Very often the Americans torpedo themselves. There's no need to do anything about it. A little while ago I took two U.S. officers to a post held by a purely Asian unit of partisans. The Vietnamese sergeant in charge had had a banquet prepared in our honor — a lacquered piglet, quantities of shrimps and *nem*,* all dripping with a particularly malodorous *nuoc mam*. At the sight of the feast the Americans shuddered: then, apologizing, they took sealed packets out of their briefcases, cellophane-wrapped germ-free food. The Annamese NCO went pale as they started to eat their hygienic sandwiches without so much as touching the dishes he offered them: he was mortally offended. The Americans will never be dangerous so long as they are afraid of catching dysentery."

In fact at that time the French were not afraid of the American shadow which was spreading farther and farther across Indochina. As they saw it they would still be the masters there as long as the Expeditionary Force remained in Vietnam. And the departure of the Expeditionary Force was not for tomorrow nor anything like it, what with the Korean War and Mao Tse-tung and everything else. There was still a long time to go.

To tell the truth, the French had a far more important concern than the mere thwarting of the Americans. This was getting the most out of them, milking them ever more and more. It went beyond cleverness, it went beyond mere cunning: it was that sort of whorish behavior that soldiers are so good at. They insisted upon guns, ammunition, radars, tanks, trucks, fighter aircraft — indeed everything that Paris would not provide. And to this end the high command, which had very little belief in the Vietminh danger and still less in the Chinese, behaved as though it were very much alarmed, and systematically put out false intelligence that was meant to end up in Washington. It spread information of the utmost gravity knowing perfectly well that it was untrue. For example, they had a secret treaty forged: it was allegedly signed by Mao Tse-tung and Ho Chi Minh and it revealed that China was building up a very large Vietnamese army of shock troops with Chinese materiel, techniques and training. This army was on the point of bursting out, perhaps accompanied by the Chinese. But having made flesh creep in the Pentagon the French high command hastened to state that the Expeditionary Force could halt a Sino-Vietminh invasion equal in volume to the attack in Korea on the condition that it was "adequately" armed. It was this "adequately" that allowed the Expeditionary Force to have itself handsomely kept for years on end.

There was subtlety everywhere. For as the Americans gave the Expeditionary Force their aid they wondered whether they were being diddled, and they half tried to diddle the French at the same time. And, to be sure, the French were by no means wholly candid. As they saw it the Korean

* *Nem* are rice-flour fritters.

War was an opportunity to be seized upon at once and to be exploited to the uttermost. So the French command said to the American command, "What is happening to you on the thirty-eighth parallel may happen to us on the Tonkin frontier. Faced with the threat of Mao, we have a common cause. Give us a very great deal." But all they really wanted was to crush the Viets and to keep Indochina for the French, making use of these Americans who were so eager to get them out. The whole ploy was to use the Americans as a cover against China, to let MacArthur's and Lin Piao's armies fight it out in Korea — and in the meantime to wage a full-scale war against Ho Chi Minh and Giap. To do all this with American money, with American materiel, but without American command.

The most curious aspect was that without suspecting it the French were diddling themselves. For all this alarming information that they spread, believing it to be entirely fictitious and devoid of foundation, all this intelligence about the imminence of a great Red offensive, about Giap's divisions, the Chinese camps and so on, turned out in the long run to be true, catastrophically true. And it was this, this ruse which was also an egregious error of appreciation, that was to lead straight to the disaster on the crags of Dongkhe, the most fatal defeat of the whole Indochinese war. And yet all this had not been wholly useless: for it was the materiel wrung from the Americans on false pretenses that was later to allow de Lattre to stop the rush of the victorious Vietminh towards Hanoi.

Those spring months of 1950 were the season of high optimism for the command. Never had Carpentier and Alessandri given Paris such hopeful assurances — they competed to see which could please the government more. The authorities were still so utterly convinced that a few French units would be enough to annihilate the whole of Giap's army if only he would accept a pitched battle! And yet behind this cheerful front, behind all these ostentatious certainties, there was not quite the same unshaken conviction of superiority that there had been before. Little doubts had crept into the generals' minds in spite of everything, little doubts that were hidden altogether or at least carefully camouflaged. That was why Carpentier decided that it would be better to postpone the sending back of the first section of the Expeditionary Force for a little while: yet it was a return that had been asked for by the government, that had been approved by the general staff, and that was then being worked out for implementation.

To be sure, officially this delay had only one aim — that of allowing the victory to be won even more quickly and even more completely. Furthermore it is true that Carpentier and Alessandri, and practically the whole of the Expeditionary Force with them, believed that victory was just at hand.

But nevertheless the prudent commander in chief was afraid of some local setback that might throw a shade over the expected triumph. He wanted to win — which was characteristic of him. Characteristically he wanted to win with all precautions taken. As for Alessandri, he wanted to charge to victory; and for that he needed a great many men.

The fact of the matter was that these apprehensions, these first stirrings of apprehension, were but pale reflections of the true situation. For alongside all the success that had been achieved there had also been certain events that it was more agreeable to overlook as insignificant but which nevertheless possessed very real importance. But for those whose eyes were open they were quite enough to justify General Revers, that unfortunate prophet of woe. He was still in complete disgrace, however, crushed by a completely bogus scandal: and in Indochina everybody was blind, or very nearly so.

The prophet of woe

PROPHETS of woe are rare birds. General Revers was Indochina's Jeremiah. Or perhaps it would be better to say that in those early days of 1949, when Bao Dai was installed, he had wanted to smash the whole system, everything that had crystalized there into a kind of block, with His Majesty, Pignon, semicolonialism, the piaster, Pacification and the war on the R.C. 4. But in the end it was the powerful Revers, the chief of the general staff, who was smashed.

He was not the traditional kind of soldier; he had been a reserve officer who transferred to the active list, and during the war he had belonged to the army's Resistance movement, succeeding its chief when the Germans captured him. He therefore started with great advantages after the liberation; furthermore the Fourth Republic with its political parties suited him well, and he attached himself to the left wing — not of course a left wing with anything revolutionary about it, but the left of the Socialist SFIO, the Freemasons, certain big business circles and men who favored NATO and America.

Poor Revers! In spite of all his hand-shaking and business luncheons and haunting of politicians he was a decent fellow and a patriot — and he loved the army. And indeed with all his cunning he still retained the simplicity of the soldier who forms his own notions of the great world and imagines that he really knows his way about. He was useful to people and people were useful to him. That was the way to succeed, he was sure. Besides, had he not taken de Lattre's place? He was chief of the general staff of the French army. What glory! He knew a great many people, from the President, the prime minister and General Mast (his admired friend and mentor) right down to some very curious loiterers in the corridors of power.

It began when he was in Washington. He was quietly discussing the problems of the Atlantic Pact with the Americans when the order came from Paris, "Go and have a look at Indochina and see what's going on there." At first he did not care for the idea. In spite of his position he was still almost unknown at the Pentagon: to the American generals, those neophytes in militarism, immature and formidable with their worship of pure energy, virility, toughness and war, he was but a dubious product of decadent French civilization. It was imperative that he should set their minds at rest, make friends and win them over. What could be more inopportune than this distant mission concerned with a colonial war that, in those days, Washington disliked very much indeed?

However, Revers returned to Paris and made ready for his journey to the Far East. From this time on everything becomes extraordinarily obscure. Very briefly the main lines were these: a bitter struggle was going on between the anticlerical SFIO and the MRP, the young left-of-center Catholic party that had emerged from the war and the Resistance with so much glory. Ramadier, the Socialist war minister, and many of his friends felt that no good would come of Indochina and that the French should get out. The MRP, on the other hand, insisted upon a strong policy in the name of France, the West, civilization and Catholicism. Pignon was their man and the Bao Dai solution their policy — and the MRP Coste-Floret was minister for overseas territories in the coalition government.

Before Revers started for Indochina his hangers-on had appeared in Saigon: presently Pignon's intelligence men learned that they were making some very strange contacts. When Revers arrived he brought a whole mission with him, and very soon it became evident that his purpose was to get rid of Pignon, Bao Dai and the MRP policies, to hand over power to the army and to return to the line laid down by Leclerc — the working out of a kind of "peace of the brave" with Ho Chi Minh. Revers's underlying notion was that Ho Chi Minh was afraid of the Chinese, and instead of throwing him into Mao Tse-tung's arms it would be far better to come to an understanding with him for an independence that should not be a mere disguised protectorate but a real friendship, favorable to the interests of France, her culture and her trade.

Tirelessly he hurried about, seeing bankers, Vietminh envoys, businessmen, collecting material for a devastating report, a top-secret report of the very first importance. On the way back he stopped off at Bangkok to charm the dictator of Siam, Marshal Pibul, a ferocious and quick-handed anti-Communist who was completely under the control of the United States. But even more important, he made a little halt in Rome — the notorious Freemason wanted to bring the Pope into action. In a private audience His Holiness displayed a "sympathetic understanding." There was a great deal at stake for Revers. How much easier everything would be if the Vatican were to issue appropriate orders to the Vietnamese Catholics on the one hand and to the French MRP on the other!

But his opponents had not been idle all this time: they knew very well what he was about and they had taken their measures. One day a soldier and a Vietnamese quarreled in a Paris bus: they came to blows just as it reached the Gare de l'Est and of course they were arrested — not by the ordinary police, who do not operate in railway stations, but by the DST, who do. And at that time the DST was under Wybot, in whom the MRP had every confidence. To the astonishment of one and all (or very nearly one and all) a copy of Revers's secret report was found on the Vietnamese. Incompetence on Revers's part, folly, even perhaps treason! Might he not have shown the document to Ho Chi Minh's agents in order to sabotage the government's official policy in Indochina and impose his own? At all events the scandal was launched and Revers was done for. And, having wished to overturn the current French policy in Indochina, Revers had, though indirectly, succeeded only in consolidating it.

Yet the report itself was a magnificent piece of work: everything was analyzed in the smallest detail, from Bao Dai, the R.C. 4, the Vietminh and the Chinese right down to the most commonplace questions of supply. And although it was weak on the positive side it was nevertheless a most remarkable cry of alarm. And that was its essence. Much would have been different if the rosy spectacles had been set aside at that time and if harsh reality had been faced. With extraordinary precision Revers foretold what would happen if things went on in the way they were going.

Later Pignon's slow realization that Revers might have been right was an agony to him; but an agony that he had to keep to himself. Revers had been wiped out; he was forgotten and despised; and yet he, or at least his ghost, was everywhere: and he had been right. He was at Dalat: he had condemned Bao Dai, and Pignon had vouched for Bao Dai. And now there was the Emperor, who owed Pignon everything, displaying all his corruption, his neuroses, his Machiavellism and his sense of importance. And all at once Pignon's conception of the independence of Vietnam turned out to be hollow, worthless, devoid of scope. At the political level, everything had failed.

But Revers was also on the R.C. 4, and there his presence was far more obvious. At his urging it had been agreed that Caobang should be evacuated, so that the Expeditionary Force might be reorganized and regrouped in defensive positions where it would stay until the negotiations. But this had to be done quickly, while there was yet time. The decision had not been officially canceled after the scandal, but it had been indefinitely postponed. So the French were still in Caobang. Soon it turned into a deadly trap, for it was there that Giap's new army struck its first hammer blows — not mere ambushes any more but great offensive movements, battles, large-scale planned assaults. The French were unable to stay, but they could no longer tell how to get out. That was how the military disaster began: and that was how the "happy war" turned into the "hopeless war."

Strange, strange year of 1950! The French moved from success to success, but the gulf was there. Nobody chose to see it; yet at the same time, and in a rapidly worsening atmosphere, everything led straight towards the precipice. After the fall into the political void of Dalat, the battalions stationed on the R.C. 4, among the cloud-topped crags of Dongkhe, were to plunge into the abyss.

Bao Dai

PIGNON's great misfortune was that Bao Dai came to pieces in his hands almost at once. As long as Revers was dangerous the Emperor was remarkably polite: once the danger was past he no longer troubled. He did not say no, but he was vague — a jellyfish; and Pignon discovered that Bao Dai possessed an extraordinary technique for not understanding, for not stirring, and for wrecking every kind of plan.

He would not live in Saigon, where he might have seemed inferior to the high commissioner, who would not yield up the Norodom Palace, his symbol of power. Nor would he live in Tonkin, although in Hanoi there would have been no question of precedence; but that would have meant engaging himself in the heart of the struggle, and he wanted nothing of that kind either. He stayed in his Dalat villa, immovable.

And there was another aspect. Pignon perfectly understood that Bao Dai would wish to make the most of the situation and become a millionaire, a more than millionaire. But why not do so in the usual unambiguous fashion, with the usual, unambiguous, enormous profits? It was suggested that important firms should be set up — banks, steamship lines, airlines, import-export houses — with fifty-one per cent of French capital, the rest being Bao Dai's without his having to produce a penny piece. But he did not like that idea either. He preferred the Asian traditions of extortion and squeeze; and his first great plan was to turn Dalat into a gambling hell, for since the decline of Macao the position had been vacant. Huge hotels and immense casinos were to be built, with a shuttle service of planes to bring in the customers, all the millionaires from Hong Kong, Singapore and elsewhere. But the French were of the opinion that the head of state ought not to be a supercroupier. It was then that Bao Dai came to his understanding with Bay Vien and had the Grand Monde at Saigon allotted to him.

The atmosphere of Dalat was profoundly corrupt, and this was particularly noticeable at the hotel where all the place seekers gathered. There were Vietminh "observers" too, as well as journalists, old acquaintances from the French and British intelligence services and a whole raft of OSS agents who were there so as to be able to answer the question "Is Bao Dai a playboy or not?" Yet on the surface everything was very proper, discreet and hidden — very Vietnamese. No nation on earth is so addicted to grave protocol, even during the haggling over the basest kind of deal. The only false note was struck by a spectacularly pneumatic peroxide blonde, the chief of His Majesty's cinematographic service, brought specially from France to make a film about His Majesty. Her team was made up of swarthy gentlemen from the bars of the Côte d'Azur who were utterly incapable of handling a camera. When the blonde and her friends got drunk and a muted criticism reached Bao Dai, he replied, "Yes. I know. But really that girl is quite extraordinary in bed." And he added, "She is only plying her trade. Of the two I am the real whore."

For in his drowsy villa Bao Dai was busy charming the whole of Vietnam, all the Vietnam that counted, that is to say; and the car that carried off the wench in the morning served to bring up the first of the Emperor's visitors. They came one after another all day long, and with unfailing penetration Bao Dai detected the most ignoble weakness in each. The heart of the matter was of course to reach an understanding, but the interviews were always conducted on the most elevated tone. Bao Dai had a well-rehearsed line of talk which he delivered in French (he did not speak Vietnamese well). He stated that he was primarily a Vietnamese patriot: one had to know how to make use of the French without becoming their tool. The visitor would then proclaim his loyalty and lay his allegiance at Bao Dai's feet. It was thus that Pham Cong Tac brought the Emperor his two million "sheep": but so that the sect might depend less upon the French could not His Majesty on his side provide the Caodaist army with a subsidy or at least bring a Caodaist into the government, giving him the treasury, for example, or the ministry of war? (For as Pham Cong Tac saw it a ministry and a subsidy were the same thing.) Bao Dai was full of praise for this independent spirit: he added that he would have to consider the matter and reflect deeply upon the country's best interests (above all he did not want to give any money). That was how it went: and in a few days Bao Dai had built himself up a following by means of playing upon avarice and greed. It was only when he detected sincerity or disinterestedness in a man that he had no use for him — such men were dangerous.

So Bao Dai concentrated on his great project. For he said (and this time it was true), "I do not want to be a mere figurehead." The project was to set up a Bao Dai system that would make him the master of events. He was obliged to use his wits, to have recourse to cleverness of every kind, because he had not been able to come back as a genuine emperor. He would so have loved to return as a legitimate sovereign, as though his abdication of 1945 had been void. "For then I should have had a place," he explained, "and everything would have been easy for me." But the French had not wanted this: it is difficult to see why, since they had decided to stake everything on him — some idea of caution, no doubt. At all events, Bao Dai was only in power as a consequence of a dubious deal with the French instead of being there by unquestioned right. It was their fault that he, the descendant of so many emperors, was little more than an upstart or even a usurper. He was called Your Majesty, but majesty was not really the word — he was only the head of state, and that by virtue of proclamations signed by himself, without the slightest popular mandate or any kind of true legality. Again and again he said to Pignon, "Coming like this, I am nothing: I have to be my own maker." In short, Bao Dai, brought back by the French, was full of bitterness against them. He said it often. "I like the French, but they force me to be against them. I perpetually have to prove that I am not their puppet. So much the worse for them! It would not have been like this if I had been able to sit properly on my throne."

Bao Dai was possessed with the idea of "making himself": it was an obsession and for him it was also a disaster, because for Bao Dai "making himself" meant advancing by devious paths, being cunning and full of guile, deceiving people, corrupting and deluding them; whereas in fact all he had to do was to walk straight forward in the open. For in the whole of the country that was not Vietminh there was nothing; there was a vacuum of power, without a single political party, a single political line of thought or even any form of public opinion to fill it, and Bao Dai could have done whatever he wished. But in order to do so he would have had to master himself — to be his own ruler. He would have had to launch into the adventure of action, to become the commander, the dictator, the man who would lead Vietnam either against Communism or against colonialism, whichever he chose. That was what a normal man would have done. But Bao Dai was not a normal man: he was paralyzed, inhibited by an anxiety that abated only when he was in the midst of some tortuous squalid deal: in order to get nowhere at all he squandered the treasures of his intelligence with a lavish hand.

He saw more clearly than anyone that the real forces opposing one another in Vietnam were international Communism and the U.S.A. France was too weak, too far away, too lacking in purpose and political stability to play a decisive part in Asia. The right course therefore was not to be too friendly with her, nor yet to oppose her too systematically, since after all she was there, holding the field, and without the Expeditionary Force there would be a Vietminh avalanche. As Bao Dai saw it, the result of this was an unstable situation that would last until the great underlying realities of the world had decided Indochina's fate. He had to hold out until then by the use of intelligence. He had to obstruct everything. He had to obstruct France, which wanted to draw him along too far; but he also had to obstruct the U.S.A., which wanted to make use of him before the time was ripe. "I will neither be the puppet of the French," he said, "nor a lemon for the Americans to squeeze."

In Vietnam itself he was also opposed to everything, not with any sudden violence, but with a heavy inertia. He was against the people and everything to do with them, for he had a morbid horror of the masses, so much so that he could not bear to come into contact with them at all. So he was utterly opposed to elections and anything that could awaken the common people: for if they were to feel their importance, what might they not demand? This stubbornness was all the more odd since the Vietminh were doing everything they possibly could to improve the lot of the enormous yellow proletariat. And in the end the nha-qués, who would have followed a Bao Dai who was concerned with them, went over to the Vietminh who did in fact take care of them, even if it was too much, too often and too severely.

Bao Dai was against nationalism. He said that he was a great Nationalist, the leader of all the Nationalists of every kind; but this was only in order to obstruct more efficiently. His contacts with the Resistance never led to any results whatever.

Bao Dai was utterly against Communism and Ho Chi Minh: he knew only too well what his fate would be if they won, for they would not miss him a second time. But he showed none of this hatred, nor did he speak of it. In the beginning he even allowed some vague dealings with the Tongbo Committee. It disturbed the French and it made him more important, for it proved that the Reds were afraid of him and that they did not look upon him as someone who could be left out of account. But that was all, except that Ho Chi Minh promised that he should not be murdered. Very prudently Bao Dai saw that the main purpose of this promise might be to lull his suspicions so that he could be killed the more easily, and he surrounded his villa with an Imperial Guard. He even wanted a Vietnamese army of his own — this was his solitary constructive idea. Later he managed to get one; but by then it was so corrupt that it was of little use for anything in the war.

For the moment the one real enemy was the rich bourgeoisie of Cochinchina, who had meddled in the Revers affair and who could get along very well without the Emperor. It was for that reason that Bao Dai was against any sort of Assembly; for he knew very well that the members, influenced by the intellectuals and the wealthy men of Saigon, would very soon come to the conclusion that he was quite useless. And he could do nothing about that, or very little. But on the other hand he was perfectly willing to hand over the government to these bourgeois. There was no risk in doing so, for everything had been worked out so that they would be ruined, discredited, destroyed. It was a game in which he was always sure to come out on top.

It was played like this. There had to be a head of government: it could be Bao Dai, but he did not want that. He did not want to be in the limelight: he preferred staying behind the scenes. He said to his intimates, "All men who are greedy for action and responsibility come to a wretched end. Power kills. The clever ones who remain hidden hold the real keys of the kingdom." Bao Dai's cleverness kept him peacefully at Dalat and placed the government far away from him in Saigon. To lead this government he appointed an enemy, a man who had to be got rid of. For the government was his pitfall, his lethal trap. This was the great theory of wearing out — of wearing out all the troublesome people until there should be none left, until the day His Majesty could form a good government in which he had confidence, a government of his own gang.

At its height the Bao Dai system consisted of a handful of men around His complex Majesty. There was Nguyen De, the imperial cabinet's little Machiavelli; there was Bay Vien the gangster, who exploited the Grand Monde at Saigon for himself and for Bao Dai, and who ended up as head of all the police and intelligence organizations; later there was General Nguyen Van-hinh, another curious piece of work who was to build up a

Vietnamese army rather too much in Bao Dai's image; and at all times there was his clown and factotum Giao, the former pharmacist, the governor of Annam and the man nearest to the Emperor.

The system was to last several years longer. But already, in this spring of 1950, when Bao Dai, in a bantering tone that had a certain amount of fear in it, asked Pignon, "What do you think of the presence of the Chinese Reds on the frontier?" the high commissioner realized that he would be alone before the danger. In spite of his good fortune Bao Dai could no longer help him — he could do nothing but harm.

Nothing was left to Pignon, the civilian, the good administrator, the somewhat Jesuitical Catholic, the slightly easternized European, the specialist in politics and in policy, nothing except brute force and General Carpentier's mercenaries. From now on events had gone beyond his control: he was only a looker-on in the war that was beginning. A war between the Expeditionary Force and a People's Army modeled upon the armies of Mao Tse-tung that had risen from the proletariat and that had nevertheless beaten both the Japanese and the Kuomintang.

Pignon felt himself powerless: he thought of resigning. His heart was racked with doubt. The French high command was still optimistic, but already the frontier was cracking. Could it be that from the military point of view too General Revers had been right?

The Caobang hedgehog

It was in these days that the disaster of the frontier began.

Even before the strength of Red China had made itself felt, before Mao's armies had settled down all along the border, before Giap's striking force was ready, the French high command at last decided to carry out the discarded Revers plan. But it did so with several months' delay and it did so only partially — a half measure that only increased the mess. They were ashamed of it: they carried it out secretly, talking about a "redeployment of forces."

The R.C. 4 was evacuated — but only one end of it. All the posts beyond Caobang were withdrawn, the absolutely impossible positions, remote and lost in the mountains, Traling, Nguyen Binh, Backan and Anlai. The thin ribbon of the R.C. 4 itself was abandoned for twenty-five miles of its length between Thatke and Caobang. But two hedgehogs were maintained in the midst of this jungle given over to the Viets — two fortresses completely cut off by land and connected with the rest of the world solely by air, by airfields and airlifts. The one was Caobang itself and the other Dongkhe.

The French held these as long as they could. At Caobang Colonel Simon said, "For my part I shall not draw in a single man or give up a single yard of ground." This was the famous colonel with a bullet in his head. But his savage obstinacy and all that he underwent himself and made his men undergo was in vain. He still had to haul down the French flag, blow up the outposts and retreat with the besieged, famished, powerless garrisons. It was impossible to hold out any longer. Things had reached an absurd pitch: the snake was eating its own tail. It became a system of posts to protect the convoys and then convoys to supply the posts. The men were entirely taken up with these duties and worn out. There was no one left for operations, for pushing the enemy a little farther back. The Viets did whatever they liked. And it became more and more impossible to supply Caobang by the road.

In the end the situation grew so bad that they heard of it in Saigon. One day a super colonel was sent to Langson, a scientific strategist called R, and his mission was to help the worthy plain colonel Vicaire, who in the ordinary course was in command of the frontier.

"I will show you how to organize a rational logistic system in the jungle," said R to Vicaire. "After that you will have no further trouble."

The super colonel organized a superconvoy with a magnificent deployment of troops, materiel and machines: every motion was synchronized to the second. The prodigious column, making its long, methodical and scientific progress, arrived at Caobang intact, without so much as a single man wounded. Just as the shower of medals was about to pour down upon the heroes of this exploit, the unpolished Vicaire said to R, "What is the aim of a supply operation, then?"

"Why, to carry in supplies, of course!"

"In that case the whole thing is a failure. Your convoy was so heavy and so slow that it has consumed everything it was meant to carry in. Instead of bringing gasoline, for example, it had to be given some from the wretched little reserve at Caobang so as to get back to Langson."

By the end of this period the garrison at Caobang came to look upon the arrival of the trucks of the convoys with horror, and they called their crews the locusts, for as they ate everything they possessed on the outward journey, they fell upon the meager provisions of the legionaries.

Finally, then, there was the withdrawal. It was A, the administrator of Caobang, who told me about it — I ran into him in Saigon. "I have been evacuated too," he said. "Just like the women and children and the old men. There was an army order to bring all the civilians who were not absolutely necessary back to Langson. They didn't think I counted as essential. The only ones allowed to stay were a few hundred shopkeepers and a score or so of whores. I came out with the last convoy from Caobang — the people's exodus. Apart from those few shopkeepers there's nobody left in the town except for about a thousand Moroccans and legionaries. When I went they were settling down as though there were going to be a permanent siege. They were digging trenches and pulling down houses, laying mines everywhere and putting up barbed wire. I built up that town, as you know, and it had grown really beautiful: now my poor Caobang was being wrecked. But the soldiers seemed to be enjoying their new arrangements — they looked perfectly happy. And yet these fellows behind the machine guns are under sentence of death already, condemned to be swept away by the Viet wave whenever Giap gives the order and his tens of thousands of regulars sweep forward. Their cheerfulness filled me with pity; but with admiration too. For after all they really had no hope, with nothing but one little airfield as their only link with the rest of the world.

"I knew I was saving my life by going. Already, all through 1949, the R.C. 4 had been in its death throes. Each convoy had been a battle, a harder, longer battle than the last. It was not ambushes any more, but head-on collisions: now the Viets were standing up and blocking the road. All the troops on the frontier had to be thrown in, in a full-blown war, for every convoy. This went on for weeks. Every peak had to be won in succession, and every yard of the road. Then one day there was no getting through. I was there in my jeep. Several thousand Viets were dug in at the Luong Phai Pass, between Thatkhe and Dongkhe. After a week of unceasing drives to get them out — and whole battalions went in to the attack — Colonel Vicaire said to me, 'We can't get through. I've tried everything. I've thrown in everything I possess. The Viets are still holding their positions.' At the bottom of the pass the blocked convoy was waiting in vain. So then, to get it through in spite of everything, we tried a desperate shift. It was possible because the Viets were not occupying the road itself, where we could have bombed them, but the mountain caves, from which they commanded the road with scores of machine guns. We decided that each vehicle should try its luck, running over the pass alone without protection. Only when it had reached the other end would the next set off, and so on until the last truck.

"It was my turn — for I went through too, in my jeep. It was a crazy run. I drove up those three miles of zigzags like a lunatic. There were bursts of machine-gun fire, and you had to go through curtains of bullets skipping off the surface of the road. All the way I kept saying that if I was hit that would be the end — no hope. I was not hit. That day the Viets were surprised, taken aback, and one by one everything got through. A month later another convoy tried it. Eighty-five trucks out of a hundred and ten were destroyed. They were burning all over the road. From then on the road was cut at Luong Phai as far as we were concerned.

"That was when the high command made up its mind to abandon the R.C. 4 beyond Thatkhe — it was already impossible for us to use it, anyway. But in that case why leave troops in Caobang? The top authorities in Indochina asked me whether a Caobang hedgehog could be held. I sent in a long report saying no. But nevertheless these same authorities have decided to keep a garrison there as a point of honor, for the prestige of the thing and to guard the cemetery, because they could not bear the idea of the Viets taking our dead and our white crosses. The high command is still full of optimism — they just suppose that things are difficult on the R.C. 4 but that it's not as bad as all that. They are sure our hedgehogs are strong enough to hold out. My report has been shelved."

So it was not as a consequence of an analysis that the high command had stirred — not because Mao's divisions were approaching, for example. It had only done so out of utter necessity, because it was no longer possible to move along the R.C. 4. In fact, as far as it could it persisted in spite of everything — it had only given up the "linear" system of the R.C. 4 in order to adopt the still more dangerous idea of hedgehogs. It took even greater risks — entirely useless risks. The army was there on the frontier in order to keep it closed, but even when it held the whole of the R.C. 4 it could not manage the task at all; so how could it possibly do so with two hedgehogs, two strong points lost in the enormous landscape? The truth of the matter was that everything was ruled by the general staff's sentimentality: there were those graves at Caobang; there was General Carpentier, who had just taken over the command and who wanted no retreat or as little as possible; and there was General Alessandri who was quite determined to come to grips with the Viets as soon as he was ready, even in the heart of the jungle. There was also the consideration of high policy — Pignon, who reflected upon the unfortunate consequences of a withdrawal just as the Vietnamese were being told "We are the stronger side: join us"; and the government in Paris, which wanted some return for its billions of francs.

To put it briefly, the authorities broke Revers and then adopted his plan, but only half of it, and then so clumsily that the army was committed even further upon these dangerous frontiers, facing the Viets and the Chinese. For the army would never be able to allow these hedgehogs to be taken. But how could the army defend them? As usual those in charge comforted themselves with logical and fallacious reasoning worked out by the intelligence sections for that very purpose. It was simple enough. The Viets knew how to hide and to dig themselves in — that was acknowledged. They could lay ambushes and even manage to render the R.C. 4 impracticable. But what they could not do was to take fortified positions by storm, for they were no good at maneuvering and they did not possess the necessary fire power. So Carpentier committed the mistake that was to be committed by all the commanders in chief who came after him until Navarre, with the one exception of de Lattre. This was to underestimate the Viets. And because of this underestimation Carpentier set up the Caobang hedgehog, just as in later years Navarre was to set up the "land-air" base of Dien-bienphu: the one was to be as disastrous as the other, and for the same reasons.

Giap's new army

FOR the force that was about to make its sudden irruption was the opposite of what the high command had foreseen — perfectly trained and equipped Vietminh regiments and even divisions, formidable in their maneuvering and their striking power. Giap's regular army, as it had been known hitherto, had been good but still not far removed from a guerrilla force. The Chinese had needed only a few months to turn it into a People's Army on the Mao Tse-tung model.

Everything happened exactly as I had been told it would happen when I was at Monkay, watching the arrival of Marshal Lin Piao's troops on the frontier. The Chinese had not attacked Indochina: except for one occasion, there had been no incidents, no clashes with their troops. At this period they were being twice as cautious, for they were getting ready to throw their countless divisions against the Americans across the Yalu, far away in the north. They were already incurring very great risks, and the leaders in Peking had no wish at all to see a second front in the south. They knew perfectly well that at the slightest direct intervention in Tonkin American marines and bombers would be there too. The whole of China would be ringed by American forces — it would mean a general war. That was something Mao did not want. At all costs he had to have peace in his southern provinces while he committed himself in Korea, where he would have to hold his ground by dint of manpower, sacrifice and blood.

But this did not prevent indirect action. For where was the danger in making war on the French imperialists, the Americans' allies, if it were done through the Vietminh — if it were done by making the Vietminh capable of waging war? Thus Mao Tse-tung's "faultless" China gave diplomatic recognition to Ho Chi Minh in his jungle. Ho Chi Minh decreed general mobilization and the build-up began.

The work was carried out in a mixed zone on either side of the frontier — a special region. First came the underpinning, the substructure: the plan called for roads leading from China towards Ho Chi Minh across the backward provinces of Kwangtung and Kwangsi — main lines of communication. For this purpose a human mass was brought together; it was made up of more than a hundred thousand Nationalist prisoners and Tonkinese coolies, and they worked with their hands and their little baskets. More than half of them died, but by force of numbers four roads were finished in a few months. They led to the key positions on the frontier, Laokay, Caobang, Langson, Monkay; and they were roads made for heavy trucks and guns.

Then came the flesh-and-blood materiel. This was trained in China, in huge camps at Nanning, Trungkhanhphu, Montseu and elsewhere. The first step in these camps was political reeducation. As Giap put it, it was a question of "raising the army's ideological level so as to link the national revolution with the international revolution that is in full progress all over the world." In other words Giap's army, which refused the Communist label, was becoming a Red army just like all the others. Nationalism was "democratized": from now on it was the main theme for mass agitation; but what was called bourgeois nationalism was done away with. For this purpose there was a great purge of the armed forces. The unsound elements, employed up until now because of their technical abilities, were replaced by the entirely reliable members produced in thousands by the camps. The political emphasis ran through the whole organization, and the political commissar was placed firmly over the military officer. The army's political department, under Nguyen Chi Thanh, had rights over Giap's general staff.

But the military reeducation was equally intensive. The indoctrinated Vietminh learned how to handle modern weapons and they were taught Chinese tactics. Henceforward, for them war was no longer to be a matter of roaring forward to the attack, but of perpetually maneuvering about the countryside, silently, making the utmost use of the terrain, never showing the least weariness or discouragement. It was at this time that the five shock divisions were formed — the 304th, 308th, 312th, 316th and 320th — the divisions that were to carry the Indochinese war right through to the end and to win it.

The teaching method was that of automatism: that is to say each man was taught the few necessary movements and reactions and then he was

made to carry them out so often that they became part of his nature. It was
the mass production of simplified, perfect soldiers, completely fanaticized,
completely unfeeling, knowing only their particular task but carrying it out
like so many robots even if it amounted to suicide. When a man was
promoted he was taught a few extra movements and reactions, all of which
had been exactly worked out as suitable for his new rank.

The system called for the continual promotion of those who survived.
Every approved fighter who was not killed was put through another
conditioning course after the engagement, given fresh political and military
reeducation and provided with the additional motions and reflexes that the
next rank required. In this way even the simplest of those Viets who
continued to improve and who remained alive in spite of the appalling
losses, reached high positions. Thus there were Vietminh colonels who
carried out their functions exceedingly well and who were nevertheless
barely literate.

In all this not the slightest weakness was allowed. Fear had to be
extinguished. Zeal and obedience, on the other hand, were pushed to the
utmost extreme. When they came back from a campaign the men of every
unit were compelled to admit their faults, accuse themselves and repent.
They learned how to do better; and those who were incapable of progress
were punished, submitted to every kind of reeducation, or shot.

As the survivors rose in rank, the losses, including those from enemy
action or political and ideological liquidation, were made good by the
guerrilla fighters, the men from the people's militias, who were sent to the
camps. There they became regular soldiers, and from then on they took
part in the continual movement of death or promotion. Meanwhile *nha-
qués* were drawn from the mass of the people to take their places,
becoming guerrillas in the militia units: later these men would reach the
camps to be turned into regulars.

In the course of the war in Indochina the French killed very great
numbers of Viets, hundreds of thousands, and not only guerrilla fighters
but regulars too. But they always found just as many facing them, because
of these camps and their production of replacements for the soldiers killed.
Giap never had to worry about the question of manpower. The camps were
factories deep in the jungle. Everything was so well organized that they had
a whole civilian population close at hand, brought in to cultivate the
vegetables and the rice that the soldiers were to eat. Farming ants
nourished the fighting ants. Each camp was a huge Red base. The recruits
poured through by thousands, by tens of thousands. They worked by day
and by night, ideologically, militarily, in the workshops and in the "fac-

tories": and each soldier also had to be a discoverer, a poet, for it was faith that was the true knowledge, the science that allowed the people to accomplish anything, even miracles.

As Giap's army learned its trade under its Chinese advisers, so from China it received weapons and ammunition. Two hundred heavy Molotova trucks ran continually from Canton, across southern China and on to these roads that were being built by the innumerable coolies. They fed the huge dumps set up a few hundred yards from the frontier to act as distribution centers for the retrained Vietminh units that were going back into Indochina for action.

The fact that the Vietminh were from now on supplied and maintained was to change the face of the war more than anything else at all. Up until then they had had to manage for themselves — to be self-sufficient. It gives some idea of their exertions when one realizes that they had had more than a hundred "factories" — jungle huts — in which, without special steels and virtually without tools, they managed to produce mortars and even recoilless guns called SKZ's. They could turn their hands to almost anything. They even had flying bombs, which they launched by means of ramps. For the raw material of these singular contraptions they made use of liquid-air containers, big aluminum bottles bought cheap in the French towns. Yet these primitive machines which had so astonished the Expeditionary Force were already exceedingly dangerous. But still this was only homemade stuff and on a very small scale. Then suddenly Giap's army had the same fire power as the French — a Viet battalion had as many submachine guns, heavy machine guns, mortars, bazookas and recoilless guns as an Expeditionary Force battalion. And these weapons were equally modern. Furthermore, with the supply line coming from China the appalling shortage of ammunition was gone forever. And gone were the days when the members of the Vietminh networks had to go after blasting powder in the quarries for their explosives, or even lay hands upon the butchers' chlorate of potassium — the chemical they were allowed for preserving hams. In those days the Viets carefully salvaged every unexploded French bomb as a source of precious raw materials. They even had divers who went down for the stocks of Japanese shells sunk far out in the open sea. Now the Molotova trucks brought small-arms ammunition, machine-gun belts, mines, grenades, mortar bombs and bazooka charges up to the frontier by the ton. Formerly the Viets could only fire with the utmost economy, when the shot was certain to go home. From now on they too could blaze away with abandon, laying a tremendous barrage.

The Chinese supplied the Viets with as much as they could take, saturation being the only limit. It might even be said that the Viets were better equipped than the French for the jungle war, for they only had light and deadly weapons, those which a man could always carry, even along the highest mountain tracks and through the forest. What is more, accompanying the soldiers there were always endless columns of coolies who carried all that was needed for the battle on their backs. Everything was worked out — and henceforward on a huge scale — for secret approaches, long marches, shattering and unforeseeable attacks; and for sudden disappearance in the event of failure or exhaustion.

The only superiority remaining to the French was in heavy weapons Apart from a few guns the Viets had almost none. In the first place because they were not in a state to make use of them — they needed a hundred men to operate a single seventy-five. And secondly because for the moment they did not want them: their tactics were fluidity combined with shock — men suddenly erupting and keeping up a violent fire close at hand. And that amply compensated for the lack of the French guns, planes and tanks, which enslaved their possessors: for these only theoretically terrifying machines could not manage to overcome the tropical vegetation or the Viets who moved about among it; and these machines were blind.

By the summer of 1950 Giap's divisions were almost ready — the French had knowledge of this. What they did not know was who was really in command, who would lead them in the war, and how. The French intelligence services frequently said that the plans were drawn up by Chinese and Russian generals. Names were produced — that of Chen Keng for example. It was established that there was a Chinese military mission three hundred strong, including some important advisers, with the Viet high command. There were also a few Russian experts. But it was not known who made the final decisions.

Perhaps the man in charge of the war was quite simply Giap — that Giap who had plunged so enthusiastically into Napoleon's campaigns when he was a schoolmaster in Hanoi. At all events, Giap, in his uniform with no badges of rank, sitting there in the hut that served as his headquarters, presented himself to all Vietnam as a man who was going to strike and who was going to conquer. It was not a mere promise: it was a certainty. In his own way Giap was humble too. For in the events to come there was no question of personal genius on his part, but rather of the infallible dialectic which led to the "correct solution" that the people would conquer within six months. And this he proved in an analytical report a hundred pages long. This masterpiece of logic is the fundamental document of the Indochinese war.

The reasoning is simple. The French were trying to win the race with their Pacification: the Viets with their power of attack. The Expeditionary Force was spreading over Vietnam: but as soon as it was ready the People's Army would launch a massive attack. The battle had to be won as soon as the monsoon was over, in the autumn, or in any case before the beginning of 1951. For the times would never be so favorable as in 1950: and indeed, the Chinese aid to the Vietminh was well ahead of the American aid to the French. Furthermore, the People's Army had built itself up into a powerful modern fighting organization, whereas the Expeditionary Force had remained weak, having scarcely begun to regroup and to receive its first consignments of American materiel. Quite accurately, Giap said, "French strength is growing but little, whereas ours increases every day. But we must act quickly, for if we allow the enemy time to reequip and reorganize himself we shall be faced with enormous difficulties." And he went on, "We are about to begin the third phase of our war. First there was the spontaneous guerrilla fighting; then the organized guerrilla warfare. Now we are going to pass from the defensive to the offensive by means of a war of movement. In the impending counteroffensive our troops will have to surround the enemy, strike home right to the vital center and force him to beg for quarter. It is essential that within a few months the last bases of colonialist resistance should be liquidated."

It was indeed a question of staking everything, for the Chinese aid did not solve the problem of the missing rice. On the contrary, there was such a shortage in southern China that it was the hungry Viets who had to supply rice to the even hungrier Chinese. And Giap knew that the deltas were slipping farther and farther out of his grasp.

But Giap was confident. He proceeded very methodically: thus, as soon as a body of troops had been reeducated in the camps he sent them to carry out maneuvers in Upper Tonkin. The purpose was to strike at the French and to attack their morale; but above all it was practical training, exercises, the application on the battlefield of the lessons learned, the dress rehearsal for what was soon to be performed on an enormous scale.

Warning shots

MEANWHILE, all through that spring, fate kept firing warning shots, more and more of them. A great many were needed to jerk the French high command out of its complacency. On March 21, 1950, General Carpentier, in a personal and secret directive, wrote: "The situation in Tonkin has definitely been clearing up in the past several months." He was even delighted that Mao's forces should have taken Hainan, as a preliminary to taking Formosa. As he saw it the liquidation of the last Nationalist refuges was the consolidation of a "good" Communist China. For once this China was steady on her feet and satisfied she would be able to devote herself to the immense labors of reconstruction at home; she would want peace on every hand.

The conquest of Hainan was carried out with ludicrous ease. The Chinese Communists, who had managed to seem so few in number, suddenly appeared in the little creeks along the Kwangtung coast: junks ferried some thousands of Red soldiers across, and tens of thousands of Nationalists surrendered without a fight.

Saigon thought the news rather good than otherwise. And yet a glance at the map would show that Hainan commanded the whole of the Gulf of Tonkin, at the bottom of which there lay the delta, its human ant hill, the big towns, and the jungles and mountains in which the French were fighting. It was a terrible threat. From now on the French forces in Tonkin were virtually prisoners: it was as though they were held in a trap. If the Communist armies were to break through the R.C. 4 and appear before Hanoi, the Expeditionary Force could no longer be evacuated by sea in the direction of Saigon: Hainan would bolt them in.

But the French staffs' continually repeated refrain was that Mao was full of good will. So Carpentier was surprised when he recognized Ho Chi Minh and his People's Republic of Vietnam. This was the moment when the slow-witted commander in chief did nevertheless begin to grow uneasy.

Yet on the Chinese side everything went along very well: after the taking of Hainan, Mao's armies stirred no more. The frontier was quiet, unnaturally quiet. But then the French discovered Giap's armies, farther off in the northwest, near Laokay and in the Red River valley, in a huge zone where they had come to train before moving against the R.C. 4. The Expeditionary Force's powerlessness against these armies in the jungle was discovered too: but this particular discovery got lost in the reports intended for the general staff.

Yet this was the real turning point, the wholly unknown turning point, of the Indochinese war. The fall of the post at Pholu in the valley of the Red River about twenty miles east of Laokay was the forerunner of all that was to be repeated over and over again in the years to come. It was not so much the fact that it was taken that was important as the way it happened.

Pholu was the most isolated, remote, forgotten post that can be imagined, and the most wildly picturesque — a post made of logs, standing by the side of an immense lake with nothing but the limitless forest beyond. There was nothing: only solitude, the infinity of trees, the impenetrable forest and the deadly Red River flowing in its ill-omened valley, that huge straight gash full of fevers and almost devoid of men. Everything had been infinitely peaceful there for an infinite number of years. But this was the spot where one day Giap launched his first massive, meticulously prepared offensive — an offensive mounted by a whole division, the 308th, the best known and the most formidable. Suddenly they emerged from the forest, battalion after battalion. This was the 308th's first appearance: presently it was to become the French soldiers' nightmare, the shock force in all the great battles to come — it was the 308th that dealt the final smashing blow at Dienbienphu.

At Pholu, Giap's new style of war was seen. As before there were swarms of Viets everywhere, but now they were formed into powerful units which attacked and maneuvered with a wonderful knowledge of the terrain, according to principles that combined military practice and Red dialectic. To begin with, during ten days of incessant attack Giap's battalions stormed the heights that commanded the Pholu basin. Then came the hammering, the destruction of the post in the hollow below by the fire of bazookas, mortars and recoilless guns, a mass of arms that had never been seen among the Viets before, an armament that nobody had ever imagined they could possess. The organization was perfect. Before beginning their shelling, the Viets had dug whole systems of shelters in the jungle-covered limestone peaks for their artillery and their ammunition: they were camouflaged, and planes could neither see nor touch them. And throughout the whole length of the battle the Red supply trains, columns of coolies plying to and fro between the front and the dumps on the frontier, ran with clockwork regularity. There were convoys of sampans on the Red River as well, and they too moved with perfect synchronization.

Pholu was held by one company, and faced with a whole division it fought with great courage. Furthermore, the high command did its utmost to save the post and to send in reinforcements. Parachute troops were dropped, as usual; but they were unable to accomplish anything. Then a relief column was sent from Laokay, but it got lost in the mountains and never arrived. The last act saw the post going up in flames: the Viets took it, burned it and vanished.

But the real disaster was that the high command did not understand what had happened. For the command the whole affair was incomprehensible. The only thing headquarters did was to accuse the paras of cowardice: not only had they not saved the post, but in order to save themselves they had abandoned their dead. And in General Carpentier's eyes that was an unforgivable crime.

The man who had led them, Lieutenant Planey, told me how it happened and what he had had to do; he told me about his dreadful moral dilemma, and the feeling of shame that had haunted him for months.

"We had not been dropped over the post itself, but in the jungle on the other side of the Red River nearly twenty miles away. There were a hundred and fifteen of us altogether, all belonging to the 3rd BCCP. We marched along the track for hours until we reached the riverbank over against Pholu, which was still holding out — but we stumbled right into the middle of the Viet concentration — a very dangerous concentration. Fifteen battalions were attacking Pholu, but two had been left on our side of the river. They closed in on us at once, firing as they ran. We were completely unsupported and we were almost in the trap. We could not resist and we had to get out by the only gap that might still be open. We destroyed our equipment and our loads and practically all the radio so as to move faster. But we couldn't get along fast enough, not nearly fast enough. We could see thousands of Viets, the ones on the other side, swarming across the river to join in the kill: they were crossing at a ford, up to their necks in the water, holding their rifles over their heads. It was then that I made the appalling decision that we had to abandon our dead. We left them by the side of a track, covered with leaves. We went on a little faster, but we were still helping our wounded along, and that kept us back. Whole battalions of Viets were closing in nearer and nearer from every side. What saved us was six fighters that saw the white strip signal I had had spread: coming lower they saw the masses of Viets, the thousands of men on our tracks, and they bombed and machine-gunned them. At that point night fell and we succeeded in making our way up a height. There we managed to disengage and get as far as Laokay. I had saved my men, but what I had done was considered dishonorable. I never stopped telling my chiefs, 'The Viets aren't the same any longer: these are really tough ones,' but they did not believe me. They said, 'Your nerve cracked. Look what happened at Nhado.'

"It's true that Nhado, a post just like Pholu, was also attacked by the whole of the 308th and yet it was saved. But to save it a whole battalion, the 5th BCCP, together with a company of my 3rd BCCP, had been dropped right onto it. I don't know why, but this massive drop frightened the Viets, although they could have smashed the lot if they had wanted to. And it was a short-term victory, don't forget. A few days later the whole garrison was ordered to evacuate the untenable position: but this was a withdrawal that had been made for strategic reasons and not under direct enemy pressure, so honor was safe, and no illusions were shattered.

"At the beginning the high para officers could not believe it either. But in spite of themselves they were soon forced to acknowledge the facts, to some degree at least. It began with my own captain in the 3rd BCCP, Cazeaux, who came to Laokay with two companies, as keen as mustard, and took them off as a relief column for a post called Banlao: it was a miracle that he came back alive. He too ran into whole battalions of Viets. He said to me in so many words, 'Planey, you're right. I had no notion of Viets like that.' The next was a colonel by the name of Daboval. He didn't understand anything of what was going on. He was a brass hat from Saigon. Every day he was getting these messages with astonishing news — Viet battalions all over the place, almost all the posts on the Red River abandoned, the French units and garrisons withdrawn in the Pakha mountains, a safe region with thousands of Man and Meo partisans. The colonel thought, 'People are going to say that my paras are afraid of the Viets. I'll go myself and give them an unholy rocket.' No sooner said than done. He dropped at Pakha, made some dreadful speeches, and then said that he was going back to Saigon. He was told that it was impossible: there were five Viet battalions on the tracks leading to Laokay, the nearest airfield, and there was no question of getting through. The colonel flew off the handle, but then realized that it was serious. In the end they got rid of him by buying a poppy field and making it into a little airstrip so that a Morane could land and fetch him.

"Nevertheless there we were, close on two battalions of paras surrounded in the Pakha region by the 308th Division. This state of affairs infuriated the high command. They gave us the order to force our way through the Viets and reach Laokay. To do that we first had to take Baonai, a ford that could not be by-passed. We tried once, and we came unstuck. We tried again in greater force, and we came worse unstuck. We went back to Pakha. Fortunately the 308th went off of its own accord in April, moving up towards the R.C. 4 after this trial period, with different, more important work to do. But for the high command this was a sign of the enemy's failure and his weakness. So everything was in order, everything was splendid, except for the paras' extraordinary lapse."

Thus for months on end Giap's battalions had been taking posts, not by suicidal charges or stratagems any more, but as the result of slow, relentless blockades that steadily ground the defenders down to a state of impotence, prevented outside help from getting through, and led unfailingly to a Red victory. And thus for months on end Giap's battalions had completely dominated the weak French columns sent against them along the tracks and the ridges of the jungle, obliging them to flee ignominiously to avoid being wiped out altogether. And all this went on over vast areas, with the distances running into hundreds of miles, and in huge sectors — not only on the Red River but even as far as the region of Hoabinh on the Black River, not much above fifty miles from Hanoi, right next to the delta. There too the posts fell — the little scattered isolated huts where one lived so snugly surrounded with girls and bottles of chum. The situation at Hoabinh was even more desperate than at Laokay: but this was the realm of the Foreign Legion — a Legion that was giving itself over to the dolce vita without caring even about its own disasters. What saved Hoabinh was the fact that it was the place where Vanuxem began his extraordinary career — Vanuxem, who was nicknamed the Professor and who had passed from an aggressive antimilitarism to the most complete and logical militarism, to him a way of life, a philosophy in which man was ruled by his primeval ancestral instinct, which was not for peace but for war. Vanuxem therefore gave himself up to war with all the earnestness of a profound theoretician, with all his immense appetite for life and with all his condottiere's brazenness. But for him war had to be total: pitiless, of course, but above all waged with both intelligence and masculine vigor, the natural consequence of which was delight in work well done. He was against the pompous foolishness of the staff just as he was against the artificial doping of the parachutists and the too-passive heroism of the legionaries. He was above all an individualist. He therefore recruited a nurse, who in due course bore him ten children; and then he recruited two famous battalions from the highlanders of the region, the Muongs. Vanuxem was not afraid of Giap's insect battalions, but he knew their terrible power, and with a cruel delight he observed, "It'll be quite a job."

But from now on most of the units that had fought against the 308th in the jungle felt a chill in their hearts. It was a feeling they did not acknowledge but expressed in conscious dash — they were braver, but braver only by an inner struggle against themselves, their nerves and their imagination. Even the paras were affected: henceforward they knew that in the forest it was the Viets who were the stronger.

But the powerless high command had not the least suspicion of its powerlessness. For headquarters these events, in the remote, not very important regions of the Red and Black rivers, were merely skirmishes. With the clearest conscience, the command preserved its unruffled, optimistic calm. Yet the situation was in fact so serious that a man whose character and profession combined to render him prudent took his courage in both hands and warned the authorities. This was a civil servant, a little administrative officer at Laokay — little in size, too, almost a dwarf and somewhat misshapen, but an intelligent, calculating, ambitious man who always knew what ought to be done and what ought to be said. Yet nevertheless one day he took the plane for Hanoi and presumed to say to General Alessandri the very thing that ought not to be said: he tried to sound the alarm. He had hardly begun before the general (who was also a very small man) assumed his wooden expression, his stubborn, irritated, preoccupied, impatient air. He was the one who knew. He silenced the incautious administrator, crushed him with a few crisp, thin-lipped, scornful phrases. "You have lost your head. The situation is not grave; it is not even worrying. When the time comes I shall take the necessary steps — then you will see what happens."

Meanwhile the 308th, after its distant campaign against Laokay and the northwest, vanished. In fact, its soldiers and coolies in their thousands and tens of thousands were moving up along the tracks towards Ho Chi Minh's quadrilateral, towards China and the great bases. Suddenly, after a few days of rest, it burst out again on the R.C. 4 at the end of May, just before the monsoon. It was a fast-moving, violent catastrophe: in forty-eight hours came the fall of the Dongkhe hedgehog, that air-supplied fortress between the great stronghold of Caobang and Thatkhe at the end of the road.

This time it was an unbelievable shock to the French high command, the confirmation of all they had denied — the existence of a powerful Red army. For Dongkhe was immense, both physically and as a symbol. It was a bastion in the heart of the French military system, a huge fortification whose name was familiar to the whole Expeditionary Force, a staging point where so many convoys used to stop to take their ease under the shelter of the French flag. Dongkhe was something that could not fall.

The most frightening aspect was the way in which the Viets had taken it — with mathematical precision and ludicrous ease. With the rest of the 308th serving as a holding force, one heavy and four light battalions appeared on the peaks commanding the basin and smashed the fortress with scores of mortars and guns, shattering the blockhouses and the inner fortifications and destroying the garrison's artillery. Only then, after a softening-up of two days and two nights, did they storm the place, coming in through the breaches in close-packed ranks. At three o'clock on the night of May 27–28 all resistance came to an end.

And there was nothing to be done, in spite of the calls for help over the Dongkhe radio. There was nothing the distant staff could do except be present at the death bed by the radio link, listening feverishly in map-strewn offices to the messages as they came in one by one. For no help was possible. No relief column could ever arrive in time. And, above all, the clouds were sitting right down on the mountains, eclipsing them. The sky was entirely covered. The Viets had chosen these days of bad weather and thick drizzle in which planes could not be of the slightest use. On the Langson and Hanoi airfields the fighters stood waiting in vain for a break to take off; and instead of smashing the Viets the pilots played cards or stood at the bar, gazing at the low, unchanging sky.

It was a revelation for the French command: the very nature of the war had changed. But then it took comfort. For now came Giap's turn to perform his autocriticism and to acknowledge his errors; for the bare hundred defenders of Dongkhe had made a desperate sortie from the blazing post and they had escaped. And even more than that, the Viets were the conquerors, those who held the field, for only half a day. The Dongkhe that they had taken was taken back almost at once.

For at last the sky cleared and a whole parachutist battalion, the 3rd BCCP, was dropped from some thirty old Junkers: they regrouped before Dongkhe, flung themselves upon it, and took it after an hour and a half of hand-to-hand fighting in the ruins. This was done against an unprepared enemy who was busy looting and who never believed in a retaliatory blow. It had been exceedingly risky — each one of the Junkers had been hit by antiaircraft fire while it was dropping its stick or circling slowly over the basin, always making the same round, lower than the ridges where the Viet machine guns were installed. A proper old circus. But all the French arrangements worked well. The relief columns from Thatkhe retook the heights, retook the grim pass of Luong Phai, and joined the paras sitting at their ease in the wreckage of Dongkhe. And the Viets fled leaving three hundred dead behind them and a great deal of equipment — two guns, three heavy machine guns, grenade throwers, automatic weapons and rifles. They vanished, dissipated, evaporated into the jungle a great way off — no one could tell where. A far more solid Dongkhe was built; a stronger garrison was put into it; and the waiting period began.

This was the way fate's warnings were not understood. And yet they had been written down in black and white. On the body of a political commissar killed at Dongkhe there was a notebook that read: "Towards September 20 we shall attack once more. We shall be far stronger. Up until now there was only the 308th — by then there will be two or three other divisions ready. We shall take Thatkhe, then we shall take the completely isolated Caobang, and then we move in full force against Langson. That will be easy, because the Expeditionary Force's morale will have been very deeply shaken by our earlier victories."

But the French generals did not know the meaning of dialectic, that analytical art in which, after a failure or even after a success, everything is minutely examined, the participants engage in self-criticism, deviations are hunted for, and the old "correct solutions" that have been used are replaced by new and better ones that will allow an improved performance next time. If they had known the Communists, the French generals, far from rejoicing over their "victory" of Dongkhe, would on the contrary have been very much alarmed. For when a plan has failed the Communists always begin again. And they do so in such conditions and after such preparations that the next time they are as it were betting on a certainty — they are almost compelled to succeed.

The staff drew sanguine conclusions from this taking and retaking of Dongkhe. It was acknowledged that the Viets were capable of fighting and of hitting hard. But for all that it was considered fortunate that at last they were no longer invisible, intangible, and that they were giving the Expeditionary Force the chance of counterattacking, meeting them face to face and utterly destroying them.

In the end nothing was done, nothing was decided. And that was how the one right moment was missed. For after the retaking of Dongkhe it would have been possible to evacuate the hedgehogs without danger — Giap's army was not yet strong enough to prevent it. But weeks and months were let go by; and then, when the thing had to be done, when the move was forced, it was too late.

Nothing happened. The only war was the one between the French generals, the open struggle between the stunted Alessandri, more dogged and sure of himself than ever, even more convinced that he was the man of destiny, and the big easy-going Carpentier, inflexible in his easiness, who was beginning to be very much afraid that something was exceedingly wrong. And it was this war, with its absurd circumstances, its infinite complexity and its mean-minded childishness, that was to deliver up the columns of the Expeditionary Force to the slaughter when the autumn came and with it the other war, the real war, the war against Giap and his army.

PART IV

The Mountains of Dongkhe

THERE is something like a mechanical sequence of events in defeat. Starting with the initial errors, the mistakes of individuals and departments, it goes on increasing, squaring itself at every stage — the geometrical progression of disaster. This is what happened in the mountains of Dongkhe. It was called bad luck: in fact the catastrophe had been laid on, called forth, provoked.

Some thousands of men died deep in the jungle, among the rocks. Some were coming from Caobang, which they were evacuating. The others were going out to meet them. They joined up only to perish together, to die wretchedly; and there was nothing that could be done for them, no help that could reach that far. After five days of fighting they were overwhelmed, so beset on all sides that there was nothing for them but death or capture.

How can this have come about? For the French were perfectly conscious of the Viets' strength and of their intentions. But in spite of that, they plunged into a deadly trap: and in spite of that, for almost the whole of the Expeditionary Force, this disaster was a complete surprise, not only strategically and tactically but also from the political point of view.

To be sure, from 1950 on nothing would have made much difference: all the young men in France might have been called up and all sorts of other steps might have been taken, but the result would have been the same. Henceforth the French were up against something stronger than themselves. But although in the long run they would have had to acquiesce or give in they were still not forced as a preliminary to undergo such disasters as Dongkhe — nor Dienbienphu some time later. They could have lost without so much humiliation and suffering, and without so many victims: they could have sat tight until they had understood the situation and come to the necessary conclusions. But instead of that they offered themselves up as a sacrifice on the R.C. 4 — they went out of their way to court disaster.

It was not the Viets' strength which was the cause of it all, for this strength was barely coming into existence: the Viets were still clumsy and unsure of themselves. But they were handed an unhoped-for opportunity and they had won even before they had fully come to believe in their superiority. They had merely profited by the extraordinary politico-military mess into which the French had plunged themselves.

Dongkhe was the disaster of total incoherence. It was the punishment for years of third-rate thinking, third-rate behavior and gross hypocrisy. In Paris the government was still foolishly complacent, waiting for victory. Apart from that, it never took any notice of Indochina: it relied upon its generals. The two military chiefs detested one another. During the monsoon, while the Viets were getting ready, they set off one after the other to carry out their separate campaigns in France. The first said, "Everything is fine, but I would rather beat the Viets on the edge of the delta; perhaps it would be better to evacuate Caobang first." The second said, "Everything is fine. But I am going to smash the Viets in their lairs. Caobang must be kept at all costs." The government had no opinion on the matter. Pignon, the high commissioner, the only man who could really see the whole thing clearly, was desperate; he too came to France, but as a good civil servant he dared not express his fears too openly. The government said that Carpentier was right, since he was commander in chief; but to his enemy Alessandri, who was busily touring the ministries in Paris, it said, "You go back to Indochina: you are the one who understands it best."

Nothing was done. And when at last the Viets struck, when they took the stronghold of Dongkhe for the second time, nothing was ready. Carpentier, with an eye to his own reputation, mounted a tremendous phony operation with a great number of battalions to take an alleged Vietminh capital (which contained no Viets) by the name of Thainguyen, which was conveniently at hand, just next to the delta. This was designed to impress public opinion throughout the world and to throw a smoke screen over the evacuation of Caobang, which took place at the same time: he made his decision because he was afraid of something worse, ten times worse than the fall of the hedgehog. Alessandri too had an eye to his own reputation: he was filled with rage and bitterness, and he spent whole days in protesting, uttering cries of despair and trying every possible maneuver against his chief's order. He did not succeed in having it canceled: on the contrary, it was he who had to command the withdrawal. The plan adopted was a two-year-old study according to which the two French columns were to make their junction at twice-taken Dongkhe, where the whole of Giap's army was gathered. And it was beside that ill-omened fortress, in a tremendous, grim, brooding landscape of limestone crags and jungle, that the French soldiers of the R.C. 4, attacked on all sides, suffered the first disaster of the Indochinese war, the defeat that sounded the death knell. Nothing could be done to help these few battalions that were being overwhelmed by the Vietminh numbers, because the mass of the French battalions was a great way off on the edge of the delta, gloriously conquering an empty Thainguyen that would presently have to be abandoned.

It was far more absurd than Dienbienphu was to be in later days. The commanders of the two colums that were to meet on the R.C. 4 loathed each other. One of them, Colonel Charton, the Legion's idol, feared nothing on earth, least of all the Vietminh: the other, Colonel Lepage, a sickly gunner, was convinced that he was going to the slaughter and he earnestly said his prayers. Carpentier was at Saigon, in his air-conditioned room. Alessandri flew over the columns, but without ever seeing them or talking to them on the radio. As for handsome Colonel Constans, in command of the frontier zone, he did not see fit to stir — he did not care for flying. In any case this curiously theatrical personage did not obey Alessandri, his immediate superior, but the many-starred General Carpentier, who had brought him from Paris because of his contacts in society. Lastly there was the worthy General Marchand, who wrote comic songs and who, on learning that he was to stand in for Alessandri during the long summer's wait, cried, "Oh God in heaven, what a blow!"

The responsibility lay with the incompetence that had gradually permeated the Expeditionary Force, gumming up its works entirely — a total incompetence, though filled with cunning plots and subtleties, an incompetence that was to make de Lattre go red with shame and fury when he arrived in Indochina, an arrival all too late.

The long wait

IT lasted all the summer. From July to September the monsoon was at its height. There was what amounted to a truce, and the Indochinese war came to a stop in the wet. The rain fell perpetually; it was the season of storms and overflowing rivers; the whole of Upper Tonkin was drowned in the flood. Men could no longer manage to come to grips in the spongy, saturated jungles, nor even on the vast watery surfaces of the deltas. The soldiers were overwhelmed and blinded by the forces of nature, by the soaking vegetation, the mountains that vanished in the clouds, the rivers swirling with turbid, dangerously rapid water, by the mud, the heat, by everything. It was a formless green-gray world, devoid of outline, inimical, a world in which every movement, even eating, was an effort. But this intermission was also a great vigil of arms.

Nothing happened. The large-scale attacks were halted. There were just a few Viets — not very active, but always on the watch, always there. So all along the frontier the soldiers waited; for they knew that things were going to happen. Nothing was altered in everyday life, but everyone knew that over there, beyond the mountains and beyond the everlasting forest, the Viets were getting ready, that they were in their training camps, doubling and tripling the number of their battalions for the next campaign. It would be for the end of September, or at the latest in October, when the monsoon would die down. Until then the monotony of the long, fever-ridden days would be unbroken, with all their boredom, routine and fatigues. And in the face of the impending danger nothing was done, nothing was changed.

I thought of all those frontier posts, hovels made of mud and planks, with their heterogeneous populations of partisans, *congai,* bearded Moroccans, kepi'd legionaries, cheerful Senegalese. Still no barbed wire, still no mines! In spite of their loneliness these handfuls of men cut off from everything on their hilltops or in their hollows, supplied by parachute or by very occasional columns, recognized the signs of danger in the midst of this ill-omened summer calm. Around Caobang the grip was tightening. The legionaries had but to look through their field glasses to see the black-uniformed Vietminh sentries who were also standing guard. Often the Viet loudspeakers would start shouting, "You are prisoners already! In a few weeks you will be in our power." There was intense watchfulness on either side of the no-man's-land a few hundred yards wide that surrounded the town. Time was running out. All the legionaries who were not on guard duty erected defenses, new works built with cement made on the spot and with stone or anything else that would withstand shells. There was scarcely any time for sleep in the surrounded town; but for all that morale was high in Caobang.

All through the summer the Reds pushed on feverishly with their preparations. Both in China and in Tonkin there was much grading and road work. In China the airfields of Kunming, Kweiling and Hainan — the most remarkable airfields in the world, built by the Americans with their bulldozers in former days to support Chiang Kai-shek against the Japanese, and long since overgrown — once more became great sheets of concrete. The permanent way of that old masterpiece of French colonialism in China, the Yunnan railway, was turned into a military road that ran down from the mountains and the high plateaus of Yunnan to the Red River valley. In Tonkin the Viets carried these Chinese roads on to points in front of their eventual objectives, Thatkhe, Dongkhe, and Caobang, all at the end of the R.C. 4. In the Chinese camps Giap had models of these towns set up: a life-size Dongkhe was built, an exact reproduction; so were all the forts and defenses of Caobang. The Vietminh shock troops practiced taking them day after day, an endless rehearsal. Finally, after all these preparations, the Vietminh divisions left their camps and gathered on the lines of penetration; they were still invisible, hidden in the jungle, but they were now ready to strike.

And behind them there were the Chinese troops in still greater number — two hundred thousand men at least. In principle they were not to intervene; but nevertheless they would attack Indochina if everything went badly, if the Korean War, which had just begun, developed into a blaze covering Asia and perhaps the whole world. How little was needed for that to happen — one single man's decision! All that was needed was that the former haberdasher, the worthy President Truman, that civilian, should let himself be impressed by the proconsular MacArthur and follow his imperious advice. For MacArthur wanted to attack People's China itself. And if the American bombers laid industrial Manchuria waste, if the Seventh Fleet shattered the ports and the coasts of Mao's republic, even if Chiang Kai-shek's army, built up again in Formosa, appeared on the mainland calling upon the people to rise, then it would be the beginning of a chain reaction. Among the Chinese Communists there were weeks full of dread and foreboding: by way of precaution, to forestall any rising, they coldly and methodically executed between twenty and thirty million bourgeois and "enemies of the people" in the course of three great mass campaigns. Nevertheless, if the worst were to happen and if America were to go all out, then China, no longer having anything to lose, would throw her armies, her militias, a vast mass trained in people's warfare, against all the colonialist, capitalist and imperialist countries within reach, beginning with what had been French Indochina.

I thought of everything that was piling up over there; and I thought of the French side of the frontier, where there were still only a few thousand men. They were given no orders, no special instructions: it was as though they were being abandoned to their fate. They were not reinforced. On the contrary, battalions were taken away — six were removed from Tonkin to be sent to Laos and Cambodia, whose rulers complained of infiltration: for political reasons it was necessary to please them.

In the top circles, everything was ambiguity and intrigue. But all the men on the R.C. 4 knew what was afoot: they were condemned to win if they did not want to burn alive in their posts or die in the bush. But how could they not be overwhelmed by the flood that was going to break over them? The tidal wave was no longer a mere hypothesis, as it had been before: it was now a certainty.

But on the frontier everyone, in spite of their tense anxiety, remained silent — no voice was raised to sound the alarm or ward off the danger. The crack troops, the legionaries, the paras, the Moroccan tabors, were perfectly capable of showing a splendid contempt for danger. Among the staffs there was a silence, not of pride, but of self-interest and ambition. An accusation of defeatism would mean disgrace and the end of a career. So they had to truckle to these generals who did not want to know the truth and who in any case would not believe it.

That was how Giap's hour came. The rainy season was not yet over when suddenly, in the Communist fashion, there came the sudden shattering blow. On September 18, Dongkhe vanished like a ship sinking in the open sea, vanished without a trace, without any apparent survivors to be rescued. The rehearsal in May had been useful: so had the autocriticism. This time it was done without any mistakes. It was thought that no one had escaped; and there was no question of retaliation.

It was a disaster. The dying of the rebuilt, strengthened post, held by the finest troops in the Legion, had lasted sixty hours. The death throes were known only by a few radio messages; then came the great silence of the end. For that was what the war in Indochina was like — the fighting men died alone and the high command did not even know the manner of their death. The signals that were picked up had that curious, utterly commonplace military tone that is so far removed from the genuine agony and the real death that is gasping itself out somewhere far away, very far away. One Saturday at noon came the first message from Dongkhe, the one that said that Giap had set things in motion, that he had begun his "general counteroffensive." It was like the attack of May, with the Viet battalions on the heights battering the lower ground; but this time the enemy fire was far heavier, and so was that of Dongkhe. This was the first of the artillery duels — later there were to be a great many — with the Viets firing from above with scattered guns and the French firing from below with guns grouped together. At Dongkhe the duel was won by the Viets, just as the same kind of duel on a larger scale was to be won at Dienbienphu.

On the first day, however, the outcome was not clear. The messages from Dongkhe said that losses were very small, and even that the garrison's artillery had silenced two Viet guns. But the second day, a long drawn-out Sunday, the messages became progressively fewer and shorter, and they ontained all the formulas of a "deteriorating situation": by twilight on hat Sunday more than half the legionaries had been killed or wounded. There was one last not entirely desperate message, but the coming of night rought an unbroken silence — Dongkhe no longer answered. There was still his silence on Monday morning, and the sky was so low that Upper Tonkin was nothing but a gray sheet, the mountains entirely lost in the clouds. Nevertheless a Junker was ordered to go and look at Dongkhe — an almost impossible flight through the monsoon and among the mountaintops. The pilot had to fly through the cloud-choked Luong Phai Pass, thrust on, and dive into the hollow of Dongkhe: the news had to be brought back. And the Junker, when it had at last pushed through, when it was circling over the Dongkhe basin, knew what that news was. The French flag had disappeared from the shattered mast; great blackish flames were still rising from the post; there was nothing but ruin and desolation. The Viets were still there, for puffs of antiaircraft fire burst all around the slow old plane as its crew gazed down at the catastrophe. But this time the Viets were invisible: they were not pillaging but hiding there in battle order to wipe out any paras who might drop from the clouds or any column coming along the R.C. 4. There was no doubt that they hoped for still more victims.

This time the command began by doing nothing. It did not dare retake Dongkhe with parachute troops as had been done the first time. It was afraid of a trap. How far away it was already, that spring of 1950, only a few months earlier, when defeats were made good by daring, scornful counterstrokes, as though the Viets were still very inferior opponents!

As Giap could neither kill nor capture any more of the Expeditionary Force because of the prudent French inactivity, he triumphantly announced over his radio that he had taken ninety-eight prisoners. It was not a very high figure: but, alas, it was the first of those communiqués in which, during the months and years to come, the Viets were to proclaim that they had taken hundreds and even thousands.

At that time it was thought that all the rest of the garrison was dead. It was only long after, weeks after, in the midst of the disaster of the frontier, that a very small, half-dying group came out of the jungle — an officer and a few men from Dongkhe. People had forgotten that in the jungle flight too is terribly slow, a tormented progress of a few hundred yards a day, with starvation all the way. And the story these unhoped-for survivors had to tell was yet another confirmation of what the Viets had become and of their inexplicable strength. What had happened was the destruction of the thoroughly exposed post by guns that could not be seen. It was done most methodically: first the four blockhouses were knocked out one after another — direct hits that shattered the concrete and killed the crews at their guns. But in the ruins of the outer line the wounded fired on the waves of Viets until they were overrun. Then those who could, the few untouched men or the more lightly wounded, retreated to the central redoubt. There everything began all over again — the hammering, the explosions, the caving-in, the roaring, disciplined Viet masses charging in the night storming the breaches. Then came the final moments when the ammunition ran out, the radio went dead and the score of men who were still capable of fighting were locked in the last hand-to-hand struggle. A handful of them tried a sortie, flinging themselves into the darkness and the forest while the victorious, shouting Viets swarmed over the citadel.

Not only did this second fall of Dongkhe utterly discredit the system of hedgehogs; it also showed that the whole frontier was cracking: it was the proof that Giap's army was a formidable reality. The French fought this army, of course; but they did so with a strange mixture of the complexes of inferiority and superiority. This resulted in the giving of absurd orders: troops were engaged in madhouse conditions. In the end the courage of the officers and men in the field, which enabled them to succeed in carrying out unbelievably stupid orders, only led them to a more bitter defeat when all was done.

But military stupidity is not, as one might suppose, uncomplicated. There is nothing more complex, more crammed with subtlety and shabby, Jesuitical casuistry. Totally false theories are built up: they are based on commonplace, third-rate intrigue, a mixture of cunning shifts and simple-mindedness; and they are nevertheless put into practice. The catastrophe of the Chinese border in 1950 can be explained only by the generals' irresponsible foolery and all the tricks they played on one another during the preceding months, at every possible and imaginable level. The greatest danger lay in the fact that beneath their selfish motives each was equally convinced that he was right and that he was acting in the best interests of France and the Expeditionary Force: this meant that both cast all restraint aside and became capable of anything whatever.

During the few months that separated the first taking of Dongkhe from the second and from the great disaster of the R.C. 4 everything that an underhand, dishonorable conflict between generals can produce was produced.

This extraordinary quarrel was long and complicated, but I must give at least a simplified version of its main lines, because it was the underlying cause of all the subsequent misfortunes.

Back in May 1950 Alessandri was putting the finishing touches to his masterpiece, a wonderfully exact and detailed plan of great scope — nothing less than a project for carrying the war into middle and Upper Tonkin, into the deep jungle and the heart of Ho Chi Minh's quadrilateral itself. It was staking everything. The conquest of the delta was over. In their hideouts the Viets were short of food. They were desperately preparing for heavy fighting, for their general counteroffensive, but they were not yet ready. This was the moment for striking the decisive blow by going after them in their bases and their camps, wiping them out, destroying their installations and their dumps and preventing the movement of Chinese supplies. Alessandri's plan was the only valid conception; and nothing that had been done before his day was of the slightest worth. The earlier misfortunes did not signify, for they were the result of an erroneous strategy. What could be more absurd than clinging to a single road, than having nothing but the R.C. 4 as a battlefield? All these posts and convoys were so many victims offered to the watchful Viets, who moved about unchecked, doing whatever they liked. It was a system that had been produced by famous generals like Valluy and Salan; but he, the modest Alessandri, would do what they had not dared attempt. He would launch his columns into the jungle and the forest, sending his men along the tracks and the ridges, making his battalions maneuver and fight against the Viets in the Viets' own fashion; he would occupy the whole of the jungle, he would clean up the terrain, and that would be the end of Ho Chi Minh.

Everything was ready. He had a striking force of fifty battalions. He was going to throw them all simultaneously against Giap's army. In the first phase they would seize the approaches and the lines of access, and in the second they would fan out in the mountains and the forest in groups of from five to six battalions. Six destroying operations would be carried out together: they would set out from Yenbay, Vietri, Thainguyen, Langson, Caobang and Backan and drive into the heart of the enemy jungle. The blows were to come everywhere at once, otherwise the Viets would slip through his fingers like quicksilver.

Everything had been worked out to the last detail. Parachute troops were an important element, and so were fighters; but there was to be no artillery — it was essential that the men should travel light, that their movements should be rapid, and that everything should be carried out at great speed. It was to be pure fighting, man-to-man combat in the tradition of the columns of the colonial days.

Everything had been arranged, including the friendship and support of Alessandri's old companions the Mans, the Meos, the Nungs and all the strange, formidable mountain tribes, whom Alessandri had loaded with presents, buying their opium at twice the normal price.

The plan had been prepared with the utmost secrecy: not even the commander in chief or the high commissioner knew of it — or at least that was what Alessandri supposed. He meant to keep it as a delightful surprise, and it never even remotely occurred to him that they could say no: after all, was he not bringing them victory, handing it to them on a plate? All he asked for was a few extra battalions. Then a few days later, on June 1, 1950, came Carpentier's reply — the briefest of notes, an arrogant, direct, total refusal — any offensive whatever was forbidden. Carpentier added that Monsieur Pignon agreed with him in condemning these reckless schemes: and that was the crowning injury, the true stab in the back; from the earliest days Pignon had been Alessandri's constant protector, friend and partner.

It had taken a considerable time for things to reach this point. To begin with, Carpentier had not come altogether willingly to the Far East, in spite of the urging of his patron Juin; he had been afraid for his reputation, and for a long while he had remained motionless in Saigon. But gradually the notion came to him that he was not merely Juin's understudy but a commander in his own right. Yet still he did nothing; and when he went on a tour of inspection he saw nothing either. But back in his office he would indignantly point out that his inkwell was dry.

In his own way Carpentier was a complicated being, full of surly confidence and yet at the same time extremely fearful of something going wrong. He was modest and vain, swashbuckling and timid. He insisted upon rank and prerogative, but he had an odd notion of a commander's role. As he saw it he was not there to command. He left that to the regional generals: it was their duty to carry on the war, to come and pay their respects to him and to tell him that everything was fine. He had no general ideas on the Indochinese war or on how it should be fought. He might almost have said that it was none of his business. What in fact he did was to allot forces and equipment to the men who pleased him, and then wait for results. His role was to keep Paris informed, or in other words comforted.

But he had a very capable chief of staff, Colonel Domergue, who wanted to turn this rear-line general into the real leader of the war. To a certain extent he succeeded, by needling his vanity on the subject of Alessandri. Everything was against the little Corsican: not only had Carpentier been obliged to rely upon him to begin with, and not only did he dislike him, but now Domergue told him, "Alessandri is right when he says that the fate

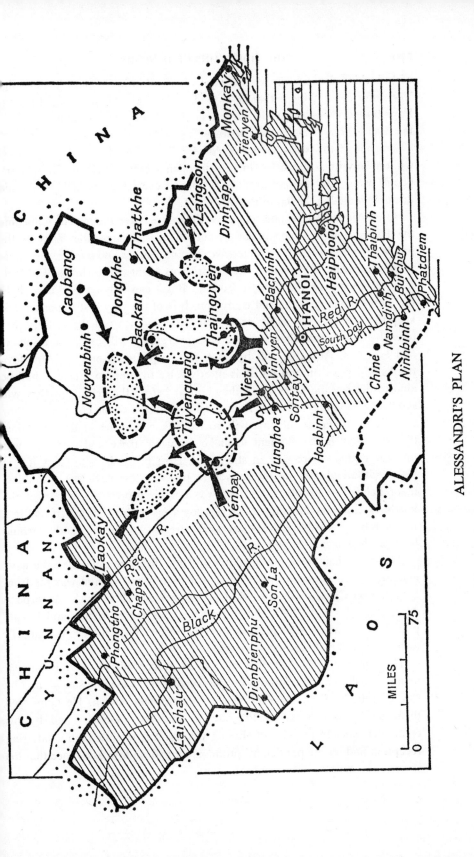

ALESSANDRI'S PLAN

of Indochina depends on what happens in Tonkin in the next few months. The unfortunate thing is that he is mad. It will be a disaster if he drags the Expeditionary Force into the Upper Tonkin mountains and jungles against the Viets: he will either be cut to pieces or he will accomplish nothing.' The result of this was that while Alessandri was working away in Hanoi without any idea that his plan was an open secret in Saigon, Carpentier's people were busy finding arguments against everything he advanced: and this culminated in the flat refusal of June 1.

After Alessandri no one, not even de Lattre, ever thought of launching the Expeditionary Force in an all-out offensive against the Viets in the jungle. From now on it was defensive fighting, harder and harder, more and more desperate. Logically, Alessandri was right when he said, "It is essential to stay on the Chinese frontier. But it can only be held if we hold the whole upper region. That is my aim. It is of the very first importance to keep the Viets far off, as far as possible from the heart of the country. My offensive is the last chance: otherwise everything will crack at Caobang and Langson. And that will be fatal, for Giap's army and the Molotova trucks will push on and on. It is utterly false to suppose that we shall be able to destroy the Viets when they appear before the delta. For they will sap everything, they will undermine and corrupt the whole country; and the Expeditionary Force, at bay, will go from defeat to defeat until the final disaster. Now is the moment to make a daring stroke and carry the war into the region where we can still smash Ho Chi Minh — to carry it into his quadrilateral. As the future was to prove, Alessandri was a faultless theoretician and prophet. And yet was not his proposed invasion of the jungle by the Expeditionary Force already a mere pipe dream? In reality it was surely impossible. The Viets were already too strong, and it would have finished in catastrophe.

Alessandri had some powerful allies. The officers commanding the navy and the air force were both in favor of fighting; and Pignon was far from certainly on Carpentier's side. So Carpentier went off to Paris, to torpedo Alessandri: he came back, having seen all his many friends and having pulled all his wires, very pleased with the result. Then it was Alessandri's turn to go to Paris to torpedo Carpentier.

The surprising thing is that he almost succeeded. He was unknown, unconnected, and unimportant, but he convinced the men he saw — and he saw everybody, from the President of the Republic down. He convinced them by his knowledge of the country and the situation, and by his completely sincere promise of shining victory. Yet in spite of his flattering reception and all the politicians' promises he had no firm assurance that his policy should supersede Carpentier's. After all his exhausting visits he took a holiday at Cannes, and while he was there Bao Dai, who was also on the Riviera, telephoned him. "Come and see me," he said. "Monsieur Letourneau [the new MRP minister for overseas territories] and Monsieur Pignon would like to talk to you."

Letourneau was wearing his most solemn expression. "General, you have made a deep impression on President Auriol. He asks you to leave for Indochina at once. Your experience is urgently needed there. You are the man the situation calls for: only you can carry out the operations planned."

Alessandri asked about the military policy that was to be followed — was it to be his? Letourneau was evasive. Yet the General weakened. "Am I to understand that the President's wish is an order?"

"It is."

There was nothing left but for Alessandri to obey the dictates of his conscience. He was in fact vain enough to be certain that once he was there, on the spot, he would be able to impose his own views. On September 17 he took the plane for Saigon. There he found that he was completely mistaken. Carpentier had strengthened his grip; he had turned himself into an imperious, commanding warrior; and Alessandri was confronted with the choice of leaving or committing himself to a policy and a campaign that he abominated. Most unhappily for him he stayed.

Carpentier's plan was summed up in a document dated August 18, 1950 and entitled "Secret Personal Directive for the Defense of the Sino-Tonkinese Frontier." The R.C. 4 was still to be defended: the strongholds of Caobang, Thatkhe, Langson and Dongdang were to act as breakwaters against the enemy offensive. Caobang and Langson were to be held firmly: the minor posts might be withdrawn. The Viet columns that crossed the R.C. 4 would be attacked as they moved through the jungle by "delaying elements." Finally the decisive battle would be joined at the edge of the delta, "with all available forces." The plan might have been drawn up for a European campaign: it paid no attention to the nature of the jungle nor to the nature of the enemy — it chose to overlook the whole "people's war" aspect. The whole thing was nonsense. Carpentier did not like the idea of evacuating the R.C. 4 because that would have a bad effect in Paris. He had two reasonable alternatives, either to strip it completely or to strengthen it adequately; but instead of either he abandoned a few thousand soldiers there — the one way to make sure of a crushing defeat that would make the enemy seem far more dangerous than he was and break the heart and spirit of the whole Expeditionary Force. And in the almost certain disaster the evacuation of the little posts and the withdrawals would either be headlong flights or ignominious surrenders. As for the "delaying elements," they had virtually no existence: at the most they amounted to a few companies who were completely overwhelmed by the mass of the invaders.

That was not all. After the foreseeable catastrophe of the frontier, the main body of the Expeditionary Force was to be so astonished, amazed and discouraged that it would no longer have the morale to resist before the delta. Nor would it be able to do so from the material point of view, for in his failure to realize the true state of affairs Carpentier did not send troops into Tonkin, although he loudly spoke of the great battles to come: not at all, he took them away — at Haiphong, battalions were to be seen getting on the boat for Annam and other distant parts of Indochina.

Carpentier's only positive measure was to set up an immense press section, for he did not like professional journalists; he was persuaded that newspapers would be delighted to print articles written by his own officers if they were provided free, and that they would therefore no longer send their own men — cynical, dubious characters.

In Saigon, then, there was a good deal of activity and preparation, at least among the people who surrounded Carpentier. But where the fighting was going to take place no one stirred. In Hanoi no one did anything — Alessandri might or might not come back, and there might or might not be reprisals. But in Langson, the capital of the frontier zone, everything was splendid. To be sure it was a histrionic splendor — one of those plays in which halfwits play the knight errant before collapsing in blood and ridicule — and it had nothing to do with real military preparation at all. Langson was the stage permanently occupied by Colonel Constans, one of Carpentier's creatures: he was the hero, the whole town was the scenery, and the legionaries were used as subsidiary mummers. Everything was calculated for its theatrical effect. When an important person came to see Constans at Langson — some worthy American general wanting to form a judgment on the spot, for example — he would telephone all his departments, saying, "Lay on the full treatment." How could anyone resist him, how could anyone fail to believe him when he put on his big act in the map room, with all his officers at attention, all deadly serious while he explained, with his enchanting, noble simplicity, the whole of his military disposition on the frontier? And everything he said he proved with facts, figures and those incredibly exact details that do so delight American soldiers who arrive filled with doubt. It was a most remarkable act, for Constans knew nothing whatever.

In Saigon Carpentier was beginning to believe in the Viets; but Constans was of the opinion that they had no existence. Two journalists appeared at Langson one day, warmly recommended by Carpentier, who had once known the mother of one of them. "Do you think you will be able to stand out against Giap's coming offensive?" they asked during the splendid dinner he gave in their honor. Ironic smile from Constans, imitated by all his staff officers. "The big bad Viets, Giap's divisions — it's an invention of your colleagues, the gentlemen of the press. It's bluff. They are still nothing but guerrilla fighters, and we shall soon settle their business for them. Don't you be afraid for us, but rather for them."

All through this summer of 1950 no decision came from Saigon, where Carpentier declined to commit himself, however badly this apparent lack of policy might affect the troops in Tonkin; yet Carpentier had made up his mind, and on September 16 he issued Order No. 46. "I have decided upon the occupation of Thainguyen at a date as close as possible to October 1. I have decided that the evacuation of Caobang shall be undertaken as soon as the Thainguyen region is seized." But to carry out his intentions he thought that two pieces of bluff were necessary. France had to be bluffed into thinking that the taking of Thainguyen was a triumph — that Thainguyen was worth Caobang and more. And the Viets had to be bluffed into thinking that the R.C. 4 was being reinforced for a last-ditch defense.

A column was sent up the ill-omened road from Langson as though the threatened Thatkhe were to be strengthened or even as though Dongkhe were to be retaken. And everything that could be provided for a total, relentless battle in Caobang was provided. Charton was sent in to command, for as everybody knew, including the Viets, he was a perfect symbol of out-and-out pitiless war; he was also sent (though this was carefully concealed) because as second-in-command at Langson he scarcely troubled to hide his view that Carpentier's pet Constans was a wet-legged drip. Everything, really everything was done to deceive Giap and to make him believe in an unshakable resistance. Every possible flying day, an airlift carried out the useless mouths that might hinder the remorseless battle, all the sick, the whores, the shopkeepers; and more fighting men, more Moroccans, were flown in.

Carpentier's idea was to wait until Giap should be thoroughly deluded and then lay his cards on the table: as quietly as possible, without giving the alarm by blowing things up, the garrison of Caobang would take French leave, hurrying down the R.C. 4 before the Viets understood what was happening. Everything was to depend on the speed of their march; and near Dongkhe they would be met by the column that had left Langson a fortnight earlier without even its leader, Colonel Lepage, having any idea of what it was intended to do. Secrecy, everything depended on secrecy according to General Carpentier. In fact, in spite of all his trumpeting, his silence and his cunning, the commander in chief did not display much imagination; all he was doing was to revert to an old plan that had been lying about in the files of the staff since Revers's time, when the evacuation of Caobang was first mooted. But in those days Giap had no army; there were no countless Viet divisions sitting across the line of retreat, all along the R.C. 4. "It doesn't matter," said Carpentier to the few men in the know. "They will be taken by surprise."

At this juncture Alessandri returned from France and found himself face to face with the horrible reality. Everything was ready: the evacuation of Caobang was to begin in a few days' time. Alessandri reasoned, stormed, threatened, called for a meeting of the Defense Council. But he could do nothing, and Carpentier was the victor, at least as far as the battle over the council table was concerned.

Little need be said about Operation Phoque, the taking of Thainguyen, except that it was carried out in continual rain, that it was behind its timetable from the word go, and that as there was no resistance worth speaking of, it was successful — if taking an undefended, useless town with close on ten thousand men and virtually all the Expeditionary Force's heavy equipment can be counted a success. The real importance of the operation lay in the fact that it pinned down a great number of men a hundred and twenty miles away at the crucial period when Giap was setting about the annihilation of Charton's and Lepage's few unsupported battalions on the R.C. 4. And of course Thainguyen was evacuated for the defense of the delta as soon as Giap had made his breakthrough.

But Operation Thérèse, the evacuation of Caobang, was something else again. There were three possible solutions, airlift, retreat down the R.C. 3 to Thainguyen which had just been taken, or retreat along the R.C. 4. In spite of everything that poor Alessandri could say, Carpentier insisted upon the R.C. 4 — but by now Alessandri was only a shadow of his former self. The plan that Carpentier had resurrected called for the crossing of the sixty mile gap between Caobang and the still-held post of Thatkhe: it provided for a relief column from Thatkhe to meet the retreating column at Dongkhe. The plan had been worked out when the Viets were still weak and when Dongkhe belonged to the French: the one modification was that now the relief column should move farther up the R.C. 4, the rendezvous being the tiny village of Namnang, some twenty miles from Caobang. When the two columns met they would return to Thatkhe together.

But this plan necessarily assumed that the strongly fortified Dongkhe

ould be taken from the Viets by the relief columns on the outward
urney. No one had worked out what should be done if the Vietminh
uld not be dislodged. And even if everything went perfectly, the success
f the operation still depended upon Giap's being deceived, and upon
ecrecy. However, Giap had never been taken in by Carpentier's peasant
unning for a moment; nor had there been any secrecy worth talking about.
here had been so much shilly-shallying about this evacuation, so much
lk in the staffs at Saigon, Hanoi and Langson. Officially only a few top
en were in the know, and the whole Expeditionary Force and the whole
f Vietnam had been vehemently told that no such thing would ever take
lace. But in these cases everybody knows. There is always a leak: and
hether it is mere gossip or downright treason the result is the same. At all
vents Giap knew what was going to happen, and he remained in Dongkhe
ith all his divisions, waiting for a minimum of seven or eight battalions to
rop into his hand. And he was certain that he would be able to destroy
hem, for he was also aware that the mass of the Expeditionary Force —
ixteen battalions, two squadrons of tanks, four groups of artillery, eight
undred vehicles and practically all the planes — was involved in the
apture of Thainguyen. Far away in the delta, the French fired eighteen
housand 105-mm shells into the empty air during the first three days of
Operation Phoque. And on the R.C. 4 they had no guns.

Caobang

AT Dongkhe Giap did nothing: as a place for lying in wait it could not
ave been improved. And day by day he saw his prey coming closer. To
egin with it was Lepage's column moving from Langson towards Thatkhe
nd Dongkhe: it was weak, but Giap was in no hurry to attack and destroy
t. He waited, because he hoped for a double success — he also wanted to
ipe out Charton's column at the same time, and he was certain that it
would presently leave Caobang for the deadly rendezvous.

The Lepage column had set out on the R.C. 4 of evil memory as early as
he second fall of Dongkhe, with no exact instructions. The troops were all
North Africans, three tabors and the 8th RTM: it was a tactical unit
hurriedly put together with bits and pieces, made up of tired men, no
longer of any great value and not very well officered. The men's morale
was low, and so, it seems, was that of their chief. He was an almost
unknown gunner who possessed no authority, who had never done any
jungle fighting and who had nothing of the warlord about him at all. No
one ever knew why he had been appointed. But he was a conscientious

man, for all that: he was also a religious man, and before leaving he praye
and took the sacrament, as though he were leading a forlorn hope.

The column moved off into the unknown, and fear went with it. Fror
the beginning, as early as just after Nachan, there were roadblocks an
clashes with the Viets — men were killed. Farther on, the road wa
nothing but a line of destruction. Mine craters everywhere, landslides
blown bridges: no possibility of getting the guns, the trucks and the heav
equipment along. It was all sent back to Langson. The column had to g
forward on foot, marching interminably through very dangerous ambusl
country: but there were no big Viet formations. At last, on September 19
after four nights of exhausting march, the worn-out soldiers of the colum
thought they were safe — far off, at the bottom of the Thatkhe depression
they could see the still-undamaged citadel and, even more important, the
most famous battalion of the Expeditionary Force, the 1st BEP, Foreig
Legion parachute troops who had been dropped there in two waves the da
before.

It was a curious situation. Thatkhe was closely invested by the Viet
minh, but it had not been attacked. One of the tabors was sent back to the
base, and the BEP took its place. But its young officers, men of iron lik
Jeanpierre or Faulke, did not know Lepage. They thought him soft
Furthermore the paras, almost all of whom were Germans, had littl
confidence in the tabors. This haphazard gathering received the name o
Bayard. There were still no orders. Everyone asked "Why are we here?"
Nobody could tell, not even Lepage. For a week, by way of keeping the
men busy, there were little operations all around Thatkhe. One was a
success. After a long night march near Poma the paras, who were leading
came upon a train of coolies in the misty dawn, carrying mortars. The
legionaries made a slaughter of them, but the Viet regulars counterattacke
in the rear, engaging the tabors, and presently everything was in a bac
state of confusion. Officially the affair was announced as a victory; but it
psychological effects were disastrous. More and more the paras felt tha
they were on their own, for they had no belief in Lepage as a commande
and they did not trust the Moroccans' courage.

At the end of a week it turned out that the high command did after al
have something in its mind. The Thatkhe airstrip, a little patch on which
even a Junker could not land, was improved; and more important all sorts
of supplies were dropped, including boots. The soldiers found that they
were not new but repaired. Lepage still did not know what the whole thing
was about.

He found out the next day, September 30. A coded signal from Constans

THE THREE PLANS FOR EVACUATING CAOBANG

1. Airlift to Langson
2. The R.C. 3 to Thainguyen
3. The R.C. 4: meeting of Charton's and Lepage's columns near Namnang, before the withdrawal to Thatkhe.

ordered Bayard to take Dongkhe by noon on October 2: it said nothing further, nor did it say why. For Lepage it was tantamount to an order to commit suicide. He desperately radioed Langson, pointing out all the dangers of the mission — the colonel was too well disciplined to speak of its madness. With scarcely more than two thousand men he was required to plunge into the unknown jungle to take a place of which nothing was known except that it was a heap of ruins. Furthermore there was an utter lack of intelligence of any kind; nothing was known except that this terrible, apparently empty landscape contained huge Viet concentrations that possessed artillery. For their part the French had no guns. To be sure, there were a few in the citadel of Thatkhe, but it was impossible to take them far along the R.C. 4 and they could never cross the Bascou bridge, which had been destroyed. More than ever before everything along the R.C. 4 was in ruins. The men who were to move forward could count only upon themselves and upon what they could carry — it would be very difficult to bring up supplies or reinforcements with such unsure lines of communication. It was only planes that could help them; but now once again it was hopeless flying weather — drizzle and a zero ceiling.

Langson's answer was imperative: the operation must be begun at once. In a last attempt Lepage asked that the start should be postponed for twenty-four hours in the hope of a better weather report. Refusal.

During the afternoon of September 30 there was a formal meeting of the commanding officers of Bayard. Together with Lepage there were Major Secretain of the 1st BEP, Major Arnaud of the 8th RTM, Major Delcros of the 11th Tabor and Captain Faugas of the 1st Tabor. It was a dismal assembly. Having told them of Langson's orders, Lepage said, "My only hope is that the Viets are not holding Dongkhe. Otherwise I do not see how we can set about taking it." The officers went out and gave the troops their orders. The young officers of the BEP and the ordinary paras laughed — their usual way of taking a challenge. The Moroccans wore their fatalistic expressions; but was not their fighting spirit deeply touched? There was a rumor among the soldiers that Lepage had said "We shall never come back," that he had wept and that he had then taken Communion.

That same evening the column pushed into the night, into the horrible mountains — four battalions going to fight thirty. They marched with different units taking turns to lead. Most of the time the paras of the Legion were on the road, with the Moroccans scouting along the sides. Once more the French climbed up the bloody pass of Luong Phai. And this time without any resistance from the enemy, without any Viets firing from the shelter of the jungle, the ridges, the caves or the rocks to stop their advance. Uneasily the soldiers said, "It's too easy." The sun had been up for hours when the long train of men, having crossed the main range, reached the top of the pass. The column's speed was slow, and the BEP was very much ahead. From the top they saw a landscape made up of hundreds of little peaks — not a single Viet. The French pushed on, passing the former post at Napa, empty now, dismally empty. It was then that a half company of the BEP under Lieutenant Faulke stumbled upon an enemy patrol on a rocky spur high over the road. They killed three Viets but two managed to get away — they would raise the alarm at Dongkhe.

Captain Jeanpierre said to Faulke, "Go on at full speed with your squad. It's the last chance of taking Dongkhe by surprise — if it's empty."

The platoon raced forward, followed by the company of the BEP. The miles stretched out and there were a hundred men running: suddenly, far below them, they saw the unchanging basin with its unchanging checkerboard of paddy fields; but in the middle, instead of the post, there was nothing but a blackened heap. Was the enemy hidden there in great strength, or was there no one? Faulke and his platoon plunged down the R.C. 4 into the plain — not a living soul, not a beast, nothing. And no one knew whether this strange emptiness was good or bad. A handful of paras were within eight hundred yards of Dongkhe and still nothing had appeared. It was about five o'clock in the afternoon. They had to cross a stream by a little bridge at the foot of a crag. At this point the paras were stopped in their tracks, pinned down by a very exact machine-gun-and-mortar fire. It came from the ruins of the former post and from a pagoda that the Expeditionary Force had turned into a blockhouse. Some way behind, the BEP company that had been following formed itself into a battery to counter the fire of the Viets' automatic weapons, but it was no use — it was still impossible to cross the barrage. Captain Jeanpierre joined Faulke and said, "There are certainly not a great many Viets in the Dongkhe basin at this moment. If Lepage throws in everything — if he maneuvers and runs the whole column in to the assault, we shall take it." But nothing appeared. Everything was halted. The colonel, having seen that the surprise had failed, decided that a full-scale operation would have to be mounted. It was put off until the next day, for it would need planes and artillery. Langson was asked to parachute two guns.

The situation that night was very strange. The Dongkhe hollow seemed deserted. It was as though each side was afraid of the other, as though each was afraid of being smashed in the bottom of that round valley. The French dared not go down: they stayed on the heights and camped there on the peaks and the ridges, in a scientific and unmoving disposition. On their side, the five Viet battalions that had taken Dongkhe a fortnight before had withdrawn from it almost at once, and they too were sitting on the crags near at hand, not where the R.C. 4 came out, but at the entrance to their own supply line that linked them with China. And behind those five battalions there were many others — practically the whole of Giap's army was there in reserve. All these men were a few hours at the most from Lepage's column as it camped there on point 615, on the Nachiang, the Nakeo, the Ngaum and the old Napa post, the last peaks that hemmed in the R.C. 4 where it began its plunge towards Dongkhe.

The next day, October 2, the French began their attack in due form. Lepage's idea was to take Dongkhe with a pincer movement, the one jaw to the east and the other to the west. They therefore left the R.C. 4, and the BEP, the tabors and the 8th RTM made their way along the ridges that dropped to the plain. It was dense jungle, a chaos of peaks, caves, sudden precipices. No one could see more than a couple of yards. No one knew where the Viets were. But they were there all right, and there were a great many of them.

It was an extraordinary battle. The BEP's task was to infiltrate a huge limestone mass to the east of the R.C. 4, a mountain that ended in an abrupt cliff a few hundred yards from Dongkhe. The first company was in the lead. At first there was nothing — nothing at all until a thirsty sergeant major went to fill his water bottle at a stream and came face to face with a Viet who was also drinking there. The two men, each as surprised as the other, both fired and ran. The sergeant major said to his captain, "There are Viets right here." But the vegetation was so inextricably thick that the company had no room to bring their weapons into action, to fire and kill. They crept on yard by yard. Suddenly a patrol found a clearing with some Viets in it, sitting on the grass and passionately arguing over the maps they had spread out. The light machine-gun carrier carefully pointed his weapon and opened fire — a butchery. But the jungle all around was overflowing with the enemy, and the reply was devastating. The paras had only wiped out a regiment's fighting post, and the whole of the rest of the formation was hidden next to it, lying there for an ambush. The paras were being shot at from every direction — a furious hail of bullets coming from all around them. Their only protection was to lie flat in deep, entangled foliage. They could not see the Viets, but it seemed that the Viets could not see them either — they kept up a tremendous fire, but it was more or less haphazard, scarcely aimed at all. Nevertheless the paras had to draw back twenty yards or so. They crept back to the clearing, where they could take their bearings and find out where they were. But

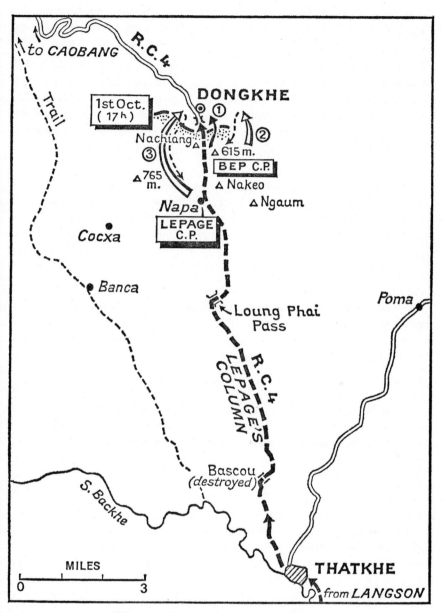

LEPAGE IS CHECKED BEFORE DONGKHE

1. Evening of October 1: Faulke's reconnaissance.
2. October 2: Lepage tries to bypass the town on the east with the BEP.
3. Simultaneously, the 8th RTM and the tabors move up on the west.

there was no room for all of them: the captain set five machine gunners along a twenty-yard line with the rest of the company behind them, in the shelter of the jungle. The engagement lasted more than an hour. After hammering the position with their mortars, the Viets tried to storm it in two separate waves, but each time they were pushed back. Only two paras were killed. The Viets withdrew, but they were there in great force, waiting for their chance. There was no possibility of moving forward. Reinforcements would be no use, for there was no room to deploy them. In the end the paras also disengaged and made their way back to the BEP's forward HQ. The mission had failed.

It was failure for the 8th RTM and the tabors as well. They too had advanced at first in spite of the extreme difficulty, and one Moroccan unit had even reached the edge of the Dongkhe airfield. But they had been counterattacked and forced to retreat. It was all the more disturbing since the planes — the weather was rather better and the fighters had been able to come out — signaled the presence of huge Viet columns, advancing at full speed. There was no longer any question of seizing Dongkhe by force, although the two guns that had been asked for had been dropped, together with their crews.

This was the decisive moment. At this point the French high command could still give up the evacuation of Caobang by way of the R.C. 4, since the necessary condition, the taking of Dongkhe by Lepage's column, had not been fulfilled. It seems that at this juncture Alessandri wired Carpentier: "CANCEL EVERYTHING. IF YOU CARRY ON IT WILL BE A CRIME." But Carpentier persisted. Since Lepage had not been able to take the Dongkhe basin he would turn the column west, thrusting into the heart of the jungle, amidst the limestone crags, in the depths of the most savage region. Running through the virgin forest there was a faint, almost unknown trail that led towards Caobang and came out onto the R.C. 4 just at Namnang, the very spot that Charton's column was to reach, having had no more than twenty miles to travel. The meeting was set for October 3. And that was the news that reached the unfortunate Lepage at half-past two in the afternoon of October 2, by means of a message dropped in his operational HQ.

At last, after a fortnight, he learned what his column was there for — that it was to join up with the garrison of Caobang. But he learned it in the most disastrous circumstances: he had failed at Dongkhe and he was ordered to thrust into the appalling mountains, where the Viets, who already outnumbered him, were at an even greater advantage. It was murder.

Lepage's column was being required to plunge into the limestone chaos to the south of Dongkhe, a country that was ordinarily considered impossible for human beings. Everything had to be carried, even water, for there was none in that fissured wilderness. The French were to march into an appalling countryside, a natural labyrinth, without guides, without supplies, without anything but inaccurate maps and their own courage. The Viets, on the other hand, were perfectly at home — this region had always been one of their haunts. And they had thousands of coolies to bring their men everything they needed, jars of water and baskets of ammunition. The supplies came in from China, which was just at hand, not more than a few miles away.

This was Giap's great moment. His guess had been entirely right. He had refrained from action so long as the matter was not absolutely clear. But from now on everything was certain; and now was the time for the kill. During the first two days of October Giap still remained on the defensive, preventing Lepage from taking Dongkhe. But on the second he too learned something of the first importance — he learned that the Caobang garrison was on the point of setting out. It would travel quietly along to Namnang, and there it would find no Lepage, no relief column, nothing at all. Then, advancing by itself, it would take two or three days to reach the neighborhood of Dongkhe. The work had to be done during that period; Lepage's column must be continually attacked as it wandered among the limestone crags, pursued, surrounded, crushed, wiped out to the last man. So when Charton's column arrived, exhausted by its march, it would not find a single Frenchman to receive it but rather thousands and tens of thousands of Viets ready to leap out: and in its turn this column too would be easy to destroy.

Giap's plan was almost wholly carried out. By a miracle of heroism a few French battalions were able to hold out in the mountains of Dongkhe longer than he had foreseen, but the result was what he had expected — a disaster for the French, a rout in the most appalling circumstances. Only a few hundred men escaped. It was an event of incalculable importance: for the first time in Indochina the Asians had crushed the Europeans; and for the first time Red dialectic had triumphed over the strategy of the Ecole de Guerre. The gods had fallen from their pedestals.

But let us see how it actually happened. To begin with, let us take notice of the contrast between Lepage's column, which was attacked almost at once and which was doomed, and Charton's, in which everybody was optimistic, although to be sure they were sorry to leave such a happy little town as Caobang.

Everything had been going along very well in Caobang since Charton's return as chief. Now that it was an air-supplied hedgehog and there was no more sweating along the R.C. 4 life was even pleasanter; and the civilians who had been evacuated a year before had made their way back, so that there were now at least three thousand of them — everything that was needed in the way of whores, cookshop women, keepers of shops and gambling dens. Caobang was full of brothels, cinemas and bars; there was everything the Legion loved — girls, drink, war, and even peace, in the sense that nobody, no top brass from Saigon or Hanoi, ever appeared. Morale was splendid. Almost every night the Viet loudspeakers bawled "Surrender! For in a few days we shall attack Caobang and we shall take it. Then woe to the mercenaries and the traitors!" But nobody gave a damn, because nobody believed it. Both naturally and by fortification the town was exceedingly strong, and Charton had much improved the garrison, changing the unimpressive 8th RTM (which now formed part of Lepage's column) for a battalion of the Legion, the 3/3 REI. It was not the cream of the Legion; it had little experience of jungle fighting and its officers were all new, straight from France or Germany; but Charton trained them in his own way, mounting as many as fifteen ambushes in a single night. The Viets scarcely dared approach Caobang; and in the town trade had never been so good. Charton had his own way with civilians too: he told them they could either stay or go, just as they pleased, but if they stayed they must not enter into contact with the Viets. "You have a fortnight to think it over. But if after that I find that anyone has had the slightest contact, direct or indirect, with the enemy, I shall have him shot out of hand." It seems that after this speech there was not a single request to return to the Vietminh, nor a single betrayal. On the contrary, the entire population proclaimed its loyalty. Thanks to Charton, at Caobang, that pinpoint in the midst of Viet territory, all was happiness, both from the military and the capitalist point of view.

But at the end of September unfortunate omens began to appear. Not the Viets, whose main force was a good way off (only the watchers and two or three of Giap's battalions stuck close to the town) but the unexpected arrival of generals. One day the commander in chief himself flew in, cheerful, kindly, very much the "soldier's father." Carpentier made a patriotic, high-sounding speech to the troops, telling them that there would be no evacuation and that they would defend Caobang to the last. To Charton he said, "Your task is to keep Caobang for France. Tomorrow I shall give orders for an airlift to bring you in a tabor and to take away all these women and children, so that you will be in the best shape to fight and to deal with the attack of the regiments that have Caobang as their next objective, as I know very well."

And so Caobang was openly put into a stage of siege, to be defended to the last. The airlift brought in strength, took out weakness. But in the midst of all this warlike show Charton received his first warning. Another plane with stars on it* — but fewer — landed at Caobang. It was Alessandri. He was sick at heart, and he was physically unwell too — weakness, fever, amebic dysentery. But what really hurt, what really gnawed at him, was that he had to conduct Operation Thérèse, the evacuation of Caobang that he so loathed and that he had so struggled against. He had come to see things on the spot and to prepare it all. What is more his conscience was giving him no rest: he had had formal orders to put on the same "last ditch" act as Carpentier. He was to say nothing of what was really being got ready, not even to Charton. The orders for withdrawal were only to be given twenty-four hours before the retreat began. Meanwhile he was to deceive Charton.

Poor Alessandri! He was caught between military discipline and what he thought his higher duty. For how could Charton set about evacuating a town like Caobang on such short notice? So Alessandri disobeyed his commander in chief and told Charton what was going to happen. It was a dramatic conversation, and a most affectionate one too, for the two men were friends — they had liked one another for many years. Alessandri could not master his feelings: there in Charton's office he wept as he said, "They are going to play the Judas on you. Caobang is to be evacuated by the R.C. 4. What do you think about it? For my part, I can't see that you can possibly succeed."

"It is madness," said Charton.

They discussed the matter a little longer — its folly, the underlying reasons for it — and then Charton said, "I know this country. It can scarcely be done with the forces I have. The relief column will have to come and meet me at the twenty-eight-kilometer mark, or preferably even the twenty-two kilometer. Over that distance I will undertake to open the road and get my men and equipment along: but not beyond."

"I give you my word that you will be met at the twenty-eight-kilometer mark," said Alessandri.

Theoretically everything was straightforward. Charton's job was to reach kilometer 28. But he was afraid that no one would turn up. He had no confidence in either Lepage or his troops. So day after day he badgered Langson to strengthen Lepage. He asked that the road between Nachan

---

* The chief generals' planes had their stars painted on them.

and Thatkhe should be repaired so that guns, supplies and men — everything necessary — could be sent up to him. He asked that they should wait for a good weather forecast, so that there could be air cover. Operation Thérèse could easily be postponed a few days, just long enough for all the conditions to be right. Besides, for his part Charton still had several little jobs to do in Caobang — for example, he had to fly out one hundred and eighty invalids and forty women, most of them pregnant; and because of a cyclone there had been scarcely any planes for the last day or two. There was really no hurry. It would be far better to prepare and organize everything properly.

But at Langson Colonel Constans was not at all of the same opinion. Carpentier suspected that Alessandri had betrayed him and more and more he kept him out of everything: it was Constans who, like a robot, relayed the orders of the commander in chief, who was now back in Saigon. For Carpentier the success of Thérèse depended entirely on secrecy and speed. Because of this, no obvious preparations could be made nor could there be any destruction of equipment, even if it might be of use to the enemy afterwards. At the last moment it was allowable to carry out some rough and ready measures, such as tossing equipment into the river or leaving delayed explosives. And as for speed, the essential thing was to march, to move so fast that the surprised enemy should not have time to close in. So it was pointless to carry too much in the way of weapons, ammunition and equipment; for the intention was not to fight but to slip away. At all events, whatever happened and whether there were Viets in the neighborhood or not, Operation Thérèse was to begin on October 3 at the latest.

In a word, there was total lack of understanding between Langson and Caobang: it was made worse by the fact that all the exchanges were by coded signal. Even at such a time Constans remained in his comfortable HQ at Langson instead of coming to talk face to face with Charton at Caobang. The only thing he did was to send his chief of staff, which accomplished nothing; the only decision taken was to fly out the various units' clerks — and not even this was done, because there was no room in the planes.

Constans did do something else, however, and that was to send out signals announcing victory during the first few days — victory both at Thainguyen and on the R.C. 4. But suddenly the tone became less sanguine, and Charton understood that things were going badly with Lepage. More and more Charton was afraid that the rendezvous would not be kept, and in a last effort he asked that he should not be required to leave Caobang until Lepage was near kilometer 28. Could not Thérèse be begun on October fourth rather than on the third? In any case he was still encumbered with his sick and wounded. He needed eight Junkers to fly them out. Otherwise he would have to take them with him, limping along or being carried on stretchers; and that would hold back the column appallingly.

The reply was no. D day was still October 3. So then Charton, having tried foxiness and cunning so long, returned to his more natural self, that of a magnificent legionary. He was not going to leave his town, his Caobang, like that, with all its wealth and splendor intact for the Viets. The delighted Legion blew it up, or at least a great deal of it. It was an enormous destruction — at one moment a hundred and fifty tons of ammunition in the citadel all went up together — and the waters of the Song Ba Giang turned the color of saffron. Charton's only regret was that he had to leave the bridges standing, but his orders were absolutely firm on that point.

What did it matter if the enormous din warned the Viets? Charton had no illusions about that. He knew that the whole of Caobang had known what was going on for days past — for a great while now the whole Expeditionary Force had been oozing leaked information. Poor Carpentier, who did not realize that if he sent his secret plans down through the usual staff channels he might just as well have had them announced by the town crier! In any case, the news had been brought to Caobang very early by the Junkers of the airlift. The Legion knew, the people knew; and so did the Viets. For the Viets' pure reasoning and the information of their spies coincided, and it is said that their loudspeakers wished the garrison a happy journey the day before the evacuation began. As for the Legion, it made no attempt to hide its going. Charton even tried to profit by all the excitement to spread the rumor that the column was about to take the R.C. 3, passing by Backan.

Charton also did all he possibly could for the civilian population, taking with him those who could walk and who wished to come, and letting out all who were in prison.

The next day, October 3, came the evacuation: it was a fine example of the big operation in the Legion's own manner — slow, heavy, massive, systematic. It was a thorough piece of work in which everything was directed towards dealing courageously with any eventuality rather than towards slipping quietly away. And again, just as Lepage's column had been discouraged even at its setting-off, so Charton's began its march with great confidence — too much confidence. Only Charton was uneasy, but he put a good face upon it; besides, he did not really believe in a great disaster — not in total catastrophe.

Officially H hour was midnight. But it was not until about noon on October 3 that the column got under way. All night long the destruction had continued, and everything that could be carried off was carried off. The whole morning was spent in putting this mass of men and materiel in order. The fifteen outlying posts of Caobang had to be withdrawn one after another, and above all the column had to be formed. It stretched out for miles — an incongruous gathering — proud looking Moroccans (the 3rd Tabor was a good unit), splendid legionaries, partisans (most of whom were old, wrinkled, faithful creatures, but more houseboys or beps than warriors), and then the civilians, practically all Asian bourgeois, mild, inoffensive shopkeepers and businessmen — about five hundred of them, and a few of the city's whores. And almost all these people, in uniform and out of it, were loaded down with enormous bundles — all their most valuable possessions, their little personal treasures or what they had picked up in the abandoned town. And then in the middle of this enormous caravan there were two guns, the one a 37-mm and the other a 105-mm, together with a whole train of trucks piled high with victuals, ammunition and all the equipment that could be crammed into them. They also contained the wounded, for however strange it may appear, there had not been time to fly them all out. Only the dead were not there: in spite of Carpentier's fine speeches of earlier days they had been left in their cemeteries to the Vietminh. Apart from that, the evacuation of Caobang was, to begin with, a house removal.

How bitterly Charton was to be reproached for taking this artillery and these trucks! It is true that he did disobey: it is true that his orders were to leave on foot, taking nothing or almost nothing — at all events a minimum, so as "to go faster." But he, an old soldier through and through, thought that was all nonsense; he knew the deadly R.C. 4 too well, with all its traps and ambushes. Along every kilometer of it, wherever there was a peak, an embankment or a gorge he could say to himself, "There we had so many killed: over there it was bloody murder. There I lost my best friend." So now he carried out the same procedure that had been employed for all the convoys moving up or down the bloodstained road: he "opened it up," that is to say he sent men to occupy all the dangerous points in the immediate neighborhood. And now he took all the more precautions since this was not a real military convoy but rather an evacuated mob making its exodus, an easy prey with all these civilians dragging along behind. It made a huge caterpillar winding along the road, a horde of people with relatively few real soldiers. In the midst of all this weakness, how Charton congratulated himself upon having brought his guns and trucks. For as an experienced fighting man who had seen trouble in every shape and size, he did not care to launch into any venture unprepared.

So it all wound along the R.C. 4. Obviously a crowd like this does not move brisky — it drags. However, close to Caobang the Viets had not even destroyed the road. Nothing happened, scarcely so much as a very slight engagement — a few blasts of automatic fire, a few rifle shots near kilometer 10. The Viets were on the watch, but there was nothing they could do. The crowd traveled along in better heart than ever, quite contented. There was plenty to eat and drink.

They crossed one of the bad passes of earlier days without incident. At nightfall they stopped. Charton set up his HQ at kilometer 16. The rest might have been one prodigious great family; the soldiers kept vigilant guard all around, but the whole length of the road for thousands of yards was a mass of sleeping people. They slept peacefully, too — still no incident, still no attack. When the sun rose they set off again, with no particular hurry. Why should they race along, since Charton knew that the relief column was still very far from the meeting place? He did not know exactly where it was. Indeed he did not know anything. All went well until midday, when at last they reached kilometer 28, the rendezvous: there was nobody there. But what was far worse, what struck home hardest, was Constans's signals, two signals that came one after the other, loaded with madness and disaster. Lepage had not taken Dongkhe. Lepage had been heavily attacked a few miles south of Dongkhe just as he was beginning to make his way along the Quangliet track so as to reach the rendezvous at kilometer 28 in spite of Dongkhe. In fact he was surrounded, at bay, completely unable to move; and he was being cut to pieces. It was now up to Charton to take the Quangliet track and go to the rescue of Lepage. To do this he must move as fast as possible, jettison all useless weight and march day and night — he had to be there within twenty-four hours.

It was a cry of distress. But why had these two messages, which had been sent to Charton on the third, only reached him on the fourth? Who can tell? It would have changed everything if he had had them on the third. He would have acted in quite another way. But now he would have to plunge into the thickest, most unbroken, least-known jungle, the kind of jungle where you cannot tell where you are nor where the enemy is; and he would have to make a long march in it — without guides. If he had known he would have found some; and he would never have brought such a train with him.

During the next few hours everything was confusion. The officers and NCO's asked every partisan and every civilian, "Do you know the Quangliet track?" And the reply was always no.

But at all events weight had to go. The destruction lasted all afternoon: the two guns and their shells were blown up, together with the trucks and everything they contained. Each soldier was issued light rations and ammunition. There was a certain amount of disorder during this distribution, for the partisans were not happy about it — they wanted more to eat and more to fight with. However, every man got rid of his encumbrances, all the private belongings that he had brought with him, keeping nothing but money, hidden deep. The road presented not so much the appearance of a disaster as that of a ragfair, a flea market with no buyers. The soldiers still looked firm and cheerful, but the faces of the wretched civilians were stricken: they knew very well that from now on it was very likely that they were going to die.

But the huge column was still in good order. There was still one last problem that had to be solved, however — the finding of the Quangliet trail. They discovered that it no longer existed. The jungle had eaten it. At one time the Viets had used it, but then they had made another farther to the east for their long trains of soldiers and coolies: and in the rioting vegetation of Upper Tonkin anything that is left to itself vanishes in a few months, returning to its natural state.

At last, after a great deal of searching, they found the beginning of what had once been a track. The whole column moved along it; a line of people miles in length pushed one by one into the green prison that was to be their grave. They went in single file, and that made the line even longer. But there was still a fair amount of order. Ahead there were the partisans as a light covering force, placed there because it was thought that they would be better at finding the way and spotting the enemy; then came the legionaries of the 3/3 REI, followed by Charton, his HQ and his civilians; and lastly the 3rd Tabor, which formed the rear guard. As the Moroccans in their turn moved into the forest the Viets of the R.C. 4 began to harass them. But that was of no importance. What was to be dreaded was the Viets who were already there in the jungle and the tumbled limestone country in their thousands and tens of thousands. It was just before nightfall by the time the whole great length of Charton's column was in the forest at last — a twilight in which nothing could be seen, so that the Viets were invisible and the line of people could scarcely make each other out two yards away.

The Quangliet trail

ON the previous day, October 3, the disaster was rapidly coming to a head: one column was at bay, surrounded, and the other was hurrying to its destruction through the vast stretch of jungle. I was in Saigon, in a completely unperturbed Saigon where no one knew anything, except in the staff, and that was deep in its own secrecy. General Carpentier was working in his air-conditioned room: he was so devoid of apprehension that he had specially summoned his handsome spokesman — a captain he had recently appointed — to tell him how he should announce the coming victories to the press and how to give them their full value. During the first days of October the captain told the journalists nothing: silence, silence. Then on the fourth he ecstatically announced the great news, and it was thus that we heard how the operations were going so well. To begin with it was said that the meeting of the columns would happen "at any moment now." On the fifth we learned that it had not yet taken place, but that it was still just on the point of happening. On the sixth it was stated that the junction had been made — the whole of Charton's column had reached the "collecting point." I remember the captain's remarks: "Now it can be said that the hardest part is over, that the daring operation of withdrawal from Caobang has succeeded. Even in their own domain, the jungle and the mountains, the Viets have not been able to prevent the movement of two isolated French columns marching through the heart of the country, very far from their bases." On the seventh we were told that the first elements of the two closely linked columns were within a few miles of Thatkhe. On the eighth, that the whole of both was under the protection of the guns of Thatkhe. On the ninth, that the vanguard was in Thatkhe, and the captain spoke of a feat of arms. And yet at the very moment he said these words thousands of French troops were dead or dying there in the jungle. The tragedy had already been consummated, and already the red ants were eating out the eyes of the dead.

And the worst was that no doubt the captain was not flatly lying, that he partially believed what he said. It took a long time for General Carpentier and the staff at Saigon to realize what had happened: they were victims of that military art of "putting things properly" — an art that had been lavished on the dispatches from Hanoi and Langson. Besides, even there nobody really knew. The meticulous General Alessandri flew over the jungle all day long, day after day, seeing nothing but the impenetrable screen of trees — never Charton's column. He never managed to discover it all through its everlasting, tragic march. Furthermore in the deep forest and among the mountains the little radios worked badly, very badly. Often they could neither hear nor be heard. Occasionally there would be an exchange of very short messages, sometimes hauntingly terrible in their brevity but most of the time unconnected, meaningless, incomprehensible.

It was only on October 8 that "informed circles" had their first misgivings. They began to talk about hard fighting and even about terrible battles. General Carpentier took his plane for Tonkin, looking concerned, but still perfectly confident. And the next day the plane brought him back, with defeat and shattered vanity written all over him: all he could manage to say was, "Everything that could happen has happened." No one could drag another word out of him or make him explain this mysterious phrase. It was only in the evening that the meaning of his words was known, when the spokesman, the same one who had so convincingly spoken of a feat of arms the day before, gave the fatal news. "The vanguard elements are the only considerable units that are in Thatkhe at this moment: and no others will get there." I shall not quickly forget that despairing voice suddenly telling the world that the columns of Lepage and Charton had been wiped out by Giap's divisions.

In fact by the evening of October 4 the entire situation was already virtually hopeless. That evening Colonel Constans, suddenly panic-stricken, signaled to Charton from Langson, "March without stopping. Get to Lepage within a few hours, this very night." In reality it was to take Charton's column three days to get through; and it was just in time to be overwhelmed by the disaster as though by an avalanche, swept away and destroyed.

What an appalling march during those three days! "Faster, faster," said the rare signals from Langson: but there was no track, and they had to push through the full-grown jungle, cutting their way with machetes along the valleys and over the ridges, among enormous rocks and trees a hundred and fifty feet high, continually haunted by the fear of an ambush in this monstrous vegetation. And then there was also the intense anxiety of never knowing exactly where they were, whether they were not astray in this world where every single part looked like all the rest. The column dragged on forever, and soon weariness seized the men and turned them into burdens that they themselves had to carry, always pushing forward, under pain of death. Presently the laggards at the far end began to collapse, particularly the civilians; yet some of them recovered and struggled on for miles. The universal dread was being unable to keep up. Whenever the Langson radio came through its message was always "Faster." But it was not possible to go faster: the advance could only be a few miles a day. And the farther the column went the more clearly it sensed the phantom presence of the Vietminh becoming tangible. So in order to carry on, the leaders took tactical precautions, obliging the exhausted troops to make reconnaissances or sending them to occupy the heights; and this made progress even slower. Indeed, everything in the jungle means delay: the slightest mistake, the slightest difficulty, and hours are lost — hours that may mean salvation.

They were supposed to be level with Dongkhe at five in the morning of the fourth to come to the help of the relief column. What nonsense! On that particular day Charton's column moved scarcely more than six miles: and in unimaginable conditions. The ghost of a trail that they had found petered out, vanished without the least trace. In the appallingly dense jungle there was only a stream three yards across, blocked by hanging creepers and branches coming down from the solid greenness that hemmed it in on either side like the walls of a prison. That was where they had to march, a file of men along each side, blundering along with the water up to their knees and sometimes up to their waists, surrounded by great clouds of mosquitoes. The soldiers, carrying ammunition and rations, labored terribly; what is more, they had to help the sick along and sometimes carry them. The forest became so thick, so impenetrable, that finally it overflowed the riverbed, and the stream had to be searched for, opened out yard by yard as they made their way along. The column, advancing through this low-lying country, could see nothing, not even the peaks rising above it — peaks that might hold Viet regiments about to attack.

The partisans were in the lead, entrusted with opening the path and trying to see a little of what lay ahead. But in their role of watchdogs they advanced slowly, far too slowly, and they were ordered back into the ranks. Besides, the legionaries of the 3/3 REI were outstripping them; though they were not moving fast either, for their commanding officer, Major Forget, found it very hard to march because of an old wound. It was in vain that Charton barked "Hurry up, hurry up!" — the pace remained slow. And again, how could such a column be commanded, stretching out as it did over three miles and more in this constricted gully? How could orders be got to the units? Charton's problem was to know where best to place himself to get the maximum of response to his commands. In the end he chose a point about the middle of the interminable train, together with his HQ and his protégés, the civilians.

Night fell. It was completely dark. The legionaries asked for a halt: in this utter blackness they were afraid of an ambush. Charton agreed. The people lay there on the banks under the protection of the sentries. The place was called Quiron. All was quiet.

At the first light of dawn on October 5 the column moved off again. After a few hours the stream dried up completely. They were in a chaotic landscape, and its main lines were completely hidden by the vegetation, which only allowed a glimpse here and there of rounded humps — the peaks and ridges that underlay the jungle. In this featureless world the problem was to find the pass that led into the Quangliet valley on the other side. Major Forget, in the lead with his legionaries, vainly tried to discover it from his maps, sending patrols out in every direction. While the whole column waited Charton and the officer in command of the 3rd Tabor, de Chergé, joined him to help in finding the way. Furiously Charton muttered, "Oh, if only we had a Morane to guide us! I asked for one, but I dare say all the planes are over by Thainguyen." At one moment a Morane did pass overhead; but the pilot did not understand the situation in the least, and all he did was to drop bales of English cigarettes.

Finally, after great difficulties and a long halt, the pass was discovered. Unit by unit the whole column crossed it and marched down into a beautiful broad valley, the valley of Quangliet. There was a track. Everyone was relieved, for the Lepage column was no longer very far off, and everyone knew that beyond Lepage's men there were the guns of Thatkhe. Then came the clash. The legionaries, going along the middle of a thin band of rice fields, were suddenly stopped by machine-gun fire coming from the wooded peaks commanding the eastern side of the little Quangliet basin. Charton said to Forget, "Send a detachment to find out how strong the enemy is." For that was the whole mystery of jungle warfare — there might be no more than a handful of Viets on those heights. But there might also be a whole division.

In any case the Viets were close at hand, and no doubt in great force. It was suicide to stay in the valley, down in the low ground. They had to climb. Looking to the west, where there had been no signs of activity so far, Charton saw a line of ridges, a long, continuous line running in the direction of Dongkhe, where Lepage was engaged. Quickly he made up his mind: that was the way they must go, following the high land. Leaving the legionaries below as a holding force to stop any formation that might attack from behind — perhaps a few score of Viets, perhaps some thousands — he ordered the long, long column to climb the mountain range and then to make its way along from peak to peak. His aim was to circumvent the enormous ambush that the Viets had no doubt laid along the Quangliet trail. But now, in this vertical climb among the screes and the cliffs and through a thorny jungle, the march was even more horrible than it had been in the riverbed of the day before. Gradually the endless line separated into groups, into handfuls of men far away from one another, scarcely able to give any mutual support. The Moroccans were in the best shape, and they were put in the lead. Their task was to reach and hold point 590, the highest of the mountains, according to the map — but only according to the map, for in this landscape all the heights were exactly the same: it was impossible to tell one from another, for they were all identical green masses with whitish precipices. Dusk was falling. The 3rd Tabor, having reached the top of a peak, signaled, "We are firmly dug in on point 590." There was an empty space between the tabor and the rest of the group, stretched out in this order — first Charton, his headquarters and the civilians, then the partisans and then the Legion. The men were utterly exhausted. They staggered as they moved through this pathless wilderness. Many had nothing left to eat, and they could find nothing to drink either. The soldiers were at the end of their tether, and they had thrown away everything but their arms and ammunition. But everybody felt protected by the tabor on the main summit, and they bedded down on the rocks for the night. Charton set up his HQ on an easily defended spur: there were no soldiers with him, only his civilians, whom he led himself, feeling bound by his word as an officer and a legionary. He was uneasy.

In fact an error had been committed. And in war errors have a cumulative effect, as subsequent events were to prove. Suddenly the tabor realized that it was not on the right peak. Point 590 was farther on, much farther on. Taking advantage of the faint light that lingered before the coming of complete darkness, the Moroccans made their way towards it. Then the ink-black night forced them to stop when they still had a mile and a quarter to go. But there below them the rest of the group no longer had any covering force. The civilians, legionaries and partisans got up again and began to climb so that at least they should gain the ridge above them. Another terrifying progress. Charton was the most desperately eager; he was almost out of his mind, being convinced that he had made an appalling mistake by staying in the rear. At all costs he wanted to get to the tabor — his place was there, ahead, right in front. And following him, everybody advanced — an unreal, nightmarish march. It was all the more dramatic because Charton had just had his first radio link with Lepage, who was just at hand, in a desperate position and calling for help. And yet so impenetrable was the darkness that even Charton was forced to give the order to halt: he was afraid of getting lost and of losing his whole column in the maze of the night and the jungle.

Miracle. Everything remained calm until dawn. Then Charton gave this direct, unqualified order: "March along the ridge at full speed, without stopping for anything; get along somehow, even if it kills you. But we must be there in time to join up with Lepage." In spite of the very great difficulties of the terrain everything began well. The men — caricatures of human beings now — pushed on. The 3rd Tabor occupied point 590, the real one. It was then that fate intervened in the form of a couple of trifles; but they were those trifles which become death sentences in conditions like these. There was, above all, not a minute to be lost: and hours flowed by, because of these two trivialities.

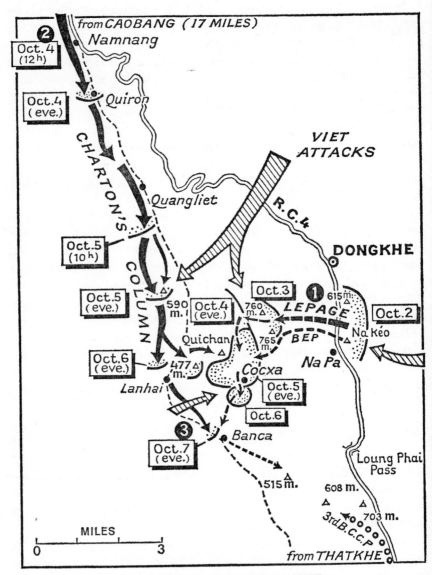

THE FATAL MEETING POINT

1. Lepage turns westward, under Viet attack, to meet Charton.
2. October 4: Charton receives orders to leave the R.C. 4 and race along the Quangliet trail to rescue Lepage.
3. October 7: The survivors of the two columns meet, and are destroyed.

It was not until eleven in the morning that Charton himself reached 590. And there he found a worrying situation. Moving up before Charton, three companies of partisans took the trail along the valley and reached the point almost at the same time as the Moroccans. Their leader was a fine soldier of the colonial army, and he said to the commander of the tabors, "I want to be the first to shake hands with Lepage's men. They are certainly on those peaks opposite. I am going to meet them with one of my companies." The tabor officer replied, "If Charton were here he would be against it." They tried to get through to Charton on the radio, but could not. The colonial officer went off with his men and ran into the Viets just where he had expected Lepage. A long engagement was needed to extract him from the trap.

This was a catastrophic delay. And there was another, even worse and even more foolish. The civilians had been growing more and more stubborn, more and more difficult to control. Suddenly, without anybody knowing why, they stopped, without any order given. The two companies of the Legion behind them stopped too, thinking that this was a halt. Charton was on 590 with Forget, the commanding officer of the 3/3 REI. He said, "Push the two companies you have with you towards point 515. They will be under the guns of Thatkhe there: they'll be safe."

But Forget replied, "I cannot abandon any of my men. My two companies here will wait for those in the rear."

It was absurd and disastrous. The Viets were all around, ready to attack. Lepage's column was in its death throes a few miles away. And yet Charton and Forget argued: they stood there wrangling as though they were in the mess or on a barrack square. Forget even went so far as to say, "You don't trust me. I tell you it's of no importance. My men will be here any moment now."

They did not come. It was impossible to find out what was happening — the radio would not work. Heroically Forget made up his mind to go and see. He went to the rear, making his way along the huge column that straggled out for miles: but he limped and he was moving more and more painfully. It all took an immense amount of time. Forget left at about one or two in the afternoon. Remaining on 590, Charton was consumed with impatience. It was an appalling wait. The hours went by, and still no news . . . And Charton knew that these were the decisive hours, for he could thrust at least half his party forward — the tabors, the partisans and some of the legionaries — as far as a point where they would be out of danger, as far as the place that he knew had been reached by the garrison of Thatkhe, advancing under the cover of its guns and reinforced by a battalion of paras, the 3rd BCCP, that had just been dropped. That would be the joining up. Perhaps joining up in that manner would amount to a flight: but in certain cases was not successful flight in itself a victory? This was Charton's terrible moral dilemma.

But this pushing on with the men he had under his immediate control, this movement towards safety, was something that he could not do. Forget had to appear first, with his two lost companies. And then he, with his columns still intact, though in grave danger, was not meant to take shelter in Thatkhe; instead he was to act as the receiving force for Lepage — an extraordinary situation. As we shall see, it was this attempted sequence of links that was to bring about total destruction, because of the way each force waited for the other.

The unending, pitiless afternoon, during which nothing happened and Charton felt that everything was being lost! He was all the more powerless since he had been put under Lepage's orders; yet he could not see Lepage's column, hidden as it was in the bottom of a dreadful hollow and almost destroyed. It was surrounded on all sides; but the next day, October 7, it was to attempt a sortie, to try to break out and climb to Charton's ridge.

At last, at six in the evening, Forget arrived, having found his two companies and the detachment of civilians into the bargain. All these people had been doing nothing all these hours, still imagining that a halt had been ordered. And when Forget did find them and move them forward, there was heavy rearguard fighting. For the Viets suddenly burst forth, attacking in waves. Some legionaries and a great many civilians were killed.

The night of October sixth was about to fall. Charton's group was still unbroken and still in good order. Later Charton said, "If I had gone on in the night I should have got through. There was still a gap on the high ground that the Viets had not yet plugged." Once again he made an attempt at escaping from fate. He sent Lepage this radio signal: "I request permission to continue along the ridge. Column still almost intact: about ten wounded and five or six killed. Once I reach Thatkhe I will return with all the forces I find there: I will return by the R.C. 4, opening the road, and I will get through to your hollow, where all you have to do is to wait for me." Lepage was not of the same opinion: he refused.

But how could he have agreed — how could men as desperate as his have agreed that the Charton column should move off as though it were abandoning them? From down there in the gorge where they were miserably imprisoned they could see the massive column up there on the ridge, even though Charton could not see them. What a huge relief it had been when the column was first seen — it was the return, the flooding back of life and hope. When there had been the first radio contact on the night of October fifth and Lepage's radio operators had heard voices coming from Charton's side they had cried, "We're saved!" And in their joy they had answered, uncoded, "Lepage here: come quick." And since then what was left of Lepage's force had been surviving on hope and on hope alone.

So at twilight on the sixth the whole Charton group stayed where it was instead of going away; it remained immobile on the ridge between points 590 and 477. The Legion held 590 and the neighboring heights. The 3rd Tabor held 477 and the slopes around it. The partisans also held some peaks along the edge of the position: two companies were sent to the Quichan peaks near the Cocxa gorges, where the remnants of Lepage's column were to come out; and one company was sent to the summit of Banca, beyond the 3rd Tabor, the nearest point to Thatkhe. The other partisans were distributed among the legionaries and the Moroccans. The civilians sheltered where best they could. In short, the whole disposition looked solid enough, even if there were not many defenders — mere handfuls of men against all the Vietminh who were about to attack.

As early as six in the evening the offensive against Charton's column began. The Viets, with an enormous amount of equipment — guns, mortars of every kind, automatic weapons — attacked point 590. This lasted all night, but the legionaries thrust them back and killed great numbers of them. By the morning the slopes were covered with their dead. None of the positions held by Charton's group had been penetrated. But Charton himself was more and more uneasy: he knew very well that the whole business was only just beginning.

Before dawn the whole jungle was filled with strange gleams. They were the lights of all the Viet regiments hurrying in to the kill; they no longer troubled to hide themselves, as though their victory were already certain. But Charton's greatest anxiety was to find out what had happened to Lepage and his men. Lepage had warned him that in the dead of night, at three o'clock, he would stake everything on a breakthrough — he would use everything he had in an all-out, desperate attempt. And indeed at three o'clock Charton heard a tremendous din of weapons, shattering explosions coming from the Cocxa ravine. These prodigious noises, echoing from one limestone crag to another, went on until daylight; and no one knew anything — no one could even guess what had happened. But not a single man appeared. It was exactly as though the breakout had been a total failure and as though the whole of Lepage's column had been destroyed as it fought to get out of the ill-omened gorge of Cocxa.

And then at six in the morning Charton had other worries. This time it was a full-scale attack by the Viets — huge artillery preparations and then massive waves of assault. His disposition lost its cohesion. The partisans lost the Banca peak, which commanded the ridge in the direction of Thatkhe. But far worse the 3rd Tabor panicked. The Moroccans let themselves be driven almost without fighting from a cliff-defended ridge and a cliff-defended mountain. "They ran," said Charton later. "I saw the Moroccans run for it when the Viets were still hundreds of yards away. I learned that it was one of their own lieutenants who gave the example." The only really sound troops left were the 3/3 REI. Charton threw them in to counterattack, to win back the lost positions. They retook one peak, but they could not manage the other. And Major Forget was mortally wounded leading his men in the tenth charge. Ten times he tried to scale the sheer wall with his legionaries before he was hit. Ten times he attempted that impossible climb: and it should be remembered that even walking was hard for him.

In spite of everything Charton's column still held out and still fought on. And it was then, a little before dawn, that there appeared the survivors of Lepage's group, those who had broken out. They came in one after the other, in little bands: they were in the most appalling state. They were not men any longer. They were out of their minds. They were in a walking nightmare. Nothing is so fantastic as the courage of the Moroccans; but nothing is so fantastic as their fear when they break. Like a stone dropping over a cliff, their courage is gone, absolutely and at once. And it so happened that most of the men who had got away were Moroccans — panic-stricken and exhausted, shameless in their terror and hatred — bearded specters with staring eyes, everything lost in madness save the primeval urge to stay alive. And they howled as they ran, firing at everyone, friends, enemies, other Moroccans, as though gunpowder alone could comfort them, as though, when everything else had gone, even the stoicism of despair and the power to die decently, gunpowder still retained some magic.

This dead weight of demoralization fell heavily upon Charton's force. Between these heights that were captured by the Viets from the 3rd Tabor there was a saddle about a thousand yards long. It was there, in a state of total disorder and confusion, that Lepage's men mingled with Charton's, infecting them with their own delirium. Along this narrow ridge there was packed a hysterical mob, crammed together and howling in panic: the Viets had but to fire into them to produce a horrible butchery. Only the 3/3 REI still held firm, and Charton continued to send them against the heights, although the Viets were everywhere now, in every crack in the rocks, behind every bush and every boulder. And at each attack the 3/3 REI lost so many men that soon there were hardly any of them left.

Meanwhile the leaders of the Lepage force flung themselves upon Charton and his staff as upon a lifebuoy. They believed that now everything was going to end well; they became talkative; they told the stories of their lives. Lepage raged against Constans, holding him responsible for everything. For his part, Major Secretain, in command of the BEP, said, "Lepage has treated us abominably." After all this talk and all these private remarks the various members of the group at last made up their minds to get their men together and re-form their units. As if it were possible! Charton, leaving Lepage, went to the spot where things were at their worst, the saddle with its milling crowd of fugitives who did not know where to flee nor what to do nor yet how to do it. He tried to reorganize them: but it was no good. The last heights held by the French were taken. Countless Viets rushed in — it was the end, the death agony. I shall give an account of it a little farther on: but first we must see how Lepage's column had been almost entirely destroyed in the mountains to the west of Dongkhe while Charton's was marching towards it.

The Cocxa gorge

IN the course of the five days from the second to the seventh of October Lepage's force had been systematically hunted, attacked, pushed back and finally smashed in the bottom of a ravine.

It will be remembered that in the early afternoon of October 2, Lepage, who had not been able to take Dongkhe, received the order to bypass the valley by way of the mountains. It was an order that meant pointless sacrifice, and the utterly exhausted men were very much aware of it. Giap had already worn down the spirit of the column: psychologically it was already doomed. There had been that fortnight at Thatkhe and Dongkhe when the men's nerves were terribly frayed by the presence of the Viets — the Viets everywhere, not yet attacking, merely keeping watch, merely killing a few now and then. In that fortnight there had been almost no fighting but everything was already extremely difficult — shortage of supplies; the near impossibility of sending back the wounded; the lines of communication with Thatkhe virtually cut. The jungle and all its real and imaginary horrors overcame Lepage's men without ever a shot having to be fired. With every day that passed they had a stronger feeling that they could look for no help. Every day they knew that the tracks coming in from

China were more and more crowded with the unseen swarms of the enemy, thousands of soldiers hurrying along in forced marches, tens of thousands of coolies bringing in ever greater quantities of arms and amunition. "There was no way of escaping from the atrocious anxiety of the Viet preparations," one of Lepage's men told me afterwards. So even though the Viets could not be seen they were as much of a reality as the jungle, and the whole column felt weak and isolated. And Colonel Lepage was not a man to inspire those around him: more and more they saw him for what he was — an old, sick gunner, very tired already, very worn.

Yet the column did its duty bravely when it attacked Dongkhe. It was after it had been stopped outside the fortress and while it was making its way through the mountains that the Viets, who had been hovering around it for so long, suddenly showed themselves. There were thousands of them, with greenery in their helmets, rising up from behind every rock and every tree. The whole countryside was lethal: everywhere there were machine guns set up to rake the narrow passages through the rocks; there were guns that had been hauled up onto the ridges; there were mortars hidden in the green jungle. All this had been made ready in the course of the preceding days, only a few hundred yards from the unseeing French. Most of the time the Viets had come down from the mountains opposite, over against China, had traversed the Dongkhe valley itself and had climbed the slopes where the French were advancing. And there they had carried out all this immense labor of turning the landscape into a trap: then they had waited patiently in the huge expanse of the jungle, with nothing showing, nothing giving itself away.

To be sure, the French had strong suspicions that this movement of men and weapons was taking place. But they were not really sure of it until they were pinned down — they realized it fully only when it killed them. And they had nothing to oppose to this great force but their courage; and then again for almost the whole length of the operation there was a thick persistent drizzle over the dark, cloudy mountains, that once more prevented any planes from helping. As soon as the French tried to maneuver, to change position, they were immediately forced to throw themselves to the ground and to flatten themselves against it; and immediately the colorless mass of the Viets, blending with the surroundings, would go into action against them. Battalion after battalion of silent automata, things, that advanced creeping or in rushes to the blast of a whistle. There was an impersonal strength in these assaults that inspired far more dread than the old human wave. For now in this discipline and this machine intelligence there was scarcely anything human left.

How simple it was, the plan for the destruction of the French! Lepage's olumn took refuge on the crests, just as one escapes from floods by limbing to high ground; but now the flood rose as high as the ridges, and here were terrible battles. The ridges changed hands again and again; but ach time the French soldiers were beaten, and from now on the movement vas a flight. Scattered, in several groups, the column fled westwards, where here was still more jungle, still more mountains: the order was to head hat way in the hope of joining up with Charton — of joining the column hat had been diverted from the R.C. 4 and that was coming intact along he Quangliet trail. But in this force that was supposed to receive Charton's olumn there were now only two or three thousand men in every degree of vretchedness, completely on the run. At night, when it was impossible to narch in the mountains and the jungle, they went on marching neverthe-ess, marching beyond the limits of human endurance as they tried to scape and get ahead of their pursuers. This marathon went on by daylight oo, until the Viets found them again and caught up. Then the column, or ather its scattered fragments, took refuge on a peak, or on several peaks, to old out until the following night, which would perhaps allow it to disengage nce more and flee farther off. But in the end the Viets were there every ime; and what is more the hunted men were often obliged to stop to let .epage rest — he was an aging man, and he was not made for these extraor-linary exertions. And then sometimes Lepage would also order one unit or nother to halt on some particular position, because from his reading of the nap it appeared to conform with sound tactical considerations. This flight, his pursuit, this hunt was carried out in such a chaotic landscape, such a dreadful confusion of cliffs, ridges and peaks that it was very difficult to ake any bearings — the column advanced in zigzags, not knowing where it vas. Lepage grew more and more exhausted: he had to be dragged along. One evening, when thousands of Viets were about to close in on the main ody, there was no nearby height to be climbed for refuge — nothing but a yawning limestone ravine, one of the gorges that are so usual in those mountains. Lepage gave the command to go down into it: the hunted troops carried out this order given by a man at the limit of his endurance — it was tantamount to suicide. They huddled together in the bottom of the ravine for the night, and for the next day and the night after that; but as early as the dawn of the following day the Viets were along the rims of the gorge with their automatic weapons, and all they had to do to make a great slaughter was to fire from up there down into the mass. Only the BEP had not gone down into the chasm. But presently they were so harassed on the edge where they had remained, so pressed that they too had to plunge into the great hollow; and where they were forced to make their descent the walls were so steep that the soldiers had to cling to lianas to get down. The enemy grip tightened steadily around the remnants of the column in its ravine. But then on a splendid ridge opposite them there appeared Charton's force, advancing magnificently. To get out of the gorge, to reach Charton marching along his ridge, what was needed was an absolutely desperate charge that should take one of the slightly less sheer walls of this mortal trap, pass a kind of limestone arch, and above all force a terribly deep and narrow cleft, an almost subterranean gulley. And for this impossible assault — the attack upon which the life or death of all that remained of his force depended — Lepage had only the BEP, whose numbers were already gravely diminished but whose spirit was as magnificent as ever. It was at this juncture, therefore, that the paras of the BEP set out into the night and clambered up the slope — faint shapes going to their death. The Viet machine guns riddled them like so many targets and their bodies fell back into the ravine. But there were still a few left who climbed on and on, reached the edge of the gorge and attacked the enemy emplacements with grenades. The battalion was almost entirely wiped out; but all that was left of the Lepage column could now escape once again, plunging into the cleft and making its way out. But the men who emerged were the hysterical tabors, the Moroccans who on reaching Charton's column destroyed it more thoroughly with their infectious panic than ever the Viets could do. This was the last rendezvous, the rendezvous of the two columns at point 470; and a few hours later there was nothing of them left.

The end of the two columns

As soon as Charton's men saw the ravaged, shattered look of the survivors from Lepage's column they understood the extent of the disaster. But Charton, leaving Lepage and his garrulous officers, went forward, beyond the defeated huddled mob, to play his last card. This was the 3/3 REI, the battalion of the Legion that he had brought from Caobang, the only organized unit left in this human mess. It was with the 3/3 REI that he tried to break out — break out was a continually recurring word in this campaign, with the columns being perpetually surrounded, separately or both together. In this case it was a question of breaking out along the ridge that led as far as the position, only a few miles away, where the receiving force from Thatkhe was dug in. That morning the 3/3 REI had charged and charged again to retake the lost peaks that stood in the way. Charton threw them in once more, and presently the battalion was in the same situation as the BEP at dawn — it had virtually no men left alive. Then in short, desperate signals to Langson Charton asked for a fresh parachute battalion to be dropped to him where he was: with a fresh battalion he would get through. But now the high command's first consideration was to cut the losses: it was thinking about the casualty list it would have to send to Paris. It had dropped a battalion, the 3rd BCCP, but not where the fighting was, only at Thatkhe, from which point it advanced but little, not very far, so as to stretch out a hand without running any risks. Not that this prevented it from being wiped out too — but a few days later. Charton asked for every available plane; but none came, or almost none. It was abandonment.

And at half-past four in the afternoon Charton learned that 477, the vital peak upon which all hope depended, had in its turn fallen to the Viets. What he did not learn was that two companies of partisans, the despised partisans, had taken it back again. Meanwhile, judging that all was lost, Charton set out: he advanced alone towards the jungle, the little hills, the streams, in what he thought was the direction of Thatkhe. It was a magnificent, desperate, insane attempt (and one that was already doomed to failure, as he knew) at bypassing the peaks which had been taken, or which he believed to have been taken, by the Viets. Before leaving in this way he turned and shouted, "Everyone follow me!" The men looked at one another and came along after him. It was a mere mob that followed. Only three or four legionaries advanced with Charton in proper fighting order. The rear was an indescribable mess. Lepage was not there, nor was the remnant of the BEP: nearly all were North Africans. Charton bawled at them, "Who's in command of this miserable crowd?" No one answered. It seems that the officers among them had taken off their badges of rank.

The mob advanced about a mile without being stopped. Charton was right in front, the spearhead: suddenly he felt himself at the top of his form, superhumanly fit and alive. He was guiding himself with his compass. A splinter hit him — the second that day — but he did not stop. As they went under one peak the Viets caught them in a heavy fire. In the forest Charton heard the sound of a foreign language: was it Germans talking or Viets? He said, "Halt for a reconnaissance." But behind him there arose a huge bellowing from the wretched herd. "It's the Viets! It's the Viets!" Within seconds there was an utter rout — the crowd that had been following Charton vanished. Only a few legionaries and Moroccans stayed with him. It was indeed the Viets, and they opened fire. Charton was hit again twice, one shot breaking his nose and the other giving him a flesh wound in the belly. He shot one Viet with his carbine. But the handful of men was

surrounded by an ever-increasing number of Viets, coming in with th
bayonet and throwing grenades. Charton's batman thrust himself forwar
to protect him and was killed immediately. Next to him Sergeant Schlum
berger fell, but in two pieces, for he had been cut in half. Charton was in th
midst of a rain of splinters and they hit him all over, knocking him dowr
A Viet rushed forward to kill him but a political commissar stopped him
"It's a French colonel. We must take him alive for questioning." And s
the unconquerable Charton, the idol of the Legion, the man who alway
won, began his long captivity: and that is the way he has recounted hi
defeat.

There is in fact no such thing as the truth about a great disaster. Every
thing is too incoherent for that, as though the world had suddenly lost al
logical sequence, as though it had dropped into a hell of impossibility an
contradiction, a horribly brutish, incomprehensible afterworld. All that ca
be established later is a few facts: for the rest, everything is uncertain
everything varies. It is for this reason that I bring forward another witness t
recount the end of Charton's column, one of his lieutenants; and hi
account is both the same and yet different.

"In a matter of seconds, when I saw what was coming from the Lepag
column, I realized that we were already on the beaten side — that the Viet
were stronger than we were. These broken men were afraid: they spread
fear all around them among our people. Soon we were no more than a
silent, dejected herd. Everyone was thinking how the Viets were crowdin
nearer somewhere out of sight for an enormous ambush. And still w
remained there, not moving off. Lepage's men had been among us fo
hours; but they were too exhausted even to talk. They could scarcely ge
more than a few words out. Lepage had flung himself into Charton's arms
saying 'And I who thought I should have my fifth broad stripe this year!'*
At four o'clock we were still there on 470, unable to understand why w
did not go: we said to one another that the Viets were being given ver
valuable time. A little after four we began to march towards Thatkhe
about twenty miles off. The track began to rise to a little pass: this wa
not high mountain like the country around Dongkhe, but more like a
inland Bay of Along — shattered limestone. The column was very long
and in the rear there were still some Caobang civilians! Charton wa
wounded by a grenade thrown from a thicket and he disappeared. Whe
the column came up close to a pass the ambush opened fire — it was al
over very quickly. Tens of thousands of Viets rushed at us. It was a sudde
storming operation with no precautions or maneuvers, to get it over an

* The insignia of a full colonel.

lone with — liquidated. An execution. For a few minutes the column ought back furiously, waving to and fro and breaking into thousands of separate personal battles in the midst of this wild tumble of rocks and greenery. Once again the confusion of boulders and vegetation was so great that men fought almost without seeing one another, and a machine gun covered hardly any ground. But there were too many Viets: the ones who were killed didn't count — there were always more, coming from behind every bush and every rock. Each of us had to go through those appalling seconds when you feel that there is no possibility of resistance any more and that now you are merely something to be killed off. And with some of us this was mixed up with the realization of an impossible state of affairs — that Europeans could be wiped out in this way by Asians. But the column was already in its death throes — thousands of separate agonies, each man in his private solitude in the midst of the horde of enemies who had disrupted everything and who were now finishing off their work. We were attacked with everything that could kill — there were still shells coming in, but now they were reaching us at point-blank range. And then it was the grenade and the knife; and above all there were these huge numbers of Viets rushing at us — they kept coming out of the jungle, little smooth men with green leaves on their helmets. Yet there was still time for some bitter unhappiness. Just next to me I saw a captain collapse, weeping; and a little farther off a sergeant who was wandering about, careless of the bullet that would kill him, waiting for it. There were officers who got their men to shoot them. Some completely surrounded Moroccans charged, singing a battle chant until they were all killed. There were a few last words of farewell between friends; then everything stopped.

"There was a silence over the destroyed column: and a smell. That silence, you know, with groaning in it; and that smell of bodies which comes when there has been a great slaughter — they are the first realities of defeat. Then presently there was another reality, and a far more surprising one — that of the Vietminh discipline. I had expected barbarity; but within a few moments after the last shot what I saw was an extraordinary scrupulousness — the establishment of exact order. Viet officers moved about all over the battlefield, but not at all as conquerors — merely as though one operation had been finished and another was beginning. I could not make out any vanity in them — no triumph. They looked into everything, they took notes, they gave orders to their men. Viet medical orderlies with a cotton mask over their mouths sorted out the heaps of dead and wounded lying on top of one another on the track and the green hollows all round it. The dead were piled up. The wounded were tied to bamboos and carried by coolies. The coolies went in pairs, each one shouldering an end of the bamboo on which the wounded man was slung, and moving with that particularly jogging pace of Asians carrying a burden. Elsewhere soldiers with submachine guns herded the prisoners together, formed them up and led them off. It was all done without savagery, without brutality, and without pity either, as though everything that had to do with humanity or inhumanity did not count: as though one were in a world with new values.

"I was face to face with the ethics of the Communist order; it was something of an absolute nature, a thousand times beyond anything we call discipline. Instead of knocking everybody on the head, from now on the Viets were caring for the wounded and taking prisoners; for they had learned a new technique from the Chinese for dealing with men, an infallible, irresistible technique that worked even better when it was applied to the worst, most atrocious enemies, including colonialists. This was reeducation. The Viets needed particularly worthwhile raw material for reeducating; and it was to get it that they were so methodical in exploiting the battlefield. As night came on the jungle filled with the torches of the conquerors in search of 'subjects.' And I thought of the few soldiers on our side who had managed to get away into the jungle and who were hiding, slipping away in the hope of reaching Thatkhe. Alas, one by one almost all of these fugitives were captured."

Indeed for days and nights some men tried to make their way through the jungle in which they had been defeated, gliding like shadows towards Thatkhe. Among them were the hundred-odd survivors of the BEP. After the two columns had joined up on the morning of October 7 they had remained on the ridge, in the rear, with Lepage. They suddenly noticed that Charton had disappeared — he had in fact gone forward to fight and lose his last battle. They were alone, but defeat was all around them, and Lepage said, "There is no longer any possibility of fighting. I give each officer full liberty of movement to get back to Thatkhe with his men." So it was a matter of escaping in little bands, hiding in a countryside filled to overflowing with Viets. And even in this way, even with this "shameful" solution, how slight they were, the chances of success!

This was the last great adventure of the BEP: there were still to be men killed and taken prisoner, but nevertheless twenty-three got through. Among these men who came back, these ghosts, was Captain Jeanpierre. In the Legion everything, even a flight, is always very well organized. At the time of setting out the BEP, or what was left of it, was too big. It was broken into five detachments of twenty men, each under the command of an officer with a map and a compass. The troops followed a track that ran along a stream. Corporals Hallert, Constans and Hai, all remarkable fighting men, formed the vanguard. At about five in the afternoon they found a corpse stranded on a little beach — a sign that the Viets were not far off. Orders were given to march along the bed of the stream. It was deep and the current was terribly strong; the noise of the water did at least drown the noise of the men's passage, but still they made immense efforts to be silent. These strong, tough men had a dread of existing physically — of being seen, heard and so killed. This intense desire to be invisible, to vanish in order to survive, grew and grew until it reached the edge of madness. Suddenly Major Secretain roared out, with all his strength, "Silence!" to these men who cherished that very silence more than anything. And Jeanpierre had to turn to him and whisper "Shut up, for God's sake. Shut up." Secretain was even more unfortunate than most: for days on end he had been making superhuman efforts to rise to the emergency — he had gone off to this frontier war suffering from sciatica. (By a strange chance the BEP, like the 3/3 REI of Caobang, was under the command of a man who found even ordinary walking difficult — and this at a time when they had to undertake these great cross-country races through the jungle.) But now the heroic Secretain was at the end of his tether.

Everyone hoped that this shouting had not been heard by the Viets. When night came on the men lay on the edges of the stream. Suddenly in the darkness there were shouts: a first burst of light machine-gun fire swept the stream and its banks; then came a longer burst, and after that all sorts of automatic weapons opened up. The legionaries flung themselves into the shelter of the jungle. Secretain, hard hit, stayed where he was in an angle of the bank, telling the others to go. "Every man for himself," he said. He repeated this order to Corporal Constans, who wanted to stand by him. He stayed there by himself, badly wounded in the belly. Later the Viets, who had been told by the men of the BEP they had captured, came and found him dying there alone. They took him on a stretcher as far as Dongkhe, where he died. It seems that at that time the Viets promised to hand over his body to the French; but they never did so. He is said to have been buried with military honors.

In the end nothing was left in the jungle except isolated men or groups of two, three or four. They crept rather than walked, like wild animals at bay, never gaining more than a hundred yards at a time, and hiding for a long while at the slightest suspicion. Some reached Thatkhe in time. But how many others got there too late, out of their minds with happiness after their appalling journeys — how many reached the first houses of Thatkhe and saw the citadel rising before them, heart-lifting safety at last! But as they hurried in they found not the French but the Vietminh: the garrison had been evacuated. These men had made efforts far beyond anything one might suppose the human spirit or body could bear, only to walk straight into their own prison. Instead of the marvelous welcome of friends and companions they were led into a little office, before an unknown Viet, with no name, no badges of rank, nothing, who said to them in perfect French, "What do you think of the war you are fighting in Vietnam? Don't you think it is an unjust war? It is an unjust war. Why won't you admit it?"

An officer of the Legion replied that he was only doing his duty as a Frenchman and a soldier. But that had no meaning for the Vietminh. He understood only Marxist reasoning — dialectic. And according to this reasoning the Frenchman was in the wrong. From the very outset he was in an inferior position, since his mind was sick and his intelligence unsound, both being given over to Evil: he was incapable of understanding right conduct, and he would have to be healed, to have his way of thinking and his whole nature changed by means of collective treatment, by brainwashing, by psychoanalysis carried out by the people.

One captured Frenchman escaped. He was caught and taken before the Vietminh, who very calmly shrugged his shoulders and said, "What you have done is quite pointless. You are fortunate enough to be in the hands of the people, who will look after you. Time no longer has any importance for you. Learn to be patient. It needs a great while for a man as corrupted as you to become good. But good you will become. And when the people have completely won the war against the colonialists you will be sent back, an entirely new, entirely regenerated being. You will form an integral part of the people and you will serve the people wherever you are, especially in that France which we are fighting but which we do not hate. One day France too, the whole of France, will come over from the side of falsehood to that of truth."

Questioning. Questioning for hours and days on end. And always the same words, the same phrases. "You have killed, tortured and massacred in Vietnam. Perhaps you expected to be shot. That is what your people do in such cases. You will not be shot. You will not be punished. Because for us you are not a prisoner in the capitalist sense of the word. For us you are only a man who has been deceived. You don't understand yet — no doubt you are only thinking of how to escape. It's natural and it's of no importance. We are going to give you the chance of improving yourself. But if you remain stubbornly devoted to your wrong way of thinking and go on trying to escape there will be no pity for you. For you will then have proved that you are nothing but a harmful, corrupted animal that has to be destroyed. I speak frankly. Now here at Thatkhe do whatever you like. Ask for anything you need. Take these vouchers for food and clothing."

They were strange days when the Vietminh were in Thatkhe. The town was bursting with the supplies left by the French army. There were huge quantities of clothing and victuals. Vietminh soldiers with notebooks in their hands counted it all up. And every day there appeared French soldiers and officers, singly or in groups, brought in by Vietminh troops. When there were enough of them they were formed into two long columns and marched ten days through the jungle to the camps where everything had been prepared to change their way of thinking — camps in which they were to fight an even worse battle than that which they had fought before their capture, a battle against dialectic, a battle against the very soul of Communism. And again and again they were to ask themselves, "Should one refuse and die, maintaining the integrity of a French officer? Or is it not one's duty to use cunning, to pretend to be converted in order to live through it and fight again for one's country another day? But is it possible to pretend without being dragged in, without being a traitor in spite of oneself, and without becoming despicable?" It was a terrible dilemma, and one in which even the strongest ended up by no longer knowing what he was doing, what stage he had reached, or even what he really thought. The men who went through this were marked forever.

In fact the only people to escape from the disaster of the two columns were a few hundred tabors, the men under Major de Chergé, who for his part found the gap and reached Thatkhe with his unit before the evacuation. But these Moroccans, who were evacuated to the delta at once, were permanently branded. It was they who, telling what they had seen and undergone, gradually infected all the North African troops in the Expeditionary Force, who grew less reliable as each year went by. And still later it was these Moroccans, back in their own country, who supported the revolution. The seeds of the tactics and the ideas that eventually led to the independence of Tunisia, Morocco and Algeria were sown by the Vietminh on the Chinese frontier.

The evacuation of Thatkhe

AFTER the destruction of Charton's and Lepage's columns in the mountains of Dongkhe there was a sudden panic. The one reaction was to evacuate. Everything was evacuated. And first of all Thatkhe, which was abandoned on October 10 in deplorable condition — a wild, feverish scramble. And in spite of all the hurry still another battalion was lost, the 3rd BCCP.

The high command, the inefficient high command, was confronted with a tragic problem: should more battalions be thrown in to save the last fragments of the columns as they dragged their way across the countryside? But would that not mean being dragged farther into defeat, condemning still more men for nothing and ending up by increasing the Vietminh victory? So they let the tragedy play itself out, for fear of something even worse. The only gesture (like Pilate's handwashing) was the dropping of one small battalion, the 3rd BCCP, over Thatkhe with orders not to fight but merely to gather the fugitives. Some hundreds were collected. But on October 10 Thatkhe was evacuated, leaving all the others who might have escaped to their fate, since the 3rd BCCP never came back alive.

It was at Thatkhe that there began the shameful chapter that was not to end until the coming of de Lattre. Later one of the garrison told me what the flight from Thatkhe was like.

"In that post we amounted to two companies of legionaries: it was a traditional fort, like the one at Dongkhe — and it was like Dongkhe in being badly made and set down in the bottom of a hollow surrounded by mountains. There day after day we lived through the death agony of the two columns: we relayed command's impossible orders to them on the radio and we got back their desperate answers. And it was we who were to receive them, for we were the last outpost of the civilized world: at the very beginning we prepared champagne and foie gras for the party that was to welcome them. And then when it turned to disaster we had nothing but the feeling of our own powerlessness, the appalling feeling of not being able to do anything. And yet it was all going on not ten or twenty miles away! For some days we did try to keep up our hopes in spite of everything: then came utter despair. Everything was over. All there was left for us do do after the catastrophe was to go out into the jungle — though we could not go far — and look for those who had escaped. They were mostly Arabs, isolated men; and they were all obsessed with terror. We made long patrols, all day long, creeping through the jungle, climbing the peaks, searching among the rocks to find those who were coming in and to bring them to the post. But alas now they were only the odd fugitives; and there were so few of them! We knew very well that almost all the others were dead or prisoners far over where we could not go; but still we had hoped for more to be saved. And we also saw the first victorious Viets who were coming after them. Every hour we had to take more care.

"All through the days of the eighth, the ninth and the tenth, Thatkhe filled to overflowing with defeat, with those who had escaped; they were in an indescribable state of exhaustion, to say nothing of their wounds. The entire post was a refuge, a hospital. The doctors worked nonstop, relaying one another. Little Moranes came down on the tiny airstrip to fly out the worst cases. And it was not only the remnants of the columns that were crowding into Thatkhe. Every living soul in the neighborhood who was frightened of the Viets took refuge inside our lines — the town's whores and shopkeepers, hundreds of Annamese with children or bundles on their backs and all their higgledy-piggledy possessions. And there were priests and nuns. All these piled up in Thatkhe.

"But we learned that the main body of the Viet army, advancing by forced marches, had already gone beyond Thatkhe, that thousands of coolies were finishing off the destruction of the road leading to Langson, and that the Viets were probing minor posts. They were closing in on us: we had to go before it was too late. We were much too weak to hold out, even after the 3rd BCCP had been dropped to us. It was a horrible moral conflict — men from the broken columns were still coming in and they were out of their minds with joy at finding us still there — they told us how terrified they had been at the idea of our having left already. And there was no doubt that others were making their way through the jungle haunted by the same dread and we imagined what it would be like for them to find the post abandoned, with the Viets in it — a trap instead of their salvation. But then again every hour we stayed at Thatkhe might mean death not only for our garrison but also for everyone who had reached the post and who now thought himself saved. And it was essential not to go too late, for the departing column would be incapable of defending itself: it would be heavy, slow and very long, made up primarily of men who had emerged from the defeat, the sick and wounded, and then all the civilians, whose numbers were continually increasing.

"The minor garrisons from all around had come into Thatkhe, with the administrative people and auxiliaries, bringing their equipment. During the night the order for evacuation came through. It was a strange raggle-taggle that set off in the darkness, a kind of gypsy train five or six miles long. It was formed in a slapdash way, and some people were forgotten — there was a medical unit, for example, that found itself all alone and had to run to catch up with us. This crowd was hardly strong enough to walk, and there were close on forty miles to go. It was made up of thousands of people, and the only real fighting men were the legionaries from Thatkhe and the paras of the 3rd BCCP, who had gone as close as they could to the battlefield and who had come back after the disaster. The Thatkhe legionaries were the main framework of the column, and the 3rd BCCP formed the rear guard. It all began badly, from the very setting-out: about half a mile from the town the Viets had blown up the bridge across the Song-kykong, and it took all night to get the huge procession over the river in boats. We only just escaped. In one narrow gorge the Viets suddenly appeared in force: the paras sacrificed themselves to hold them back. They asked us by radio to turn and disengage them, but we could not: far from it — we had to advance, to hurry the mob along. The paras were wiped out in this ambush, but the column got through. After that there were no more heavy engagements, which was fortunate, for we no longer had the least possibility of fighting back. The column went on in a martyrdom of weariness with only one thought — to go faster than the Viets and to get by before they were there, for that was our only chance. When the R.C. 4 seemed too dangerous we went by the mountain tracks or even right through the jungle, with all the herd. Sometimes people gave up and lay down, but a great many kept on going, even pregnant women and the wounded who could no longer be carried on stretchers. And yet the fatigue was terrible: it was worse than heavy fighting. After we had gone up one mountain there was another in front of us, and so on indefinitely; and we had to climb on hands and knees like animals, bleeding and torn by the ragged limestone. There was also the horror of thirst and hunger — we had nothing to eat or drink. This lasted two days and two nights, because we had to go so far out of the direct line. The civilians stood up to it better than the legionaires — they were all desperately eager to live. Though, it is true, that for ten days we had never stopped searching the jungle around Thatkhe for fugitives — and a fugitive in the jungle is like a needle in a haystack. So in this wretched convoy we soldiers were in an even worse state than the people we were protecting. By the time we reached Dong-dang, where there were lines of trucks waiting for us, we should have cracked if we had been made to go another few yards. The crowd that reached Dongdang might have been something out of the Apocalypse: but they were all loaded onto trucks, then onto planes and taken a great way off, cleaned up, sterilized, treated, hidden, as though it was essential that nothing should be known about the column. Every trace of its history was wiped out. It was only us, the soldiers, who were kept at Langson."

This pitiful crowd, these sweepings of defeat — fugitives and broken men of every kind, the wounded, the panic-stricken and nerve-shattered, and also all those who had profited by the piaster and who thought of nothing but saving their skins now that the piaster system was falling to pieces, all these notorious businessmen and whores, all these "good

Asians" who were required in every place where the Expeditionary Force settled — had only been able to escape thanks to the destruction, almost to the suicide, of the last crack battalion on the R.C. 4 between the murderous battlefield and Colonel Constans's headquarters in Langson, that splendid city. I was also told about this annihilation, the result of daring and magnanimity carried too far; and this time by an officer of the 3rd BCCP.

"The battalion had been in the field for months in the Samnes jungle, right over against Laos, a great way from the R.C. 4 and the frontier. It had been very tough, even in those parts, and we had come down to less than half our establishment, down to two hundred and eighty men, all of them quite worn out. But we were at the end of our tour of duty, and after the exhaustion of those endless, monotonous sweeps — it is always the same wherever you are in Indochina, the jungle and the Viets — we were just waiting for one order, the word to go and get on the ship at Haiphong. Instead of that we received another: we were to come back to Nasan and Hanoi by forced marches. There we learned that we were to be dropped at Thatkhe. Of course we were proud of going to the help of our friends, our hunted comrades on the R.C. 4; but still we did wonder why such a depleted, exhausted battalion as ours should be chosen for such a tough mission — a battalion that no longer amounted to much from a military point of view. Furthermore in Hanoi itself nothing was ready. There were not even any sound parachutes. In the end we managed to find some, but they were wretched things — damp, filthy, and not even folded. They were packed up hurriedly, and the result was that when we were dropped at five in the afternoon two of them did not open — a bad omen: everything was beginning badly. We buried the bodies at once.

"Thatkhe was a dismal spectacle. The commanding officer had made his will and he was looking for a pilot of a Morane to fly it out. You felt cold feet all around you. People were saying, 'We'll never get out of this one alive.' Nobody knew anything, either about the Viets or about the Charton and Lepage columns, except that they were done for. But we did not linger in the Thatkhe hollow, which was filling up with all the bits and pieces of the defeat. We thrust in the direction of Dongkhe along a ridge, and there we dug in to receive anything in the way of survivors that might appear. The whole day went by and nothing happened. We had no idea of what was going on. That night there was gunfire below us, towards Thatkhe — the Viets had just blown up the Songkykong bridge a little beyond Thatkhe, to cut off all the people who were accumulating in the post — to cut off their retreat towards Langson. 'That's going to block everything,' we said. During the night we received the order to disengage: and that was easily done. A few miles before Thatkhe we stopped on the R.C. 4 itself, and stayed forty-eight hours. It was there that we saw strange creatures coming out of the jungle and down the mountainside, running toward us — the first survivors from the Charton and Lepage columns. There was Jean-pierre and about thirty legionaries, and several hundred Moroccans. We hoped that there would be a great many more, but that was all. It was as though the jungle had closed upon itself; nothing more came out — except the Viets.

"We took all these men down to Thatkhe as they came in. There we learned that we should have to get ready for evacuation. Speaking from Langson Constans had given this order, 'Destroy as little as possible, so as not to give the impression that you are going to withdraw. The Viets must not be warned, as they were at Caobang.' Thatkhe was out of its mind with worry. In the first place the order of the column for the great flight had to be established — how the various units were to be placed. The argument between the field officers went on for hours. Some said, 'The legionaries must be put in front and the tabors behind.' Others replied, 'If they are behind, the tabors will run.' These were the Moroccans who had escaped from the Lepage and Charton columns, and who were still in a very bad way. The whole argument sounded as though each speaker wanted to be in front.

"The catastrophe was that right at the beginning we had to cross the Songkykong. With the bridge gone, the only way of getting this motley crowd of soldiers and civilians across the river was to use the few dinghies that belonged to a squad of sappers. What an endless time it took — and at any moment the Viets might rush out on all those who had not yet crossed and who were still waiting on the dangerous bank for their turn. Having an early turn might mean the saving of one's life. After a great deal of shilly-shallying an order of priorities was laid down: the legionaries were to cross first so as to open the road, then HQ, then the 3rd BCCP, then the seven hundred North Africans of the two columns, then the partisan companies of Thatkhe, and pell-mell in the middle of it all the civilians. So in short the weakest were left in the rear.

"The operation began at six in the evening and it took all night. Just imagine that human mass crammed together on the edge of the broad river, trying to make out the miserable little overloaded boats that crept very slowly to and fro, almost invisible — you could only detect them by the splash of the oars. What happiness for those who went aboard, and what anxiety for those who had to wait still longer, working out when it would be their turn, how many hours, how many minutes. To begin with it went quite well, except that it was slower, infinitely slower, than had been planned.

"The 3rd BCCP was still holding the Thatkhe basin. They had to leave their positions once again, and they came down to the river very much behind their time. The tabors were supposed to wait for them and let them pass. But the Moroccans had been given pep pills, and this had revived them: they took advantage of it to seize the boats and pile into them without giving a damn for anything except getting away. When the 3rd BCCP arrived it found that its turn had been stolen. There were shadowy figures busy on the bank — a cavalry lieutenant and his men trying to destroy their armored cars without setting fire to them. The wait dragged on — midnight came, then three o'clock, and then five. In spite of all their haste the Moroccans were taking longer and longer to cross the Songkykong. They had to row themselves, for the sappers were quite worn out; and it is true the tabors were very weak. Every crossing took still more time. At one moment everything came to a complete halt. Instead of six boats there was only one in service. And when it had taken the last Moroccans across it remained stranded on the other side. There were no boats left for the BCCP.

"A few paras swam across the river and brought back the six dinghies that the utterly careless Moroccans had abandoned. By rowing hard the whole battalion got across to the other side in one hour. It was high time, for the Viet machine guns were beginning to fire on us.

"In full daylight the enormous, miserable column marched towards Nachan and Langson. It was a race, with us down on the road and the Viets up on the ridge. We knew beforehand that the dangerous place would be a little plain whose farther end was closed by a narrow gorge. As we came into it we saw some tabors running back: there were only a few of them — they belonged to the last platoon of the last company. They said, 'The column has been cut in two, just in front of us. When we were in the middle of the gully machine guns suddenly opened fire from the top of the mountains, laying down a barrage on the road. Everyone on the far side of the barrage — most of the column, thousands of people — rushed forward at once and escaped. We could not get through.' The 3rd BCCP said, 'There's only one solution. There are close on four hundred of us. The whole battalion will charge and break the Viet's hold.' At nine in the morning the 3rd BCCP entered the gully. It was a most impressive place, with the gorge of the Songkykong on one side and the sheer wall of the mountain on the other. The first company had scarcely advanced a few hundred yards before there was a cataract of fire. Everyone flung himself into the ditch. There was no possibility of forcing a way through. What had happened was perfectly simple, and perfectly disastrous too. On those heights there were two French posts, 41 East and 41 West, that commanded the road. But their garrisons had left too soon, before the whole column had passed through. So the Viets had rushed in and set up their machine guns: they only had to press on the trigger to turn the R.C. 4 into an inferno.

"The 3rd BCCP withdrew to the little plain with its wounded. There was no longer any question of forcing a passage — there were at least two Viet battalions of heavy machine guns up there. But what was to be done? The dreadful moral dilemma came up once more — the problem of the wounded. Among the officers there was a dramatic discussion. One lieutenant said, 'We can't stay here, unless we want to be surrounded in a few hours. We have to move at once, bypassing the gorge by the jungle tracks.' But the officer in command of the battalion, Captain Cazeaux, replied, 'No. We stay.'

"He knew that his decision was something very like suicide for him and his men. But there was a weight on his mind, the memory of something that had happened only a few months before, although it now seemed so far away as to belong to another world. But that was of no importance to Cazeaux: for honor was something that did not change at all. When his officers pressed him he said, 'We stay. Remember the Pholu affair, gentlemen, and the shame we had to endure. I don't want that to happen again.' So here was the obscure Pholu affair coming to life again on the R.C. 4 at the moment when the whole frontier was cracking, the moment of total disaster. At Pholu in the Red River valley thousands of Viets had surrounded the 3rd BCCP, and in order to escape the battalion had left its dead behind — only its dead, not its wounded. But in those days that had been enough for General Carpentier to excoriate the unit, to accuse it of cowardice and dishonorable conduct. And now on the R.C. 4, in order to get away, the 3rd BCCP would have to leave not only its dead but also its wounded. That was something Cazeaux would not have at any price. He remembered the reproaches made against him too well.

"But more than ever his officers tried to dissuade him. They said, 'What would be the point of fighting another Camerone in this war?' Finally he agreed that a detachment should make a reconnaissance in the mountain to try to find a track. The men came back and said, 'There is a place where it seems possible to get through, along a ridge.' This was at five o'clock in the afternoon. Suddenly Cazeaux agreed — perhaps he had received permission on the radio: nobody knew. The wounded were dressed and treated and lined up carefully along the edge of the road: and they were left to the Viets. The least badly hurt decided to follow. The 3rd BCCP plunged into the jungle. Cazeaux, for his part, would not leave. He stayed there: yet a little later he rejoined his unit. The whole day had been lost.

"The weather was horrible. It was a night march with no guides, no bearings, no maps. The column moved in a circle through a bamboo forest. At four in the morning someone said, 'I know this place. We went by here yesterday, a little before midnight. We have looped the loop, we're biting our own tail, that's what we're doing.' At dawn the 3rd BCCP found another track and marched and marched until the evening. They emerged in a limestone amphitheater with no way out. Yet there was a post quite near, the post of Lungai. The radio operator picked up an order for this post: 'Wait for the 3rd BCCP until midnight: then, even if it has not arrived, you will leave.' And at midnight the battalion heard the trucks start their engines and go off.

"All night the battalion remained on the side of the mountain, the soldiers sleeping in scattered groups. The next day it took until eleven o'clock to find a way out and to leave the chasm. At that moment a plane flew over them. It made signs and dropped a parcel containing aerial photographs and the message, 'Take such-and-such a trail and be at Nachan tonight before three o'clock.' Everyone's spirits revived. The battalion followed the line of a ridge; but it was cut by a valley and a road. Each man thought, 'If the Viets are waiting for us, that will be the place.' It was, indeed.

"Down in the valley the road, which led northwards towards China, crossed a stream by a bridge. The column prudently hid under its arches. Scarcely had the leading company stepped onto the bridge before the Viets sprang up from all sides. In a few minutes the 3rd BCCP was in complete disorder, cut to pieces, divided into fragments that the Viets wiped out one after another. This was the kill. A few men had managed to cross the road: they were chased and slaughtered. Part of the battalion, giving up any idea of getting through there, plunged back into the jungle. One group marched all night, but every time it reached the road again it found itself face to face with the Viets, who had strung out three, four or five regiments all along the road. Out of the 3rd BCCP there were no more than forty men in fighting order, then twenty, then no more at all — only a few isolated individuals.

"One survivor went towards Dongdang. But civilians appeared and surrounded him, waving jungle knives. One of them leaped on his back and brought him down. Another survivor met a little boy who showed him a road — and it led him straight to a group of Viet soldiers. There were Viets everywhere. Yet a few paras did get as far as Nachan. There on a bridge they saw some men they took for French: they were Viets, and the paras killed them. Then they went as far as the citadel, but there too there were Viets, and this time there was no killing them: the paras were obliged to surrender. Nevertheless some did manage to get beyond Nachan, and they were very near their goal. But then a terrible rain fell, and they were stopped by a torrent: the Viets gathered them in. Finally, from the whole of the 3rd BCCP, five men reached Langson."

Langson's noble constancy

INDOCHINA knew nothing of all these catastrophes. When the news broke there was first total amazement and then panic. The one followed the other in a few hours. It was the Expeditionary Force that was most affected, and in the Expeditionary Force the highest-ranking men, the command. It seems to be a natural law among soldiers to be too confident to begin with and then, when things go wrong, to plunge to the opposite extreme. Now for weeks on end there was an immense flight, a retreat without fighting, with generals saying "Get out before it's too late." The communiqués called it evacuation or withdrawal.

It is true that the position was serious. By October 9, after all the exterminations on the R.C. 4, the whole frontier was open, and Hanoi would be threatened within a few weeks. To oppose Giap's army, coming from China and out of the jungle, the French had no main striking force: the few existing bodies of shock troops had just been destroyed, and all the rest were useless for a pitched battle, being scattered over practically the whole of the country in countless little posts.

The worst was the psychological disaster. To begin with there was sensible retreat, as at Thatkhe: but was not flight going to become an end in itself, a continually repeated automatic gesture? I was going to find the answer to that at Langson. For the Expeditionary Force's disease, this contagious dread, could be cured only by an almost instant victory. And what could be better than a victory at Langson, one that should crush Giap's divisions, already marching on the capital of the frontier, that splendid city of a hundred thousand souls? A considerable effort would be necessary, for there were only six small, battle-weary battalions in Langson, and heavy reinforcements would have to come up from the delta — a dangerous business. Abandoning Langson would mean losing face; it would be a catastrophe from every point of view — military, strategic, political and psychological. But was holding it possible? The high command said nothing. Carpentier made no statement to his troops; he did not even go to see them. He was busy in Saigon sending explanations to Paris, proving that he was in no way to blame.

Would Langson be defended or not? One had to go there to know, and unbelievably on October 14 I got a permit to fly in. The town looked the same from the air, but as I drove through it, it was dead, totally dead. No living creature moved except those who were hopelessly compromised with the French, and they crowded the airfield, waiting for planes: everyone else had gone to ground, silently, behind locked doors. I talked with some officers of the Legion: they were shocked by the force of the Vietminh, shocked and very deeply impressed by what the Vietminh were capable of doing to reach their ends. They were in favor of the only solution that occurred to them. "There is only one thing left for us," said a captain, "and that is to do our duty according to the traditions of the French army and fight honorably to the last man. I should rather see another defeat than another evacuation."

The next day I was received by Colonel Constans. He had the splendid expression of a soldier who is caught up in a disaster but who is standing firm. Sadness for the dead was balanced by the steadiness of the leader; the outcome was a noble gravity, rather sad and overcast, but full of the up-to-date charm of the war hero, and very human. And it was with this expression that Colonel Constans, speaking earnestly and yet with heroic fire, disclosed to me that he would defend Langson. He gave me reasons at length, clear, exact explanations: he also spoke of the technical aspect — all the nearby mountaintops were bare, devoid of jungle, so that the attacking Viets would have to make their assault without any cover. His conclusion was both moving and full of confidence. "So when Giap's divisions charge I shall crush them with my guns and my fighters. And even if all my communications with the rest of Tonkin are cut I shall hold out with an airlift. I have huge reserves of stores and ammunition — plenty to carry on the war here for months and even for years."

I returned to my plane almost entirely convinced, and a few hours later I was in Hanoi, where I heard the news that Langson was being evacuated at that moment. Colonel Constans had lied to me; for the decision had already been made when I was there. Later he told me that it had been necessary for him to deceive me. Perhaps so: however that may be his act was very successful. It was then that I learned never to trust soldiers any more, for it is often their duty to say that which is the reverse of the truth. And they grow so very good at it!

At all events, I saw the evacuation of Langson in the midst of official splendors — the splendors of the defeat! There was a great gathering of most important people who had come hurrying to the disaster. Juin was there, and Letourneau, the archetypes of the soldier and the civilian — they had flown from France; Pignon and Carpentier and all their assistants — quantities of people who shook hands and whispered among themselves, looking mysterious, and who never stopped having committee meetings and banquets. And I noticed that these important people with their pomp and circumstance produced an atmosphere in which everything was deadened, everything lost its urgency and became almost normal. The disaster of the R.C. 4 and all its consequences dwindled to unfortunate contingencies.

I went along with the procession — that was all there was left for me to do, in any case. We drove; we flew; and in time we reached Phulangthuong. This was the great meeting place, and I saw Colonel Constans, in full fighting kit, leap beaming from a jeep and shake hands in all directions. You would have said he was a conqueror. While the troops ate their rations in the village he was magnificently received in the church, which had been turned into an HQ of more than unusual splendor. The dimness glowed here and there with the colors of the saints, mostly bearded and all primitive: a huge map was stretched out in front of the altar. And here, before all these great men Constans nobly and eloquently explained his maneuver — how his speed in deciding to evacuate Langson and the suddenness of the operation had frustrated the Viets' plans and saved thousands of men. Farther off, in little groups scattered about all the corners of the church, the less important people — colonels, journalists, Letourneau's worthy young assistants, Pignon's civil servants — waited for the end of the confabulation: it was long, very long. They noticed with astonishment that General Alessandri was not admitted to these solemn discussions. Yet he was there in Phulangthuong. He had not come with the official caravan but in a Morane, following and overseeing the march of the column. To get him to Phulangthuong his plane had had to land in a dangerously small field. He stepped out, haggard, pale, exhausted, with a ten days' beard. But no sooner had he emerged than he was the unwanted person, the man nobody wanted to see or hear. He was excluded from the unending assembly in the church. To his protests one of Carpentier's officers replied in a whisper, "It will be arranged so that you are not questioned." "But I command in Tonkin!" "You will keep your command. But for the moment it is preferable that you should not speak."

Meanwhile, as the meeting dragged on in front of the altar, the faces of the great men grew darker and darker. Constans spoke into an ever more disapproving void. Apart from the proscribed Alessandri, there were some fifty important soldiers from Indochina and France, gleaming with stars and gold lace, smiling and nodding to one another. But now they were settling deeper and deeper into a rigid, gloomy silence. Juin looked grim and sullen. After Constans there came Carpentier, to say how necessary the evacuation of Langson had been, and how urgent. Then other officers appeared to give earnest, intense explanations. Juin said nothing, but his expression grew ever more lowering. Increasingly the ministerial face of the enigmatic Letourneau expressed the gravity of outraged civil power. All trace of satisfaction and pleasure had vanished, not only among the great men and their followers, but among all who were in Phulangthuong, officers, NCO's and ordinary soldiers. Suddenly it was as though all hearts were wrung — as though a cloud of remorse had descended upon the Expeditionary Force.

Carpentier and Constans struggled bravely on, trying to justify themselves and put a good face on it all. But now, after what they had disclosed, everybody knew that the evacuation of Langson, as it had been carried out, was henceforward the French army's shame, even if it was its only shame in Indochina, where it had fought so bravely and so desperately over so many years for a doubtful cause.

After a short period of relief the Expeditionary Force fell back into a dejection that the feeling of cowardice made worse than ever. Nothing was left to it but remorse and humiliation; for information kept coming in about the Langson affair, and now everybody knew. They knew that all that had been stated, put forward and proved to justify the flight — a flight intended to avert a massacre — was false. The whole thing had been nothing but a hallucination provoked by fear, cold dread, and a shrinking heart.

So Langson had been evacuated before there was any cause. But the most depressing news was that it had been abandoned virtually intact with all its immense stores, on the principle of not warning the Viets of the impending departure. The magnitude of these stocks was unbelievable: Giap's divisions (when at last they walked into Langson, long after the French had left) found all they needed in the way of food, clothing and medical supplies for years. Far, far more serious was the question of arms and ammunition. Almost everything that the Viets fired at the French in after years came from Langson: there were 11,000 tons of ammunition, including 10,000 75-mm shells (and the Viets had 75-mm guns); there were 4000 new submachine guns; hundreds of gallons of gasoline — an incalculable treasure of military stores.

To be sure, there had been some arrangement for blowing it all up: it seems that a little squad of sappers was left to set the fuses going but with the strictest instructions to do nothing without a written order brought by one of Constans's staff officers. The order never came, and in the end the sappers moved off. Later, when the scandal of Langson burst forth, the military security force looked for the lieutenant in command of the squad — a scapegoat was wanted. But his comrades hid him in the back room of a bar and finally the authorities gave up the idea of the arrest — the injustice would have been too flagrant. Then the most strenuous efforts were made to bomb what had not been blown up: everything in Indochina that could fly appeared over Langson. But it was all in vain — the stores were lying in magnificent underground chambers with fifty feet of clay and sand over them.

And now that everything was known, now that it was clear how lamentable it had all been, and now that people were acquainted with all the shame and the consequences of the evacuation, inevitably there arose the question: who was responsible? It was found that the panic that had seized upon the Expeditionary Force and that was still affecting it, had come from above — from among the generals. To unwind the skein of guilt in this ugly business one must go back some days, to the period after the defeat in the mountains of Dongkhe but before it was known what was going to be done with Langson. It was then that the panic-stricken generals, including Alessandri, made all the others lose their heads — the government in Paris, the high commissioner's office in Saigon, and also their own people, their own officers and men. It was the high command that cracked first, and that caused the cracking everywhere else.

Juin's attitude was strange: he seemed unwilling to do anything positive about the situation, as though he were afraid of becoming involved and of seeing his great reputation tarnished. One of the few things he did was to uphold Carpentier in public — indeed, at first he refused even to see poor Alessandri. But he judged the situation with remarkable perspicacity, and before leaving he told the truth about it — he explained it at a great council of war at Hanoi, he wrote it in a report for the French government, and he even told the journalists about it. The whole structure of the Expeditionary Force had to be changed: it was nothing but a scattering of innumerable posts, useful for the Pacification but powerless in war. As quickly as possible it was essential to build up powerful mobile groups that could maneuver and strike in the open country. There had to be what he called a striking force of planes, for that was the essential arm in the destruction of the Viets, the one that would allow their supply lines and their concentrations to be hammered. But very great numbers of planes were needed, hundreds and even thousands, to strike effectively in spite of camouflage, invisibility and the screen provided by the jungle. He said, "In order to attack, the Viets have to concentrate. That is the moment when they can be smashed by blanket bombing — bombing in which no particular targets are aimed at, no fine work, but in which high explosive is poured into a given area until nothing can remain alive inside its perimeter." But a powerful Expeditionary Force and a big air force were not enough: the very first need was the creation of a Vietnamese national army. Juin was the first to say forcibly, "I believe that the solution to the Indochinese war lies in the strength and the faith of a Vietnamese army. In the first phase we shall progressively hand the sectors over to this army: it will carry out the Pacification, and we shall get back French troops to fight Ho Chi Minh's regular battalions. But in the second phase the Vietnamese army must also take them on, and then there will be thousands of Asian regulars against thousands of other Asian regulars, all fighting in the same way."

That was not all. For the present moment it was essential not to lie down under the blow: the withdrawals had to be halted for an "offensive defensive." Faced with these Viets who thought they were the winners, the French must carry on a war of movement, just as the enemy was doing. There were some places that might still be abandoned, but there were others, such as Langson, that would have to be retaken. Mere defense would inevitably lead to total defeat: it would mean withdrawal after withdrawal, and the Expeditionary Force's morale would collapse for good and all. So there had to be an offensive, first from the strategic point of view, and then as a means of healing the spirit of the officers and men who were still suffering from the humiliation of the R.C. 4 and all the complexes that come from defeat — they had to be given back their pride.

Such was Juin's diagnosis, and such were his drastic remedies. But to apply them the whole French nation would have to make an immense effort: France herself would have to fight the war instead of leaving it to the mercenaries of an Expeditionary Force. This meant an infinitely greater sacrifice in men and treasure — it meant behaving as though the war were really of vital concern to the nation. But was it? Juin himself asked the question in his report. He did not answer it; but he wrote that unless the essential measures for fighting properly were taken it would be necessary to look towards other solutions — either to treat with Ho Chi Minh and leave, or to turn the war into an international conflict. And Juin ended, "It is for France to choose."

So Juin had plainly stated the case. He did not believe that France would fight the war with heart and soul; nor did he think that she would make up her mind to negotiate with the Viets or manage to induce the Americans and the United Nations to fight in Indochina. He thought that she would do nothing, or almost nothing, so that the Indochinese war would last, dragging on from year to year until it came to a very nasty end. And he wanted no part of it. The soldiers of the Expeditionary Force understood his attitude, and it discouraged them bitterly.

After Juin's departure the Expeditionary Force seemed to have recovered its calm, but, in fact, beneath the surface the gangrene was creeping fast. Constans vanished, universally despised; but Carpentier remained, and so did Alessandri, and with these two defeated men the Expeditionary Force was sure to go on to fresh defeats, to the loss of Tonkin and of the whole of Indochina.

The first of the defeatists was Carpentier himself. One day he showed me a huge map and said, "My staff has been at work. From now on we can set about successive withdrawals. For we cannot hold Tonkin against Giap's divisions backed up by the Chinese. I have provided for seven lines to fall back upon, and the last is in the middle of Annam, in that place where the country is squeezed into a gully, near the twentieth parallel. There we would be able to form a real front and stop the Vietminh advance: we should have only a little more than sixty miles to defend, and we should still possess all the wealth of Cochinchina." But the commander in chief dared not profess this perfectly defensible strategy in public: he felt that he had to envelop the politicians and the country in a cloud of vague, comforting words.

For weeks and weeks no one knew what to do or how to set about it. I saw a perfect example of this total incoherence at Monkay: I had gone back because I wanted to be there once again before its evacuation, which had been decided upon. (It was countermanded as soon as I arrived.) The little garrison, one company of the Legion, was extremely uneasy: over on the Chinese side there were now three thousand Viets and two thousand Chinese, with quantities of heavy machine guns and artillery. Was it worth staying and being killed when the high command might abandon the whole thing in a few weeks? There was no possibilty of defense, so would it not be better to slip away by sea before the attack? The officers did not know whether their duty required them to live or die. At this point a plane landed and out stepped the breezy Carpentier, looking as though no problem existed; but in spite of his good humor he was far thinner, no more than a bony frame — no flesh left, only those big bones. The captain in command of the company, a sort of human buffalo, stood to attention: respectfully, firmly, he asked the general for orders. "Please may I have instructions, sir? I have none at all at present. If the enemy attacks, are we to fight to the end or try to withdraw by the Bay of Along? And should I fire into China if the Chinese support the Viets?" I shall long remember Carpentier's bewildered look and his gesture: he raised his arms in the air. At last he said, "What do I know about it?" And he left without another word.

The evacuation of Laokay

FACED with the mounting tidal wave of Viets the Expeditionary Force was too weak: it could not hold everywhere. There had to be a concentration so that at a few points it would be strong and capable of defending itself. More and more every day that was Carpentier's line; and he even seemed to feel something resembling pleasure at each successive withdrawal. It was not really masochism, but rather the effulgence of his common sense that made him say, "Once again I have avoided a trap." His mind was filled not with depression at being defeated but with satisfaction at his own wiliness: it was as though the men at the top could never feel ashamed.

So Monkay was held, but everywhere else there was a shortening of the lines of communication — that was the chaste military term for evacuation, for in the army things are never called by name. Scarcely a day passed without the news of some "withdrawal" for "strategic reasons." But who was not aware that this hypocritical language was that of calculated, accepted, though perhaps not acknowledged, failure and decay?

It began with Thainguyen, whose capture without a fight had been celebrated as a French triumph only a few weeks before. But as soon as the slaughter on the R.C. 4 had taken place the three useless columns that had taken the town with sheathed swords went back to Hanoi quicker than they had come. Thainguyen had been French for ten days or so; and never again until the war ended were the French to return. More than ever it was Ho Chi Minh's capital, the Vietminh's holy place, Hanoi's rival and its near neighbor.

Next came the leaving of Hoabinh, a much more important renunciation. For this was the place where the Black River made its way through a last rocky spur before joining the Red River and flowing into the plain. And it was from Hoabinh, from that hollow surrounded by abrupt cliffs, that the French threatened the Viets' *via sacra,* the track that connected the jungle quadrilateral of the Tongbo and Giap's divisions with the storehouse of men and rice — the great Red area of northern Annam. But this road

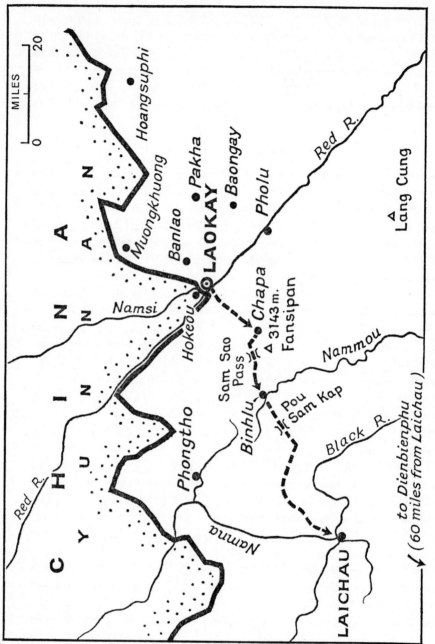

THE EVACUATION OF LAOKAY

crossed the gorge of the dangerous Black River just upstream from Hoabinh, and for months the French had been fighting a battle of the fords, trying to cut the enemy's vital artery in the waters of the river itself. They had built posts on the banks well beyond Hoabinh, everywhere where the Viets might cross the dark, troubled, fast-flowing stream. From then on the Viets had attacked them furiously; and from then on the French had attached the enemy convoys and caravans crossing the broad river with what came to hand — often on the trunks of banana trees. How many Viet soldiers and coolies had been shot or carried away by the current of that splendid but inauspicious river!

Holding Hoabinh meant strangling the Viets. Leaving it meant giving them back total freedom of movement. From that time on not only were they sure of their supply lines but they could also maneuver their divisions all around the delta in a kind of hide-and-go-seek for the attack of that rapidly diminishing territory. The French shut themselves up in the delta as if it were a shell, and the Viets all around it did whatever they chose.

But the most important evacuation after that of Langson, the front door to China, was that of Laokay, the back door on the other side of Tonkin, over against Yunnan. Once Laokay was gone all the invasion routes were in the hands of the Viets. With Laokay lost they held the valley of the Red River, that immense straight cleft through the mountains. This opened fresh possibilities, immense possibilities for them — now they could carry on two wars at once or alternately, one in the jungle and the other in the plain. And that was one war too many for the French.

The fall of Langson had given the Vietminh the keys of the delta: henceforward Giap's divisions could thrust straight at Hanoi and come down the R.C. 4 from the mountains for a frontal attack upon its rice lands and its swarming cities. But Laokay delivered up to them the limitless expanses of the jungle: from now on the Viets could attack the Thai countries and their little rulers who were allied to the French, they could attack Laos and the royal city of Luong Prabang with its sacred pagodas, and they could strike beyond that, far beyond, over the Mekong, at Siam and the whole of southeast Asia. There were no longer any limits: nothing was left to stop their movement through the forests and the mountains — a movement that would lead them, after hundreds and even thousands of miles, to the strategic heart of the continent.

That was the essential fact: in the future the Vietminh could wage two wars — that of the rice fields in the delta and that of the deep jungle with a perpetual flow of columns thrusting farther and farther, without the French having any way of stopping them. To begin with Giap waged now the one and now the other; but the moment of the French defeat was to come when he was strong enough to carry on both at once.

In the first place the French command hesitated over giving up Laokay. Such shuffling and beating about the bush! But how could a hedgehog nearly two hundred miles away be defended, particularly at a time when every sound man, every soldier capable of fighting, everyone the Expeditionary Force could possibly spare was needed for the delta? At the end of October the decision was made.

Then, in addition to the drama of the war, there appeared the drama of military obedience among the officers and men of the garrison: they did not want to go. Although there had been so few of them, they had withstood all the Viet attacks simply because of the loyalty of the mountain tribes. The chief at Laokay was Colonel Coste. I always thought of him as an Alfred de Vigny kind of hero, an iron-hard leader of immense energy, but too clearly aware of what was going on, and apt to wonder sometimes whether it was all worth it. He was an exceedingly distinguished man, reserved but affable, tall, lean, fine featured, with sadness in his blue eyes, in his voice and his entire person. A man who spoke little, yet a charmer: with so delicate a pride that the result was modesty.

Coste entered into a long exchange of signals with Hanoi. In fact, Alessandri wanted Laokay to be held and the town to be fought for; but Carpentier ordered him to evacuate it, and now he was afraid of Carpentier. He no longer stood up to him, either directly or indirectly. When Coste signaled, "We can hold out," he replied, "You must leave: form a column to move through the Thai countries." At this Coste almost mutinied, sending as his official reply, "We are betraying all those who have trusted us: after we leave heads will fall." Hanoi merely repeated, "You must leave."

The fighting was already coming closer to the town. Two Vietminh regiments, part of those trained in the Chinese manner, were reported not far off. There was scarcely more than one battalion in Laokay: and it was Moroccan. Then once again on the edge of China there began the familiar sequence, the preparations for a flight, an evacuation. There was the airlift of Junkers and Dakotas carrying out the equipment, the sick, the women and children. A very large stock of opium, some tons of it, also had to be flown out. The pilot who took the drug aboard cried, "I'm a swine. My chiefs are swine. Instead of saving people they save this muck first." As for the civilians who could walk, they were formed into two columns and sent off without protection along the tracks towards Phongtho, that paradise, the capital of the old warlord Deo Van-anh. The pitilessness of abandonment was becoming familiar.

While the useless mouths of Laokay were disappearing, the garrisons of the remoter posts came in — those from Pakha, for example, and Hoangsuphi, which was so deep in the jungle and which had seen such a great deal of fighting. At Hoangsuphi the officer in command of the post, Captain de B, spoke with shame in his heart to his terrible ally, Chao Quan-lo, the chief of the Muongkhuong Mans, and said, "We are going. Come with us. Bring your people." The one-eyed Chao Quan-lo replied, "France promised never to leave us. She is leaving us. You go: but I shall stay, and my people will stay. For this is our country. We shall carry on the war against the Viets without mercy until I am killed and until all my people are slaughtered."

All night Captain de B pleaded with Chao Quan-lo to leave: he could not be shaken. As a last service he saved the French garrison. For Hoangsuphi was already surrounded by Viets on all sides, and it was the old chief himself who guided the French column along a secret trail — which, incidentally, wandered into China. When they were out of danger the captain and the Man chief embraced each other with tears: the Man returned to his mountains and his domain. And for two years, as he said he would, he carried on a savage struggle against the Viets — he was elusive, unreachable, in his own country and his jungles. French planes dropped arms and ammunition to him. Then there was no word of Chao Quan-lo and his people any more. For at the beginning of 1952 the powerless Viets asked for Chinese help to deal with him, and tens of thousands of Mao Tse-tung's soldiers spread over the region of Muongkhuong — finally the avalanche wiped out Chao Quan-lo and his men.

All that was left was the last act, the actual leaving of Laokay. The real difficulty of the evacuation was the choice of the right moment — it had to be as late as possible but not too late. For in these matters there was one exactly right moment. Too late, as at Caobang, and it was annihilation. Too early, as at Langson, and it was ignominy. After these disasters the high command no longer dared give the signal itself. So it was for Coste to decide: he alone was to have the huge responsibility of saying "This is the time." In Hanoi they were afraid that he would take too many risks in this wager — for a wager it was, and a terrible one. So they never stopped sending advice: there were continual signals that read, "Bear in mind that the safety of your troops is your first duty. Above all leave in time. The slightest error of appreciation could be fatal." There was the danger of a massive attack upon Laokay: there was the far greater danger of the Viets lying along the line of withdrawal in an ambush that would wipe the column out. For the garrison not being outstripped was a question of life

or death. And all this was happening in the jungle. Coste knew nothing — and yet he was to guess the right moment.

The Viets concentrated before Laokay; they took up their positions; they
commanded the airstrip with their fire. Planes could no longer land. But
strangely enough they displayed a lack of conviction in their attacks, and
this more than anything else made the garrison want to stay on. But was it
not a ruse to persuade them to stay in Laokay while other Viet troops were
on their way to cut the line of withdrawal? Whether that was so or not, the
French launched a counteroffensive on October 31, and after hand-to-hand
fighting they thrust the Viets back some miles. The airfield was out of
enemy range, and the French removed the white cloth cross on the ground
which meant that nothing could land. A Junker came in at once, and in a
matter of minutes it had taken away the sick and the men wounded in the
recent fighting. After this success Coste firmly signaled to Hanoi, "There
is no longer any question of evacuation. The defense can be carried
on." The generals pondered long and heavily in Hanoi that evening: were
they to make the most of this improvement at Laokay to strengthen the
fortress and hold it, or should they on the other hand evacuate it directly,
with the greatest likelihood of success? In the end they were incapable of
making the choice and the decision was left to Coste — his was the burden
and the responsibility.

It was in the middle of this shilly-shally, with Hanoi making no hard
statement and Coste more alone than ever with his problems, that a piece
of intelligence decided it all. News was brought to Laokay that the Vietminh regiments were moving in long narrow files down the paths that
followed the southern bank of the still-flooded Red River. They must
therefore have made the formidable thousand-yard crossing, and now they
were racing towards the place where the French were to be slaughtered, the
spot chosen for the great massacre. The Viets were making forced marches,
for they had to reach the first spurs of the Thai mountains, where the
killing was to take place, before the French. What was planned was the
traditional outflanking movement, and its goal was an ambush in which
some thousands of Viets hidden in the jungle should rush out upon the
French column drawn out all along the trail. And all this was genuine
intelligence, brought by the partisans who had been watching and listening
in the forest. It was in no way the result of an overheated imagination, as it
had been at Langson. Coste therefore gave the order for withdrawal. What
was beginning was a race for life in which a few hours or even a few minutes
were to be all important. The Viets had moved off with a day's start, but as
their point of departure was farther off they had an extra thirty miles or so to
march. The odds were even, terribly well balanced on either side.

At dawn on Wednesday the Chinese soldiers in their fort on the other side of the frontier saw the French column move out of Laokay in the midst of flames and explosions. The disengagement was well carried out: furthermore Coste had already taken the precaution of sending covering forces to the dangerous parts of the track. He had to march through the stifling vegetation of the Red River valley, then make the long climb up the mountains towards Chapa, rising from the thorny jungle at the bottom to the pines up on the heights. In the background rose the great mass of Fansipan, the holy mountain, streaming with waterfalls and torrents. There were a few shots from the jungle as the column made its way through its green walls: but then suddenly it was learned that the main body of the Viets was just behind, not half an hour away. Now the great hunt began. The exhausted men could not stop: they had to push on more desperately than ever. But still minute by minute the enemy gained ground, coming closer and closer. Chapa, the old hill station, was reached and left behind. Without a halt, marching day and night, the French thrust on towards the great ridges that separate the Red River basin from the Black.

Coste's plan was to turn when he reached the right place, to stop the Viet attack at the Sam Sao Pass, a ravine between limestone screes at the top of a great mountain range. But the enemy did not give the French time to take up defensive positions: two minutes after the exhausted battalion had reached the pass the Viets attacked, using the most modern techniques. They charged in little groups with commando weapons — grenades, sub-machine guns, automatic rifles. Meanwhile others made their way above the pass and opened fire with heavy machine guns on the flanks. Added to this there was accurate, heavy mortar fire coming from unseen positions. After several hours of fighting the Moroccan battalion had used up all its ammunition and it had to continue its flight. The enemy forced the Sam Sao Pass, and henceforward all the Thai country was open to him.

The Viets harried the retreating column more savagely than ever. A storm made air-drops impossible, and food, ammunition, everything ran out. Some Vietminh groups pushed forward and attacked the convoy in the flank as it struggled on in the mud, while the main body hammered it from behind. The paths were mere scratches on huge, jungle-covered slopes: some were cut in steps that ran down and down to the bottom of marsh-filled valleys; others climbed to ridges covered with lilies. One Frenchman who took part in the retreat told me later, "It was as though you were on the teeth of a saw, each tooth being seven thousand feet high." At last, after several days, the column reached safety: it crossed the ridges of the Pou Sam Kap, which were held by the army of Deo Van-long, the despot of Laichau. The Viets in their turn had run out of food and ammunition — their supply line of coolies had failed them — and at last they gave up. And that was how their prey escaped.

For the French this successful fighting retreat was almost a victory. In reality it was still a defeat, even though honorable. For the pursuit had brought the Viets into the heart of the Thai region, and this time it was not a question of guerrilla fighters but of Giap's own regulars, who seized Phongtho and Binhlu, beyond the first passes, and held their positions before Pou Sam Kap, that range which encloses Baichau, the cradle of the Thais.

It was in this way that another great jungle war began for the French. Its beginnings were vague and obscure: yet it was this war that was to reach its tragic culmination in 1954 at Dienbienphu, a mortal struggle in which the picked troops of either army, the European and the Asian, destroyed one another where fighting itself seemed impossible, in the unspeakably remote heart of the jungle. It was to be the greatest jungle battle the world had ever seen.

Now, in the autumn of 1950, the new war was already taking shape. It was not merely a question of sending convoys along a road, as it had been on the R.C. 4 — of getting them through until it became impossible, and until a disastrous retreat took place. Henceforward it was to be savage infighting anywhere in the natural terrain — all over the landscape. The French columns making their way along the jungle tracks would have nothing but a few airfields as their link with the outer world. Wingate's campaigns behind the Japanese lines in Burma during the Second World War were going to be fought again, this time on the scale of Indochina. It was to be a prodigious undertaking. To supply, guide and protect the troops engaged there would only be planes taking off from the delta — planes whose course would have to take them through all the dangers of the monsoon and all the natural hazards of the country. Would the French be capable of fighting this jungle war? At that time no one asked the question: no one even thought of providing the powerful air force that it would require.

I went to Laichau, to see what was going on. The first thing I saw was Deo Van-ahn. He had fled from his town of Phongtho, invaded by the Viets, and he was stepping out of his royal canoe, which had brought him down the rapids of the Red River. He was as dignified as ever, with his wrinkled face, his white, drooping moustache and his black skullcap. Poor man! He gave me a melancholy smile. His lovely Phongtho was in ashes and his people had taken refuge in the mountains. A great wave of fear had broken over the town even before the arrival of the Viets, for a man who had escaped from Laokay spread the news of what they had done there. It seems that the French were scarcely out of sight before special Red commandos rushed in, slaughtering people right and left. Deo Van-ahn told me sadly that the Communists wanted to break the resistance of the Thais by terror.

But the misfortunes of Deo Van-ahn did not move his cousin Deo Van-long, the despot of Laichau, in the very least; indeed, he was rather pleased. He was in the thick of the fighting, in a high state of warlike exaltation. His ardor reached an ever higher pitch when planes flew over the rocky walls and dived down into the Laichau gorge, bringing him an unbelievably vast quantity of arms and ammunition — more than that formidable character had ever hoped for. Furthermore, he managed to squeeze even more out of the French, both in arms and money: the whole thing seemed to him an excellent piece of business.

The Thais were quite certain of destroying the Viets. They had in fact only met the Vietminh guerrillas, and they had no notion of the terrible power of Giap's regular battalions. But personally I thought at the time that if the Viets went on building up their numbers, and if they launched a real jungle offensive, then it would be a landslide, a general rout. Although the French often talked about Wingate they were even less ready for the forest than they were for the rice fields. At that time they had no specialized troops for striking along the jungle tracks — they had not expected that kind of war at all! In the Thai country the best they could do was to arm the little tyrant Deo Van-long against Giap.

But the alarm at Laichau only lasted a few days. It was not there that the storm was gathering, but in the delta — and it was the delta that the storm threatened. The time had not yet come for the Viets to scatter their armies throughout the whole immensity of Indochina and its jungles in a complex kriegspiel. Giap wanted to start with a great blow, a mortal heart blow, to finish everything at once. He wanted to take Hanoi.

From the beginning of November the French knew one thing for certain: that the Viets were maneuvering with scrupulous, unremitting care to set up positions all around the delta for a great attack. The French were certain of this, for now they knew how the Viets went about things. The military intelligence racked their brains in vain as to Giap's precise intentions. The French knew only that one day the whole thing would blow up, that perhaps there would still be nothing to be done about it, and that, in spite of all their foreknowledge, they would be taken by surprise.

Now the whole of the Expeditionary Force, staff, officers and men, felt a most painful inferiority. What could they do against the Red avalanche?

Weeks passed and nothing happened. But everyone knew that in the mountainous jungles of Upper Tonkin the hordes of coolies were carrying their crushing burdens towards the edge of the plain. There were a hundred thousand of them, two hundred thousand, as many as were needed. These human ants made their invisible way day and night under the impenetrable camouflage of the forest, along the countless paths, and along the roads that had been won. The Viets were still very short of trucks, and the coolie was their means of transport, in accordance with the slow and sure methods of the past. They were known to be carrying Chinese supplies from the frontier to the forward dumps of food and ammunition which were mounting up somewhere in the last jungle-covered hills at the rim of the unending flatness of the plain. But who could tell where they were? Once the dumps were assembled it would be the turn of the soldiers to come and surround the delta. They too would march as the coolies had done, thirty-five miles a day through the secrecy of the forest, with leaves hiding their helmets; and they would carry nothing but their weapons and a few riceballs. When they had come they would stay in the jungle where they could not be seen and where nothing could threaten them; and yet they would be within reach of the crowded, densely populated delta, and of Hanoi, that splendid prize.

So Giap's People's Army gathered in the almost impenetrable secrecy of the Communist world and the obscurity of the jungle. The French, who knew everything in general and nothing in particular, did their utmost to pierce this secrecy wherever they could and gain some scraps of strategic intelligence from it. Planes took aerial photographs, but the results showed only the uninterrupted sea of forest. Patrols went out on reconnaissance, but they did not push far enough, to the places that mattered, for that would mean destruction. If prisoners were taken during these raids, they never knew anything, even if they could be induced to talk, not even the names of their officers or the number of their unit. This was often a genuine ignorance, for nothing had a name in the Vietminh army; or if it did, then it was a false name, and often changed. Of course, as usual the intelligence sections bought information from their agents, that particular little underworld that really never changed, since the foolish or incautious members who got themselves knocked on the head by one side or another were immediately replaced by more of the same kind. But how difficult it was to check and evaluate their wares, their alleged intelligence: even when it was genuine it was not much use, for it could not be trusted, and no one dared base any decision upon it. Distrust was all the stronger since it was known that some of the professional informers were working for the Viets, repeating what they were told, giving false information or rather a very little truth mingled with a great deal of falsity: but it was not known which these men were. It seems that there was an entire Viet cell made up of nothing but French intelligence agents.

There ensued a great battle of false information. For the French the whole question was to guess where the Viets were going to strike: for the Viets it was to prevent it from being found out. The Expeditionary Force was like the blindfolded man in a game of blind-man's-bluff, stretching out to catch hold of something, some hint of the truth. The Expeditionary Force was in the open, in the delta; its movements were thoroughly known and well in sight of the Viets all around, lying there hidden, unseen, elusive, on the edge of the jungle. In fact the French were so desperately eager that the Viets, instead of letting them probe to find out, provided them with hints, information that they would accept as sound so that on D day the Viets would be able to launch their offensive just where the French expected it least. It was an exceedingly complex game. In order to confuse the military intelligence even more, Giap's divisions, or selected units, devoted their time to ruses, maneuvers, false marches and phony concentrations.

What the French did know by the end of November, what little they really did know, was quite frightening enough. Giap had already assembled the greater part of his forces: something like a hundred battalions were ready. There were three main concentrations, one for each side of the triangular delta.

The most lethal threat was about twenty-five miles away, due north of Hanoi, where the roads from Langson and Caobang debouched into the plain. In this direction the Vietminh country came very close to the capital: from the streets and avenues of Hanoi one could see the foothills in which the troops were gathering in the hope of taking the city. These were the victorious frontier units, Giap's iron divisions: their task was to carry out the strike, the short, violent charge, the decisive thrust into the heart of Hanoi.

An almost equally serious threat came from the west, at the head of the delta, the meeting of the waters, where the Red River was joined by the Clear River on the one side and, only a little way off, by the Black River on the other. This confluence was dominated by two huge sentinels, two abrupt mountain ranges at the edge of the plain, the Tam Dao and the Bavi. It was their flanks that hid the second concentration. This was made up of the troops that had been fighting in central Tonkin, those that had taken Laokay and had fought the war of the fords on the Black River. When Coste and his Moroccan battalion had escaped, the main body of the pursuers, instead of carrying on to Laichau and Laos, turned back for the great objective, for Hanoi itself. Here again the city was not more than twenty-five miles away, and all one had to do to get there was to follow the Red River as it flowed through the delta.

In short, everything looked as though Giap intended to take Hanoi by a pincer movement, the northern and the western concentrations being ready to close on their splendid prey, so near at hand.

The third concentration, that in the south, was quite different. It had not been brought together for delivering the fatal blow but for the huge work of subversion. A glance at the delta shows that everything of immediate vital importance lay to the north — Hanoi, the road from Hanoi to Haiphong and Haiphong itself. The south, on the other hand, has the appearance of an enormous appendix. Strategically it was less important, yet it was there that the great mass of people lived: the south had the world's highest density of population, and it was there that the greatest poverty was to be found. This was the Asia of the *nha-qués,* as opposed to the northern fringe which was that of the towns, with their European economy, European influence and European physical presence. It was in this southern region, upstream from Hanoi, that the huge Red River lost itself in the delta, changing the whole landscape into one vast flood of yellowish water for six months of the year. In the south everything was in the Viets' favor — its comparative remoteness, the lack of roads, the confusion of land and water, the mass of humanity, the poverty, the famine and the traditional revolutionary ferment. But it was not there that the decisive battle could be fought: the southern concentration could do no more than help in the decision, but by using the right methods it could help a great deal.

All Giap's plans were ruled by this physical and human geography. While the northern and western armies were to strike the French in their vitals, the army in the south was to spread out among the paddy fields, dominate the *nha-qués* and take possession of the masses. It was to be an undermining, a subversion upon a scale never seen before.

The task was entrusted to the forces that came up from Red north Annam: they were poorly armed, as they had not been to China, but they were formidable because they were exceptionally close to the people. Their hideout was the Chiné range, one of Indochina's most romantic landscapes. It was a great mass of wild rocks, the land's equivalent of the Bay of Along, full of grottoes and pagodas, and it rose sheer from the southern end of the delta — an utterly flat expanse of muddy water or a sea of rice, according to the season. There the army was immediately above the plain: the troops had but to come down, cross the Day River, and they were in the midst of the ant heap.

It was here that the new war began. While the regulars from China were moving into position around Hanoi the semiregulars from north Annam insinuated themselves into the rice fields. Before making a frontal attack upon the delta, Giap organized it from within. The fighting in the neighborhood of Namdinh and Thaibinh was like guerrilla warfare, but on a much larger scale, with battalions and even whole regiments involved. The French communiqués only spoke of infiltration. In fact the Viets from Chiné smashed all the connecting links of French rule: the notables were killed, the roads cut: even the posts were taken. All at once in this pacified delta everything collapsed, and nobody knew how to stop the spread of the appalling, invisible disease. It only needed a few of Giap's soldiers to appear, in uniform or not, for everything that had been hidden and buried to come to life again — the agents, committees and political commissars, the associations of every kind, the messengers, bringers of supplies, guerrilla fighters, killers, provincial and regional militias. Within a few days the whole Vietminh apparatus was functioning once more in the south of the delta, and once more the whole population belonged to Ho Chi Minh. The most convincing symptom of this repossession was the appearance of the fortified village — a village that became a Red citadel with its earth walls, its emplacements for automatic weapons and its labyrinth of tunnels.

The first post that fell was called Hoitung: it was held by a Vietnamese garrison under the command of a Vietnamese lieutenant who had just come back from a military school in France. It was one of the most forward posts in what was called the Day line, which faced the enemy base in the Chiné range. Five battalions attacked it, hammering it with bazookas. There was no hope. The Vietnamese officer was wounded. He ordered his men to crawl through the Vietminh lines at nightfall and make for the nearest French post: and having done this he killed himself.

Against the infiltrating Viet battalions the French high command mounted the first big mopping-up operation in the delta: but this was real war, a huge, heavy, soldier's operation. It had nothing in common with the earlier sweeps and the screening that had been so familiar in Cochinchina and which really amounted to no more than policing. Now it really was the army against the people — the ponderous, massive army carrying out combined operations with all its fire power and all that was needed to crush opposition by weight of equipment. Each time there were thousands of tough soldiers, sticks of parachutists, the amphibious machines called crabs, columns of artillery, observation planes and fighters. The aim was to retake the fortified villages where the regulars had dug themselves in, and even to win back the mass of the people. In theory the procedure was simple. The first thing to do was to smash everything with the guns of the artillery or the naval vessels. Then the amphibious machines were sent across the rice fields, followed by infantry, for the attack upon the villages. If there was resistance, the fighter planes would intervene.

It all seemed easy — unnaturally easy. But it was not. It was wretchedly, dismally hard, and it called for an unvarying monotonous cruelty. For there was no coming to an end of these regulars mingled with the ordinary people: they might have been indestructible. In an attempt to destroy them nevertheless, thousands of combined operations were mounted in the years that followed — operations for which all sorts of tricks, dodges and new angles were invented. The result was the wiping out of thousands of *nha-qués* every week and every month. Day after day, millions of men, women and children were forced to live under the threat of death, to live with bombs dropping all around: thus they took to hating the French, and sided with the Viet regulars for good and all. It was a psychological defeat. And to arrive at this end, how many men was France to lose along the dikes and in the mud; for the war was to be terribly bloody for the Expeditionary Force as well.

The dreariest days

In a certain sense horror and dreariness are the same: horror is when nothing happens and when there is no hope left. All through November 1950, all through those endless empty weeks, there was a bogging down of the spirit, an acceptance of imminent and disastrous fate. The waiting became more nerve racking every day: everyone knew that the long taking up of positions just north of Hanoi was coming to an end. There was now a general certainty that it would be for the end of December or the beginning of January — that was when the regulars would thrust forward in their tens of thousands for the final stroke: for then the drizzle would lie like a dirty shroud over the delta; the planes would no longer be able to fly; the tanks and the guns would sink in the mud on the roads; and the equipment of the French would have lost half its value.

There was no longer even a show of command. Pettiness, anonymity and mediocrity reigned in the citadel of Hanoi, which housed the headquarters of Tonkin armed forces. It was a strange place, on the site of the ancient Annamese fortress the French had conquered a century ago. A drowsy, parsimonious protectorate had built its offices there about 1900, shabby brick pavilions decked out with "Eastern" touches: roofs with glazed, upcurving tiles, plaster dragons, and plenty of staircases in the style of Angkor Wat. Now it was a dirty, neglected-looking bureaucratic backwater, where countless clerks and countless officers who looked and behaved like clerks, plodded along the narrow routines they knew so well. General Carpentier had finally got the better of Alessandri at the beginning of November and the little Corsican was about to leave for France. Ugly, miserable intrigues! Alessandri's departure caused little emotion in the Expeditionary Force, except among a few particularly loyal friends: whether he was responsible or not he was too deeply marked, too worn out by the disaster — the very type of a man who has reached his end, and a bad end, at that. The only comment was, "But why doesn't Carpentier go too?"

But Carpentier was there, still there. And he did not even know how to replace Alessandri: to begin with there was virtually no one to fill the vacancy. One General Garbey — a strong man, it was said — was sounded out; but having come to look at the situation at first hand he quickly vanished.

To be sure, this void, this shocking absence of vision, of command or preparation, did not prevent the high command from blossoming out with fresh theories. I have always been astonished by the intellectual capacity for inventing brilliant justificatory and explanatory arguments that is to be found in staff officers. It was this period that saw the spreading of the notion that the Pacification was out of date: a change, a reconversion for war, was essential. The basic idea was to form a real hitting force with mobile groups, important artillery formations and an air force for carrying out strikes — everything that makes up firepower. The Expeditionary Force was still at the battalion level while the Viets had reached that of the regiment or even the division: what was needed was to move on to the stage of the mobile group. This was a small army provided with everything necessary to fight its own war: it had three infantry battalions, a few guns, a few tanks and some engineers. Some complementary ideas also appeared. The systematic employment of commandos, for example, of French murder committees, by way of using surprise and terrorism against the Viets. And then there was the idea of the White Zone, a belt of scorched earth all around the delta that would prevent the enemy from infiltrating and cut off his supplies.

But all this remained in the form of words; no one even began to apply the program. Furthermore there was a great battle of different schools of thought — it raged throughout the country, from Hanoi to the remotest section. No one agreed with anyone else. Everybody acknowledged that a positive war had to be fought and that the mobile groups were necessary. But as soon as an officer in command of any section was asked for a unit or even a single man to start building them up, he would fling his hands into the air and cry, "I can't. If I strip my territory, what's going to happen to my Pacification?" There were obstacles everywhere. The men in the offices found it physically painful to make any sort of change whatever. So in general there was a very cautious approach: people did nothing, as though they had all the time in the world before them, and as though the bill of life and death were not to fall due in the next few weeks. The situation was known, understood; yet people behaved as though the outcome was pre-determined, as though nothing could be done about it.

This passive conduct was all the more alarming because now it was not only a question of the Vietminh — the Viets who were massing against Hanoi and those who were undermining the delta. In November there suddenly appeared another danger, a thousand times worse. Dread of the Viets was replaced by the dread of the Chinese. For thousands of miles away, by the Yalu, Mao's armies had suddenly flung themselves upon MacArthur's splendid troops, the ultimate perfection of the Western military idea. And the swarm of little yellow men, the homogeneous, fanaticized mass, had overwhelmed the much bigger, much better fed, much better armed American soldiers. Far away in the north it was disaster for the Americans: but everyone in Hanoi wondered whether the storm that was battering Korea might not spread over all that surrounded China, beginning with Tonkin.

The effect of the American catastrophe in Korea was immense. Everyone thought, "This is the final struggle between the Asians and the whites. It is the end of the whites in Asia." Henceforward China was a cauldron with six hundred million people in it, all at the highest pitch of emotion. Inside the country this was the time of the great purges, the destruction of all opposition, in which millions of men and women were delivered over to the people's courts and put to death with an extraordinary technique of hatred. Outside the country this was the time when floods of men in greenish uniforms rushed into the inferno of American fire, confronting American strength and falling by thousands, by tens of thousands, beyond counting, but still advancing — men who could not be stopped and who carried everything before them. Thus, after slumbering for hundreds of years the Chinese dragon had awakened — and woe to those who were near at hand, within its reach!

Hanoi was obsessed by the idea that the Red armies were going to intervene in Tonkin as they had in Korea; and here in this remote delta, where nothing was done, the Expeditionary Force bogged down in a sort of masochistic fatalism. What was the use of trying anything, of making any sort of attempt at a solution? If a boundless flood of men were to come rushing furiously out of China, then this hopeless place, this Tonkin that was so far from anything, would be a trap in which the surrounded French units would be utterly destroyed — wiped out.

If the French were beaten by the Viets alone, no doubt they would manage to evacuate the greater part of their men by way of Haiphong. But if Mao's soldiers were to combine with Giap's, if they were to burst over the frontier, then there would be measureless disaster — one from which not a single unit, not a single man, would ever return.

The deluge might come at any moment. There would be no warning. Hundreds of thousands of men might make their way through the secrecy of the jungle unseen, breaking out all at once upon Hanoi and cutting the Hanoi-Haiphong road. It would all be over in three or four days. No resistance would be possible: there would be nothing but death, massacre, captivity. There would not even be a chance of retreating.

Tonkin was indeed a deathtrap of a country. It thrust into China, and in the nature of things it was already almost surrounded. Furthermore it was virtually cut off from the rest of Indochina: it was six hundred miles away, and its only communication with the rest of the world was by ships or planes. So in the event of a Chinese avalanche the Expeditionary Force would not even be able to flee. Where could they run to? Precious few men would get as far as Haiphong, the only outward port, for an Asian Dunkirk. And no doubt those few would be wiped out on the quays before they ever got on board. For in order to have a Far Eastern Dunkirk some foresight was called for — planned preparations were needed, a fleet of transports, a great number of aircraft carriers. And even if all these elements were brought together it would still be a shockingly dangerous operation, because of the Chinese island of Hainan, which commanded this whole stretch of water, the whole of the Gulf of Tonkin.

So if they chose, Mao's Chinese could win a total victory in Indochina; and they could do so far more easily than in Korea. The Expeditionary Force was in fact at their mercy. Would there even be an attempt at a hurried embarkation? The French would never even get as far as Haiphong in the first place: they would be cut to pieces far earlier, in the rice fields, on the roads and among the waterways of the delta.

Still nothing happened. The days went by, each more dismal than the last, and men's minds were filled with ever more horrifying suppositions. Now, after so many assurances of peace, Tonkin's neighbor was no longer the China of gentleness but the China of wrath. Chou En-lai, speaking on the radio, declared, "Indochina is now nothing but a base for American aggression. We can no longer tolerate this state of affairs for any length of time." In Canton all the walls were covered with the slogan, "We are going to cut off French imperialism's bloody talons." The Chinese as well as the Viets made huge military preparations. They put the southern provinces on a war footing, especially Kwangtung, Kwangsi and Yunnan, which all bordered upon Indochina. They carried out enormous troop movements: the Chinese 2nd Army concentrated in Yunnan and the 3rd Army in Kwangsi — that is to say on the two lines of invasion, the one by Laokay and the other by Caobang and Langson. They set up an immense staff at Nanning, little more than a hundred miles from the frontier: it was said to be that of the famous General Cheng Keng, who would be in command of the whole offensive.

In southern China the convoys were now far larger than would be necessary for the support of the Viets alone. And the nearest Chinese cities (no doubt out of fear of the American air force) were plunged into the sinister atmosphere of war. More and more precautions were taken. The political commissars organized huge meetings to warn the population. They dug trenches, dismantled factories, carried away records and evacuated the families of important civil servants — everything that was valuable, whether people or things, was moved off to the interior. In Canton anti-aircraft guns were set up on the roofs.

In fact the intelligence services knew that the Chinese would not attack Indochina for itself — not for what the country was worth. But they might strike there as a counterblow to what was happening elsewhere. An intelligence officer said to me, "The Chinese are in no hurry for Indochina: they believe it will drop into their hands one day by means of the Viets, giving them the power they want at the moment they want it. That is their ordinary program. But they have an extraordinary one, too. And to switch from the one to the other — to the Chinese attacking instead of letting the Viets deal with the situation under Chinese guidance — only a very little is needed, and that little scarcely depends on us at all. If ever the Americans carry the war into China by air raids or the atomic bomb, the Chinese are determined to retaliate. And this is where they'll do it in the first place — this is the easiest, after all. Our fate is being decided thousands of miles away: it all depends on the doings of MacArthur in Tokyo, Truman in Washington, Mao Tse-tung in Peking and Stalin in Moscow. But if ever the Chinese decide upon moving against Tonkin it will be a lightning victory for them — they have everything laid on for it. They know our numbers and our strength exactly, and they have only had to work out what is needed to smash us. And at this moment everything is in place."

So at the end of that year of 1950 Indochina was in the midst of the Asian drama: the Vietminh attack was certain; the Sino-Vietminh offensive was very likely. And the men who really understood what was afoot, the men who had none of the splendid immobility of those in high circles, were the officers of the units in the field: it was their skins that were at stake. But they did not want to die like that, through the fault of others and by reason of ineptitude. Once when I was there, a colonel of shock troops, a hero, cried, "The Expeditionary Force in Tonkin knows that it is being sacrificed beforehand — and sacrificed for nothing. Fair enough, death is our trade: but not the kind of death that is being got ready for us at this moment. If morale is so shockingly low it is because there is not a single officer or man who is not saying to himself, 'Who do they think they're taking in?' If we were told, 'You are in a hopeless position: we can do nothing for you; do your best,' we should accept it. But the high command asserts that equipment and reinforcements have come and that everything is perfectly ready — and that is absolutely untrue. Not a single extra man has arrived in Tonkin since the disaster on the frontier; nor a single extra gun or plane. And even if they had, even if what has been promised and provided for were here, how would that change the course of events? They say that the battalions wiped out at Dongkhe will be replaced in January and that there will even be two over: but what does that amount to when the Viets are turning out six a month in the Chinese camps? The B-26 light bombers the Americans were supposed to give us weeks ago have not come — they haven't even left the States. In any case this so-called powerful air force would only amount to eighteen in all. And MacArthur can't stop the waves of Chinese with twelve hundred! At present we still have nothing but dilapidated old Kingcobras, and the pilots complain that as often as not they have no shells for their cannon and that when they fire the machine guns the bullets come out in a corkscrew because their tubes are changed only after twenty thousand rounds instead of the regulation five thousand. Do you know that there is nothing in the army's ammunition dumps either — scarcely enough to sustain a single major battle?

"So of course we are angry. We feel that everything that is most loathsome on earth — falsehood combined with stupidity — is dragging us on to a fresh slaughter. Who would not be discouraged by these speeches and orders that make no sense? What is worse for morale than feeling you are at the mercy of ludicrous instructions? A young fellow came to me this morning and said, 'I have a handful of legionaries in a post that is being virtually thrown away. I am perfectly willing to be sacrified, but I should like to know what it's all about. No one has been able to tell me.' And then there is this wretched feeling that France knows nothing and doesn't want to know anything — is just not interested.

"If I were General Carpentier I'd shout the truth out loud. I'd warn everybody. I'd make a tremendous noise. But no doubt he confines himself to sending in reports that please the government. During these past weeks the great decision ought to have been taken — the decision between giving up and going on. For it could perfectly well be maintained that the Indo-chinese adventure is too costly, and that, to begin with, Tonkin ought to be given up entirely — that we ought to get out while there's time. Then on the other hand it could be said that this war is in the interests of France: but that should only be said in full awareness, knowing what is involved and accepting the necessary commitments. But nothing of the kind takes place: France is silent, and the high command lets itself be forced into battle just when it wants to retreat. In short, the high command has not had the courage to prepare either for battle or for retreat. So the battle is going to be fought in the worst possible conditions. It will be lost, and then the retreat will be a shameful running away, a rout. And we shall be precious lucky if the flight carries us as far as Haiphong and on board a ship."

General Carpentier's whole philosophy was summed up in a few homely phrases addressed to Colonel Gambiez, the curious figure whom he had chosen for the taking, and later for the evacuation of Thainguyen, and who now stood in as commander at Hanoi. "I have one bloody mess on my hands. I don't want any others. You shift for yourself." And obviously that was the best possible way of getting into even bloodier messes.

The false savior

AT this juncture there appeared a savior: but he was not the genuine article. What was called for was blazing enthusiasm and integrity, and General Boyer de La Tour was essentially ambiguous. Simple-looking, rough, jovial soldiers are often extraordinary complex within, and this was the case with him. His service had been mostly in North Africa, but he had been in the Far East before: it was he who had won over the sects in Cochin-china two years earlier, and the Pacification was his invention. The government seized upon him in Paris and put him on an airplane, telling him to go and save Indochina, but without saying how — he had practically no orders or instructions. However Juin, always Carpentier's patron, up until this time, had hinted to La Tour that he might be due for replacement.

By December 16, he had made up his mind and he wrote a report. His idea was to tiptoe out of Tonkin and wage a full-scale war for the far more easily defensible Cochinchina, where there was the rice, the wealth, the economic interests and the money. Naturally he did not speak his whole mind: he just suggested that a hundred Vietnamese battalions might be formed, and that they could be left to carry on the war in the north while France's fine Expeditionary Force should take up positions far away in the exotic south. At the same time he began to build up a striking force in Tonkin and to strengthen the Hanoi front with fortifications and earthworks in the 1914 style, only smaller.

Unfortunately the Expeditionary Force's morale did not rise: on the contrary, it fell. The officers and men sensed that La Tour did not believe in what he was doing — that he thought the game was lost in the north and that his one concern was to get out.

The general lassitude persisted. The danger mounted continually: that of the Chinese faded, but the Vietminh threat grew terribly oppressive. After the long wait the time had come when Giap's divisions began pushing harder every day. They had already launched a preliminary offensive, only a minor action with a single division and that far away; but it was a forerunner of the avalanche, and it showed that the Reds' machinery for destruction had started to run. It was on the coast of the Bay of Along, towards Tien Yen and the start of the R.C. 4; and once again there had to be an evacuation, with the posts and the garrisons falling back. Binhlu tried to hold out, but it lost a hundred and fifty men and even so it had to be abandoned.

The crushing weight of the Vietminh increased, and so did the private burden each man bore within — the weight of resignation or of hopelessness. In spite of it all the Expeditionary Force still fought well: and now, after the pause, the nightmare began. Giap's regulars probed the ring of positions north of Hanoi. Once again the French were shown just how far Asian fanaticism and Asian obedience could go — how far it could reach beyond what was human or even inhuman, in that strange vacuum of a world where ordinary living no longer counted. The Viets advanced in spite of their increasing losses: they came in against machine guns as though they were drunk (many of the French survivors asserted that they were in fact drunk on chum: but there is no proof of that). Groups of three linked their ankles, so that the dead or wounded would still advance, carried on by the others. And then there were all those who blew themselves up with their yellow-powder bangalores, with packets of sulphur tied to grenades, or with strange Chinese weapons full of holes that poured out gas — they died to smash the posts, to burn them or to smother them. In some places everything was so furiously burned that the French and Vietminh bodies could no longer be told apart, their ashes or at least their remains being so tragically alike.

The French held out against this Asiatic state of mind, this total indifference to everything, by their courage, by forcing themselves to be brave. For their part they had by no means lost their awareness: they retained all their love of life and their longing for it, and therefore they needed an even greater inner strength to fight on the inhuman level of the Viets.

And yet what was the point of fighting heroically? Everyone knew that these were only the last convulsive jerks before the death agony. It was then, in December, that Hanoi's great fear began. It came slowly. To begin with the town had not believed in the threat. It was like an Asian subprefecture carrying on with its subprefectorial life in the midst of the strangest of wars, making a profit out of it and yet not being fully aware of its existence. Formerly Hanoi had been a great administrative center. After the "troubles" of 1946 its population had slowly grown again; but from that time on the city's prosperity was only that of small people — bar keepers, tradesmen, prostitutes, government employees. Everything was small in Hanoi, this curiously sluggish city under its lowering sky, with its charming little lake and its glass-windowed houses, quite unlike exotic Saigon. The pleasures of the town — the sort that soldiers needed — were drowned in the melancholy of Asiatic mandarinism and French provincialism — Confucius at Romorantin. Its avenues were perfectly straight, wide, well planted with trees; and almost empty. The trim, neat houses were well built, and thoroughly ugly. There was none of the life-giving scandal and the rotting heat of Saigon. It was ill-natured gossip, narrow-minded opinions, humdrum existences: the people of Hanoi did not live at all, except for those who were there to die in the war. Some worked in administrative offices; others traded with the soldiers. Nowhere was any imagination to be found; there was not even enough speculation to stimulate it.

The French civilians were relics of a former age, imprisoned in their memories — veterans of the 1914 war who had then done thirty years in the colonies. They were all more of less Asianized; yet they had an immeasurable contempt (though it was tinged with kindness) for the Asians. Nothing could change their attitude, and they spent their days proving that "Asiatics had no idea of how to fight." And in spite of all the power of the Vietminh, the Vietnamese of Hanoi were not yet convinced that a French army could be wholly beaten by Giap and his Asian soldiers — indeed, they were very skeptical about it. At the beginning the whole of Hanoi was splendidly calm, out of mere stupidity.

Then gradually doubt began to seep in. It was not the Vietminh propaganda that brought it, but the French army's fear, all the staringly obvious marks of anxiety among the soldiers and the officials. Eventually

Hanoi began to wonder whether what the Viets said might be true, whether they would enter the city on December 19 as Ho Chi Minh had announced. The omens were of the most unfortunate kind. It appeared that an immense turtle, five feet long, had risen from the depths and shown itself for a few moments upon the surface of the Little Lake beside the Holy Pagoda before plunging out of sight once more. That evening the whole city worried over the interpretation of this augury — for the people knew perfectly well that it was one. The tradition was that the ancient creature never appeared except on the eve of some catastrophe, when a new era was about to begin. So the Vietminh agents who proclaimed the taking of the town within the next few days had confirmation from on high.

Under its drizzling sky Hanoi passed from its ordinary torpor to that deathly coma which precedes battle in a threatened Asian city. It is the direct opposite of excitement: paralysis spreads over the town. No gathering in the streets, no wrought-up faces, no urgent, feverish talk: but the population bows to the facts.

The French civilians' collapse could be seen in *L'Entente,* the local rag, where whole pages were filled with For Sale notices. An entire district turned into an open market in which the whole of the French civilization and everything that represented it was put up for sale, without finding any buyers. A strange foreshadowing of what was to happen four years later; only then the day and hour of the Viets' appearance was to be known exactly, for it was all put down in the agreement.

There was only one man who bought — bought everything he could lay his hands on, and bought it for a song. This optimist was the celebrated Monsieur G. (who was to be host at a luxurious farewell feast, after Dienbienphu). "I'm not a fool," said this gambler, pokerplayer, and jack-of-all-trades, "I grant you, someday the Viets may smash the French, and the French may quit. But not yet. There's a few good years left. They'll finally send a really big man, don't ask me who, and he'll beat the Viets. I could lose my shirt on this . . . but I don't think so." Apart from him the whole city was panic stricken. There was an immense carrying away of goods and chattels: General de La Tour had been very successful with the piaster worshippers of Cochinchina, but he was obviously not the great man who had been expected here — he provided no reassurance at all.

As soon as he reached Tonkin everybody, including the civilians, knew what he had come to do. He certainly proclaimed that he would defend Hanoi to the last: but what he actually did was, "as a precautionary measure," to evacuate. He sent huge convoys of trucks loaded with administrative personnel and heavy equipment down to Haiphong. This, it seemed, was in order to free Hanoi of unnecessary clutter when the fighting began. But everyone knew that once an evacuation had begun it went on: it did not stop.

Furthermore, de La Tour was obsessed by the Doumer Bridge, a great mass of iron more than a mile long, the only way out of Hanoi, the only way of getting across the Red River: if that were destroyed, the Expeditionary Force would be cut off. Everyone knew that it was poorly defended. De La Tour's obsession was to keep it intact: he increased the precautions to the point of using something like a whole division to guard it. And what sickened the people of Hanoi was a warning from the General. It appears that he advised them to settle their affairs quickly and go; for if ever the army were to pull out in earnest it would not trouble with them. It would reserve the exclusive use of the Doumer Bridge and the Hanoi-Haiphong road for its own huge convoys, and no civilian would be allowed to accompany them.

The final blow to the morale of the civilian population was the order for the evacuation of the French women and children. For the first time in Indochina, after so many an Asian exodus, I was to see the Europeans in flight. The state took charge of the very poor, and these amounted to close on four thousand. It must be added that most who left in this way were yellowish white people, very nearly Asian: the wholly European families were rich enough to flee unaided. It was pitiful. At Haiphong I saw an embarkation center for these "French citizens": there were betel-chewing *congai* and *nho,* in short all the families and relatives of French people who were themselves more Annamese than European. They were leaving for the unknown, without a penny; and they were going to end up God knows where — the whole tragedy of mixed blood was there. Yet among all these different shades of yellow I did see one completely white couple, an elderly pair. Anxiously the man asked me, "Shan't we die of cold in France? We don't remember, you see: we haven't been back for forty years."

December 19 came nearer. The Vietminh proclaimed a week of revenge and said, "Kill the French to make ready for our coming." But there were no murders in Hanoi, only the agonizing question, "When will it happen? How will it happen?" The future was wrapped in mystery. The rhythm of the evacuation grew faster: at the Gialam airfield a stream of special planes flew out everything that could be flown out while there was yet time. They droned over the blood-drained city, which still went on emptying. The café terraces were the last places where any life was to be seen — it was there that those who were staying provided themselves with courage. The authorities undertook to defend the town street by street, house by house, if necessary. Military intelligence said that Giap's divisions were completely ready and that the hammer blow might be struck from one day to the next, from one hour to the next. The French troops were in position. But there was almost no hope left.

In this desperate situation Bernard de Lattre wrote to his father, "What we need is a leader who leads, fresh blood and new machinery, and no more niggling, small-time warfare; and then, with the morale that we still have in spite of it all, we could save everything."

From the depth of humiliation, of all these humiliations, and in this extremity, it was a desperate appeal to the Father. And the miracle was that the Father came. The radio proclaimed to the whole of Indochina that General de Lattre de Tassigny had been appointed French high commissioner and commander in chief of the French forces in Indochina. And this coming had an exact, clearly defined, absolute meaning for all the officers, all the men, in the messes, canteens and places where they gathered to talk, in the posts under attack and in the threatened front line. It also had a very distinct meaning in the staffs whose members had been so very much mistaken and which had turned out so many erroneous, flabby and disastrous plans. It meant that France — or rather its disjointed, ignorant governments — had nevertheless refused to accept defeat, and had turned her face to glory rather than to shame.

Everything was on the edge of the precipice. And intelligent people wondered whether any single man could, by his mere presence, alter the unrelenting course of history: we shall see how he thought he could succeed in doing so, how he undeceived himself, and how it killed him. Nevertheless this was to be the last of the great romantic epics, the most splendid tale of modern times.

The great choice

IN order to put everything right in Indochina, the French government (which still understood nothing whatever about it) sent a hero there, as if that were the solution, as if that alone were enough. And for a time he did drag the Expeditionary Force up out of its wretchedness and give it back its dignity and its self-confidence. But his mind was too clear for him not to perceive that all he had created was a great illusion — and to perceive this very soon. He flung himself into his task with all his strength; he tried every possible method; he lavished all his vital powers, all the energy, strength of will and intelligence that he possessed, spending himself beyond human limits in a paroxysm of effort. He wore out his fire and his iron strength, and his death was as it were an indirect suicide. But before he died he said, "If everything fails, I shall take the Expeditionary Force back to France rather than let it be destroyed by the Viets either piecemeal or in one great catastrophe."

De Lattre rescued the Expeditionary Force from its humiliation in 1951: what would he have done if he had lived? No one can tell. But he would never have let it fall into worse humiliation; he would never have let it be brought to bay in a Dienbienphu of any kind: by hook or by crook he would have prevented that. In fact de Lattre came too late. For the defeat on the R.C. 4 — the destruction of the columns, the flight from Langson, the investment of Hanoi — was fate writing on the wall "It is over, it is over." In itself this defeat was far more important than Dienbienphu, which was only the inevitable, disastrous conclusion. But the surrounding blindness and incoherence was so general that nobody chose to read the message.

The choice of war had been made in the first place in 1945 when it was decided to retake Indochina, occupied first by the Japanese and then by the Viets: the French had tried gentleness and negotiation to begin with, and that had quickly turned to bloodshed. The choice of war had been made in the second place after the coup at Hanoi in December 1946, when Ho Chi Minh tried massacre as a solution. It was then that the Expeditionary Force had been launched against the forces of the people: the French thought they were on the very brink of victory; and then, brought face to face with a reality that had been denied, everything fell to pieces on the Chinese frontier. But in December 1950 war was chosen for the third time — and that at a moment when everybody ought to have known what that war implied. They should have seen clearly that it was an impossible undertaking, lost before it was begun, because it had to be fought against the huge potentialities of Chinese Communism and against Asia's almost universal xenophobia. The whole continent abhorred any kind of direct or indirect colonial reconquest; the Europeans were yielding ground everywhere; yet the French wanted to maintain their hold in Indochina. And then in spite of a certain amount of help from the Americans, France was scarcely supported at all by the other Western powers, each of which was concerned only with cutting its losses in its former possessions by giving up the outward appearance of power so as to try to stay there on another footing — modest and subfusc. France was tragically alone in her out-of-date enterprise; not only were immense physical forces against her but also the whole tide of history.

Yet the French persisted. For a while de Lattre blazed like a splendid comet — the embodiment and the symbol of the refusal to accept defeat. But what did his means amount to? Himself, his own genius, and some mercenaries — far too few mercenaries. He turned the meager Expeditionary Force into a magnificent weapon; but what could an Expeditionary Force do against the spirit, against the wind from the east that was blowing with hurricane force? To be sure, at some levels and in some branches, particularly the SDEC, the intelligence, there were men who saw the blind alley, the fatal trap into which the French were marching. But they said little or nothing at all; and then they were quickly silenced or sent away. The French government wanted a victory, a victory after the manner of Verdun. But they wanted it absurdly cheap, without even trying to provide the means for winning it and without noticing that the world was changing in a way that nothing on earth could reverse. And then there were also murky, shameful elements in this stubbornness, such as the piaster, for example, and business prosperity.

Should there have been negotiations with the Viets in 1950? But that was impossible, for they would not accept any kind of compromise or arrangement — and they had to have a "long war" in order to forge their people on the Red anvil and to make them entirely Communist. But what might have been done was to dig in in the strong zones where there was a possibility of playing for time, instead of fighting all over the country. That was Carpentier's theory; but his one concern was to avoid "bloody messes." It was also de La Tour's more clearly thought-out theory; but he dealt so much in subterfuge that he dared not express it.

And then there was another aspect. None of this was feasible in an atmosphere of shame. What was needed — since total victory was not to be won — was at least a victory on the battlefield to give the Expeditionary Force back its pride in itself. This was something that de Lattre understood, and at Vinhyen he cured the soldiers' spiritual malady, their yellow disease, by providing them with thousands of Viet corpses and by chanting the hymn of glory. But what then? It was clearly seen, and de Lattre was the first to see it, that all this led to nothing. Another card should have been tried, any other card at all. But with the General dead those who remained clung desperately, insanely, to what he had accomplished, without choosing to see that it was continually dwindling and that it too carried within it the seeds of death and defeat.

De Lattre meant not only a tremendous name, an unparalleled epic, a total sacrifice. His name also stood for going on from victory to victory without ever winning the real one, without solving the basis of the problem, because it could no longer be done and because interests that were too important stood in the way. But what he accomplished in those few months — and restoring its human dignity to an army is no trifling feat — should have been used to the full in order to reach an honorable solution. This was not even attempted. De Lattre died in vain: and the result of his dying was Dienbienphu.

But at least, because of him, there was to be one splendid chapter shining among the unhappiness and the squalor of the war in Indochina: and this is the chapter that I have yet to tell.

Historical Summary

NOTE: This summary has been prepared by the American publisher for the convenience of the general reader. Therefore, any errors of fact or interpretation are the publisher's, not the author's, responsibility.

The Annamese, a Mongoloid people, with some Indonesian blood, form eighty per cent of the population of Vietnam, and have done so since its earliest history when most of what is now Vietnam was called Van Lang. The Chinese acquired the country about 110 B.C., and ruled with difficulty until 939 A.D., when the Annamese achieved their independence and began expanding southward. The official language was Chinese, and Annamese was not a written language until the thirteenth century. Chinese influence, particularly in Vietnamese Buddhism, has always been strong; Chinese expansion has been a constant threat; and the million Chinese, living mostly in the south, are the country's largest minority.

By the sixteenth century the Annamese had absorbed the highly civilized kingdom of Champa and were taking over part of the declining Khmer (Cambodian) empire. At about this time the country was discovered by Portuguese mariners, and both Portuguese and French missionaries came, spreading European influence, and inventing the *quoc-ngu* method, still in use, of transcribing Annamese into Roman letters. By the nineteenth century, French churchmen and French merchants were numerous and influential in Vietnam. By 1802 the Nguyen dynasty, with unofficial French aid, had united the countries of Tonkin, Annam, and Cochinchina under its rule. Cochinchina, where French influence was earliest and strongest, became a French colony in 1862; and in 1887 Cochinchina, Annam, Tonkin, Cambodia and Laos were united as French Indochina under a governor-general. This conquest had been accomplished in the course of "punitive expeditions" and of protecting one faction from another, or from the Chinese (in particular the Black Flag bandits of Tonkin). Resistance, at first Annamese but soon spreading throughout Indochina, was always lively; and after 1900 Nationalist uprisings were frequent. Nevertheless, the country prospered: with the draining of the Mekong delta, a fertile rice-growing district was created; rubber, sugar, tea, and other crops were intensively cultivated; coal and tin mines were opened; Saigon became a rich commercial metropolis, and Indochina, the richest element in France-d'Outre-mer.

1890   Nguyen Van Thanh, later known as Nguyen Ai Quoc, and later still as Ho Chi Minh, was born in Annam, son of a minor civil servant who was eventually dismissed for anti-French nationalism. He went to France in 1911, worked on steamships around the world, and joined the French Socialist Party. He became intimate with Communist intellectuals, went to Moscow for Marxist study in 1922, and by 1925 was a delegate to the Comintern's Fifth Congress. He then went to China, set up a solid Communist Party in Indochina, and was active in Party work throughout Southeast Asia. His orientation was always toward old-style Leninist Marxism, rather than Stalinism.

1919   Founding of the Caodaist sect.

1932   Bao Dai, age eighteen, returned from France to be crowned Emperor of Annam, the last of the Nguyen dynasty.

1934   Mao's "Long March" began in Kiangsi.

1939   Founding of the Hoahao sect.

1940   Expecting Japanese pressure, General Catroux, Governor-General of Indochina, tried to acquire arms in Washington, and was refused. The Japanese wanted to pass through northern Tonkin in order to attack the Chinese rear in Yunnan; moreover they wanted to bar American shipments to Chiang Kai-shek from the port of Haiphong. In September the Japanese attacked. The Vichy government agreed to collaborate with them, and appointed Admiral Jean Decoux as governor-general.

1941–1943   Ho Chi Minh was the Kuomintang's prisoner. In 1943, he promised his support to a Kuomintang warlord who was also a rival of Chiang Kai-shek's. Secretly released, Ho became head of the Dong Ming Hoi, an overall Vietnamese resistance organization in which the newly formed Vietminh was one of several groups, and which was subsidized by the Kuomintang. Ho and Giap, however, built up an independent 10,000-man Vietminh army; and in 1944 they sought aid from the O.S.S., in return for harassing the Japanese in Tonkin and Yunnan, and for rescuing American pilots. They did receive some aid from the O.S.S. unofficially, from American ex-businessmen in Indochina, and from Great Britain.

1945 FEBRUARY: de Gaulle issued a statement reasserting French sovereignty in Indochina.

MARCH 9: The Japanese captured the French administration in Indochina, and interned all French troops (of which 2000 escaped and, led by General Alessandri, made their way to Kunming, where they received O.S.S. help). The Japanese also captured Bao Dai, whom they forced to declare Vietnamese independence. He was soon forced by Ho to abdicate, and was paraded in the north as Ho's "Supreme Counselor."

SUMMER: Bay Vien, head of the Binh Xuyen sect, seized control of Cholon.

AUGUST: Vietminh troops entered Hanoi. The O.S.S. Major Patti parachuted in, accompanied by the Free French Major Sainteny (later commissioner in Tonkin). Both were sympathetic to the nationalistic ideals of the Vietminh, which in September proclaimed the Democratic Republic of Vietnam. Much of Ho's support was non-Communist, and in November he dissolved the Communist Party of northern Indochina. (Eventually the Laodang [workers'] Party arose in its stead.)

SEPTEMBER: as agreed among the Allies, Kuomintang troops took over northern Vietnam, while the British arrived in Saigon to disarm the Japanese (of whom 70,000 remained in Cochinchina), and to rearm the French. On September 23 in Saigon, while the British and Japanese stood aside, 1500 French troops under Colonel Cedile (just named commissioner in Cochinchina) expelled the Communist-inspired Committee of the South. The piaster was pegged at seventeen francs, and this remained its official rate, despite extreme depreciation.

1945–1946 A million people perished during a famine in Tonkin.

1946 JANUARY: Cambodia was recognized by France as an autonomous protectorate.

FEBRUARY: Cedile appointed a Consultative Council in Cochinchina, consisting of four Frenchmen and eight Vietnamese, seven of whom had French citizenship.

MARCH: The British forces officially transferred to France responsibility for law and order in Indochina, except of course for Tonkin. The Chinese agreed to evacuate their troops from Tonkin in return for special customs concessions there, and for French renunciation of extraterritorial and other rights in China. Ho agreed to permit Leclerc, the French commander in chief, to bring troops to Hanoi; in return, the French recognized the Republic of Vietnam (Tonkin and Annam) and promised to hold a referendum in the South.

APRIL: A conference was held at Dalat, preliminary to one at Fontaine-bleau. Refusing to hold a referendum until guerrilla fighting in Cochin-china had ended, the French proposed to confederate the governments of the South. Giap, as head of the Vietminh delegation, demanded more, but not full, independence from the French. Nothing was settled. The Vietminh sent Nguyen Binh to organize the Cochinchinese Resistance.

JUNE: Admiral Thierry d'Argenlieu, High Commissioner for Indochina as a whole, set up a "Provisional Government of Cochinchina," with Dr. Nguyen Van Thinh as President, and incorporating the much-expanded Consultative Council. Immediately thereafter, the Fontainebleau Con-ference began. Ho was personally very popular there, but the Conference broke up over Vietminh insistence on the inclusion of Cochinchina in the state of Vietnam, and ended inconclusively in September, with the signing of a weak *modus vivendi* agreement by Ho and Moutet (Minister of France-d'Outre-mer). In Ho's absence, the extreme left, led by Giap and Dang Xuan Khu, had purged non-Communist nationalists both north and south; and on Ho's return his allies found fault with his moderation and with his willingness for a rapprochement which would maintain French economic interests in Indochina.

NOVEMBER: Dr. Thinh committed suicide and his government resigned. Ho, as Prime Minister, formed a government: Thuc Kang, Minister of the Interior; Nguyen Giap, Minister of Defense; Pham Van Dong, Minister of National Economy.

DECEMBER: The French Union was set up under the new French con-stitution: a consultative body of 75 French members and 75 elected from overseas territories, which was to advise the French National Assembly. Natives of Associated States within the French Union did not have full French citizenship, but were equal with Frenchmen before the law.

Open warfare broke out in Hanoi and Haiphong. Seventy-five thou-sand more French troops were ordered to Indochina.

1947   MARCH–JUNE: The French negotiated with Bao Dai in Hong Kong.

MIDSUMMER: The Radical Socialist Emile Bollaert replaced d'Argenlieu as high commissioner. The overall status by this time was:

Cochinchina a colony, its capital Saigon, Dufour its commissioner.

Annam a protectorate, its capital Hue, General Lebris its commissioner.

Tonkin a protectorate, its capital Hanoi, Sainteny its commissioner.

Laos a colony, its capital Vientiane, de Raymond its commissioner.

Cambodia a protectorate, its capital Phompenh, its king, Norodom Sihanouk.

General Valluy (who had replaced Leclerc as commander in chief in 1946) conducted large-scale operations against Ho's quadrilateral in the north. Garrison towns and strongpoints were established, but the Vietminh still moved freely between them, and hopes of a purely military solution waned. The policy of Pacification was gradually introduced.

1948 JUNE: Bao Dai signed an agreement with Bollaert which recognized Vietnam (including Cochinchina) as an Independent Associated State within the French Union. A reorganized provisional Vietnamese government was proclaimed, with General Nguyen Van Xuan as its head. The other Associated States were Laos and Cambodia. (Their powers were not fully defined until late in 1950, nor fully implemented until the following summer.) The press was censored and the French retained broad supervisory powers in such areas as immigration, foreign trade and negotiations, customs, banking, and finance.

OCTOBER: Léon Pignon, with MRP support, replaced Bollaert as high commissioner.

1949 MARCH: The "Elysée Letters" were exchanged between Bao Dai and President Auriol of France; Vietnam was to have its own army and its own bank; other matters were postponed.

APRIL: Bao Dai returned to Vietnam, and set up his court in Dalat.
The Revers affair.

SUMMER: Bay Vien acquired the Grand Monde gambling establishment.
Carpentier became commander in chief.
The Catholics in the Tonkinese delta began to arm.

AUTUMN: The Vietminh terror in Saigon.
In the north, the French abandoned their posts beyond Caobang. The Chinese People's Republic was proclaimed, with Chou En-lai as premier, and Mao Tse-tung as Party leader. In the late autumn, Mao's armies reached the Yunnanese frontier.
The Vietminh aligned itself with the Moscow-Peking axis (having heretofore stressed nationalism even above Party discipline).

1950 JANUARY: the French National Assembly ratified the agreement proposed in the "Elysée Letters."

FEBRUARY: Great Britain and the U.S. recognized the Associated States of Vietnam, Cambodia and Laos. A conference between these Associated States and France was held at Pau, to formalize their internal relations.

MARCH: Tam was appointed chief of the Vietnamese Sûreté in Saigon. Edmund Gullion came to Saigon as U.S. Chargé d'Affaires, pending the arrival of Donald Heath as Minister. (The U.S. Legation later became an embassy.) Shortly thereafter, U.S. aid began. Ho Chi Minh's regime was recognized by Moscow and Peking.

MAY: The Vietminh took Dongkhe and the French retook it.

JUNE: Carpentier turned down General Alessandri's plan.

North Korea attacked South Korea, and the U.N. intervened.

SEPTEMBER: Carpentier took Thainguyen. Caobang was evacuated.

OCTOBER: Charton's and Lepage's columns were destroyed near Dongkhe, which was retaken by the Vietminh. Thatkhe was evacuated, then Langson.

NOVEMBER: Laokay was evacuated.

DECEMBER: Boyer de La Tour recommended retreating. De Lattre de Tassigny was appointed both high commissioner and commander in chief.

In May 1954 the French were defeated at the battle of Dienbienphu. In July, Premier Pierre Mendès-France signed an armistice at Geneva, which divided the country at the seventeenth parallel into two autonomous nations, the Democratic Republic of Vietnam in the north, and the Republic of Vietnam in the south. The partition was provisional, pending a plebiscite, which has never been held.

Index